THE CHANGING
AMERICAN LEGAL SYSTEM
Some Selected Phases

THE CHANGING
AMERICAN LEGAL SYSTEM

Some Selected Phases

By Francis R. Aumann

DA CAPO PRESS · NEW YORK · 1969

A Da Capo Press Reprint Edition

This Da Capo Press edition of *The Changing American Legal System* is an unabridged republication of the first edition published in Columbus, Ohio, in 1940 as Number XVI of the Ohio State University Contributions in History and Political Science.

KF 352 ,A87 1969

Library of Congress Catalog Card Number 77-87664

Published by Da Capo Press
A Division of Plenum Publishing Corporation
227 West 17th Street
New York, N.Y. 10011

Printed in the United States of America

THE CHANGING AMERICAN
LEGAL SYSTEM

THE CHANGING AMERICAN LEGAL SYSTEM: SOME SELECTED PHASES

By

FRANCIS R. AUMANN
Professor of Political Science
The Ohio State University

•

COLUMBUS - - - 1940

Graduate School Series

CONTRIBUTIONS IN HISTORY AND POLITICAL SCIENCE

NUMBER 16

•

Printed in
United States of America

TABLE OF CONTENTS

FOREWORD

Professor Aumann has written extensively during the last decade about the development of law and the legal system in the United States, considered from the colonial, state, and federal viewpoints. His name is well known in the periodical literature dealing with the legal system in America. Herein, he builds a book on the subject, bringing into a compact volume a study extending from Plymouth Rock simplicity to present-day complications and confusions. This is no easy task, for the writer must base his study upon numerous sources and a myriad of writers and commentators, with a baffling diversity of deductions. He has critically and with intelligent purpose threaded his way through them, as his copious footnotes and comprehensive bibliography demonstrate. He has footnoted probably two-thirds of his bibliographical items. He compares the views of his authors, he presents their conclusions, frequently interspersed with illuminating or reconciling views of his own, constantly keeps the reader in the presence of the best American legal writers of three centuries, and closes his chapters with brief but pointed summaries containing his own thought.

The panorama is exciting: Colonial America gradually effecting a political cleavage from Britain, which is reflected in the judicial aberrations especially noted in the post-revolutionary period; the spirit of personal liberty which marks the pioneer era; the efforts to simplify law and procedure and to fix it by codification; the passing from an era in which the prevailing concept is "rugged individualism" to an era in which social values dominate, and the resultant new emphases in the legal system; the impact upon all life of an age of speed and the urge toward swift and direct administrative agencies in preference to courts and the "law's delays"; and the vigorous struggle in progress for fifty years between the legal system of a rural agricultural America and an urban industrialized America, with common law methods in the background, and statutory authorities and devices in the foreground. He has given each movement a "day in court," and his treatment graphically sustains his title "The Changing American Legal System."

Law students, teachers, and lawyers alike have felt an embarrassing uncertainty, if not ignorance, about the growth of American law in its state environment. The vast number of references to be consulted, with only local coloring, most of them unavailable, in order to acquire merely a fragmentary understanding, has been a very discouraging circumstance. As a result we know far less of American state systems than we think we do of the English system—and there perchance we imagine that Blackstone's *Commentaries* apply to twentieth century England.

We have here, then, a handbook—a mirror—of the development of the legal system of the American states, with much detail and a persistent purpose of weaving these threads of experience together into a multi-colored pattern steadily trending towards uniformity. For this stimulating study of the changing American legal system, lawyers, publicists, historians and lawmakers will unite in commending Professor Aumann; his work will prompt a larger interest in this fundamental juridical area, and will afford firm footing as we go forward in an effort to comprehend the significance and the orientation of the accelerating movement toward administrative methods and tribunals.

GEORGE W. RIGHTMIRE
President Emeritus
The Ohio State University

PREFACE

It is the purpose of this study to consider in brief fashion some selected phases of the development of the American legal system. The major trends of these developments are familiar to most legalists and it is not expected that specialists in the field of American legal history will find much that is new, either in the substance of these materials or in the manner of their presentation. To those members of the bar, students of political science, and members of the general public who are interested in the American legal system in a more general way, however, it is hoped that this study will further a better appreciation of some of the problems which have attended its growth. Needless to say, this study does not attempt to treat all phases of this growth, nor to explore all of the materials in the areas with which it is concerned. To do so would require a thorough-going exploration of colonial legal sources not readily available and a far-reaching survey of widely scattered materials in the still neglected field of local legal history in the periods after the Revolution, as well. Limitations of time and resource have precluded any extensive attempts in either of these directions. For the purpose of emphasis, it is repeated that no attempt has been made here to break new pathways. The purpose throughout has been to follow the main-travelled roads as closely as possible. The plan of procedure followed involves a brief consideration of some of the problems of colonial justice, including the several views as to the nature and extent of common law reception in the seventeenth and eighteenth centuries; the effect of the War of Revolution and reconstruction upon the legal system; the interest in the civil law and its influence in the post-war period; the up-thrust of the common law system in the formative period of American life and its expansion into the newly formed commonwealths of the nation; including a supplementary survey of early court organizations and procedures; the role of legal education, etc. Also involved is a brief analysis of the course of American legal development in the period of industrial growth which intervened between the Civil War and the turn of the century, including a consideration of some of the changing concepts and contents of American law brought about by the conversion of a simple, agricultural society into a complicated, industrial order. Following this excursion into the period of legal maturity, attention is turned to the changing patterns that appear in the legal order during the first third of the

twentieth century. In undertaking this plan of study the writer has
been greatly assisted by the sound judgment and wide legal scholarship
of Mr. Walter F. Dodd of Chicago. In the midst of a heavy program
while a member of the Yale Law School faculty and at the Chicago
bar, Mr. Dodd has found time and patience to encourage the preparation of this manuscript in countless ways. For his generous and wise
counsel, the writer is deeply grateful. Dean Carl F. Wittke of Oberlin
College, formerly head of the Department of History at The Ohio
State University; Professors Homer C. Hockett, Francis P. Weisen-
burger, and Henry Simms of the Department of History at The Ohio
State University; Professor Oliver P. Chitwood of the Department of
History of West Virginia University; Professor A. A. Morrison of the
University of Cincinnati Law School — all have read portions of the
manuscript and have offered valuable suggestions, as have the editors
of the *Ohio Archaeological and Historical Society Journal*, the *Journal
of Criminal Law and Criminology*, the *American Political Science
Review*, the *American Judicature Society Journal*, the *Cincinnati Law
Review*, the *Kentucky Law Journal*, and several other journals in
which some portions of this manuscript have been published from time
to time. Various staff members of the Library of Congress and The
Ohio State University have been most helpful and the assistance of the
publications committee and staff of the Graduate Council has been of
the utmost value. Mr. Ceph L. Stephens of the Department of Political
Science of The Ohio State University has contributed particularly valuable assistance in the preparation of the index. For all of these gifts of
time and effort the writer is most grateful. For the errors which undoubtedly will be found, the writer must take full responsibility despite
the wise and generous efforts of scholarly friends. In doing so, however,
he joins hopefully in the quaint and often-repeated petition of the old
Bellewe. "Beseeching you," he writes, "that where you shall finde any
faults, which by my insufficiency, the intricateness of the worke, or the
printers recklessness are committed, either friendly to pardon, or by
some means to admonish me thereof."

PART I

THE PERIOD OF COLONIAL LEGAL BEGINNINGS, 1608-1776

CHAPTER I

CONFLICTING VIEWS CONCERNING THE NATURE OF COLONIAL LAW

"Legal development," says Samuel Eliot Morison, "is probably the least known aspect of American colonial history. Judicial opinions were not recorded in the colonies, no year books were issued, and the printed materials for legal and judicial history have been so scanty as to preclude the more cautious historians from dealing with this important side of colonial life; while less cautious historians have indulged in generalizations for which slight support can be found in fact."[1] The difficulties attending a proper understanding of the subject are increased by the fact that the colonies were established under widely differing conditions, by dissimilar groups of people, and at intervals covering a stretch of one hundred and twenty-five years.[2]

It will be remembered that Virginia was founded by a trading company, Plymouth by an earnest religious group, Maryland by a Catholic proprietor, and Pennsylvania by a wealthy Quaker magnate. The settlers themselves were drawn from many diverse religious groups, social classes and nationalities. In Massachusetts there were Puritans; in Virginia, Anglicans; in Maryland, Catholics; in Pennsylvania, Quakers; in Rhode Island, Separatists; in South Carolina, Huguenots; etc. Along with younger sons of noble families and religious devotees were found indentured servants, victims of press gangs, and the outpourings of English almshouses and debtors' prisons. The English predominated but other nationalities were also represented, including the Dutch in New York and New Jersey, the Swedes in what is now Delaware, the Germans in Pennsylvania, the French Huguenots in New York and South Carolina, and the Scotch Irish along the frontier.[3] Despite a number of unifying tendencies, the colonies formed originally

---

[1] *Records of the Suffolk Court*, 1671-1680. I. Publications of the Colonial Society of Massachusetts, vol. 29, Preface.

[2] The first colony was established in 1607 and the last in 1733.

[3] Despite this diversity of background, it has been estimated that in 1790, nine-tenths of the population of 3,172,444, was of English or Scotch or Scotch-Irish descent. When broken down these figures include: English 2,605,699; Scotch, 221,562; Irish, 61,534; Dutch, 78,959; French, 17,619; German, 176,407; all others, 10,664. Since no questions as to nationality were asked in the census of 1790, these estimates were made by the Census Bureau at a later date on the basis of the surnames of heads of families. *A Century of Population Growth*, 116 ff. Bureau of the Census (Washington, 1909).

in separate settlements, grew up in a condition of geographical isolation
which tended to emphasize the difference in their social and economic
life and in their political organization as well.[4] In short, many factors
are present which discourage attempts to consider the condition of law
and law administration in the years between 1608 and 1776.

Nevertheless, this period is an important one since many of the
institutions which underlie the American judiciary have their origins in
colonial as well as English sources.[5] Some of these beginnings are seen
in the early charters and ordinances[6] of the original colonies.[7] While
these instruments are of variegated types, they provide in a general way

---

[4] It will be remembered that these settlements were drawn out along a north and
south seacoast more than twelve hundred miles in length and that there were marked differences between the plantation states of the south and the farming and trading states of the
north. Men came to speak of themselves as Virginians or Pennsylvanians and by the eve
of the Revolution most of the colonies had developed a political self-consciousness all
their own.

[5] Julius Goebel, Jr., *Cases and Materials on the Developments of Legal Institutions*,
(1930), pp. 294, 310, 329.

[6] *"Ordinances of Convention*, May, 1776, C. V. (Virginia). 9 *Hening Statutes at
Large*, 127. VI. And be it farther ordained, that the common law of England, all statutes,
or acts of parliament made in aid of common law prior to the fourth year of the reign of
King James, the first, and which are of a general nature, not local to that kingdom,
together with the several acts of the general assembly of this colony now in force, as far
as the same may consist with the several ordinances, declarations and resolutions of the
general convention, shall be the rule of decisions, and shall be considered as in full force,
until the same shall be altered by the legislative power of the colony." Goebel, *ibid.*,
p. 330.

[7] "The first century and three quarters of American legal development," writes
Julius Goebel, Jr., "is bounded by two landmarks which have served as monuments to
those historians who have attempted to survey the field of colonial law. The first of these
is the royal charter, the second is the so-called reception statute. The former with its
mandate that the law in the lands granted should be agreeable or not repugnant to the law
of England, (see, e.g. the Virginia charter of 1609; cf. 2 Poor, *Federal and State Constitutions* (2nd ed. 1878) 1901, 1902, 1905; the Pennsylvania charter of 1681, 2 *ibid.* 1509,
1511, the Georgia charter of 1732, 1 *ibid.* 369, 372-3; the Massachusetts Bay charter
1 *ibid.* 932, 940; the New York charter of 1664, 1 *Colonial Laws of New York*, 1. 2.)
is commonly regarded as a forecast of what was to transpire. The latter, with its declaration that the common law of England, in so far as it had been adopted at a particular
date was the law of a state, is held to have marked the consummation of the forecast.
(The so-called reception statutes vary in form, in the date chosen as the deadline, and as
to the implication of the extent of reception. Compare the Virginia provision, *Ordinances
of Convention* (1776) C. V. (VI), 9 Hening 126, 127; 9 Pa. *Statutes at Large*, (1777)
art. XXXV, now art. 1, sec. 16.) There has been no comprehensive discussion of the relation of these statutes to the judicial elaboration of the actual details of reception. In 1926,
at the meeting of the American Law School Association, the writer (Goebel) in a paper
Courts as Historians pointed out that judges acting on the assumption that their function
to declare the law, embraces a knowledge of its history, undertook after the revolution,
to decide what rules had been adopted in colonial times. Since little was known as to
what actually transpired in colonial America, the results of the courts are frequently worthless as history. This theory persists. A saner view would seem to be that actual proof as
to what colonial practice had been should be required. There is some discussion of the
matter in Goebel, *Cases and Materials on the Development of Legal Institutions* (1930),
293 et sig." "King's Law and Local Custom in Seventeenth ˚Century New England."
Columbia Law Review, vol. 31, 1931, p. 416.

for the reception of English law and legal institutions,[8] and require the colonists to adopt and follow the policies and forms of laws, customs, and manners of administering justice as they existed in England.[9] Since England, then as now, was a country "where freedom slowly broadens down from precedent to precedent," these requirements meant the adoption of the English Common Law.[10] In Virginia, for example, the settlers of Jamestown were required to "adhere" as closely as they could "to the common law and the equity thereof."[11] These requirements meant the adoption of English court forms also.[12] The highest court in England was the House of Lords. In the colonies the legislative body was given a similar position and the historical English justice of the peace became the model for a similar office in the colonies.[13] The grand and petit juries were also introduced into the colonial system.[14]

In theory the colonists had little opportunity to escape conformity

[8] Some charters used the expression that they must "be agreeable to" the laws of England; others that they must "not be repugnant to" and others that they must "not be contrary" to the laws of England. Goebel, *ibid.*, pp. 311, 312.

[9] Goebel, *ibid.*, pp. 323, 324.

[10] For several views as to the reception and applicability of the English common law in this country see Goebel, *ibid.*, pp. 331-338; see also Pope, "The English Common Law in the United States," 24 *Harvard Law Review*, 6; R. C. Dale, "The Adoption of the Common Law by the American Colonies," *Amer. Law Reg.*, N.S., XXI, 554.

[11] Atkinson, "Origin and Growth of the Jurisprudence of the Two Virginias," 2 *Va. Law Reg.* (N.S.), 721, see also Chitwood, "Justice in Colonial Virginia," 32 *W. Va. L. Quart.*, 204.

[12] In Virginia, the judiciary was closely allied to the other departments of government. Before 1682, the legislature was the highest court of appeal in the colony. During the entire colonial period it was closely connected with both the superior and inferior courts. The judges of the General Court constituted the upper house of the assembly, and the justices of the county courts were often elected to seats in the lower house. As members of the governor's council, the judges of the General Court performed executive duties for the colony at large and the justices of the peace performed administrative duties in their respective counties. The authority of the judiciary was subordinate to the legislature at all times. From 1682 to the Revolution, the people had no choice, either directly or indirectly, in the selection of their judges. Before 1682, the assembly was the only court in which the judges were elected directly by the people and the justices of the county courts were appointed with the consent of the assembly. This practice was short lived, however. Throughout the period, the office of judge in both the superior and inferior courts was an influential one and was usually held by men of ability. A legal education was not required for the office, however, "and apparently many, if not most, of the judges both of the superior and inferior courts, came to the bench without special legal training." Chitwood, *op. cit.*, pp. 309-311.

[13] Charles A. Beard, "The Justice of the Peace in England," *Columbia University Studies*, 1904.

[14] The judicial organization established in the colonies was essentially the same. It was characterized by local units, usually presided over by a justice of the peace appointed by the governor. Above these in most cases were courts of quarter session, presided over by the justices of the county. Finally there was a higher court usually composed of the governor and his council and sometimes a separate body of appointed judges. From these courts appeals could be carried to the King and Privy Council in England. See Palfrey, *Compendious History of New England, 1494-1567*, pp. 276-277.

to English legal patterns.[15] In practice, there seems to have been considerable deviation from the common law.[16] In Virginia for example, the courts were bound in their decisions "by the common law of England, the Parliamentary statutes passed prior to 1607, and the statutes enacted by the Virginia Assembly."[17] Actually the Virginia courts relied to a great extent upon their own judgments for guidance in arriving at decisions rather than upon law and precedent and the results of the practice seem to have been fairly satisfactory.[18] The situation in other colonies was quite similar. It would have been extremely difficult to transplant the English system in its entirety to colonies faced with many problems that were quite different from those of the older society at

[15] Goebel, *ibid.*, p. 310.

[16] "The early colonial assemblies and courts were in theory bound to follow, as far as local conditions permitted, the legal tradition of the mother country. Actually, however, the seventeenth-century colonies, faced with many problems quite different from those of an older society, departed widely and at many points from the English law, gradually developing a common law of their own, which varied more or less from colony to colony. In the second century of the colonial era, British control of colonial practice became more effective, through royal instructions to the governors, the appointment of professionally trained judges and attorney generals, the royal disallowance of provincial legislation and the judicial review of American decisions by the Privy Council. There was also an increasing number of colonial lawyers who, whether in the English Inns of Court or under the guidance of older practitioners, were brought under conservative influence. The resultant of these forces—the transplanted English law and the practical requirements of a new society—was the development even before the Revolution, of an American legal tradition which with many local variations, departed significantly from the system of the English Common-law Courts." Evarts Greene, Foreword, *Proceedings of the Maryland Court of Appeals, 1695-1729*, (1934), edited by Carroll T. Bond. See also Thomas Pownall, *The Administration of the Colonies; wherein their Rights and Constitutions are discussed and stated*, London, 1768; *The North American Review*, vol. 21, July, 1825, p. 104 ff.

[17] "The Virginia courts were governed in their decisions by the common law of England and by the Parliamentary statutes that were enacted before the colony was settled, and not by any that were enacted after that event, except those that made mention of the plantations. (Hening, II, 43). The first act of assembly that has been found in which the common law of England is recognized as being in force in Virginia was passed in 1622 (Brown, *Genesis of the United States*, 66; McDonald Papers, I, 376. Sainsbury MSS; 1637-1649, 44. Hening, I, 44). But in all probability the common law was to some extent observed by the courts during the entire colonial period with the exception of the time which the colony was under military rule. Besides, prior to 1662 orders were issued from England from time to time directing the authorities in Virginia to follow the law of England, as far as practicable. . . . Such an instruction was given to the King's council in Virginia in 1606, and a similar provision is found in commissions to governors that were issued before 1662. As early as 1621, Governor Wyatt was instructed to do justice "after form of the laws of England." Spottswood's Letters, II, 13. Henrico County Court Records, 1710-1714, 28. Journal of the Assembly, 1699-1720, 36, 37." Chitwood, *op. cit.*, pp. 205-206.

[18] "In the documents that have been examined very few complaints against the inferior courts are recorded and it seems that these tribunals as a rule administered justice fairly and impartially. . . . There were certain latent weaknesses in the constitution of the General Court which occasionally gave rise to abuses in actual practice. But as only a few cases of such abuses have been found it may safely be inferred that justice was as a rule fairly administered by the superior, as well as the inferior courts." *Ibid.*, p. 311. See also Philip A. Bruce, *Institutional History of Virginia in the Seventeenth Century*, (1910), vol. 1, p. 478; also Hammond, *Leah and Rachel, or the Two Fruitfull Sisters, Virginia and Maryland, 1656*, p. 15; Force's *Historical Tracts*, Vol. III.

home.[19] Indeed, the extent to which the colonies could and did adopt the provisions of the common law during the course of the seventeenth century remains a question concerning which there is considerable difference of opinion.

In the view of one group of historians, including Professors Paul Reinsch, Charles J. Hilkey, and R. B. Morris, "the English common law remained largely an alien system until the middle of the eighteenth century and was then received into the colonies by professionally trained lawyers in somewhat the same way as Roman law was received into Germany after the close of the middle ages."[20] On the other hand, another group of distinguished legal scholars, including Professors Julius Goebel and Theodore Plucknett, believe that it is easy to exaggerate the slowness and incompleteness of common law reception in the seventeenth century.[21] In their view there was a "voluntary reception of a good deal of common law, freely modified to meet local conditions," during that time.[22]

The differences here seem to be largely a matter of emphasis and interpretation rather than of complete disagreement as to facts; since both groups of scholars would undoubtedly admit that the English common law had some influence during the seventeenth century, while recognizing that its institutions and rules were not completely adopted. Nevertheless, these points of difference are important inasmuch as they stimulate the search for new evidence and incidentally establish a better perspective on the evidence now available. For example, if we were to follow the Reinsch-Hilkey-Morris view too closely, we might derive the impression that colonial justice during its earlier phases tended to be largely indifferent to as well as independent of law. This interpretation is not entirely acceptable to the Goebel-Plucknett group and their

[19] In 1734 we hear this plaint in an extract from the minute book of the Supreme Court of New York Province. " . . . This is a new Colony and is yet (as it were) but in its Infancy, we cannot be thought to have everything in its full and complete perfection as they have at home, but we endeavor to imitate and come as near to them as we can. . . . *Murray's Opinions on Courts of Justice.*" Cited by Goebel, *ibid.*, at pp. 322-323.

[20] Professor Charles J. Hilkey says: "The colonists did not consider English law binding. The statutes passed by the General Courts were to them the positive, and the scriptures the subsidiary law." (*Legal Development in Colonial Massachusetts, 1630-1686*, p. 144; see also pp. 5, 66 ff.) This view is largely shared by Paul S. Reinsch ("The English Common Law in the Early American Colonies" in *Select Essays in Anglo-American Legal History*, I, 367 ff. See also R. B. Morris, "Massachusetts and the Common Law; the Declaration of 1646," *American Historical Review, XXXI*, 443.) Both of these writers consider that the English Common Law remained largely an alien system until the middle of the eighteenth century. . . . " *Records of the Suffolk County Court, 1671-1680*, vol. 1, p. xxviii. *Publications of the Colonial Society of Massachusetts*, vol. 29.

[21] *Ibid.*, p. xxviii.

[22] " 'As early as 1648,' writes Professor Theodore Plucknett, 'and in spite of the talk about judicial laws of Moses, there had been a voluntary reception of a good deal of common law, freely modified to meet local conditions.' (Review of 'Laws and Liberties of 1648,' in *New England Quarterly*, III, 157-158.)" *Ibid.*, p. xxviii.

insistence upon a closer examination of the record results in a somewhat different picture of colonial legal processes in general. The Recent studies of colonial law administration in Maryland[23] and Massachusetts,[24] seem to support their position in many ways. The net result of these studies is to dispel the notion that early colonial justice was marked by a complete absence of formality. On the other hand, the emphasis of the Reinsch-Hilkey-Morris group may lead to a better appreciation of the difficulties which attended the establishment of satisfactory legal institutions in a new land and social order. In any event, an examination of these varying views seems of value, inasmuch as it may throw more light upon obscure corners of this difficult subject.

A number of circumstances are referred to by the Reinsch-Hilkey-Morris group (if we may again so classify) as to why the immediate reception of the common law was not possible. As mentioned before, they emphasize the scarcity of trained lawyers to administer it. "The fundamental limitation on the growth of American law in the seventeenth century," says R. B. Morris, "was the scarcity of lawyers. . . . The legal profession in New England in the seventeenth century was inconsequential. Of the sixty-five men who landed at Plymouth in 1620, not one was a lawyer. Although there was some legal talent in Massachusetts Bay, there was no lawyer actually practicing at the time of settlement."[25] In consequence, it is asserted, law administration fell largely into the hands of laymen and remained there for a long time to come.[26] When trained lawyers became more numerous with the advent of the eighteenth century, the common law assumed a new importance.[27] With an increase in legal training the courts too became more prone to turn to the common law. "It is but natural," says Paul Reinsch, "that with increased training the courts should turn to the great reservoir

[23] "The number of judicial records left by the early Maryland colonists and the amount of judicial business recorded in them, may surprise those who suppose that pioneers and frontiersmen in all times and places tend to become independent of the law. For it seems to be demonstrated that, removed as these people were from the environment of their civilization, and relaxed as that civilization must therefore have been, in some degree, they were nevertheless tenacious of regulation by law, and prone to litigation." Carroll T. Bond, *Introduction of Proceedings of the Maryland Court of Appeals, 1695-1729,* (1934), at p. v.

[24] "The materials in these cases must dispel the view that Massachusetts remained until after 1700 in a period of rude, untechnical popular law. Before the colony was half a century old, its courts are shown busy with trusts for the benefit of creditors and their annulment for fraud, difficult questions of inheritance, and complex mercantile transactions afloat and ashore." *Records of the Suffolk County Court, 1671-1680,* vol. 1, p. xxviii. *Publications of the Colonial Society of Massachusetts,* vol. 29.

[25] Morris, *Studies in the History of American Law,* p. 42.

[26] Reinsch, *op. cit.,* p. 400 ff.

[27] "With the advent of the eighteenth century the number of trained lawyers in the colonies increased markedly. Many of these attorneys emigrated to the colonies; and an appreciable number of native lawyers had, by the eve of the American Revolution, received their legal education at the Inns of Court in England." Morris, *op. cit.,* pp. 65-66.

of legal experience in their own language for guidance and direction."[28] It has been suggested that the willingness of the courts to adopt the common law was increased by the fact that it virtually gave them the power to legislate for the colonies. At any rate, it is contended that it is only when trained lawyers became available during the course of the eighteenth century that the common law was put into operation to any considerable extent.[29]

In the meantime, it is said, the colonists pursued "an ideal of rude natural justice dispensed without rule by a jury or a plain man;"[30] and the actual administration of justice was in many of its phases of a popular, summary kind in which the refined distinctions and artificial niceties of the common law had no place and many of the elements of English common law procedure were ignored as they seem to have been in Pennsylvania.[31] In undertaking these various experiments, says Paul Reinsch, the colonists passed through many stages which are remindful of similar developments in the early days of the Anglo-Saxon law. As illustrative of this trend Professor Reinsch mentions "the union of powers in the councils; the petitioning against the exercise of extraordinary jurisdiction by the council in ordinary cases, which carries us back to the time of Edward III; archaic conceptions of the jury; the system of petty, popular courts which had long become obsolete, or only maintained a precarious existence, in old England."[32] In his view, the

[28] Reinsch, *op. cit.*, pp. 399-400.

[29] In the beginning of the eighteenth century, says Paul Reinsch in writing about Massachusetts, "the old popular law was still largely administered in derogation of the more highly developed rules of the common law. It is stated that after the change in the appointment of judges, practice became very captious and sharp. In 1712, the first professional lawyer, Lynde, became Chief Justice and after this we find the English books and authors frequently cited." *Ibid.*, p. 416.

[30] Warren, *History of the American Bar*, 3, 105, 140; Eaton, "The Development of the Judicial System in Rhode Island." 14 *Yale Law Journal*, 153.

[31] "The County Courts of the Province first claim notice and attention. They had their origin in 1673, under the Government of James, Duke of York, and were established in every country 'to decide all matters under twenty pounds without appeal,' and to have exclusive jurisdiction in the administration of criminal justice, with an appeal, however, in cases extending to 'Life, Limb and Banishment,' to the Court of Assizes in New York. (5 Penna. Archives, N. S. 631; 7 Penna. Archives, N. S. 738). They were originally composed of five or six justices appointed by the Governor (5 Penna. Arch. N. S. 718) and had a jurisdiction so vague and undefined that they can scarcely be said to have been bound by any positive law. The records that have come down to us, 'are not satisfactory enough to justify any attempt at analyzing the conglomerate condition of law and justice . . . with the view of accurately making out the precise code and practice.' (Historical Notes: D. of Y. Laws, 414.) Some of these courts met quarterly, some monthly, no one learned in the law presided on the bench, no attorney allowed to practice for pay, (Haz. Ann. Penn. 438) juries were only allowed to consist of six or seven men, except in cases of life and death, and in all save these instances, the conclusions of the majority were allowed to prevail. (Book of Laws: D. of Y. L. 33, 34.) In short these courts lacked almost every element of distinctively English procedure." Lawrence Lewis, Jr. "The Courts of Pennsylvania in the Seventeenth Century," a paper reprinted from the *Pennsylvania Magazine of History and Biography* in 1, *Reports of Penn. Bar Assoc.* (1895), p. 356.

[32] Reinsch, *op. cit.*, p. 400.

colonists repeated the experiences of their ancestors in many ways. In New England, he asserts, a system of popular law (Volksrecht) grew up in which the law of God had an important place.[33] In Massachusetts the criminal law was based on the code of Moses.[34] The Body of Liberties formulated under clerical auspices in 1641 was a theocratic code.[35] In the legislative and judicial spheres, the Christian Bible was frequently invoked as the source of law.[36] "The Scriptures," says C. J. Hilkey "were an infallible guide for both judge and legislator."[37] Law itself was not viewed as a human institution.[38] In one sense, it was viewed as a "brooding omniprescience in the sky," bringing peace and order to men.[39]

Another factor which retarded an immediate and complete acceptance of the common law in the seventeenth century, in the view of this first group of scholars, was the nature of the common law at the time. Highly technical in character, it was not functioning well at home. Burdened with the formal thinking of the Middle Ages, its weaknesses

[33] *Ibid.*, p. 400.

[34] "Where the Puritan influence was strong, especially in New England and East Jersey, the Mosaic code was in criminal cases frequently appealed to as subsidiary law." Chitwood, *A History of Colonial America,* p. 191.

[35] Morris, *op. cit.,* pp. 37-39. Before the Charter of Liberties was adopted in Massachusetts the administration of justice was for some years without security either of a system of statutes, or of any recognition of the authority of the common law. "The Law dispensed by the magistrates" writes John Gorham Palfrey "was no other than equity, as its principles and rules existed in their own reason and conscience, instructed by scripture." *Compendious History of New England, 1494-1657,* vol. 1, p. 279. The people desired the safeguard of a written code, but their wishes were denied. While the question was debated John Cotton prepared a small volume entitled "An Abstract of the Laws of New England as they are now established." It was not approved by the General Court. It was then that Nathaniel Ward of Ipswich proposed the code of fundamental law which was called *The Body of Liberties.* Apparently this was adopted by the General Court by an unanimous act. Ward, a minister, had studied and practiced in the common law in England. In the "Simple Cobbler of Agawam" he stated that he had "read almost all the common law of England." See Palfrey, *ibid.,* pp. 279-280; also F. W. Grinnell, *"The Bench and Bar in Colony and Province,* (1630-1776)," ch. 6, vol. 2, *Commonwealth History of Massachusetts,* p. 157.

[36] Koucerek, "Sources of Law in the United States of America in Their Relation to Each Other," *American Bar Association Journal,* Oct. 1932, p. 676; John Winthrop, *History of New England,* (a journal) edited by John Savage (Boston, 1853), vol. 1, p. 388; vol. 2, p. 332; Winslow, "New England's Salamander" *Massachusetts Historical Society Collections,* 3rd ser., II, 137.

[37] C. J. Hilkey, *"Legal Development in Colonial Massachusetts, 1630-1686."* (Columbia Studies in History, Economics, and Public Law), vol. XXXVII, No. 2, N. Y. 1910, p. 68.

[38] Morris, *op. cit.,* 24, 25, 37.

[39] "The conception of law current among the Puritans is well illustrated by the remarks of Cotton that he should not 'call them laws because God alone has the power to make laws, but conventions between men.' This theory of law as the command of God, the medieval conception uncolored by the modern sense of sovereignty seems to have been firmly held by the Puritans of New, as of Old England. (Figgis, *Divine Right of Kings,* p. 323.) The same views . . . may have prompted the general court not to call the Body of Liberties laws, but to pass them in the form of recommendations." Reinsch, *op. cit.,* p. 14.

were accentuated by the over-refinements which characterized the seventeenth and eighteenth centuries. Criticized severely by the Puritans as "a dark and knavish business" the common law was entering a new period of development. Indeed the period is one of transition and the legal order suffered accordingly. The feudal society of Medieval England was "only beginning to feel the effects of Lord Holt and it was yet to experience the benefit of the judgments of Lord Mansfield which gave our law a deserved capacity for expansion and development."[40] The work of Lord Mansfield who was appointed Chief Justice in 1756 and resigned in 1789, marked a turning point in English legal development. During his tenure of office the law merchant was incorporated into the English system and the common law was liberalized. Throughout the period of colonial beginnings, however, the common law stood in need of alterations and improvement.[41] Indeed it was the object of a veritable barrage of critical pamphlet literature as were its practitioners.[42]

Included among the books and pamphlets expressing dissatisfaction with the law and its administration were the "Speech against the Judges for their Ignorance," 1641, "The Mirrors of Justice," written before that time but printed in 1645, "The Downfall of the Unjust Lawyers," "Doomsday Drawing Near with Thunder and Lightning for Lawyers," 1645, "A Rod for Lawyers who are hereby declared Robbers and Deceivers of the Nation," 1659, and many others of a similar character. While part of the criticism was political in nature, much of it rested on the nature of the law's operation. Under the Stuart regime the Puritans witnessed English administration of justice at its worst, including a bar which gave its devotion to the crown rather than the law and resisted Cromwell's projects of law reform and opposed all improvements. They also witnessed the activities of a bench which included many "servile if not corrupt judges and law officers of the crown, the last of their kind in English history to stain the annals of the profession."[43] In consequence, they distrusted the law and the legal profession. The Puritan clergy were particularly active in opposing the legal order. These factors undoubtedly exerted great influence upon the course of the common law in the colonies.

It is further suggested by this first group of scholars that in a new land, devoid of books and facility for study, a system like the common law of that period, requiring as it did, an elaborate apparatus of technical

[40] Harlan F. Stone, "The Lawyer and His Neighbors," *Cornell L. Quarterly*, vol. 4, (1918-19), p. 175.
[41] Charles Warren, *History of the American Bar*, pp. 10-11; see also Morris, *ibid.*, pp. 45-46.
[42] Harlan Stone, *op. cit.*, p. 175.
[43] *Ibid.*, p. 175.

treatises, reports and statute books, would have been extremely difficult to apply. It was to avoid this difficulty, it is said, that the colonists in many cases formulated simple codes to take care of their legal needs.[44] This practice was first instituted in Virginia and quickly spread to the other colonies.[45] In some respects these codes resembled the ancient "dooms of the Anglo-Saxon kings." During the early years of the colonies they became an important source of legal knowledge and rules for adjudication.[46] In all the colonies except Maryland, the essential elements of the common law were codified at an early date.

In some instances, the codes departed from common law principles in important respects.[47] In Massachusetts[48] and Pennsylvania[49] the

[44] The first code at Plymouth was established when the colony had existed sixteen years. It was "not framed upon any theory of conformity to the Jewish law, or to the law of England, but consisted of such provisions as, on general principles of jurisprudence, and with the experience which had been obtained, appeared suitable to secure the well-being of the little community. It allowed authority to such laws only as were enacted by the body of freemen, or by their representatives legally assembled. It recognized eight capital official offences, and made other crimes punishable at the discretion of the magistrates. In transfers of real estate it required acknowledgment before a magistrate and a public record. . . . Every resident was to provide himself with certain arms and accoutrements. The retail sale of liquors except in private houses, was forbidden. A few other simple regulations, among which were some relating to the distribution of lands and to trespasses of domestic animals, made a body of law sufficient for the present needs of the orderly people of Plymouth." Palfrey, *Compendious History of New England, 1494-1657*, vol. I, p. 278.

[45] In 1610 Sir Thomas Gates was sent to Virginia to act as governor pending the arrival of Lord De La Warr, the permanent governor. Gates initiated a system of justice by which judicial decisions were to be rendered in accordance with law made to suit existing conditions in the colony. He wrote out certain rules and ordinances by which the colonies were to be governed during his tenure of office. These laws were posted in the church at Jamestown. They constituted the first legal code of English-speaking America. See Strachey, *A True Reportory of the Wracke and Redemption of Sir Thomas Gates, Knight*, printed by Purchas, 1748-1749. These laws were "approved and exemplified" by Lord De La Warr and enlarged by Sir Thomas Dale, who added certain stern features of the martial law. From 1611 to 1619 this phase continued. By 1619, the colony was established on so firm a basis that the need for military rule ceased and Virginians began to enjoy the rights of Englishmen. See Chitwood, *op. cit., pp.* 86-88.

[46] Thomas Lechford, *Plain Dealing.* (London, Nathaniel Butler, 1642.) This book was written by the only lawyer in the colony, "who was really a 'scrivener'." It contains much material concerning colonial society mixed with considerable criticism of church government. Lechford's *Note-book* kept by him in Boston from June, 1638, to June 29, 1641, is also of interest. It contains many forms of contracts, deeds, etc. as well as notes of his personal history as a lawyer.

[47] "In the colonial system of Massachusetts we find types of the common law; the less technical parts of its terminology are in use, forms of contracts and deeds are modeled on English precedents, although for the latter acknowledgment and recording is essential to validity. (Massachusetts Colonial Records, I, 116; and Suffolk County Deeds.) But the authority of the common law as a subsidiary system is nowhere admitted, its principles are radically departed from, its rules used only for purposes of illustration." Reinsch, *op. cit.,* p. 411.

[48] " . . . The early character of Massachusetts law has never ceased to influence the system of that state, the originality of whose jurisprudence has always been recognized. Jefferson says in a letter to Attorney General Rodney, September 25, 1810, (Jefferson's Complete Works, V. 546), speaking of Lincoln of Massachusetts, as a possible successor to Cushing as Associate Justice: 'He is thought not to be an able common lawyer, but

departure was particularly noticeable. In these states old principles were disregarded and new ones introduced. "I took a trip once," says Lord Peterborough, "with Penn to his colony of Pennsylvania; the laws there have no alterations wanted in any one of them ever since Sir William made them. They have no lawyers. Everyone is to tell his own case, or some friend for him; they have four persons as judges on the bench, and after the case has been fully laid down on all sides, all the four are to draw lots, and he on whom the lot falls decides the question. 'Tis a happy country, and the people are neither oppressed with poor rates, tythes, nor taxes."[59]

In all the colonies, it is suggested by the first group of scholars, the wide discretionary powers accorded to lay magistrates permitted the development of ideas and devices which were unknown to English practices. These developments are considered important, in so far as they foreshadow in several regards some of our characteristically lay American legal practices. Effecting a simplification of procedure that was utterly in conflict with prevailing common law practices,[51] it was apparently assumed that any man of ordinary intelligence should be able to plead his own cause before the courts.[52] The spirit of these early

there is not and never was an able one in the New England states. Their system is *sui generis* in which the common law is little attended to. Lincoln is one of the ablest in their system'." Reinsch, *op. cit.*, pp. 416-417.

[49] While justice in Pennsylvania is said to have been characterized by the simplicity and fewness of its laws, the absence of lawyers, and the informality of judicial proceedings (see 1, *Pennsylvania Law Reports*, 229; Reinsch, *op. cit.*, pp. 428-432) it must not be viewed as completely devoid of technical nicety or procedural regularity. In the opinion of Mr. Lawrence Lewis, Jr., the course of procedure in seventeenth century Pennsylvania "was much more regular than has been generally supposed." "Although," he says, "the justices were never men of any regular legal training, they were doubtless familiar by book forms with the ordinary mode of conducting legal proceedings and at any rate were invariably solicitous to maintain the dignity and propriety of their separate courts." "The Courts of Pennsylvania in the Seventeenth Century," a paper read before the Historical Society of Pennsylvania in 1881, which is reprinted from *The Pennsylvania Magazine of History and Biography*, in 1, *Reports of Pennsylvania Bar Association*, 1895, p. 356.

[50] Spence's Anecdotes, quoted by Anthony Lausatt, Jr., in "An Essay on Equity in Pennsylvania," prepared in 1825 for the Law Academy of Philadelphia and reprinted in 1, *Pennsylvania Bar Association Reports*, 229. See Reinsch, *op. cit.*, 229.

[51] "Evidence was in many colonies given in writing, or at least taken down by the clerk and made a part of the record in the action; a practice utterly abhorrent to common law ideas, not so to the popular mind to whom the evidence is the most important part of the case. Various modifications of the jury systems have been noted, but in general this venerable and highly popular institution was finally adopted in the colonies in its English form at an early date. The period of prescription was in many of the colonies lowered to five or seven years, a change that was of course eminently consistent with the conditions of an infant colony on a new continent. Executions on land were permitted, and in many cases fundamental distinction between real and personal property in the English Law was obliterated or ignored. The laws of inheritance and of tenure were, . . . very materially modified, very often leading to a system totally unlike the common law at that period." Reinsch, *op. cit.*, 55.

[52] William Duane, writing in post-Revolution days, expressed this demand for simplifications of procedure and the reasons which give rise to it, in a bitter attack on

attempts to "democratize" the working methods of our tribunals of justice lingered long after the colonial period was over, leading in some instances to very unfortunate results indeed.[53]

Other circumstances are also adverted to as to why the common law took root but slowly. It is asserted that it was retarded not only by Puritanism[54] and theocratic influences,[55] but that frontier conditions exerted an adverse influence upon it as well. The suggestions concerning the frontier influence are of interest. It is no easy task to transplant the elements of a culture to a new and rude environment. In making the transfer many losses are suffered and many modifications necessarily result. Large parts of the original cultural pattern are never successfully transplanted. Edward Eggleston in his study of the transit of English civilization to the colonies in the seventeenth century, discusses this subject at some length.[56] The movement from an organized society to one of rude beginnings, he points out, is always a perilous one for the arts and sciences. Dixon Ryan Fox agrees with him and asserts further that civilization, generally speaking, declines when it strikes the frontier.[57] He cites some interesting evidence in support of his statement.[58]

As the first group of legal historians view it, the slow and incomplete acceptance of the principles, techniques, and practices of the common law is but a part of a general tendency of a new country to accept all cultural patterns slowly and incompletely. While this tendency denies the new community many values which the older society has produced over a period of time, it is suggested that this circumstance may not be altogether undesirable. Indeed, some analysts believe that

lawyers and the legal technique. His pamphlet is entitled *"Sampson against the Philistines, or the Reformation of Lawsuits and Justice Made Cheap, Speedy, and Brought to Everyman's Door; Agreeable to the Principles of the Ancient Trial by Jury, Before the Same were Innovated by Judges and Lawyers."* Advocating a return to a system where the trial would be conducted by the jury without lawyers, he asserted that "you can never regain the ancient simple plain justice, such as is necessary for general and common use," without demolishing the whole "farrago of finesse and intricacy" imported from the continent (p. 23). This, he asserted, would be a return to the ancient Saxon system, unadulterated by Norman-Roman influences.

[53] W. F. Dodd, *State Government*, (1928, pp. 11-12; G. M. Hogan, "The Strangled Judge," *American Judicature Society Journal*, vol. 14, pp. 116-125, Dec. 1930).

[54] Morris, *op. cit.*, pp. 45-46.

[55] Reinsch, *op. cit.*, p. 54.

[56] *The Transit of a Civilization from England to America in the Seventeenth Century* (1923), Peter Smith.

[57] *Ideas in Motion*, p. 25.

[58] Mr. Fox presents a dark picture of early eighteenth century New England painted by President Samuel Johnson in his autobiography. "The condition of learning (as well as anything else) was very low in these times, indeed much lower than in the earlier times while those yet lived who had had their education in England and first settled the country. They were now gone off the stage and their sons fell greatly short of their requirements, as through the necessities of the times they could give little attention to the business of education." *Ibid.*, p. 26.

it is a good thing that we cannot transplant a complete culture. Professor Frederick L. Paxson, for one, believes that this "frontier process," as he calls it, permits the scrapping of many obsolete forms and devices which older communities are compelled to put up with. "In older, settled, established communities," he says, "we put up with obsolete conditions, with laws that cease to fulfill a useful purpose and institutions that have become cumbersome rather than profitable. We keep on putting up with them, because to change would be an annoyance and a nuisance, and because one can never be quite sure in lopping off a governmental appendix that something won't be lopped off with it that will leave the system weaker instead of stronger for the operation. But in these new communities, where they started with a great long table and a big white sheet of paper and an abundance of ink, with no solicitations as to what they should write or should not, it was easy to cut out institutions of government and to substitute others that they desired and approved."[59]

Something like this, it is asserted, happened in transplanting the common law to America; [60] and as mentioned before, many observers contend that it was very fortunate that the common law as it existed in the seventeenth century was not brought over bodily to the new world and put into effect.[61] In support of Professor Paxson's theories it should be mentioned that although demands for reforms of the common law were numerous and persistent in England, changes were slow to come, whereas in America, thanks to the "frontier process" the colonists could and did discard many of the archaic formalisms of the common law,[62] apparently to their very great advantage.[63] Among the undesirable

[59] F. L. Paxson, "Influence of Frontier Life on Development of American Law," State Bar Association of Wisconsin, *Reports*, XIII, (1919-1920-1921), p. 484.

[60] "The common law of England is not to be taken in all respects to be that of America. Our ancestors brought with them its general principles and claimed it as their birthright; but they brought with them and adopted only that portion which was applicable to their condition." Justice Story in *Van Ness* v. *Packard*, 2 *Peters*, 144.

[61] It will be remembered "that England at the seventeenth and eighteenth centuries was not in the remotest sense of the term a democratic country and the average Englishman . . . one was restricted in his thoughts and activities by the feudal customs, class, . . . constitutional limitations of his day. Furthermore, throughout the entire colonial period, the government at home enforced in America, principles of law and methods of control that were at bottom monarchial, aristocratic and feudal. Naturally such principles and methods did not take permanent root in the free soil of America, among colonists often radical in temperament, but they survived their transplanting and appeared for many years as features of the law, government, and even social relations of the American seaboard." Charles N. Andrews in Introduction to Beverly Bond's, *The Quit Rent System of the American Colonies*, (1919), p. 13.

[62] "We regard the ignorance of the first colonists of the technicalities of the common law as one of the most fortunate things in the history of the law, since, while the substance of the common law was preserved, we happily lost a great mass of antiquated and useless rubbish and gained in its stead a course of practice of admirable simplicity." Bell, J., in *B. C. & M. R. R.* v. *State* (1855), 32 *N. H.* 231.

[63] "In the colonies most exempt from English supervision the tendency to disregard

features eliminated were many phases of English procedural laws and the law of evidence. Much of the legal procedure which was established was greatly simplified. Since, as Sir Henry Maine has remarked, "the substantive law is secreted in the interstices of procedure," it is not surprising that important departures in substantive law accompanied many of these procedural changes.[64]

Turning to the substantive law proper, some conception of the modifying influence of transplantation upon common-law devices may be derived from an examination of colonial experiences with the "quit-rent." "The history of the colonial quit-rent," writes Professor Beverly Bond, Jr., who has written an authoritative monograph upon the subject, "illustrates the futility of the attempt to transplant to fresh soil a feudal charge upon the land that even in the home country was outgrowing its original justification."[65] The quit-rent was established with varying success in all the American colonies except those of New England[66] and continued to "be collected within the territory of the thirteen colonies until the eve of the revolution, and traces of its influence can be seen long after all feudal incidents were abolished by the first state constitutions."[67] It was a remnant of feudal tenure and it is well to remember that[68] "in no single particular have the customs of the past

---

the authority of the common law was frequently given public expression. These colonies were Massachusetts, Plymouth, New Haven, Connecticut, Rhode Island, Pennsylvania, and Maryland. To a lesser extent in the provinces generally frontier innovation was present in the seventeenth century; although outward deference was paid to English legal institutions." Morris, *op. cit.*, pp. 17-18.

[64] Morris, *op. cit.*, p. 61.

[65] *The Quit-Rent System in the American Colonies*, (1919), Yale Historical Publications, p. 459; see also Williamson, *History of Maine*, Belknap, *History of New Hampshire*; Burk, *History of Virginia*; Beverly, *History of Virginia*; and Bruce, *Institutional History of Virginia*.

[66] Though quit-rents were originally proposed as a feature of the land-system in New England, "they were never actually established in the colonies of Massachusetts Bay, Plymouth, Connecticut, or Rhode Island." *Ibid.*, p. 35. Indeed the Body of Liberties of 1641 forbade any such charge as a quit-rent except by order of the General Court. This regulation was adhered to and the free tenure of land which resulted in Plymouth and Massachusetts had important results. (*Colonial Law of Massachusetts, Reprint*, pp. 33-35.) For among other things "it saved the New England Colonies from the struggles which so frequently arose elsewhere, over this unpopular form of tenure, and it strengthened the habit already established among the Puritan settlers, of self-assertion in matters of government. To a certain extent it served as an example to other colonies, for wherever the Massachusetts settlers went they carried with them this idea of the ownership of the soil, which took root at once in Connecticut, Rhode Island, and New Haven, and in the end won out in New Hampshire. . . . " Bond, *ibid.*, pp. 38-39.

[67] *Ibid.*, p. 20. For a discussion of some of the legal aspects of New England land-holding see Goebel, "King's Law and Local Custom in Seventeenth Century New England," *Columbia Law Review*, vol. 31, 1931, pp. 443-447.

[68] "The tenure by which a large portion of our colonial lands was held was commonly styled free and common socage or tenure in fee-simple, the terms of which were fealty and fixed rent. Feudally speaking, fealty was the bond between lord and men, which survived only in the oath of allegiance to the crown; rent was the bond between the lord and the land, the symbol of territorial ownership, and was usually called the

been more tenacious and persistent than in the domain of real property." For example, even today, much of the law in this field "governing descent, contract, conveyance, and tenure bear the marks of their feudal origin."[69]

Despite this fact and although landholding in Colonial America was essentially tenurial in character, the common-law principles built around the quit-rent in England which were theoretically transplanted to America, were actually not "universally accepted" at all. "It was not always possible," Professor Bond asserts, "at such a distance, to enforce legal rules that had been developed in the mother country, and it became necessary to determine anew in each colony such questions as the amount, the place and medium of payment, and the means for the enforcement of the quit-rent." The establishment of this land charge in the American colonies, he adds, was in reality "an attempt to transfer a feudal relationship and a feudal obligation from the Old World, where it had meaning, to the new where it had none."[70] That such an

quit-rent, or sometimes—and there is an instance of this in the 'Fundamental Constitutions' of Carolina—the chief rent. In addition there were other incidents, such as alienation fines and escheats. The quit-rent was originally a commutation in money of certain medieval villein obligations, such as laboring for the lord of the manor a number of days in the week and paying to him a proportion of the produce of the villein's land and stock. In very early times in England, the payments of a money rent seems to have been the privilege of the class of sokemen (whence the name of the tenure), the free peasantry, which in considerable numbers survived the Norman Conquest. . . . But later the quit-rent was used to designate any form of payment, which absolved or made quit the tenant, whether vassals, freeholder, copyholder, or leaseholder, in respect of personal services or their similar obligation to the lord. The tenure there evolved became the 'freest' of all the English land tenures, and because of its easy adaptability to a changing land system, which was gradually throwing off its medieval fetters, was widely employed to meet the need of a simpler and more flexible method of acquiring landed property. The strictly feudal tenures . . . had become formal and rare by the seventeenth century . . . so that *socage tenure* was all but universal in the British world during our colonial period. (Pollock and Maitland, *History of the English Law*, Id-Ed), I, 356. As there were no copyholds in America, it applied only to freeholds and leaseholds the prevailing types of land in the colonies, and unless payment of the rent was waived, as in the case of the corporate colonies, all colonial freeholders and leaseholders were under obligation to recognize in one form or another the higher title of some landed proprietor. The payment in no way hampered the freeholder in the control of his land, for although actual ownership remained elsewhere, he was free to alienate or bequeath his real estate according to the law of his colony and to exercise all the rights of possession, provided he conformed to the terms of his tenure." Charles Andrews' "Introduction" to Bond's *The Quit-Rent System in the American Colonies*, pp. 16-17.

[69] *Ibid.*, pp. 14-15.

[70] "Except in the corporate colonies of Massachusetts, Rhode Island, and Connecticut the formula held good, *nulle terre sans seigneur*, for every acre of land was held of a lord, either the king himself, or some landed proprietor or proprietors to whom a grant had been made by the crown. Even in those colonies, though there was nothing tenurial about the way the towns distributed their land among their own inhabitants, for the Puritans were vehemently opposed to the distinction between lord and tenant and were determined to be 'supreme lords of their own lands, equal before God and the law,' there was much that was tenurial in the higher relations of town and colony with the crown. . . . Thus the feudal (in broader sense) landed relationship which was so widely preva-

attempt could meet with complete success, was to ask altogether too much. The result was that the "quit-rent in the domain of real property, like the royal prerogative in the field of government and the navigation acts in the field of commerce, was an obstacle to complete colonial independence, and a check upon the ability of the people to utilize its own resources for its own benefit and advantage."[71]

If we were to stop at this point, we would have noted that there is a distinct difference of opinion held by reputable historians as to the nature of colonial law. We would have seen that in the view of one group the English common law system was but slowly and incompletely received in the earlier colonial period for the good and sufficient reasons that: (1) there was a scarcity of trained lawyers and judges to administer it; (2) in a new land devoid of books and learning a highly technical system would have been difficult to apply if the colonists had been interested in applying it, which they were not, since simpler forms appealed to them and since frontier conditions exerted an adverse influence upon it so well; and (3) the acceptance of the common law was retarded by religious forces which were more interested in Biblical precepts than in the technicalities of the English legal system, which were disapproved of anyway. We would have also seen that in the view of a second group of historians important qualifications should be made concerning some of these conclusions. In their view it is a mistake to suppose that there was a general lack of legal formality in the earlier colonial period despite the admitted difficulties of transplanting in full the legal institutions of the homeland. Resting their case upon recent studies of early colonial law in Massachusetts and Maryland this group holds that there was a much higher degree of formality in colonial law than had been previously supposed.

While these conflicting views as to the nature of colonial law do not afford a completely satisfactory picture of our legal beginnings, it would seem that we must rest content with it, inadequate as it is, until further surveys comparable to those executed in Massachusetts and Maryland throw more light on the subject. In the meantime, a brief review of some of the evidence now available will explain, in part at least, the kind of qualification, which the Goebel-Plucknett group has in mind, and reveal some of the difficulties which were encountered in the administration of colonial justice as well.

---

lent elsewhere, had a place even in these self-governing Puritan Colonies. . . . " Charles Andrews' "Introduction" to Bond's *The Quit-Rent System in the American Colonies*, pp. 14-15.

[71] Bond, *ibid.*, pp. 21-22.

CHAPTER II

THE VARYING CONDITION OF LAWYER AND JUDGE IN THE COLONIAL PERIOD OF DEVELOPMENT

The facts asserted in Chapter I as to the scarcity of trained lawyers and judges during the early colonial period seem to be fairly well established in the records of many of the colonies. It seems clear that not only were lawyers scarce during a great part of the seventeenth century but also that the colonists were bent on keeping them scarce.[1] At any rate lawyers were made the subject matter of considerable restrictive legislation during this period, as the situation in Massachusetts indicates. In Article 26 of the Body of Liberties, which was adopted in 1641, it was provided that attorneys might plead causes other than their own, but all fees were disallowed,[2] a rule which greatly discouraged lawyers.[3] This policy did not last long, and Article 26 of the Body of Liberties was omitted from the revision of the statutes made in 1648.[4] From that year on "it was legal to employ paid attor-

[1] "During the seventeenth century," says Oliver Chitwood, "there was considerable prejudice against lawyers throughout the colonies, and the practice of the legal profession was discouraged by a number of legislative enactments. Most of the judges were without legal training, and so neither bench nor bar were versed in the English Common Law. In the first half of the colonial era judicial decisions could not therefore have followed closely the precedents of English practice even if there had been a disposition to do so." *A History of Colonial America*, p. 190.

[2] "Every man that findeth himself unfit to plead his own cause in any Court shall have Libertie to employ any man against whom the Court doth not except, to helpe him, provided he give him noe fee or reward for his paines. This shall not exempt the partie himself from answereing such questions in person as the Court shall thinke meete to demand of him." Art. 26 of the *Body of Liberties of 1641*.

[3] "As attorneys willing to practice for pure love of justice were not easy to find, the practice grew up of litigants or defendants going to some magistrate for his advice and opinion before the cause came to trial. The Reverend Nathaniel Ward, the 'simple Cobbler of Agawam,' who had practiced law in London for some ten years (as an 'outer barrister') before he entered the ministry, rightly denounced the propriety of this arrangement. After he had argued against it in his Election Sermon of 1641, an effort was made to forbid this practice of private consultation with judges. But, as Winthrop records, nothing was then done; partly on the ground that if the magistrates were forbidden to give legal advice 'we must then provide lawyers to direct men in their causes.' (Winthrop's Journal), 1908, ed. II, 37." *Records of the Suffolk County Court, 1671-1680*, vol. 1, p. xxii, Publications of the Colonial Society of Massachusetts, vol. 29.

[4] *The Laws and Liberties of Massachusetts*, Reprinted from the 1648 Edition (1928).

neys in the Massachusetts Colony."[5] The spirit of Article 26 was not so short-lived, however, as subsequent events proved.[6]

In Virginia a similar tendency is noted.[7] Various charges were urged against lawyers as a class. It was said that "they were constantly stirring up troublesome and unnecessary suits" and were "ignorant, unskillful, and covetous"; looking rather to their own profits than to the interests of their clients. In 1645, the legislature passed an act which virtually eliminated paid attorneys.[8] This act was repealed in 1656, only to be followed by a new act of 1657, which imposed a heavy fine upon lawyers for appearing in court in behalf of a client. With the exclusion of the professional attorney, "the ordinary law business outside

[5] "Apparently the number of lawyers and their influence increased more rapidly than the rulers desired, for in 1633 it was enacted by the General Court, 'That no person who is an usual and Common Attorney in any Inferior Court shall be admitted to sit as a Deputy in this Court.' (Id., p. 224.) Sanction was also given attorneys by a statute of October 1673, making it lawful for any person to sue in any court 'by his lawful Attorney Authorized under his Hande and Seale.' (Whitemore, *Colonial Laws, 1672-1686*, p. 211). Thus these seventeenth century lawyers usually sued in their own names as attorneys, and not in their clients alone as is the practice today." *Ibid.*, p. xiii.

[6] Morison and Chafee, *Records of the Suffolk County Court, 1671-1680*, vol. 1, p. xxii. *Publications of the Colonial Society of Massachusetts*, vol. 29. "After a while," says Frederick W. Grinnell, " 'usual and common' attorneys, even though not trained lawyers, become recognized as a necessary evil to save the time of the court; but even they were so verbose that in 1656 they were limited to one hour of talk on each side. Under these primitive conditions with laymen as judges and with prejudice against English law, even though needed and used, there developed what Brooks Adams has called 'the pernicious tradition' that special training was not needed to administer justice; and that anybody could be either a lawyer or a judge." "The Bench and Bar in Colony and Province, 1630-1776," ch. 6, *Commonwealth History of Massachusetts*, (Hart, Ed., 1928), vol. 2, p. 162. It will be remembered, however, that Winthrop, Bellingham, Humphreys, Dudley, Downing, and Ward were trained in the law. See *Notebook of Thomas Lechford*, XV; Hildreth, *History of the United States*, I, 211.

[7] A statute was passed in 1658 which was concerned with legal formalities. "Whereas there is and daily doth arise excessive charges and great delaies and hinderances of justice betwixt the subjects of this collony by reason of small mistakes in writts and formes of pleading; it is therefore, for the prevention thereof, enacted by this present General Assembly that all courts of judicature within the collony shall proceed and give judgment according as the right of the cause and the matter in law shall appeare unto them, without regard of any imperfection, default or want of forme in any work, return, plaint or process, or any other cause whatsoever." Hening, *Statutes of Virginia*, I, 486.

[8] "The passage of laws excluding regular attorneys from the courts," says Philip A. Bruce, "is an indication, not so much of a lack of practical sagacity on the part of the justices, at whose instigation, or at least with whose consent, such laws were probably adopted, as of the general inferiority, certainly in learning of the members of the bar during the earlier decades of the century. To shut out professional attorneys and to suffer the persons, without even pretension to special knowledge, to practice, would have been to write the same evil in a much worse form; so in order to strike at the root of the whole trouble, a serious effort was made to carry on the business of the courts without any assistance from the outside." This restrictive course was looked upon by the Governor and Council, as not only impracticable, but as an encroachment upon the suitors' rights; and in a few years, "professional attorneys resumed their former position in court, and thereafter found no difficulty in retaining it as the volume of business, owing to the colony's growth in wealth and population, rapidly-became so great, that even in the opinion of the justices themselves, only trained lawyers could properly attend to it." Philip A. Bruce, *Institutional History of Virginia in the Seventeenth Century*, vol. 1, p. 565.

of the courts," says Philip A. Bruce, "fell, to a large degree, into the hands of clerks who were rendered capable of attending to it by the legal information they had acquired in the performance of the duties of their office. It would appear from allowances made in inventories, that, about the middle of the century, numerous wills were drafted by this body of men, to whom it was only natural that persons wishing to have their last testaments drawn up should apply."[9] In 1680, lawyers were again allowed to practice under strict regulation and after license by the governor.[10]

In Connecticut restrictive measures were also passed, although not at the outset. When the original constitution, or "Fundamental Orders" of Connecticut was framed, Roger Ludlow, an English barrister of ability, who was largely instrumental in drafting the measure, borrowed extensively from the Massachusetts "Body of Liberties," but did not include the provision excluding "mercenary attorneys." Shortly thereafter, laws were adopted forbidding the employment of attorneys for the defense in proceedings for criminal misdemeanors and in 1667 this was enforced by a penalty of a fine or an hour in the stocks.[11] Certain exceptions were made, however.[12] It was not until early in the next century that Connecticut made provision for the admission of attorneys, as regular officers of the courts, and then only in a limited way.[13] While most of these restrictive measures are seventeenth century products, hostility to the legal profession seems to carry on over to the eighteenth century, as laws passed in Maryland and Georgia indicate.[14] Indeed some aspects of this dislike are continued long past the Revolution.[15]

Despite these circumstances it would seem to be a mistake to suppose that the general lack of professional training during this early period means a complete absence of the lawyer's technique. This is an important point and should be kept in mind when considering the

[9] *Ibid.*, pp. 562-563.

[10] Morris, *op. cit.*, pp. 43-44.

[11] *Two Centuries Growth of American Law, 1701-1901*, p. 15.

[12] *Colonial Records*, II, 59.

[13] Hildreth, *History of the United States*, II, 513.

[14] In Maryland an act was passed in 1725, regulating lawyer's fees with extreme strictness and giving an option to the planters to pay in tobacco or currency at a fixed rate. In 1729, despite the protests of the profession, the act was extended for three years. See Morris, *ibid.*, p. 43. In Georgia restrictive legislation was also passed. See Cardozo, *Law and Literature*, p. 155. In 1748, the position of the lawyer was stabilized when a general statute was passed providing for the licensing of all lawyers. See Warren, *op. cit.*, p. 39.

[15] "Throughout the greater part of the colonial period," says R. B. Morris, "both bench and bar remained suspect to the rank and file of the citizenry." *Select Cases of the Mayor's Court of New York City, 1674-1784*, p. 57. See William Duane's comments in his "Samson against the Philistines" and the remarks of Hector G. John de Crevécouer in his "Letters of an American Farmer." See also F. R. Aumann, "Public Opinion and the Legal Technique," *United States Law Review*, Feb., 1935, pp. 72-75.

limited and unpopular role played by the lawyer at this time. During the early colonial period, says Judge Carroll T. Bond,[16] "there was among educated men generally a familiarity with the law and its administration that is not ordinarily found among laymen today."[17] "Skill in the law," he says, "had not yet been so abandoned to professional lawyers, and just as laymen could be found who merely had skill in physic, for example, John Winthrop, Jr., in America, and Sir Francis Drake, in England, so there were non-professionals who had skill in the law. This had been true in England in the fifteenth century, when, as it had been said 'every man who had property to protect, if not every well-educated woman also, was perfectly well versed in the ordinary forms of legal processes.' "[18]

Some such circumstance as this must explain the fact that the Records of the Suffolk County Court of Massachusetts for the period between 1671 and 1680 show that conveyancing, "a phase of the modern lawyers' work no less important than appearing in court," was well developed,[19] although lawyers were still frowned upon in that section[20] and were in no sense required to meet the standards later demanded of them.[21] As Judge Bond has pointed out in connection with the conditions existing in Maryland during this same period, "no sharp line could yet be drawn between attorneys in fact and persons who

[16] Judge Bond's remarks are directed immediately to certain conditions existing in the eighteenth century. They are applicable, however, to seventeenth century conditions as well.

[17] Carroll T. Bond, "Introduction" to *Proceedings of the Maryland Court of Appeals, 1695-1729*, (1934), p. xix.

[18] See also Holdsworth, *History of the English Law*, II, 416, 556; also J. F. Baldwin, "Litigation in English Society," *Vassar Medieval Studies* (New Haven, 1923), pp. 151-182; Carroll T. Bond, *ibid.*, p. xv.

[19] "There is abundant evidence of the existence of skilled conveyancers in the complex form of the documents reprinted in these volumes." Morison and Chafee, *Records of the Suffolk County Court, 1671-1680*, vol. 1, p. xxvii, Publications of the Colonial Society of Massachusetts, vol. 29.

[20] "In the period (1671-1680) . . . the practice of law was far from being recognized as a profession, or even a reputable calling. Much of the early prejudice against lawyers as a class which characterized the founders of New England, still survived; and the conduct of some of these who are repeatedly found acting as attorneys in these records was certainly not such as to remove those prejudices." Morison and Chafee, *Records of the Suffolk County Court, 1671-1680*, vol. 1, p. xxviii, Publications of the Colonial Society of Massachusetts, vol. 29.

[21] " . . . by the year 1672, . . . paid attorneys were a recognized but hardly a reputable class. No educational or moral requirements were made of them; and they were not sworn in at the bar of the court, or in any way licensed or regulated. No one of the several persons who are found practicing before the Suffolk County Court during the period (1671-1680) had had, so far as we know, any legal training; and only one, Elisha Cooke, had had even a liberal education. . . . It was not until about 1730 that Jeremiah Gridley succeeded in imposing professional standards on the Suffolk bar. (In 1688, Andros obliged attorneys to take oath upon admission to the bar. In 1701 a statute required such an oath. Warren, *History of the American Bar*, (1918), pp. 72, 77, 78)." Morison and Chafee, *Records of the Suffolk County Court, 1671-1680*, vol. I, p. xxvii.

earned a living by appearing in court for litigants."[22] There can be no question, however, that many of the attorneys in the cases reported in Massachusetts "do correspond to the lawyers of today."[23] In Maryland, which was much more advanced than Massachusetts in this respect,[24] there is a reported instance of "the requirement of special qualifications for an attorney in 1657."[25] Indeed "as early as 1637 opinions of leading men were taken on questions of law, and brief notes of the earliest provincial court sessions show an observance of the distinction between causes of action at common law and an approximate adherence to the rules of procedure of England."[26]

While the beginning of a truly professional bar in Maryland is the subject of uncertainty, "in the decade of the 1660's the courts are found admitting what were denominated (sworn attorneys of the court), evidently men of special training in the law, and these men constituted a professional bar."[27] However, the attorneys at law who may be said to have formed this professional bar "were not at that time, nor for a century afterwards, men whose sole occupation in life was their work in the law. The chief occupation of substantially all these men was the cultivating and marketing of tobacco. Work in the law was only periodic, having been with possible minor exceptions, taken up only when the courts opened their terms, and whole terms intervened between successive steps in the pleadings. The attorneys at law were, indeed, men of expert training in the law, but not exclusively practitioners of it."[28]

[22] *Ibid.*, p. xxv.

[23] *Ibid.*, p. xxvi. It was not, however, until 1686 that "the Superior Court, which consisted of a majority of the 'President's Council', with William Stoughton as Chief Justice, began the practice, by rule of Court, of requiring 'attorneys' to take an oath." Grinnell, *op. cit.*, p. 163.

[24] "In many ways besides their knowledge of law-books, the Maryland lawyers described by Judge Bond seem further advanced than their Massachusetts contemporaries. The Maryland lawyers were sworn and admitted to the bar. They reason more like lawyers today and are much concerned with the same kind of questions. Was the Provincial Court the exact equivalent of the Court of King's Bench? How was appellate procedure to be reformed? Should judicial dissents be recorded? Altho Maryland writs were in English as were true in Massachusetts they were frequently called by a Latin title. In comparison, Massachusetts attorneys seem unlearned. Latin is used only three times in these pages to describe writs and it rarely occurs in other connections, the most interesting example being a maxim possibly taken from Coke." Morison and Chafee, *Records of the Suffolk County Court, 1671-1680*, vol. 1, p. xxxii, Publications of the Colonial Society of Massachusetts, vol. 29.

[25] *The Archives of Maryland*, XLI, 10, cited by Bond, *op. cit.*, p. xxii.

[26] Bond, *op. cit.*, p. xxii.

[27] *Ibid.*, p. xxii. "of the sworn attorneys admitted, John Morecroft, described by Governor Charles Calvert in 1672 as the best lawyer in the country (Calvert Papers, *Md. Hist. Society Fund Publications*, No. 28, 264), and who may therefore be accepted as the first leader of the Maryland bar of record, was admitted on June 12, 1666. He had appeared as attorney for many litigants before that time and had apparently acquired his training in the courts of the province." *Ibid.*, p. xxiii.

[28] Bond, *op. cit.*, p. xxii.

The condition of the legal profession in Virginia during the same period is very much the same. William Sherwood, a native of England, "appears to have been one of the few attorneys residing in the Colony who devoted his talents and energies exclusively to the pursuit of law."[29] The majority of the members of the bar combined their activities in this field with those of the tobacco-planter, and occasionally with those of the surveyor. One of their number, Jacob Johnson, an advocate of Princess Anne County, "employed a part of his time in following the business of a brick-layer, and house plasterer."[30]

In New York, the professional level during the seventeenth century seems to correspond more closely to that of Massachusetts than to that of Maryland. "The men who practiced as attorneys during the first decade of English government of New York," says Julius Goebel, Jr., "were undoubtedly self-taught."[31] After the Revolution of 1688, conditions improved with the advent of a number of persons of more extensive training.[32] It was not until 1700, or thereabouts, however, that far-reaching changes in practice were introduced.[33] While the indictment made by Lord Bellomont in 1698 may be overly severe,[34] the general standard could not have been high, and the service of an agent or attorney-in-fact as distinguished from the professional practitioner must have been frequently resorted to. They undoubtedly were employed in the Mayor's Court of New York, if recent studies are deemed conclusive. In that court, according to R. B. Morris, "down

[29] Bruce, *op. cit.*, p. 575; see also Hildreth, *History of the United States*, I, 337, 516; *William and Mary College Quarterly*, VIII, 228.
[30] See *Virginia Magazine of History and Biography*, vol. VII, p. 361; see also Philip A. Bruce, *op. cit.*, p. 575. Mr. Bruce discusses the lawyers of the seventeenth century Virginia at some length. See *ibid.*, pp. 561-587. See also "Court and Bar in Colonial Virginia," *The Green Bag*, vol. 12, 1900.
[31] "The Courts and the Law in Colonial New York," *History of the State of New York*, (Alex. Flick, ed., 1933), vol. III, p. 35.
[32] *Ibid.*, pp. 34, 35.
[33] "The profound changes which took place in the whole technique of law administration is in many ways astounding. There was never really any necessity for abolishing the Duke's Laws or the acts of the Dongan Assemblies, for upon the arrival of really learned barristers the crudities that had become the rule in the practice of the law were by mere force of example swept into the discard. There have been preserved some notes of memoranda of authority in various arguments on demurrer in the provincial courts about the year 1783, which demonstrate that the New York bar was not far behind that of England in profundity of learning and adeptness in dealing with common law precedent. Indeed one need only examine the account of the Bayard trial (1702), one of the most fully reported cases of the early eighteenth century, to realize how the professionalization of the law was advancing. And if one turns to the Zenger trial (1735) it is apparent that the practice of the law had acquired a high degree of technical perfection." Julius Goebel, Jr., "The Courts and the Law in Colonial New York," *History of the State of New York*, (Alexander Flick, ed., 1933), vol. III, p. 35.
[34] " . . . Governor Bellomont had characterized the lawyers of the late seventeenth century in disparaging tones, noting that they could hardly be considered lawyers at all." Michael Kraus, "Social Classes and Customs," *History of the State of New York*, vol. II, p. 388.

to the end of the seventeenth century, if a litigant wished to be represented . . . by counsel, he would have to make his selection from
the very small number of lawyers of questionable training who were
available. If he could not spare time from the shop or had to be at
sea when the case was scheduled to appear, he would frequently ask
a friend or a relative, possibly his wife to appear as 'attorney' for him."[35]
This practice, he adds, was frequently resorted to in all colonial courts
of the seventeenth century.[36]

With the development of greater population and wealth at the
end of the seventeenth and the beginning of the eighteenth century, an
increase in the number of trained lawyers is evidenced in a number of
the colonies. Judge Bond reports an increase of this sort in Maryland
and adds that "frequently men with the training of the Inns of the
Court were added to the bar."[37] He mentioned a number of them
including "Henry Jowles, trained at Gray's Inn; Charles Carroll, the
first of that name in Maryland, who had entered the Inner Temple
in 1685; William Bladen, also of the Inner Temple; Daniel Dulany
(the elder) of Gray's Inn; Wornell Hunt of Lincoln's Inn; Michael
Howard of Gray's Inn; Edmund Jennings of the Middle Temple;
Thomas Macnemara and Michael Macnemara of Gray's Inn; and
George Plater, 2d., of Inner Temple."[38]

Towards the end of the seventeenth century the condition of the
legal profession in Virginia was also improving. While there were no
licensed practitioners as yet,[39] the fact remains that "Law had, by this
time, become in Virginia as distinct a profession as Medicine, and the
men specially trained for it, by their practice through a long series of
years, now formed a separate body remarkable for a high degree of
respectability from the point of view of talents, integrity, and even
learning."[40] While Virginia may not boast of the number of lawyers
trained at the Inns of Court that Maryland was fortunate enough to
possess, she was certainly not without such representatives. Henry
Perrot of Rappahannock County, for one, was trained at the Inns of

[35] R. B. Morris, Introduction, *Select Cases of the Mayor's Court of New York City,
1674-1784,* p. 52.
[36] In this connection he cites Bond, *op. cit.,* p. xxi and Morison and Chafee, *op.
cit.,* pp. xxv, 52.
[37] *Ibid.,* p. xxv.
[38] "Of this group Dulany was probably the strongest lawyer. He is chiefly known as
author in 1728 of a pamphlet on *The Rights of Inhabitants of Maryland to the Benefit
of the English Laws,* (see Richard Henry Spencer,) Hon. Daniel Dulany, 1685, (the
elder), *Maryland Historical Mag.,* XIII, 20, *et seq.*). He was the father of Daniel
Dulany, the younger, (1721-1797), who is celebrated in Maryland as the ablest of provincial lawyers, or as his contemporaries in the province thought, the ablest on the continent."
Ibid., p. xxv.
[39] Beverly, *History of Virginia,* p. 208.
[40] Bruce, *op. cit.,* p. 568.

Court.[41] Moreover, the spirit which obtained earlier in the century toward restrictive legislation was now gone and there was a tendency to "encourage the enlargement of the circle of competent men who devoted the chief part of their time, as paid attorneys and solicitors, to looking after the legal interests of their different communities."[42] Indeed, in 1681, the establishment of a Law Society at Jamestown was proposed.[43]

During the course of the eighteenth century the legal profession continued to improve in dignity and strength, and came to recruit its membership by license and examination. During the earlier part of the century it numbered such men as Edward Barradal, John Clayton, Stevens Thompson, William Robertson, and John Holloway. In its latter years it produced an outstanding group, including such men as Patrick Henry, George Wythe, Peyton Randolph, Edmund Randolph, Robert Carter Nichols, Thomas Jefferson, St. George Tucker, Henry Tazewell and a number of others. These men prepared the way for an early nineteenth century Virginia bar which was to number among its membership John Marshall, Spencer Roane, Littleton W. Tazewell, Chapman Johnson, John Wickham, and Benjamin W. Leigh.[44]

In New York, a similar increase in trained lawyers took place during this time.[45] "At the turn of the century," writes Goebel, "the desire for the common law was filled with the advent of lawyers from home, and in their hands the amorphous jurisprudence of the new courts presently took shape."[46] While this group did not apply the common law technique as satisfactorily as might have been desired, they did draw up "the pleadings and forms necessary to an orderly practice, adopting the English models to colonial conditions."[47] "Precedents"

[41] *William and Mary College Quarterly*, vol. IV, p. 135.

[42] Bruce, *op. cit.*, p. 569.

[43] *Ibid.*, p. 569.

[44] Lyon G. Tyler, *History of Virginia*, vol. II, p. 563.

[45] Julius H. Goebel, Jr., "The Courts and the Law in Colonial New York," *History of the State of New York* (Alex. Flick, ed., 1933), vol. III, p. 35.

[46] "The common law as an ideal was devoutly prayed for; the law in fact—a tangle of technicalities—was just what the lawyers brought. In the early days, with a lay justice like 'Tangier' Smith, there was little hope for an intelligent application of the tortured blackness of the *Book of Entries*, but there was a rough and substantial justice accomplished. The metamorphosis from country justice to common law perfection begins with the turn of the century." *Ibid.*, pp. 34-35.

[47] "There is no doubt that the New York bar during the eighteenth century was learned," says Julius Goebel, Jr., "but the law as practiced by it, was not flexible and, in spite of certain occasional changes, it did not have that close relation to the life of the community, nor did it make that steady and minute adjustment to circumstances, which was one of the prime attributes of the judge-made law of England, and which gave to the English law its constant vitality. In New York, the task of adjusting the common law to the American wilds was an accomplishment of the legislature, and not of the judiciary; and in the statutes enacted within a period of one century lies the real record of the crown's behest that colonial law should conform 'as nearly as may be' to the law of

became important and were carefully preserved in manuscript form.[48] "The chief result of the lawyer's achievement in bringing about a more or less complete reception of the common law in the province," in Goebel's view, "was the certainty and stabilization of the practice."[49] As time passed, an increasing dependence upon identical English precedents developed, and there was little or no growth of native precedent. Consequently "the reception of the English common law tended toward a certain ossification."[50]

During the course of the eighteenth century the leading lawyers of New York joined together in a Law Society and made provisions for training lawyers in their offices. A very definite course of study was prescribed which is considered by some competent observers as far superior to that which succeeded it. "Many leading lawyers of the eighteenth century were trained in this way," says Professor Goebel, "and one can understand why these men were superior in learning to those of a later generation, whose chief pabulum was the cloying text of Blackstone."[51] That it was not always successful, however, may be gleaned from William Livingston's description of his own experiences, when preparing for the profession in an able lawyer's office during the 1730's.[52] Although he paid a substantial fee for the privilege of studying law while acting as a clerk, the training feature was almost completely ignored. It was assumed, he said, that the young neophyte is to learn the law "by gazing on a number of books which he had neither time

---

England." "The Courts and the Law in Colonial New York," *History of the State of New York*, vol. III, p. 38 (Alexander C. Flick, ed., 1933). This may explain Dean Pound's statement that "as late as 1791 the law was so completely at large in New York that the genius of Kent was needed to make the common law of that state." *The Spirit of Common Law*, p. 117. For criticism of this statement see Goebel, "King's Law and Local Custom in Seventeenth Century New England," *Columbia Law Review*, vol. 31, 1931, p. 420.

[48] Julius Goebel, Jr., *op. cit.*, p. 36.

[49] *Ibid.*, p. 37.

[50] *Ibid.*, p. 37.

[51] "In both the Smith and Livingston papers, is preserved a document dealing with law study, that probably represents the typical method of training in an eighteenth century New York law office. It tells us that 'the sciences necessary for a lawyer are: 1. The English, Latin, and French tongues. 2. Writing, arithmetic, geometry, surveying, merchant's accounts or bookkeeping. 3. Geography, chronology, history. 4. Logic and rhetoric. 5. Divinity. 6. Law of Nature and Nations. 7. Law of England.' Explicit instructions were given as to the books to be used in the various fields of knowledge. The directions for the study of law are exceedingly interesting, since the student is first expected to ground himself in the legal philosophy of the period, and only then to master the leading English text writers." *Ibid.*, p. 36.

[52] In describing the bar of the New York Mayor's court, R. B. Morris says: "The great majority of Mayor's court attorneys in colonial times merely served clerkships—a routinized siege of laborious copying." *Select Cases of the Mayor's Court of New York City, 1674-1784*, p. 57.

nor opportunity to read; or that he is to be metamorphos'd into an attorney by the virtue of Hocus Pocus."[53]

In New York, as in Maryland, a number of lawyers of this period had been trained at the Inns of Court. "Down to 1750," says Morris, "about a dozen members of the New York bar had studied at the Inns of Court."[54] A number of other members of the bar had received their preparatory training at one or another of the colonial colleges of the time.[55] In fact, the New York bar contained some very competent lawyers.[56] A respectable group of well-prepared lawyers were to be found practicing in the Mayor's Court of New York alone. The Bar was extremely limited in size however. Not more than a half dozen attorneys practiced before the Mayor's Court during the first two decades of the eighteenth century,[57] and the number was kept small for a long time.[58] During the early years of the eighteenth century, the increasing needs of the rapidly growing commonwealth of Massachusetts were likewise reflected in an expanding bar. Here as in Maryland some outstanding figures were developed, including John Read,[59] Jeremiah Gridley,[60] and Edmund Trowbridge.[61]

[53] Theodore Sedgwick, *Memoir of the Life of William Livingston*, (N. Y. 1833), pp. 126-127. Morris, *op. cit.*, p. 57. See also John Adams, *Works*, II, 52.

[54] Included in the group are Sampson Broughton, John Chambers, and Joseph Murray who were Middle Templars, and James Alexander who seems to have studied at Gray's Inn. Morris, *op. cit.*, p. 57.

[55] William Livingston, John Morin Scott, Thomas Jones, and the two Smiths came from Yale; while John Jay came into the profession from King's College in the late provincial period. Morris, *op. cit.*, p. 57.

[56] Including James Alexander, William Smith, Joseph Murray, and John Tabor Kempe. Morris, *op. cit.*, pp. 52-57.

[57] R. B. Morris points out that "it was customary in English towns of the seventeenth and eighteenth centuries to restrict the practice of law to a handful of practitioners." This usage was apparently followed in New York. In the twenties "more highly trained lawyers made their appearance; competition grew keener and the prize at stake more lucrative." Subsequently a few lawyers were actually given a monopoly of the practice in the Mayor's Court. While this was broken in 1746, practice remained in the hands of a comparative few down to the Revolution. *Select Cases of the Mayor's Court of New York City, 1674-1784*, pp. 52-57.

[58] In the Colony of New York attorneys at law were appointed by special license from the Governor. During the sixty-eight years immediately preceding the Revolution, Simeon E. Baldwin writes, there were some one hundred and thirty-six attorneys admitted to practice. See *Two Centuries Growth of the American Law, 1701-1901*, pp. 16-17; see also, In the Matter of Cooper, 22 *New York Reports*, 67, 79.

[59] John Read commenced practice in Massachusetts in 1722, after considerable experience in Connecticut. He is said to have "reduced the jarring and contradictory forms of practice to a system, taught courts the advantages of precedents, and practitioners the value of knowledge." He also attempted to reduce the "quaint, redundant and obscure phraseology" of the English "deeds of conveyance" to shorter and simpler forms. Copies of some of Read's original writs were preserved and published in the book of precedents as late as 1834. See F. S. Grinnell, *op. cit.*, pp. 171-172.

[60] Jeremiah Gridley graduated from Harvard in 1725, "and after a few years of school teaching and the study of theology, turned to the bar and rapidly made such a position for himself that he is sometimes referred to as 'The Father of the Bar.' He represented the Crown at the argument in support of the Application for the Writs of Assist

A similar tendency is noted in other colonies as well.[62] In South Carolina, for example, the legal profession increased in numbers and in distinction as the century advanced and in the years immediately preceding the Revolution is represented by some very able men including Whitaker and Pinckney. By 1771, there were thirty-four members of the bar.[63] Although the legal profession was represented in South Carolina from a very early date, these numbers are impressive.[64] It is interesting to note, however, that when Oglethorpe gave up his complete patriarchal sway in Georgia on July 7, 1733, and set up the government formulated by the Trustees, there was no provision for lawyers, as it was contemplated that Georgia should be "a happy flourishing colony . . . free from that pest and scourge of mankind called lawyers." They were content with a general court, consisting of three judges, called bailiffs, a recorder, and a few constables, or conservators of the peace. "Some of those in authority were untrained, unlettered, cantankerous, and jealous of the others. . . . Here was ample room for tyranny, and the people had reason to complain of it, John Wesley among the chiefest."[65] When Georgia became a royal province in 1752, the first of the lawyers arrived and in five years "they had multiplied so fast that they were important enough to be referred to as 'the bar.' "[66]

As the eighteenth century advanced, the number of trained lawyers in the colonies continued to increase and lawyers in general came to assume an importance in public life that is quite remarkable when viewed in the light of their position in earlier days. So extensive is the change effected that Edmund Burke in his great speech on conciliation with the colonies which was delivered in Parliament on March 22, 1775,

---

ance in 1761, being opposed by James Otis, Jr., who had studied law in his office." *Ibid.*, p. 172.

[61] Edmund Trowbridge who has been referred to by Chief Justice Parker as "perhaps the most profound common lawyer in New England before the Revolution" was born in 1709. Serving as attorney-general and justice of the Superior Court of Judicature, he also wrote an essay on "The Law of Mortgages" and taught law to Theophilus Parsons, Francis Dana, James Putnam, Royal Tyler, Rufus King, Christopher Gore, and Harrison Gray Otis. *Ibid.*, p. 179.

[62] R. B. Morris, *Studies in the History of American Law* (1930), pp. 65-67.

[63] *South Carolina Gazette*, Oct. 31, 1771, cited by Wallace, *History of South Carolina*, vol. I, p. 407.

[64] "The learned professions of the law, medicine, and the ministry," says Wallace, the South Carolina historian, "were represented in the province from an early date. The clause of Locke's *Fundamental Constitutions* forbidding pleading for reward had no more effect than the other parts of that never accepted code. Trott was practicing in civil cases in 1700 and was then jailed for his bold "contempt" of court in defending his client. (Salley, Commissions, etc., 144.) References to practicing lawyers occur in 1714, 1717, etc. (H. J. 4, 239; also Dec. 2, 1714; October 3, 1717.)" *History of South Carolina*, vol. I, p. 407.

[65] E. M. Coulter, *A Short History of Georgia*, p. 71.

[66] *Ibid.*, pp. 77-78.

held the influence of the lawyer to be largely responsible for much of
the spirit of liberty found in the new world. "In no country perhaps
in the world," he said, "is the law so generally studied" and he mentions
the great number of lawyers who were members of the continental congress. He was greatly impressed with the fact that so many law books
were being printed in the colonies for their own use[67] and that as many
copies of Blackstone's Commentaries were sold in America as in England.[68] This widespread interest in law, he believed, made the colonists
"prompt in attack, ready in defense, full of resources." It caused them
to "augur misgovernment at a distance and sniff the approach of tyranny
in every tainted breeze."

Justice Harlan Stone writes:

Burke's portrayal of the position and influence of the legal profession in
Revolutionary America was not overdrawn. The history of the Revolution
and of the formative period of the union of states is a record of leadership
and of the influence of the bar which has never been surpassed at any time or
in any country. Such names as James Otis, John Adams, Josiah Quincy, Robert
Payne of Massachusetts, Peyton Randolph, Patrick Henry, Edmund Pendleton of Virginia, Charles Carroll and Samuel Chase of Maryland, and Alexander Hamilton and James Kent of New York, recall vividly to mind not
only the remarkable development of the common law in America during the
latter part of the eighteenth century but the ascendency of the legal profession
in legislation and in the political and social life of the growing nation.
Lawyers were the most influential members of the colonial legislatures and
the Continental Congress . . . They not only kindled the flame of the Revolution, but they translated the Revolution into institutions under the form of
law with a passionate devotion to liberty and a skill and statesmanship grasp
which has excited the wonder and admiration of the historian. They profoundly influenced the formulation of the constitution and the great legislative
acts organizing the administrative and judicial branches of the government were
the creation of lawyers. The constitution itself was vitalized and made an effective instrument of government by Chief Justice Marshall aided by an able bar.[69]

The influence of the legal profession during these years of growth

[67] E. M. Coulter, *A Short History of Georgia*, p. 71.

[68] When the first edition of Blackstone appeared in 1765, there were more than one
thousand copies sold in America. This exceeded the number sold in England. Before the
Declaration of Independence, nearly twenty-five hundred copies were sold. This is an
important fact, for Blackstone became the foundation of American legal education and
was treated as an authoritative statement of the English law which was received. It seems
to have changed and facilitated legal training, as indicated by a statement made by James
Otis to his brother to the effect that "Blackstone's 'Commentaries' would have saved him
seven years labor pouring over and delving in black letter." Grinnell, *op. cit.*, p. 174.
During this same period the importation of other law books from England also greatly
increased, including such standard works as Coke on Littleton, Comyn's Digest, Hale's and
Hawkin's Pleas of the Crown, and Lily's Entries. All of these books were eagerly sought
and widely read. See Stone, "The Lawyer and His Neighbors," *Cornell Law Quarterly*,
vol. 4, 1918-19, p. 175.

[69] "The Lawyer and His Neighbors," *Cornell Law Quarterly*, vol. 4, 1918-19, p. 175.

in the late eighteenth century is in striking contrast to its role during the earlier colonial period. During much of that time members of the legal profession furnished comparatively little leadership in public affairs in most of the colonies. In New England such leadership was largely drawn from the clergy.[70] Under these circumstances it is not strange that political problems were frequently resolved in the light of Biblical lore and that secular issues were frequently discussed in the light of a divine purpose. In the twenty years before the Revolution, however, as Simeon E. Baldwin points out, the lawyers came rapidly to the front.[71] As they increased in number and influence, they became prominent in town meetings and assemblies. Participating in these lesser affairs they were preparing for larger affairs. How well they prepared may be seen from the fact that 25 of the 55 signers of the Declaration of Independence were lawyers; that 31 of the 50 members of the Constitutional Convention were lawyers; and that 10 of the 29 Senators and 17 of of the 65 Representatives in the First Congress were lawyers.[72]

Truly a remarkable change has taken place here in the status of the legal profession. What is the explanation of it? Why is it, inquires Mr. Justice Stone, that "from a vocation generally held in contempt and almost outlawed, . . . that in less than fifty years it attained a position of influence as deserved as it was assured?"[73] The reasons are close at hand. During those closing years of the colonial period increasing wealth and property demanded more lawyers.[74] Consequently, as Mr. Justice

---

[70] "The clergy, (that is to say, the Congregational ministers), and not the lawyers, were the leaders of public opinion in New England. The system which prevailed there under (the established order) or the old charter in Massachusetts, was essentially a theocracy, and so it remained, although somewhat modified, up to the time of the Revolution." Charles Stillé, *The Life and Times of John Dickinson*, vol. 13, Memoirs of the Historical Society of Pennsylvania, 1891, pp. 29-30.

[71] *Two Centuries Growth of American Law, 1701-1901*, p. 20.

[72] Charles Warren, *History of the American Bar*, p. 211.

[73] *Op. cit.*, p. 175.

[74] "Wealth was increasing, and property interests required more of his care. Law books were largely imported. (See *American Historical Association Report* for 1895, pp. 203, 206; *Documentary History of New York*, IV, 1930, 1148.) It is believed that more copies of Blackstone's *Commentaries*, during the eighteenth century, were sold in America than in England. Their elegance of literary form appealed more strongly to our bar. Blackstone was the first English lawyer, for a hundred and fifty years, who while in the practice of his profession, Lord Campbell has declared, paid the slightest attention to the selection of, or collocation of words. (*Lives of the Chief Justices of England*, III, 475.) The French writers on government and jurisprudence, of the new school, like Montesquieu, were also read in this country. Legal education was made the subject of legislation. New Jersey prescribed a term of preparation for the bar lawyer, longer as respects its highest positions, than any State now requires, and provided for finally crowning the successful competitor with the title of serjeant at law. (Sanderson, *Lives of the Signers*, III, 83, 84.) The judges wore the official gown (*ibid.*, 105) and so did those in several of the other colonies. (*Life and Works of John Adams*, II, 133.) The control of public affairs was passing from the hands of those who, like Franklin and Trumbull and Washington were not lawyers, to those who like Adams and Jefferson and Johnson, were." Simeon E. Baldwin, *Two Centuries Growth of American Law, 1701-1901*, pp. 20-21.

Stone points out, there was a marked tendency to develop "law as a science in the colonies" and to apply "improved educational methods" to it.[75] This tendency was facilitated by the fact that educational advantages in general were increasing.[76] The common school system of New England was now deeply rooted after a hundred years of experience. A number of colleges had already been established in the colonies[77] and the legal profession received a large recruitment from their classic halls.[78]

Many young men who afterwards became the best-known lawyers of the colonies went to London to study in the Inns of Court. The New England colonies, it should be remarked, did not supply many of these young men,[79] and as a result were not brought under the influence of the training furnished there.[80] At the Inns of Court, says Mr. Justice Stone, "in association with young lawyers many of whom

[75] *Op. cit.*, p. 175.

[76] Some conception of the requirements necessary for admission to the profession may be derived from a consideration of the case of John Adams. In moving for the admission of Josiah Quincy and John Adams to the inferior court in Boston in 1758, Jeremiah Gridley said: "Of Mr. Quincy, it is sufficient for me to say that he has lived three years with Mr. Pratt; of Mr. Adams, as he is unknown to your honors, it is necessary to say that he has lived between two and three years with Mr. Putnam of Worcester, has a good character from him and all others who know him, and that he was with me the other day several hours, and I take it he is qualified to study the law by his scholarship, and that he has made a very considerable, a very great proficiency in the principles of the law, and therefore, that the client's interest may be safely intrusted to his hands. I therefore recommend him, with the consent of the bar, to your honors for the oath." Having taken the oath, Adams "shook hands with the bar, and received their congratulations, and invited them over to Stone's to drink some punch." After three more years of diligent study he was admitted to the Superior Court. Adams, *Life and Works*, 1850, II, 49, 133.

[77] Harvard (1636), William and Mary College (1693), Yale (1701), Princeton (1746), University of Pennsylvania (1753), King's College (Columbia) (1754).

[78] "The lawyers at the Massachusetts bar between 1788 and 1817 were nearly all college graduates, for the most part from Harvard but with some representation of Dartmouth, Brown, and Williams. In 1805, seventy-five of the one hundred and five members of the New Hampshire bar were college graduates and in Maine, Connecticut, New Jersey, and South Carolina a large part of the bar and in New York a somewhat smaller proportion of the bar were either educated for the bar in England or were graduates of American colleges notabley Yale, Princeton, King's (afterwards Columbia) College, the University of Pennsylvania, and William and Mary College in Virginia." Stone, *op. cit.*, p. 176. See Sanderson, *Lives of the Signers*, III, pp. 83, 84.

[79] It is interesting to note that of the one hundred and fifteen American students who were admitted to the Inns of Court from 1760 to the close of the Revolution, only two were from New England. On the other hand, South Carolina had forty-seven; Virginia, twenty-one; Maryland, sixteen; Pennsylvania, eleven; New York, five; and each of the other colonies one or two. Stone, *op. cit.*, p. 176.

[80] "A learned and independent bar has always been regarded both in England and in those states which have adopted the English system as one of the great safeguards of the liberties of the people; but in Massachusetts, under the new charter their power was much lessened. Yet the tradition was still strong enough to discourage the acquisition of legal knowledge. There was, therefore, no inducement to send their young men to England, where they might gain a complete knowledge of it." Charles J. Stillé, *op. cit.*, p. 29. See C. E. A. Bedwell, "American Middle Templars," *American Historical Review*, vol. 25, 1920, pp. 680-689.

became famous at the English bar," a great number of young Americans "received their legal training profoundly influenced by the traditions of the English bar and by the notions of individual right and liberty which characterized legal thought and became our greatest heritage from the common law."

The case of John Dickinson is of interest in this connection. This Pennsylvania lawyer attended the Middle Temple with "such men as Lord Thurlow, afterwards Lord Chancellor; Kenyon, Chief Justice of the King's Bench; John Hill, afterwards Earl of Hillsborough; and William Cowper, the poet."[81] He was a prominent figure in the years immediately preceding Independence. His attitude toward war and independence according to his biographer, Charles J. Stillé, was always governed by the "legal aspects of the situation" conditioned as it was by his Temple training, as compared with Samuel Adams, for example, who was "naturally an enthusiastic revolutionist, for whom existing laws, if they interfered with the adoption of his views of independence, were only obstacles to be removed, like any others, without scruple, if he had the power to do so."[82]

A number of others from the Inns of Court were active during the same period.[83] Moreover, with their firm professional emphasis on liberty and rights they directed public thinking[84] in these channels in many parts of the country, although usually along conservative lines.[85] Many of them took an active part in the Revolutionary contest which was about to ensue, including, in addition to John Dickinson, Charles

[81] Charles J. Stillé, *The Life and Times of John Dickinson*, Memoirs of the Historical Society, 1891, vol. 13, p. 24.

[82] *Ibid.*, p. 35.

[83] *Ibid.*, p. 26; see also Foster, *The Register of Admission to Gray's Inn, 1521-1889*, (London), 1889.

[84] Sir William Johnson thought that the considerable opposition of New York lawyers to the Stamp Act was due to the fear that "their business must decrease from the duties on Law proceedings." *Documentary History of New York*, II, 823.

[85] In Massachusetts, Brooks Adams says, "a peculiarly acrimonious hostility to Great Britain" existed. Whereas the leaders in the central colonies, trained as they were in the Inns of Court, were likely to assert their grievances in the light of violations of "the English common and parliamentary law," the leaders in New England, influenced by clerical factors, were likely to claim that the violation of their charters, abrogated "rights" which rested upon something "above and beyond English law"; in other words, abrogated "natural rights," founded on the principles of natural equity. "This," says Charles J. Stillé "was the favorite thesis of the Congregational clergy, and it carried the people, whose leaders they were, very far beyond the ideas of resistance which prevailed elsewhere." *Op. cit.*, p. 31. The men trained in the Inns of Court, however, he asserts, emphasized and directed a "constitutional resistance." *Ibid.*, p. 29. "Most of these men," he says, "were English Constitutional Whigs, in whom that event (the Revolutionary contest) developed almost every shade of political opinion except non-resistance, yet they all based their theories of resistance upon the English law and English traditions which had been taught them in the Temple." *Ibid.*, p. 27. "From the beginning to the end," he adds, "they all maintained their resistance to the ministerial measures on the ground that these acts were violations of English, not of natural, law." *Ibid.*, p. 28.

Pinckney,[86] Edward Rutledge,[87] Richard Henry Lee, Arthur Lee,[88] Daniel Dulany,[89] Nicholas Waln, Joseph Yeates, Joseph Reed, William Hamilton, Richard Tilghman, Edward Tilghman, William Tilghman, Thomas McKean, Jared Ingersoll, Moses Franks, William Rawle, Benjamin Chew, and Peter Markoe.[90] These men differed in many things but agreed that the dispute with Great Britain was mainly a legal question, and should be settled as other legal questions were by "an appeal to legal principles recognized in common by both mother country and the colonies as the outgrowth of English history and traditions." Indeed the resistance of the central colonies, which was largely led by these Templars, "was at the beginning a constitutional resistance within the lines of the English law."[91]

The circumstances which produced a scarcity of trained lawyers during a considerable part of the colonial period naturally affected the judiciary as well. During the course of the seventeenth century most of the judges were without legal training. For example the records of the Suffolk County Court of Massachusetts, between the years 1671 and 1680, show that "the magistrates, except for the training derived from their experience in official duties, were as innocent of legal education as the attorneys; and we know less about their legal ability because they decided cases without writing opinions, whereas the attorneys revealed their knowledge of law in drafting Reasons of Appeal and other documents."[92] With the turn of the century, the possibilities for a legally trained judiciary were improved, but changes came but slowly. In New York, according to Professor Goebel, the supreme court and the mayor's court "acquired in the early eighteenth century, a technical perfection in doing business, comparable to the king's court, but in the counties the courts of common pleas were manned by men of little learning and, as we know from the colonial minutes, not always above reproach."[93] In Maryland, "during the course of the eighteenth cen-

[86] Pinckney, as a strongly conservative supporter of American liberty, accurately reflects his Temple training. *Ibid.*, p. 27.

[87] Rutledge opposed the Declaration of Independence to the last.

[88] Stillé, *op. cit.*, p. 27.

[89] Daniel Dulany, the distinguished Maryland lawyer, was the author "of a theory of legal resistance, founded upon the distinction between internal and external taxation, so subtle and refined, and yet so widespread in its consequences, that it was adopted by the Earl of Chatham in defending American rights in the House of Lords." *Ibid.*, pp. 27-28.

[90] *Ibid.*, p. 28.

[91] *Ibid.*, p. 29.

[92] Morison and Chafee, *Records of the Suffolk County Court, 1671-1680*, vol. 1, pp. xxiii-xxvii, Publications of the Colonial Society of Massachusetts, vol. 29.

[93] "The Courts and Law in Colonial New York," *History of the State of New York*, (Alexander Flick, ed., 1933), vol. III, pp. 24-25. "Even the circumstances that the leading barristers of the province did in fact practice in these courts on occasion," says Mr. Goebel, "was not in itself sufficient pressure to overcome the handicap of a lay judiciary." *Ibid.*, p. 25.

tury," writes Judge Bond, "there were several lawyers who became justices as their fortunes advanced. But, generally, the justices were men of no school training in the law; they had been trained in practice, with such study as they could make by themselves for the better protection of their own interests and for equipping themselves for the judicial duties of which they might be called."[94]

In Massachusetts this condition lasted for a long time. In fact a majority of the chief justices of that colony were laymen down to the Revolution.[95] For example, William Stoughton, the Chief Justice from 1692 to 1701, was a clergyman. Waite Winthrop, a physician, succeeded Stoughton as Chief Justice in 1701. He also served in that capacity from 1708 to 1717. Isaac Addington, another physician, served as Chief Justice from 1702 to 1703; Samuel Sewell, a clergyman, from 1718 to 1728; Benjamin Lynde, a barrister of the Middle Temple, from 1729 to 1745; Paul Dudley, a barrister of the Inner Temple and one of the first lawyers to sit on the bench, as a judge of the Superior Court in 1718, served as Chief Justice from 1745 to 1751; Stephen Sewall, a tutor in Harvard College, served from 1752 to 1760; Thomas Hutcheson, a merchant, from 1761 to 1769; Benjamin Lynde the younger, a legally educated person, from 1769 to 1771; and Peter Oliver, a literary man, from 1772 to 1775. Only three of the 23 associate justices were legally trained.[96]

In Virginia the membership of the county courts during the course of the seventeenth century was apparently made up of "country gentlemen who had received no education in law."[97] During the earlier part of the century, we are informed by Hartwell, Chilton, and Blair

---

[94] Carroll T. Bond, *op. cit.*, pp. xix.

[95] Morris, *op. cit.*, p. 66; see also *American Law Review*, vol. 40, pp. 436-437. "It has been stated," says William Plumer, "I know not upon what authority, that Paul Dudley, was the first person regularly bred to the law, who ever sat on the bench in Massachusetts. He was appointed in 1718, eighty-eight years after the first settlement of Boston." *Life of Plumer*, p. 159. This statement does not seem to be correct. At any rate, F. W. Grinnell asserts that in 1712, "the first trained lawyer was appointed judge in the person of Benjamin Lynde, who had studied law at one of the Inns of Court in London." *Op. cit.*, p. 171. Mr. Grinnell further states that "the second trained lawyer, appointed in 1718, was Paul Dudley, son of Governor Joseph Dudley." *Ibid.*, p. 171. "Both Lynde and Dudley," he points out, "later became chief justices and served for many years." *Ibid.*, p. 171. However, the editors of the Suffolk County Court Records for the period between 1671 and 1680, make the statement that Richard Bellingham, who was a member of the bench for a short time during that period (1671-1780), "had been 'bred a lawyer' in the reign of James I, had served as Recorder of the Borough of Boston in Lincolnshire in the following reign, and had represented the borough in the Parliament of 1628." *Op. cit.*, p. xxvii. It is interesting to note that Governor Bellingham also played a leading part in the compilation of the first published Body of Laws in the colony in 1648. *Ibid.*, p. xxvii.

[96] Charles Warren, *A History of the American Bar*, pp. 75-76.

[97] Philip A. Bruce, *op. cit.*, p. 554.

in their pamphlet, the *Present State of Virginia, 1697-8*,[98] that the personnel of these courts, included a large proportion of persons of English birth, who possessed a considerable degree of legal knowledge. Their successors, however, were born in the colony, and did not enjoy the same opportunity of obtaining such information. "Nevertheless," writes Philip A. Bruce, "the surviving records show that, in every period during the seventeenth century, the justices, whether natives of England or Virginia, had sufficient knowledge of law to conduct the business of their court according to the recognized English precedents. In pursuing this course, they were not simply following a plan approved by long experience; a proclamation of the Governor and Council issued in 1686 enjoined them to shape all their proceedings "as reasonably near as our present condition will admit to ye practice of ye courts in England."[99]

While this injunction was apparently followed, and the judges adhered as closely as possible to the long established procedure borrowed from the English courts,[100] they were nevertheless likely to become quite impatient with any attempts on the part of counsel to use such procedural methods as a means to an end. Like the judges of the General Court, who according to Beverly never admitted "unnecessary impertinences of form and nicety," they were prone to come quickly to their decision avoiding in the process all the "trickery and foppery of the law."[101] In arriving at their conclusions they were aided by the English statutes, the Acts of the Assembly and the customary list of approved legal works such as Dalton's *Justice of the Peace and Office of Sheriff*, Swinburne's *Book of Wills and Testaments* and the like.

[98] The writers of this pamphlet, two of whom had been members of the bar, were well informed as to conditions existing in the colony. They were inclined to be unduly disparaging on occasion, however. See Bruce, *ibid.*, p. 468.

[99] *Ibid.*, p. 554, " . . . there was both a common law and a chancery division to the county court's jurisdiction, and the different pleadings used in England in either branch was adhered to in the Colony; on the chancery side, for instance, there was the bill of complaint, the answer, and the decree; on the common law side, the declaration, the demurrer, the replication, and the like. From the foundation of the monthly court, it is probable that a cause came before the justices first by the ordinary petitions (see Lower Norfolk County Records, Orders, July 17, 1641); and this had to be followed up by the usual pleas. . . . Very frequently, a demurrer would follow immediately after the petition or declaration; and should it be overruled the statements contained in the forms were submitted to a jury. (A case in which pleadings were drawn with great care and exactness will be found entered in Westmoreland County Records, vol. 1690-98, p. 188. How strictly all the regular procedure was observed in a criminal case will be seen by an examination of the record of the trial of Robert Hayes and Thomas Cooke in Northampton County Records, vol. 1657-64, folio, p. 205.) No petition was allowed to be filed without the plaintiff having previously issued a summons informing the defendant of the fact that a suit was about to be begun aaginst him. (Lower Norfolk County Records, Orders, Aug. 15, 1645.)" Bruce, *op. cit.*, p. 555.

[100] See comments by Hartwell, Chilton, and Blair, cited by Philip A. Bruce, *op. cit.*, p. 468; see also *ibid.*, p. 555.

[101] *Ibid.*, p. 556.

These volumes were paid for by a special allowance in the county levy.[102] In addition to the not inconsiderable collection of law books and Acts of Assembly belonging to the respective counties, the justices had access to their own libraries, an important section of which, frequently related to law. "There were few prominent citizens of the Colony known to have served many years on the county bench," says Philip A. Bruce, "whose collection did not include many law books";[103] and he supports this statement with a wealth of evidence.[104]

[102] *Ibid.*, p. 557. "In 1669, Captain James of the *Duke of York*, was asked by the justices of Lancaster to purchase certain law books for the county's use, and a sum was raised by the levy of 1671 sufficient to reimburse him. (Lancaster County Records, Orders, Nov. 26, 1669.) In the course of the same year, a similar request was made by Major Adam Thoroughgood (then on the point of sailing to England) by the justices of Lower Norfolk; and in the letter they addressed to him they stated that they were acting in obedience to the General Assembly's injunction. (Lower Norfolk County Records, vol. 1666-75, p. 95.) In York, a like commission was entrusted to Colonel John Page, a member of the county court. (York County Records, vol. 1664-72, p. 516, Va. St. Libr.) At a later date, the court of this county complained that these books, which, by that time, had been bought, were dispersed in so many hands, that they were practically of no benefit to the justices themselves; and the clerk was instructed to have them once more returned to the shelves of the court-room. (York County Records, vol. 1675-84, orig. p. 331. In 1690, a prisoner was bailed in Lower Norfolk County because there was no copy of the statutes at large at hand for the court to consult; see orders Aug. 15, 1690.) Nicholas Spencer, about 1690, secured in England, for the use of Westmoreland county court, perhaps the most complete set of law books owned by any court of this grade sitting in the colony; it contained not only the works which the Act of 1666 required every bench of judges to obtain, but also numerous other volumes equally indispensable in administering judicial business. The value of this little library was estimated at eight pounds sterling, or four thousand pounds of tobacco; which would mean that, in modern figures, it was worth about two hundred dollars. . . . It is probable that the collection of law books belonging to each of the county courts steadily grew larger as the years passed on. . . ." *Ibid.*, pp. 552.

[103] *Ibid.*, p. 559.

[104] Among the volumes belonging to Colonel John Mottrom, of Northumberland, he says, "were a *Treatise on Wills*, *The Serjeant at Law*, and the *Statutes of Elizabeth*. (Northumberland County Records, Orders, July 4, 1655.) Colonel Southey Littleton, of Accommac, owned *Ye Body of Ye Common Law* and *Printed Laws of Virginia*. (Accommac County Records, vol. 1676-1690, p. 295.) Henry Willoughby's library contained two books relating to law printed in folio, four in quarto, nine in octavo, and twenty-three in duo-decimo. (Rappahannock County Records, vol. 1, 1677-82, orig., p. 75. Willoughby was a physician, but his library was accessible to every justice among his friends and patients.) Among contents of John Sampson's store, situated in Rappahannock, were 'ninety-one law books of this county.' (Rappahannock County Records, vol. 1677-82, orig. p. 62.) These volumes were easily purchasable by the justices, whose need of them had probably been Sampson's inducement to keep them in stock. When Captain Francis Matthews of York died, he had in his possession a copy of the *Lex Mercatoria*. . . . (York County Records, vol. 1671-1694, p. 161, Va. St. Libr.) One of the works composing the Farrar collection in 1683, was *West's Precedents*. (Henrico County Records, vol. 1677-92, orig. p. 268.) Among the law books left by Thomas Cooke, of Princess Anne County, at his death in 1697, was the *Jure Maritimo*, the *Complete Justice* and the *Laws of Virginia* (Princess Anne County Deed Book, 1691-1708, p. 162.) In 1690, John Carter, of Lancaster, bequeathed to Robert Carter his collection of works on law. (Lancaster County Records, vol. 1690-1709, p. 4.) Of the three hundred and ninety titles forming the library of Ralph Wormely, thirty-three related to law and political science among them, six sets of the Acts of Virginia, and several editions of the statutes-at-large. (*William and Mary College Quart.*, vol. II, p. 170.)" *Ibid.*, pp. 559-560.

In Delaware, no professionally trained justice held office before the Revolution.[105] The first lawyer to become Chief Justice of Pennsylvania was Guest in 1701.[106] Nicholas More who in 1684 first discharged the highest judicial office in Pennsylvania is said to have been educated in medicine.[107] In New Hampshire, Theodore Atkinson, a lawyer, became Chief Justice in 1754. Most of the New Hampshire judges were laymen, however, until long after the Revolution. "The Revolution," says William Plumer, "brought with it new men, but no increase, in the first instance, of judicial science."[108] For example, Meschech Weare, who had studied theology but did not preach, was Chief Justice of the state from 1776 to 1792. Associated with him was Matthew Thornton, a physician, and John Wentworth, who was a lawyer. During the same period, Nathaniel Peabody and Jonathan Blanchard discharged the duties of attorney-general, although neither of them was a lawyer. From 1782 to 1790, the Chief Justice was Samuel Livermore, who, though bred to the law, had little regard for its systematic or technical application.[109] In 1791, Josiah Bartlett, a physician, became Chief Justice. He was succeeded by John Pickering, a well-read lawyer.[110] The associate justices of this period also included men who were not lawyers. John Dudley who sat on the court from 1785 to 1797 was a trader and farmer; Woodbury Langdon, a judge at different periods from 1782 to 1791 was a merchant; and Timothy Farrar, who served from 1771 to 1803, was originally trained for the pulpit.[111] The use of lay judges in the post-Revolutionary period, was not peculiar to New Hampshire. In the neighboring state of Rhode Island, a blacksmith was judge of the highest court from 1814 to 1818, and from 1818 to 1826 the chief justice was a farmer.[112]

[105] Grubb, *Judiciary of Delaware*, p. 9.

[106] *Penn and Logan Correspondence*, I, 19, 48; Loyd, *The Early Courts of Pennsylvania*, (1911), The Boston Book Co.

[107] Lawrence Lewis, Jr., *op. cit.*, p. 371. "The remaining chief or prior justices of Pennsylvania during the seventeenth century were James Harrison and Arthur Cook of Bucks, John Symcocke of Chester, and Andrew Robinson of Philadelphia (Vide John Hill Martin's Bench and Bar, *Printed Slips in Hist. Soc. of Pennsylvania*). Though perhaps not as eminent as More, they were nevertheless all well fitted by temperament and reputation for the station which they filled. Their integrity was never disputed and their judgments never complained of." *Ibid.*, p. 377.

[108] Plumer, *Life of William Plumer*, p. 150.

[109] Cautioning juries against "paying too much attention to the niceties of law to the prejudice of justice," he paid very little attention to precedents, including his own. "Every tub," he asserted, "must stand on its own bottom." He once decided that English law reports of a date prior to the Declaration of Independence, might be cited, not as authorities but as enlightening by their reasonings the judgment of the court. Those of a later date he would have nothing to do with. Plumer, *op. cit.*, p. 151.

[110] Plumer, *op. cit.*, p. 151.

[111] Plumer, *op. cit.*, p. 152. The practice of appointing lay judges of the Superior Court in New Hampshire was discontinued in 1813.

[112] Pound, *The Spirit of the Common Law*, (1921), p. 113.

These illustrations of lay judges, functioning even beyond the Revolutionary period in some jurisdictions, serve to emphasize the widespread dependence upon them during colonial days. In considering this circumstance it is well to remember, however, as Justice Bond has pointed out in the Maryland study, that "it is a mistake to suppose that lack of special professional training left the lay justices lacking in all skill for judicial work, or that their proceedings were inartificial, and not judicial in nature.[113] Chief Justice Albert Mason, after a careful study of seventeenth and eighteenth century courts in Massachusetts arrives at a similar conclusion.[114] Among the educated men of the time, as suggested before, there was "a familiarity with the law and it's administration that is not ordinarily found among laymen now."[115] In consequence, where educated laymen served as judges, as in Maryland and Massachusetts, there may have been no lack of skill in judicial work.[116] Even where the lay judge was uneducated, he was not always unsuccessful. Many lay judges, of little or no formal education, were held in high esteem and seem to have merited great praise.

The career of John Dudley, the farmer and trader of Raymond, who sat on the Supreme Court of New Hampshire in post-Revolutionary days, illustrates this fact. It has been said of Dudley, that he "had not only no legal education, but little learning of any kind. But he had a discriminating mind, a retentive memory, a patience which no labor could tire, and integrity proof alike against threats and flattery, and a free elocution, rude indeed, and often uncouth, but bold, clear and expressive, with a warmth of honest feeling which it was not easy to

[113] Carroll T. Bond, *ibid.*, p. xix.

[114] Albert Mason, "A Short History of the Supreme Judicial Court of Massachusetts: Part I, Judicial History Prior to 1780," *Massachusetts Law Quarterly*, vol. 2, pp. 82-100; also found in William Davis, *The New England States*, vol. III, ch. CXXIV.

[115] Carroll T. Bond, *ibid.*, p. xix.

[116] From the time of its creation in 1692 to the Revolution four trained judges served on the Superior Court of Judicature of Massachusetts. While all of the others were laymen, there was no complete absence of legal learning. "It is a mistake to assume," says Chief Justice Mason, "that other members of the highest judicial tribunal of the province were not familiar with the legal learning of the times because not educated for or trained by practice in the legal profession. Nearly all of them were graduates of Harvard, and of ability in general scholarship. Participating actively in public affairs, they had become familiar with the organization of the government and its administration, also with the legislation of the province and of parliament affecting provincial affairs, and when appointed to judicial duties did not fail to apply themselves to studies to give them efficiency in the work. Law libraries were not then so extensive as now, and the mastery of such books of the law as were then accessible was not a formidable task for trained scholars. It is not probable that so far as familiarity with books of the law could give equipment for judicial work, the trained lawyers of the court were so much better furnished than their associates as might be hastily assumed. While it is not practicable to make accurate comparison of the legal attainments of the provincial judges, it is quite certain that the average standard was not a low one." "A Short History of the Supreme Judicial Court of Massachusetts: Part 1, Judicial History Prior to 1780," *Massachusetts Law Quarterly*, vol. II, No. 2, pp. 82-100.

resist."[117] It has also been said that he was a "resolute, strong-minded man, intent on doing substantial justice in every case, though often indifferent to the forms and requirements of law."[118] Judge Theophilus Parsons, whose legal attainments were outstanding, supports the statement: "You may laugh at his law, and ridicule his language," he says, "but Dudley is after all, the best judge I ever knew in New Hampshire." Arthur Livermore, another able lawyer of the time, was of the opinion that "justice was never better administered in New Hampshire, than when the judges knew very little of what we lawyers call law."[119]

There is not a complete agreement upon this matter, however, and as late as 1843, we hear Chief Justice Parker of the New Hampshire Supreme Court describing the nature of the judicial process in the days before the Revolution in quite a different way. "It is well understood," he says, "that the administration of justice was in general of a very inartificial character and great complaints were made respecting it, up to that period. How much of this was owing to the want of competent knowledge of its true principles, on the part of those appointed to administer the law, and how much to the alleged corruption of some of the incumbents of the bench, it is impossible now to determine. Certain it is that, true or false, allegations were not wanting in that period; and it is very clear that we cannot resort to the rulings or decisions of that time, for the purpose of determining a contested question, involving legal principles."[120]

While it is often asserted that little concern was given to the developments of precedents or to the finding of authoritative guidance

[117] Plumer, op. cit., p. 153.

[118] A copy of what purports to be one of Dudley's charges to a jury comes down to us in this form. "You've heered what has been said by the lawyers, the rascals; but no, I wont abuse 'em. 'Tis their business to make out a good case—they're paid for it, and they've done well enough in this case. But you and I, gentlemen, have sumthin' else to think of. They talk about law—why, gentlemen, its not law we want, but justice. They want to govern us by the common law of England; trust me for it, common sense is a much safer guide for us—the common sense of Raymond, Exeter, Ipin (Epping) and the other towns that sent us here to try this case between two of our neighbors. A clear head and an honest heart are wuth more than all the law of all the lawyers. There was one good thing said by 'em though; 't was from one Shakespeare, an English stage-player, I believe. No matter for that; 't was e'venmost good enough to be in the Bible—'Be just and fear not.' That's the law in this case, gentlemen, and law enough in any case in this court. It's our business to do justice between the parties; not by any quirks of the law out of Coke or Blackstone—books that I never read and never will—but by common sense and common honesty between man and men. That's our business, and the curse of God is upon us if we neglect or turn aside from that. And now, Mr. Sheriff, take out the jury; and you, Mr. Foreman, don't keep us waiting with idle talk—too much o' that a'ready, about matters that have nothin' to do with the merits of this 'ere case. Give us an honest verdict that common sense men needn't be ashamed on." American Law Review, vol. 40, 1906, p. 437.

[119] Plumer, op. cit., pp. 155-156.

[120] Pierce v. The State, 13 N. H. 557, 558 (1843). See Warren, op. cit., 136, 137. On the other hand see American Law Review, vol. 40, p. 436-437.

in the principles of the common law, where lay judges were functioning,[121] charges reflecting upon the personal character of lay judges are
not so frequent. Nevertheless, we do find them. In New Hampshire,
according to William Plumer, some of the lay judges were not only
prone to disregard known principles of established law, but were inclined
in some instances to mete out a very uncertain product of their own.
"So much, indeed," he says, "was the result supposed to depend upon
the favor or aversion of the courts, that presents were not uncommon,
nor perhaps, unexpected."[122] Nor is he without an illuminating incident
to support his position. "On one occasion," he writes, "the Chief Justice
who was also a member of the Council, is said to have inquired . . .
what cattle those were that had waked him so unreasonably in the
morning by their lowing under his window; and to have been somewhat
mollified by the answer that they were a yoke of six-feet cattle, which
Col. —— had sent as a present to His Honor. 'Has he?' said the Judge,
'I must look into his case, it has been in court long enough.' "[123]

However that may be, when the appraisals of Judges Bond and
Mason are given due consideration, we may not be inclined to view
the work of colonial lay judges in an altogether unfavorable light. It
must be recognized, however, that during certain portions of the colonial
period, the deep-seated hostility to the legal profession already referred
to was in effect against the judiciary as well and that there were reasons
for this which were quite unrelated to the lack of legal proficiency, or
to the personal limitations of a lay judiciary. Some important reasons
for this hostility were rooted in a quite different cause. The independence of the judiciary, it will be remembered, had been but lately won.
It certainly did not exist in Stuart England. Indeed it was not secured
until the Act of Settlement, of 1701. This safeguard was not extended
to the colonies. Some of the colonial assemblies tried at intervals to
secure it but were resisted by the Lords of Trade, who believed that an
independent colonial judicial tenure would "lessen that joint dependence which the colonies ought to have upon the government of the
mother country." The Zenger libel case of 1735 drew attention to this
subject throughout the colonies. That important case grew out of the
removal of Chief Justice Morris of New York by the royal governor

[121] It has been frequently asserted that where untrained men were charged with the
judicial function, during certain periods in colonial history, they administered their
task as their common sense dictated, "with some little help from the statute books and
more yet from the law of nature." Captain Bredon writes to the Council of Colonies,
speaking of the printed laws of Massachusetts, "what laws are not mentioned in this book
are in the magistrates' breasts to be understood." (Documents Relative to the Colonial
History of New York), Reinsch, *op. cit.*, p. 41.

[122] Plumer, *Life of William Plumer*, pp. 149-150. See comments of John Adams
cited by William Plumer at p. 150.

[123] *Ibid.*, p. 150.

because the Chief Justice decided a case adversely to the governor's interest. Later on, a bitter controversy arose in Massachusetts, when it was planned that judicial salaries should be paid by the Crown and judges of the superior court were forbidden to receive grants from the legislature, council, and governor.[124] This action took place in 1772 and was vigorously condemned by John Adams.[125] Distrust of judges who were royal appointees put the judiciary in a position of disrepute, from which it was not able quickly to recover. These were some of the things that led Thomas Jefferson in the Declaration of Independence to mention as one of the acts of tyranny of George III that "he has made judges dependent on his will alone, for the tenure of their offices, and the amount and payment of their salaries." It is not strange that when the Revolution came and new political institutions were established, the jury became a popular factor (in many instances becoming the controlling body as to both law and fact)[126] and remained so for some time.[127]

In short, it may be said that during the seventeenth century, the condition of the lawyer and judge was not a favorable one. There was not only a scarcity of trained lawyers, but also a considerable prejudice against a learned bench and bar in many of the colonies. Many of the judges like the lawyers were without formal legal training and consequently were not trained in the English Common Law. Despite these conditions many phases of the lawyer's technique seem to have been applied and formalities long characteristic of the English system adhered to as well. With the development of population and wealth at the end of the seventeenth century and the beginning of the eighteenth century, an increase in trained lawyers and judges was evidenced in a number of the colonies and as the eighteenth century advanced, legal training and formality advanced with it. Moreover, the closing years of the colonial period were marked by an increasing tendency to develop law as a science and to elevate the lawyers to a position of public leadership, a role denied to them during a major portion of the colonial period.

[124] W. S. Carpenter, *Judicial Tenure in the United States*, p. 23 ff.
[125] John Adams, *Writings*, p. 513 *et seq.*
[126] In the Georgia Constitution of 1777 is a provision that "the jury shall be judges of the law as well as fact." This tendency carried over to a very late date in many states.
[127] W. F. Dodd, *State Government*, (1928), pp. 297, 298; Roscoe Pound, *American Law Review*, vol. 48, 1919, p. 676; W. F. Dodd, "The Constitutional History of New Hampshire," *Proceedings of the New Hampshire Bar Association*, (1906). In Rhode Island, for example, there was no charge to the jury till 1833. See Eaton, "The Development of the Judicial System in Rhode Island," *Yale Law Journal*, vol. 14, p. 153; Warren, *History of the American Bar*, vol. 2, pp. 105, 140.

CHAPTER III

SOME TECHNICAL AND NON–TECHNICAL INFLUENCES IN COLONIAL LEGAL DEVELOPMENT AND SOME CONCLUSIONS

One of the points of difference concerning the nature of colonial law, already referred to, had to do with its relationship to the common law system of England. The Reinsch-Hilkey-Morris group, it will be remembered, advanced the idea that the common law had been slowly and incompletely received in the colonies, not only because of the scarcity of trained lawyers and judges to administer it, but also because in a new land devoid of books and learning a highly technical system would have been difficult to apply; furthermore, simpler forms of justice appealed to the colonists, influenced as they were at times by frontier conditions. While this proposition has much to commend it, it requires further consideration also. It is true that books and learning were essential requirements in the successful application of the seventeenth and eighteenth century common law system with its highly technical characteristics, and that the colonists at different times and places were apparently not desirous of applying them and were more interested in simpler forms of one kind or another. It is also true that frontier conditions presented difficulties for the reception of an elaborate apparatus of principles and practices, developed in and for a quite different environment. Nevertheless there is a sound basis for the contention that these factors may be given altogether too much weight, and even prove to be misleading if accepted without considering some of the surrounding circumstances. Indeed recent studies in Maryland and Massachusetts reveal many facts which compel modification of earlier views in this regard, as expressions from Carroll T. Bond,[1] Julius H. Goebel, Jr.,[2] Samuel Morison and Zechariah Chafee[3] clearly indicate.

In Maryland, at least, there seems to have been a supply of books and learning concerning the law, which is surprising. Judge Bond says:

[1] Introduction to *Proceedings of the Court of Appeals of Maryland, 1695-1729.*

[2] "King's Law and Local Custom in Seventeenth Century New England," *Columbia Law Review*, vol. 31, 1931, pp. 420-448.

[3] Introduction to *Records of the Suffolk County Court, 1671-1680*, vol. 1, Publications of the Colonial Society of Massachusetts, vol. 29.

For the instruction of laymen who might act as justices, or for other reasons should have need to know the law, there was an ample supply of books explaining details of practice with some explanation of principles to be applied. Lambarde's book (William Lambarde, *Eirenarcha*, first published in 1581; Holdsworth, *op. cit.*, IV, 117), the first of a succession of such books, was published in the last quarter of the sixteenth century with the purpose, as Lambarde said in his preface, of furthering somewhat (the good endeavour of such gentlemen as be not trained up in the continued study of the law). Dalton's *County Justice*, *op. cit.*, IV, 119; cf. also *Mass. Col. Rec.*, II, 212), ran through many subsequent editions, and justices in Maryland were required by statute to have copies of it, or of other like work, along with the British statutes, in their courts. (Acts, 1678, ch. 7; *Archives*, VII, 71; 1715, ch. 41, *ibid*, XXX, 239).[4]

Moreover, Judge Bond does not believe that the purchase of law books for the colonies of which Burke spoke so enthusiastically,[5] was altogether a late eighteenth century development.[6] He adds:

There are many evidences of a substantial supply in Maryland at the end of the seventeenth century. Mention has been made of the requirements that the court keep at hand copies of Dalton's *County Justice* and the English statutes, and in 1723 Hale's *Pleas of the Crown*, Hawkin's *Pleas of the Crown*, and Nelson's *Justice*, were added to the list. (*Archives*, XXXIV, 346, 654.) But some individuals were much better supplied. In 1695, when consulted by the governor and council (*ibid.*, XX, 314, 438, etc.) the lawyers asked time to refer to the authorities, and in the appendix to this volume authorities they used will be found cited. . . . Harris and McHenry, who had collected private notes of arguments made, show the use of authorities, both abridgments and early English reports, in considerable number in 1718. (Gresham v. Cassaway (1718), 1 Harris and McHenry, 34. . . . See 2 Harris and McHenry, 365.) Stephen Bordley, . . . accumulated a law library which gave him much fame. . . . Inventories of the estates of later lawyers include collections which were large even in comparison with private libraries of the nineteenth century. . . . Local precedents were found in part in the court records . . . , and for further information on the points decided resort was had to the contemporary notebooks . . ., those which had been kept by lawyers in attendance upon the court sessions.[7]

Other factors were also present, he asserts, which tended to minimize the difficulties of applying a formal system of law in Maryland. "More important than the provisions of books and the common knowledge of law and practice," he says, "was the training of actual experience gained by the provincial judges as the province grew older. Some of the men who sat on cases the proceedings of which are here recorded

---

[4] Bond, *op. cit.*, p. xx.

[5] Burke's *Works*, pp. 124-125.

[6] See *American Historical Association Report for 1895*, 203, 206; *Documentary History of New York*, IV, 930, 1148.

[7] Introduction to *Records of the Suffolk County Court, 1671-1680*, vol. I, Publications of the Colonial Society of Massachusetts, vol. 29, pp. xxviii, xxiv.

had previously dispensed justice in the courts throughout periods of twenty years; and that would seem to be an apprenticeship the products of which could hardly have been inferior to those of the Inns of the Court of the time. It was, indeed, a training similar to that of by far the greater part of the bench and bar before the recent widespread development of law schools."[8]

In Virginia, as we have seen, there were books enough on legal subjects to afford sufficient knowledge to those charged with the duties of the judicial office to apply the principles of a formal legal system. There were also enough men familiar with legal principles to serve as lawyers. In his *Institutional History of Virginia in the Seventeenth Century,* Philip A. Bruce has examined the number and character of legal books and materials available in Virginia at considerable length. Devoting several chapters to the examination of the libraries of seventeenth century Virginia,[9] he gives particular attention to the legal materials available.[10] The evidence he presents indicates a rather surprising number of useful legal materials in Virginia. Without attempting to survey the matter at length, it might be of interest to note the type of legal materials which we may assume to have been in use. This can be done by examining the inventory of the library of Arthur Spicer, a lawyer of Richmond County, who enjoyed a large practice throughout the Northern Neck of Virginia.

When Spicer died about 1701, his collection of books contained one hundred and two titles, which would indicate a total of about two hundred volumes. About fifty-two of these titles were related to legal subjects. Included among them were "the *Statutes at Large,* beginning in the year 1640, and ending with 27 Charles the Second; Pulton's edition of the *English Statutes;* Rastell's *Collections of Ye Statutes; Magna Carta; Resolutions upon ye Statute of Bankrupt; Laws of Virginia; Justinian, Third and Fourth Parts;* Totles' *Reports; Crown Reports; Terms of the Law; Directions for the Study of the Law;* Noy's *Maxims;* Wingate's *Body of ye Common Law;* Shepperd's *Epitomy;* Keeble's *Justice of the Peace;* Dalton's *Justice of the Peace; Law concerning Justices of the Peace;* Lambert's *Office of a Justice of the Peace;* Fleetwood's *Office of a Justice of the Peace;* The *Conveyancer's Light;* Herne's *Conveyances; Practical Register; The Complete Attorney; The Attorney's Academy; The Complete Lawyer;* Kitchen's *Jurisdiction of. Courts;* Wingate's *Abridgments; Mysteries of Clerkship; The Clerk's Tutor; Clerk's Guide; Office of Executor; The Layman's Lawyer;* Finch's *Law;* Judge Jenkins *Works; Jura Maritima; A Preparation to Pleading; Declarations and Pleading,*

[8] *Ibid.,* p. xx.
[9] *Ibid.,* pp. 402-442.
[10] *Ibid.,* pp. 556-560.

Fines and Recoveries; Perkin's *Treatise;* Horne's *Mirrors; Collection of Orders in Chancery;* West's *Precedents;* West's *Symbolographia; A Book of Entries;* Bacon's *Elements; Index of Sentences; Practical Part of Law; A Dispute between a Common and Civilian Lawyer;* and the *Life of Sir Matthew Hale.* (Richmond County Will Book for 1701)."[11]

Spicer appeared frequently in the courts of the justices of the peace, and his library includes five books which were useful in the work of these bodies. "But the jurisdiction of the county court in Virginia," says Phillip A. Bruce, "was much more extended than the jurisdiction of the corresponding bench of justices in England," and the attorney practicing before it, was, "in order to attain to the highest distinction, compelled to possess a very considerable knowledge of the whole field of law."[12] This requirement is reflected in the variety of subjects represented in the titles of Spencer's volumes. There is a wide range here. Nor is there reason to believe, he adds, that Spencer's volumes were "either in their number, or diversity of topics, exceptional among the collections possessed by those of his contemporaries who had won an equally high standing at the bar . . ."[13]

In Massachusetts facilities for legal study do not seem to have been as well developed as in Maryland and Virginia.[14] This may have been due in part to the dislike of the Puritans for lawyers and their technique,[15] or simply to the lack of opportunity for supplying such needs. At any rate Massachusetts seems to have possessed a much scantier supply of law books than did Maryland and Virginia. Indeed, law books are said to have been "exceedingly rare in New England until the latter part of the seventeenth century when important shipments came to Boston."[16] In support of this view is the fact that among the numerous inventories of personal effects found in the records of the Suffolk County Court between 1671 and 1680, only one law book is mentioned, that particular one being in "the list of Capt. Scotlow's property seized by the Indians in Maine."[17] In 1647, the General Court voted to purchase a number of well-known English law books "to the end that we may have better light for making and proceeding about laws." This list included two copies of *Coke on Littleton;* two of the *Book of Entries;* two of

[11] *Ibid.,* pp. 584, 585.
[12] *Ibid.,* p. 586.
[13] *Ibid.,* p. 586.
[14] Introduction to the *Records of the Suffolk County Court, 1671-1680,* Publications of the Colonial Society of Massachusetts, vol. 29; Bruce, *op. cit.,* pp. 557-560, 584, 587.
[15] F. W. Grinnell, *op. ct.,* p. 156.
[16] Morris, *Studies in the History of American Law,* p. 44, citing T. G. Wright, *Literary Culture in Early New England, 1620-1730* (New York, 1920), p. 123.
[17] Introduction to the *Records of the Suffolk County Court, 1671-1680,* vol. I, p. xxxi, Publications of the Colonial Society of Massachusetts, vol. 29.

Coke's *Reports*.[18] The only one of them cited in the records of the Suffolk Court, however, is *Coke on Littleton*.[19]

"Despite this apparent ignorance of English legal treatises," writes the editor of this survey, "English law books of another important type must have been in the possession of the colonists, to judge from internal evidence. The colonial knowledge of legal forms for conveyances and other documents has been mentioned. Some of this may have been derived from manuscript deeds, leases, etc., which the settlers brought with them from England, but it is probable that they also used books of legal forms."[20] As the eighteenth century advanced, some of the wealthier lawyers established libraries of some importance. At the beginning of the century Judge Sewell attempted to establish a good common law library in Massachusetts,[21] but Judge Edmund Trowbridge is said to have had the only fairly complete law library in New England down to the Revolution.[22]

"The middle and southern colonies," writes R. B. Morris, "were likewise lacking in books relating to the law."[23] In eighteenth century, New York, however, Professor Julius Goebel asserts that "Bracton and Coke were venerated names, and many of the New York lawyers owned and used the old Year Books at a time when they were rapidly going out of existence in England."[24] By the time of the Revolution, it would seem that whatever scarcity of law books had obtained had been partially remedied.[25] As mentioned above, a widespread interest in law and legal study developed late in the colonial period, when treatises on law and political subjects became almost as popular as religious books, and Edmund Burke could remark that "in no country, perhaps in the world, is the law so general a study. The profession itself is numerous and powerful, and in most provinces it takes the lead. The greater number

[18] "These books, at that time recent, were the main sources of information about the common law, Dalton's *Justice of the Peace*, in particular, was a very practical guide in the administration of criminal law. "Moses his judicialls" (to use John Cotton's language) were a source of law which the people in general could understand; and a mixture of Moses and Lord Coke characterized the Colonial statutes." F. W. Grinnell, *op. cit.*, p. 159.

[19] Introduction to *Records of Suffolk County Court, op. cit.*, p. xxxii.

[20] *Ibid.*

[21] T. C. Wright, *Literary Culture in Early New England, 1620-1730*, New York, 1920, p. 174.

[22] Warren, *History of the American Bar*, p. 162.

[23] *Studies in the History of American Law*, pp. 44-45. Mr. Morris mentions the fact that "the outstanding colonial library of the eighteenth century, that of William Byrd, the younger, in Virginia, contained only 350 volumes of law and statutes out of a total of 3625." It does not seem to follow, as Philip A. Bruce has shown, that Virginia can be thought of as suffering from the lack of necessary law books, for the purposes of that day and time.

[24] Goebel, "The Courts and the Law in Colonial New York," *History of the State of New York*, vol. III, p. 37.

[25] Warren, *op. cit.*, pp. 157, 158, 161.

of deputies sent to congress were lawyers, but all read, and . . . endeavour to find some smattering in that science. I have been told by an eminent bookseller, that in no branch of his business, after tracts of popular devotion, were so many books as those on the law exported to the plantation. The colonists have now fallen into the way of printing them for their own use."[26] While it appears from the slender volume of evidence available that this happy condition did not exist during a large part of the colonial period, and that the supply of books necessary for an effective administration of the common law could not have been plentiful, the situation in Maryland and Virginia indicates that the scarcity of law books as "sources of law" may be overemphasized and that such scarcity as did exist was undoubtedly offset by the knowledge of legal forms referred to, and the utilization of such manuals as Dalton's *County Justice* which seems to have served a very worthy purpose indeed.

The assertion that the colonists were interested in simpler forms of administering justice than those provided for by the common law also requires consideration. There can be no doubt that there was considerable impatience with the technical aspects of legal justice in many of the colonies. It was this spirit which led to experiments with various devices in which the formalities of systematic law were reduced to a minimum. One of the popular forms developed out of this tendency was the system of lay tribunals which came to be so widely used throughout the colonial period.[27] In New York a system of arbitration was established by the Dutch, and was perpetuated under English rule.[28] "The Duke's Laws," says R. B. Morris, "provide that in actions of debt and trespass under five pounds between neighbors, two indifferent persons were to be selected by the constable to act as arbitrators whose award was to be conclusive. Recourse to arbitration may have been somewhat more frequent in the first decade of English rule than in the period that followed, but there are included in the present volume cases which were arbitrated from 1675 to 1788 from which time it was the practice to refer mercantile disputes to the Committee on Arbitration of the Chamber of Commerce."[29]

[26] Burke's *Works*, pp. 124-125.

[27] Morris, *Studies in the History of American Law*, pp. 60-61.

[28] "A vast quantity of litigation was referred by the court to burgomasters . . . to good men or arbitrators, appointed by the bench or selected by the litigants." R. B. Morris, Introduction to *Select Cases of the Mayor's Court of New York City, 1674-1784*, p. 44; see also *Charters and Laws*, pp. 3, 4. See also A. L. Becker, "Adrien Van Der Donck, the Earliest Lawyer in New York," *Albany Law Journal*, LXVI, (1904), p. 46; O'Callaghan, II, 550.

[29] "The full scope of the activities of this arbitral tribunal, which began functioning in 1768, is disclosed in the manuscript records for the years 1779-1 now in the N. Y. Public Library and printed in a small edition. (*Earliest Arbitration Records of the Chamber of Commerce of the State of New York, founded in 1768, Committee Minutes, 1779-1792*, New York, 1913. The city of New York likewise resorted to arbitration for

A system of arbitration also "occupied a prominent place in Penn's system of justice" and "was by far the most popular method of determining civil cases during the early period in Pennsylvania."[30] In 1683 a statute was enacted, providing for the annual selection in every precinct of three persons to act as "common peace makers." In 1705 another statute was enacted which provided that persons might refer their claims in contract to persons mutually chosen by them in open court whose award should have the effect of a verdict by a jury.[31] Subsequently, writes R. B. Morris, "this statute was extended to other forms of legal action, and by 1766 there are records of elaborate decisions by referees resembling decrees in equity in real estate matters."[32] Some form of arbitration also seems to have been used, to some extent, in New Jersey.[33] Even in the late eighteenth century, there appears to have been a widespread use of lay arbitral boards in many of the colonies.[34] Indeed this type of procedure found so much favor that Dallas in the Preface to his *Reports* in 1790 made the assertion that an important portion of law administration in the late colonial period was entrusted to lay referees.[35]

The popularity of the arbitration method seems to have continued long after this time, and apparently made a deep impression upon George Washington. At any rate, he decided to refer all differences which might arise under his will to three honest men of the neighborhood, whose decision would be final, and expressly enjoined his heirs not to go to law after his death. He writes:

In the construction of this my last will and testament, it will readily be perceived, that no professional character has been consulted, or has had any agency in the draught; and although it has occupied many of my leisure hours to digest, and to throw it into its present form, it may notwithstanding appear crude and incorrect but having endeavored to be plain and explicit in all the

---

the settlement of its claims, M.C.C., 123, 125.) Occasionally, as in *Green* v. *Duncan* (infra, p. 510), the parties attempted to effect a concord before resorting to the law courts. In that case the mediators brought about an agreement that the defendant 'should spend upon him the said Arthur and their friends aforesaid four shillings current money of New York in beer and be thereof discharged of liability for ruining a suit of clothes by poor tailoring. After the brief hour of good cheer the plaintiff brought suit in the Mayor's court and denied that there had been an agreement. But the jury was quite certain that there had been 'such concord' and judgment was rendered for the defendant with costs.' John Watts, a prominent N. Y. merchant, writing in 1764 with reference to an award settling insurance claims, said: 'I could not in decency appeal from their judgment as it is contrary to all practice.' *Letter Book of John Watts*, (New York, 1928), Aug. 14, 1764." R. B. Morris, *Introduction, Select Cases of the Mayor's Court of New York City, 1674-1784*, pp. 44-45.

[30] William Loyd, *The Early Courts of Pennsylvania*, 1911.

[31] R. B. Morris, *Studies in the History of American Law*, p. 61; see also *Pa. Hist. Soc. Memoirs*, vol. VII, p. 42.

[32] *Ibid.*, p. 61.

[33] *Grants and Concessions of N. J.*, p. 455.

[34] Act of 1752, *Conn. Pub. Rec.*, vol. X, p. 201.

[35] Warren, *op. cit.*, pp. 105, 106; Morris, *op. cit.*, p. 61.

devises, even at the expense of prolixity, perhaps tautology, I hope and trust, that no disputes will arise concerning them; but if contrary to expectation, the case should be otherwise, from the want of legal expression, or the usual techni-cal terms, or because too much or too little has been said on any of the devises, to be consonant with law, my will and direction expressly is, that all disputes (if unhappily any should arise) shall be decided by three impartial and intelligent men, known for their probity and good understanding, two to be chosen by the disputants, each having the choice of one, and the third by those two, which three men thus chosen, shall unfettered by law or legal construction, declare the sense of the testator's intentions; and such decision is, to all intents and purposes, to be as binding on the parties as if it had been given in the Supreme Court of the United States. In witness, etc., (signed) George Washington.[36]

These views reflect the same critical attitude toward legal formality expressed by William Duane in his "Samson against the Philistines," in which the case for arbitration, as it operated in these earlier times, is set forth.[37]

If interest in simpler methods of justice stimulated the adoption of arbitration, it undoubtedly affected procedural forms as well, although upon this subject one must generalize at his own risk, since wide varia-tions are likely to be found in this connection, depending largely upon the time and place. In Massachusetts, at least, forms of procedure seem to have followed quite simple patterns in the earlier period. "In fact," says Frank W. Grinnell, "litigation in general probably resembled the procedure of all small claims courts today in which lawyers seldom appear."[38] There were actions of "debt" and "trespass" and "actions of case" which was "the usual method of trying almost any issue includ-ing land disputes."[39] One of "the most striking features of civil litiga-tion" brought out in the survey of the Suffolk Court was "the frequency of the action on the case."[40] Studies of the Massachusetts courts by Washburn[41] and Goebel[42] bring out the same fact. Pleadings in the trial court, according to the same survey, "must have been largely oral."[43] Attempts to require written pleadings seem to have little effect in establishing such a practice.[44]

[36] Quoted by William Duane, *op. cit.*, pp. xxiii.

[37] William Duane, *op. cit.*, pp. 36-42; see also *Appendix* I, xxiii.

[38] *Op. cit.*, p. 161.

[39] *Ibid.*, p. 161.

[40] Introduction to *Records of the Suffolk County Court, 1671-1680*, vol. I, p. xii; Publications of the Colonial Society of Massachusetts, vol. 29.

[41] Washburn, *Sketches of the Judicial History of Massachusetts*, (1840), p. 48.

[42] Goebel, "King's Law and Local Custom," *Columbia Law Review*, vol. 31, p. 437, 438.

[43] "It is true that some references to written pleadings are found in the statutes before 1660. The Body of Liberties of 1641 (No. 27, Reprinted in Whitmore's Sketch of the Laws of the Mass. Bay Colony, (1630-1686), p. 39, says that if the plaintiff files a written declaration the defendant shall have liberty and time to give his answer in

Such written pleadings as are found are in English although pleadings in England remained in Latin until 1731.[45] Apparently, Latin was rarely used in any connection;[46] technical legal phrases were also ignored. "Indeed," Morison and Chafee assert, "there must have been far less use of technical legal phrases of any kind than in the Plays of Shakespeare."[47] "However," they add, "one attorney refers to the mythical person 'John of Styles'."[48] The Massachusetts colonists, however, did not completely disregard ancient common law formalities and fictions; nor were they as unfriendly to equity as might be thought.[49] Since rules of evidence in England were still in process of formation during the seventeenth century,[50] however, "it is only natural that we should find them operating in the Bay Colony in a still more elementary fashion."[51]

Paying little attention to the need for certainty in the law, the Massachusetts colonists, through their magistrates and juries, "openly and persistently violated the elementary principles of *res judicata*."[52] "The most disagreeable characteristic of the colonist which is revealed in these pages," writes Morison and Chafee, "is their unwillingness to end a law suit. They never knew when they were beaten. The loser in the County Court sought reviews and appeals as long as he could and when these failed he started suit all over again from a different angle. Magistrates and juries encouraged these pertinacious contestants by constant disregard of previous adjudications which ought to have settled

---

writing. A statute of 1646 orders that all plaintiffs or their attorneys in civil actions shall file a written declaration at least three days before court opens, whereby the defendant may have time to answer in writing. (Mass. Bay Records, II, 219.)" Chafee and Morison, *Records of the Suffolk County Court, 1671-1680*, vol. I, p. xiii, Publications of the Colonial Society of Massachusetts, vol. 29.

[44] *Ibid.*, p. xiii.

[45] Written pleadings were required to be in English by a Cromwellian statute of 1650, "so that the Puritans on both sides of the ocean were in advance of their time. (Robinson, 'Anticipations under the Commonwealth of Changes in Law,' *Select Essays in Anglo-American Legal History*, I, 480)." *Ibid.*, p. xiii.

[46] *Ibid.*, p. xxxii.

[47] *Ibid.*

[48] *Ibid.*

[49] "The Puritan has been described as 'always a consistent and thorough going opponent of equity,' (Roscoe Pound, "Puritan and the Common Law," *American Law Review*, XLV, 825, reprinted in his *Spirit of the Common Law*. Attacks on chancery under Cromwell are described by Robinson, "Anticipations under the Commonwealth of Changes in the Law," *supra*, I, 470-472) but the material in these cases indicates that the relations were not so unfriendly." *Ibid.*, p. lvi.

[50] J. H. Wigmore, *Treatise on Evidence* (2d. ed., 1923), I, 108.

[51] Chafee and Morison, *op. cit.*, p. xlviii. "Yet, we can already detect the germs of several modern rules, and there was considerable insistence on a few principles, particularly the desirability that the main issue should be proved by at least two witnesses." *Ibid.*, p. xlviii.

[52] *Ibid.*, p. xxxvii.

the issue forever."[53] This disregard for previous adjudications was encouraged by the fact that few books of English reports existed in Massachusetts, and the decisions of its own courts were not printed and were not explained by judicial opinions. In some instances, the Suffolk Study reports, a litigant might succeed in convincing the court that "it ought to be consistent and abide by a principle which had been applied in an earlier decision."[54] These instances were rare, however.

The tendency toward litigiousness though sometimes retarded by barratry statutes[55] seems to have been general in nature during colonial days and does not end then. The Duc De La Rochefoucauld, travelling through the United States in the years 1795, 1796, 1797, asserts that all of the inhabitants of New England were exceedingly litigious and that "there are, indeed, few disputes even of the most trivial nature among them that can be terminated elsewhere than before a court of justice." He was particularly impressed by conditions in Connecticut. "The inhabitants of Connecticut," he said, "are, almost universally, of English descent, and are a sober, active industrious people. Their distinguishing qualities are nearly the same as those of the other inhabitants of New England." Then comes his observation on their litigiousness. "No state," he says, "perhaps no equal number of people in the universe, have such a multitude of lawsuits. There is, nowhere else, such a mob of advocates as here. Is it the multiplicity of lawsuits that has engendered the lawyers? Or do not the lawyers give birth to the excess of lawsuits? Be this as it may, these lawyers have, at present, very great influence among the people of the state, especially in political matters. It is even said to be greater than that of the ministers, who, in consequence of their mutual wranglings and their fierce intolerance, have lost much of the high influence which they once possessed."[56]

The simplicity which marks Massachusetts' procedural method is not evident in the procedure prevailing in Maryland. "Tenacious of regulation by law and prone to litigation," the people of this colony were

[53] *Op. cit.*, p. xxxvii. Editors Morison and Chafee make another interesting comment in this connection. "Although the evidence is not sufficient to support a charge that the colonists were as over-eager to begin lawsuits as they were stubborn about ending them," they say, "it is somewhat startling to see the son of Major John Pyncheon bringing a suit in 1673 for the value of a horse borrowed in 1646. (*Pyncheon* v. *Collecott*, pp. 319-322.)" *Ibid.*, p. xxxvii.

[54] "One of the most important sources of law today consists of the principle declared by judges in their decisions. This was already true in seventeenth century England. But this doctrine of the binding force of precedent could have little vitality in Massachusetts so long as few books of reports of English cases existed there, and while the decisions of its own courts were not printed. . . . " *Ibid.*, p. xxxiv.

[55] Whitmore, *Colonial Laws*, 1672-1686, p. 9.

[56] *Travels through the United States of North America, the Country of the Iroquois and Upper Canada in the years 1795, 1796, and 1797; with an authentic account of Lower Canada* (1799), p. 536.

not unduly averse to systematic legal forms. This fact is borne out in the surprising volume of records which come down to us.[57] This does not mean that procedure assumed a highly developed nicety and precision from the outset. On the contrary, considerable freedom of procedural action was exercised in the seventeenth century, either as a result of a "degree of learning short of the highest, or possibly a minor degree of concern with the law."[58] Nevertheless, the lawyers of Maryland "had a knowledge of common law and chancery practice" as evidenced "by the records of the session and provincial court, published and unpublished,"[59] and they tended to make use of their knowledge. As time passed, the degree of professional specialization increased and the employment of common law forms was extended in scope and assumed a greater degree of precision in application. But as late as the period between 1695 and 1729, the proceedings of the court of appeals reveal "a freedom and adaptability not permitted later."[60]

Such procedural freedom "does not, however," says Judge Bond, "mark the age as a golden one in judicature;"[61] and many instances of a remarkable insistence upon technicality are to be found in the records of this period.[62] There are wide differences in degree, however, in the technical application of the law, among the several courts of the colony. Naturally, a greater lack of formality obtains in the lower courts. The same condition is found in New York where the supreme court and mayor's court of the early eighteenth century acquired "a technical perfection in doing business, comparable to the king's court," whereas the county courts continued to be comparatively free and easy, in their application of the law.[63] In Maryland, as in New York and Massachusetts and elsewhere, the art of conveyancing seems to have been well developed.[64]

[57] " . . . In the public buildings of the state and its counties there are still stored accumulations of manuscript folios and papers, of a large sum total in which the daily work of the several courts of justice from the time of the organization of the settlement is set down. Some of these records have already been printed and published. The Maryland Historical Society, acting as an agent of the state for that purpose, has printed and made accessible to students in the *Archives of Maryland* (the *Archives of Maryland* are reproductions of old records of the province and state, published serially. Fifty volumes have been issued . . .) four seventeenth century records of a central court of common law, the 'provincial court,' and it is engaged in reproducing others of that court, of a court of chancery, and of county courts of the province. But these constitute only a small fragment of the surviving records of even that one century, and the remainder, especially records of the county courts, must remain difficult of access for some years to come." Carroll T. Bond, *op. cit.*, p. v.

[58] *Ibid.*

[59] *Ibid.*, pp. v, vi, report of the trial on a charge of treason 1682, *Archives*, vol. 313.

[60] *Ibid.*, p. xxxix.

[61] *Ibid.*

[62] *Ibid.*

[63] Goebel, "The Courts and Law in Colonial New York," *History of the State of New York* (Alexander Flick, ed., 1933), vol. III, pp. 24-25.

[64] Morison and Chafee, *op. cit.*, p. xxvi, citing pp. 14-15ff.

In Virginia, as previously noted, the judges adhered as closely as possible to the procedure of the English courts, although definitely impatient with technicalities, and prone to come quickly to their decisions.[65] Indeed they were so expeditious in their conduct of business that Hammond, the author of *Leah and Rachel, or the two Fruitfull Sisters, Virginia and Maryland, 1656*, asserted that "there was no place to be found in which justice more speedy or at a smaller charge was to be obtained than in Virginia at this time."[66] The price for this speed may have included a certain lack of formality. At any rate, Henry Hartwell, who probably wrote the chapters on the courts and their procedures in the *Present State of Virginia, 1697-8*, was disposed to criticize the General Court on the ground that it was composed of men who had little legal education,[67] and also because its proceedings were conducted "without those formal pleadings which in England had long become a regular system dear to the hearts of English attorneys."[68] Beverly also states, though not with disapproval, that the members of the court sought to "come to the merits of a cause as soon as they could without injustice."[69] While "plain methods" and lack of formality undoubtedly characterized Virginia procedure in all court levels, the fact remains that the courts of colonial Virginia apparently heeded the injunction requiring them to shape their practice as "reasonably near" as conditions permitted to "ye practice of ye law in England."

While it will not be possible to consider procedural methods in the other colonies, the evidence at hand raises a question as to whether or not it is safe to assume that such methods can be accurately described at all times and places as a system of lay justice administered by popular agencies, acting with complete informality and expedition. While a desire for procedural freedom undoubtedly was present at different times and places, it would seem that the frequent clashes of interest of a highly litigious people would tend to break down their propensity for informality. It has sometimes been said that the informality of much of our early colonial justice is graphically portrayed in the picture that is brought to us of Thomas Oliver, the governor of West Jersey, "sitting on a stump in his meadow,"[70] dispensing justice. A somewhat different impression of colonial justice may be derived, on the other hand, from the picture painted by John Adams of the case of the Writs of Assistance before the Supreme Court of Judicature in 1761, in which James Otis,

---

[65] Bruce, *op. cit.*, pp. 555-556.

[66] See *Leah and Rachel, or the Two Fruitfull Sisters, Virginia and Maryland, 1656*, p. 15; Force's *Historical Tracts*, vol. III; Bruce, *op. cit.*, p. 478.

[67] Bruce, *op. cit.*, p. 661.

[68] Bruce, *op. cit.*, p. 663.

[69] *Ibid.*, p. 663; also Beverly's *History of Virginia*, p. 205.

[70] E. P. Tanner, "The Province of New Jersey," *Columbia Studies in History and Politics*, vol. 30, (1908), p. 460.

the "flame of fire," made his great plea in behalf of the "supremacy of law."

"The scene," says John Adams, "is the Council Chamber of the Old Town House in Boston. . . . In this chamber, 'round a great fire, were seated five Judges, with Lieutenant-Governor Hutchinson at their head, as Chief Justice, *all arrayed in their robes of scarlet English broadcloth, in their large cambric bands and immense judicial wigs.* In this chamber were seated at a long table all the barristers at law of Boston and of the neighboring county of Middlesex in gowns, bands, and tie wigs."[71] A wide difference exists here between Jersey justice and that of Boston, but no wider than the degrees of informality which undoubtedly prevailed throughout the colonies, in different times and places, in the several levels of courts in existence.

The influence of the frontier on colonial law so greatly emphasized by some of the legal historians referred to has been subjected to some new interpretations in recent years. Its importance cannot be denied. That frontier conditions presented obstacles to reception of the English common law is undoubtedly true. The question which has arisen, however, concerns the degree of frontier influence and the effects of the same. If we are to regard frontier conditions as incompatible with any or every attempt to establish a scientific law, we may possibly be giving an undue and not entirely correct emphasis to its effect. Moreover, if we adopt the view that frontier conditions preclude the adoption of orderly forms of justice, patterned along familiar lines throughout the major portions of the colonial period we may possibly be taking an incorrect position also. But this view has had wide currency in the past and it has been iterated and reiterated that the colonies, manifesting a characteristic frontier dislike for scientific law, experimented with all manner of devices in administering justice without law during the major portion of the colonial period and that it was not until the middle of the eighteenth century that serious attempts were made to effect a general administration of justice according to English law.

The application of this theory to thirteen separate colonies and over a period of 150 years has its difficulties and a number of objections to it have been made. For one thing, it is pointed out that the records indicate that early settlers of some provinces were far from hostile to scientific law; that on the contrary they seem to have introduced as much of it as they possibly could; and that the amount which resulted is surprising. Professor Goebel, after investigating materials drawn from Plymouth colony, thinks that a considerable borrowing of English law took place at an early date. He advances the theory, however, that the law borrowed was "the law prevailing in English local courts such as county

[71] *Works,* vol. X, pp. 244-248.

courts and recorders' courts in London and various boroughs, with which, coming from the middle strata of English society, they would naturally have had more experience than with the King's Court."[72] These conclusions not only throw light upon the need for a further study of English local court records, but require extensive modifications of interpretation of this earlier period which have been long adhered to.[73] More recently, materials somewhat similar to his have been found in the Suffolk study, and more work will undoubtedly be done along this line.[74]

The views advanced by Professor Goebel are of great interest. "Unless we are willing to resort to the frontier theory (that *pons asinorum*) of American historiography . . .," he says, "we can make but one assumption: for the purpose of civil order in the colony, resort was had to the law with which the colonists had grown up."[75] In his opinion, it was inevitable "that the local courts and customary law would assume a position of transcendent importance in the life of the ordinary man."[76] "It was to these courts," he says, "that the small farmer or artisan would turn if he wished to replevy his cows or to collect a bill, and that turned upon him if his hogs were unringed or if he put his garbage in the street. Except what these humble men may have known of the ecclesiastical courts . . . the workings of the county, manorial, or borough tribunals were the length and breadth of their knowledge of the administration of justice, the local customs the sum of their law."[77] Historians, he points out, have not failed to observe that "in respect of the machinery of government, the local institution was that which was first duplicated in America. . . . Only a profound and abysmal disregard of the character of English law in the seventeenth century could have made them blind to the fact that in respect to the law conditions were no different."[78]

In this view, the Massachusetts colonists could not be expected to draw upon the practices of the great courts of Westminster which dominated the judicial scene in England, or to use "the law which was practiced in those courts and about which Coke wrote so learnedly when the first Puritans settled in New England." For "the small artisans, merchants, and peasants" who comprised these colonists were not familiar with these courts and their laws. "Their contacts," in Professor Goebel's view, "had been for the most part with those relics of ancient jurisdiction which still functioned in seventeenth century England—the

---

[72] Morison and Chafee, *op. cit.*, p. xxxii.
[73] *Ibid.*
[74] *Ibid.*
[75] "King's Law and Local Custom," *Columbia Law Review*, vol. 31, 1931, p. 420.
[76] *Ibid.*, p. 421.
[77] *Ibid.*
[78] *Ibid.*

courts baron and leet on the manor, the borough courts in the city, the county courts, and the quarter sessions. All but the last of these institutions had their roots in the feudal jurisdiction of the Middle Ages. They were already marked for destruction but as we know from their extent, they still handled the bulk of petty litigation. Here was administered old custom embodied in the rolls of the court or in the customals of the boroughs, customs that are as hoary as the common law, and to which the latter in specific instance or on occasion gave recognition and validity. Here were observed practices in pleading and procedure long since outmoded in the central courts. Here may be found the striking parallels between the law of old England and the law which the settlers, where there were no barristers to lead the way, presently put into operation for their civil litigation. For their criminal jurisprudence, where they were not bound by substantive provisions culled from the Bible, the colonists' models were the court leet (the police court of the manor), or the quarter sessions (the courts held by the justices of the peace in the county). The latter alone in England were endowed with the vigor of going concerns with a future ahead of them and were pushing out of the picture the moribund court leet. They were definitely part of the central royal authority and at the same time were local institutions, manned largely by laymen, and maintained practices that had no more in common with the older methods of police administration than with the practices of the assizes or of the King's Bench."[79]

The earliest deeds, crude of form as they were, indicate, he believes, "that landholding was conceived in the image of the English freehold;" and that a particular form of Yorkshire freehold, the so-called "Meerstead freehold," was known to the Pilgrims.[80] This particular form of land tenure, he points out, was used at Royston, near the home of Bradford, and was one in which the seignorial element was almost indiscernible.[81] "Certainly it is a striking coincidence," he observes, "that meerstead is used for messuage in Plymouth and that the term, so far as I can ascertain, was not used elsewhere in England.[82] It is evidence like this that makes him believe that the Pilgrims undertook to set up with "the crude imitation of inaccurately remembered things" the local usage with which they were familiar at home. This tendency, in his view, explains the use of the code form and certain aspects of lay administration. It also explains "the absence of clear-cut lines between

---

[79] *Op. cit.*, pp. 10-11.

[80] *Ibid.*, p. 446.

[81] "The Pilgrims generally came from those regions of England where the effects of the agrarian revolution of the sixteenth century had been most profoundly experienced . . . what transpired in Plymouth colony was a reflection of peasant psychoses after decades of unrest." *Ibid.*, p. 445.

[82] *Ibid.*, p. 446.

the legislative and judicial function." The Pilgrim's failure to distinguish between civil and criminal jurisdiction, is also characteristic of the county courts at home. "No one," he concludes, "who has read the records of the local courts of seventeenth century England can fail to be struck with the resemblances between the two."[83]

Recognizing many flaws in this picture of the law's growth in early Plymouth, he is of the opinion, nevertheless, that the key to a proper understanding of this early period is to be found in an analysis of the transplantation of local experience, usage, and custom. "Local custom," he says, "substantive as the Winchester measure, pretentious as the notion of the code, ineradicable as the methods of law administration, fortuitous as a form of tenure; bitter experience at the hands of a zealous bishop and his pursuivants, or a stony hearted evicting landlord; hope and salvation in the Word of God preached by word or pamphlet, these things are the materials that went with settlers to Plymouth, and out of which their law was fashioned."[84] Nor does he consider this condition peculiar to Plymouth. "The curious melange of religious ideas and remnants of English local customs and practices which pervaded the Plymouth legal institutions is not without parallel," he says, "for her neighbors in Massachusetts, Connecticut, and Long Island, exhibited similar proclivities."[85] In every colony, despite its peculiar characteristics, the basic factor "in the seventeenth century before the Leviathan common law had been set in motion" was the transplanting of "local institutions and customary law." Viewed in this light, he adds, "the first century of American law no longer seems chaotic and absurd; on the contrary the frontier theory, as I have intimated, becomes an artificial and labored explanation."[86] If Professor Goebel's findings receive additional support in future studies, they will, necessarily, require a reappraisal of the frequently accepted view that a widespread incorporation of important English legal materials did not take place until the middle of the eighteenth century, when for the first time a systematic legal order was in the process of establishment and American law, as we know it today, had its real beginning.

The influence of religious forces upon the history of the common law in the colonial period is also of interest. "From the time of Calvin's experiment in theocracy at Geneva," it has been said, "the notion that the 'judicials' of Moses were binding upon men and should be incor-

[83] *Ibid.*, p. 435.
[84] *Ibid.*, p. 447.
[85] *Ibid.*, p. 448.
[86] *Ibid.*, p. 448. "We cannot brush this century away as meaningless; neither should we invest it with greater importance for the future than it actually possesses. Yet the fact that it gave us legal institutions which the common law never succeeded in smothering is sufficient reason for devoting to it some scientific attention." *Ibid.*, p. 448.

porated in man's law had obsessed the more radical Protestant groups, both in England and on the Continent. When opportunity at last came to these zealots to regulate their affairs without episcopal or royal interference, there was no hesitation in setting these ideas forth in their codes. We can observe this in the Plymouth laws, in the Body of Liberties of Massachusetts Bay, and in the New Haven Code. It was in the main the source of the brief and ferocious criminal law drawn in Southampton in 1641."[87]

It has been frequently asserted by the first group of legal historians, referred to earlier, that the acceptance of the common law in the colonies, particularly in New England, was greatly retarded by religious influences which were more interested in Biblical precepts than in the technicalities of the English system which was an object of suspicion anyway, and great stress has been laid upon the Bible as a source of law. It is contended by some members of the second group however, that the role of the Bible and religious precept in our early judicial process has been given altogether too much importance. This cleavage in opinion, also represents a difference in emphasis rather than a complete disagreement as to the facts. It is undoubtedly recognized by both groups that the Bible had some authoritative value. The difference in the opinion of Professors Morison and Chafee lies in the relative importance which is attributed to the common law and to the Bible. "There is," they say, "considerable justification for the opinion of Hilkey and Reinsch that when the Massachusetts statutes failed to cover a situation the colonists did not resort much to the English law in order to fill up the gaps, and did make some use of the Bible for that purpose."[88] On the other hand, they assert, common law materials had a decisive influence upon the language and form of the colonial statutes. "When once the common law had been recognized as the chief basis of legislation," they observe, "the small use which was made of it in supplementing legislation possesses less significance than Reinsch and Hilkey thought."[89]

The editors of the Suffolk County Court Records also point out that "although the rules of the English law were not followed as closely as a vocal minority in the colony wished, the very argument of authorities in reply was not drawn from the Bible, and might have come from

---

[87] Goebel, "The Courts and the Law in Colonial New York," *History of the State of New York* (A. F. Flick, ed., 1933), vol. 3, p. 9. It is interesting to note that before Georgia became a royal province in 1752, the most important court for the common man was the minor court held by the local justice of the peace, called the "court of conscience." Here all petty disputes were settled and the justice likely unlearned in the law used the rule of their conscience. Coulter, *op. cit.*, pp. 77-78.

[88] *Op. cit.*, p. xxxi.

[89] *Ibid.*

English lawyers";[90] and furthermore that "whatever the theocratic inclination of the colonists they were too canny to treat with contempt the charter on which they depended for all their governmental powers and in which the King expressly authorized the General Court to make laws "not contrarie to the laws of this our realme of England."[91] "Occasional violations of this charter provision," they add, "and more frequent forgetfulness of it in irresponsible colonial talk and writing cannot obscure the importance which it must have had for every thoughtful magistrate and member of the General Court."[92]

The Suffolk study, it is interesting to note, contains several cases in which arguments based upon the Bible are used. In the case of *Holwells* v. *Butler*,[93] the question of the legal effect of the Bible is brought directly to the fore, when the rules of inheritance laid down in the Book of Numbers are relied upon by the claimant to a certain decedent's property. In the reply to this claim, it was asserted "that this part of the Bible was an unsafe basis for Massachusetts law, since it provided for a complete redistribution of property every fifty years, which would upset the title of every purchaser of real estate."[94] Other arguments citing the Bible are also found, but this does not lead the editors to believe that it was of outstanding importance. Indeed they believe that it would be unsafe to conclude that this supports the statement sometimes made that "the Scriptures were an infallible guide for both judge and legislator."[95] The Bible, they point out, was thoroughly known by everybody and was a natural source for illustrative material in the course of any discussion. Pointing to its frequent use before juries even today, they observe that it was "much more intimately entwined in popular thought in the seventeenth century." In this connection they note, that scriptural passages are found in English judicial opinions, where the Bible was not viewed as a source of law. For example, they cite the beginning of an opinion by the English chancellor, Lord Ellesmere, in the reign of James I, where he makes the statement that "the law of God speaks for the plaintiff, Deut. XXVIII, 30," and then goes on to the Year Books. Some of the references to the Scriptures found in the cases in the Suffolk study, they suggest, are thrown out persuasively

[90] In this argument it was suggested "that corporations like the city of London had 'diverse customs and by-laws different from the common and statute laws of England,' and that a similar freedom of divergence to meet local needs was permissible for the Massachusetts Bay Colony." *Ibid.*, p. xxxi.

[91] Poore, *Federal and State Constitutions*, Colonial Charters, etc., 1, 940, cited by Morison and Chafee, *op. cit.*, at p. xxxi.

[92] Morison and Chafee, *op. cit.*, p. xxxi.

[93] *Ibid.*, vol. 2, pp. 1034, 1037.

[94] *Ibid.*, p. xxxiv.

[95] *Ibid.*, p. xxxiii.

in the fashion of Lord Ellesmere, rather than looked upon as authoritative legal rules.[96]

In short the Suffolk study does not indicate that Biblical precept was the overwhelmingly important factor in the administration of justice that it is sometimes supposed to be. There were practical difficulties which stood in the way of its establishment in a central role. "Even the most intensely devout church goer," says Professor Goebel, "would have been hard put to extract from the Bible sufficient guide for the details of judicial establishment and procedure. Nor have we any evidence that the Puritan Biblicism in America was ever so broadly conceived, even among the holy men of New Haven."[97] For these matters of details, and where the incidents of daily life did not impinge upon religious beliefs, he adds, "they imitated the institutions and practices with which they were familiar." The institutions, with which these humble folk were familiar, were distinctly local in character.[98] These institutions, as noted before, were not without their technical features, nor completely devoid of the formalities of the ancient system of the homeland.

In concluding, it may be repeated, that generalizations concerning colonial legal developments are difficult to make and prone to mislead. Out of necessity they must be confined to a given time and place. Nevertheless, the roots of the American legal system are to be found in colonial America and the legal developments of that period should not be completely ignored or left entirely to the specialist concerned with one small portion of the problem. Any attempt to see the conditions of legal development in their entirety must treat the matter in a general way, despite the attending difficulties. From the scanty evidence available it would seem that the methods and principles followed, while greatly influenced by conditions obtaining in individual colonies, are properly classified as a development of the English common-law system. The transfer of that great body of principles is slowly accomplished, however, and is by no means complete. There were and are large gaps to be found. During the earlier phases of the colonial period, when colonization was taking place and the colonists were getting settled in their new homes, various obstacles to the successful transfer of English legal materials were encountered. Some of these obstacles arose out of the practical necessities of the situation, others sprang from the various attitudes of mind and tempers of the time. Moreover, the English legal system at the time of colonization had qualities which did not encourage adoption. It was the highly developed, technical system of a settled

---

[96] *Ibid.*
[97] "The Courts and the Law in Colonial New York," *History of the State of New York*, (A. Flick, ed., 1933), vol. 3, pp. 10-11.
[98] *Ibid.*, pp. 10-11.

community. In some instances the primitive new world society had to pass through several stages before it reached a condition of social organization which permitted a profitable use of some phases of the common law.

Life in colonial America, it will be remembered, was for the most part on a comparatively simple level. It had its frontier household manufacture of cloth, clothes, furniture and implements; its farmhouse processing of land and animal products; and its mills which treated grain, cloth, or lumber. It had its charcoal smelting of iron, its nail shops, its distilleries, potash plants and shipyards. It had some town handicraftsmen as well. Taken by and large, however, the average colonist relied upon others only for that which he could not produce himself. Since the legal institutions and ideas of colonial society were largely conditioned by this somewhat rude order of life, it would not be surprising if many English legal materials were not brought into use until late in the Colonial period. While a considerable body of necessary and important principle and practice arising out of their English experience were undoubtedly put into use at an early date, as Professors Goebel and Plucknett suggest and recent studies corroborate, it is possible that many phases of the technical common law system which was to become the foundation of our later system were not applied until the necessary social development required it.

While all too little of what was decided by American courts before the Revolution was reported or left in a condition to be usable in the era of growth which followed the Revolution, the spirit and technique of colonial law is said to have been not without effect upon subsequent American legal development.[99] Colonial justice, in some of its phases, undoubtedly depended upon a system administered by the men of the neighborhood, by administrative officers, and by legislative assemblies. This unprofessional characteristic comes down to us in the system of petty courts administered largely by laymen which plays such an important part in the American judicial system throughout its history, and in the prominent role that has long continued to exist for the jury.[100] It is sometimes said that Americans became a legally minded, politically minded people during the colonial period and have remained so during a large part of their history.[101] Some analysts suggest that

[99] "Some of the characteristic features of our procedure grew out of the offhand applications of common sense by lay magistrates in colonial times to the scanty stock of English law and English procedure which had come to their notice. The 'freedom and inclination to novelty' which characterize our formative period may be seen full blown in the colonies." Pound, *Criminal Justice in America*, p. 118.

[100] Eaton, "The Development of the Judicial System in Rhode Island," *Yale Law Journal*, 148, 153; also Warren, *History of the American Bar*, 3, 105, 140.

[101] A. L. Lowell, *Essays in Government*, (1889) ch. III.

popular participation in legal affairs[102] beginning in colonial days and continuing through the formative period of American law, has had a great deal to do with maintaining this popular interest in law and politics. Recognizing its obvious disadvantages, they assert that such participation is an important educational factor in the democratic process, which will remain a vital saving force just so long as this sense of direct participation and responsibility continues.

Viewed in the light of history it seems clear that powerful forces were at work which made the adoption of common law materials in the colonial period necessary and desirable. The material development of the new country was one force which assisted the adoption of systematic justice. As commerce expanded and wealth increased the simpler devices of the earlier days were not sufficient. When economic growth became too rapid for legislation or other forms to meet its demands, the tendency to speed the adoption of common law materials was undoubtedly encouraged. Political factors were also important. The same forces which led the colonists to seek separation from the mother country, caused them to turn to the common law for protection against the crown, the royal governors and even Parliament. In the struggle between the courts and the Stuart kings, the courts stood between the crown and the subject, and the courts stood upon the ancient rights of Englishmen. Sir Edward Coke, the oracle of the common law, fashioned some of the legal theories of the ancient law into political rights of the first magnitude. When friction developed between the colonists and the royal governors, or between colonial legislatures and the crown, Coke's writings became a powerful source of argument for the colonists.[103] In short, the events which tended to separate the colonists from England tended to stimulate common law development as well.

[102] It must be remembered that the informal character of some of our colonial judicial processes does not necessarily mean that the system was democratic. The judiciary of Virginia, as Oliver Chitwood points out, was distinctly aristocratic in character. The people had little or no choice in the selection of their judges, who were appointed in one fashion or another. *Op. cit.*, pp. 309-31.

[103] "The security of rights and repose of private society against general search warrants, of the conscious independence of personal liberty against arbitrary seizure or extravagant stipulation, the indemnity of individual property against acts of involuntary benevolence, or in other words, the resistance of taxation without representation; the independence of thought, together with its signs, of speaking, writing, and publishing, as well as the liberty of volition and action, within the bounds of law; these were the topics that were perpetually harped upon out of the common law, and served to fan the flame of freedom on both sides of the Atlantic." *The North American Review*, vol. 21, July, 1825, p. 139.

PART II
THE FORMATIVE PERIOD OF AMERICAN LAW, 1776-1860

CHAPTER IV

THE PROBLEM OF ADJUSTMENT CONFRONTING THE AMERICAN LEGAL SYSTEM IN THE CRITICAL POST–REVOLUTIONARY PERIOD

The half century following the Declaration of Independence was a period of great change. The world was passing through a commercial revolution almost as important as that which followed the discovery of the Atlantic routes. At the same time a long period of inventive effort was coming to a head in some remarkable technological changes which tended to produce modern industrialism. These phenomena which are sometimes said to reflect an "industrial revolution" gave rise to an increased productive power, an increased strength and resourcefulness of capital, an increase of economic freedom, an expansion of domestic and foreign trade, an improved knowledge of agricultural possibilities, and a quickened tempo in transportation activities. This combination of events led to far-reaching changes in the life of Europe and America.

In America these were the formative years. During this period important social and political patterns were fashioned which continue to have an important effect on American life. In the brief span of one life a remarkable record in human accomplishment was written. A great system of self-government was organized and put into operation, vast areas of new land were opened up for settlement, great population shifts were effected, and great experiments in social as well as political democracy were attempted. Furthermore, roads were hewn out of forests, navigable streams improved, extensive canal systems inaugurated, new commercial areas opened and trade, commerce and agriculture expanded. When the trans-Allegheny region was settled, thousands pressed on to new lands in the trans-Mississippi West.

Land was plentiful, technology had not advanced to its present perfection, and a premium was placed upon man-power. Everything conspired to make the democratic experiment a success. At the root of the matter was the fact that land was available and cheap. The basic economy was agricultural and remained so until the last half of the century, when the industrial movement gathered overwhelming force. This condition is important, for many current problems are directly affected by the fact that institutions formed to meet the needs of an agricultural society, living in part under frontier conditions, are used today to administer the functions of an industrial society, living largely under urban conditions. Certainly many current problems of law and law administration are affected by this fact, since the essential character-istics of the American legal system take form and shape during the years between 1775 and 1860. "Two periods," remarks Dean Pound, "require special study by anyone who would know Anglo-American law. The first is the classical common law period, the end of the sixteenth and the beginning of the seventeenth century. The other is the period which some day will be regarded as no less classical than the former—the period of legal development in America that comes to an end with the Civil War."[1] During this period we moved away from the colonial system of justice which in some instances was admin-istered by laymen who were unable to give full service to the rule of law and adopted a system of justice administered according to law by a trained judiciary. While colonial influences played an important part in the evolution of the American legal system, despite views to the con-trary[2] the more important developments seem to have taken place after the War of Independence.

This is a surprising fact since hostility to England and its institu-tions characterized the Revolutionary period and lingered on long after the second war with England. Moreover, the distressed economic condition of the immediate post-Revolutionary period, which Jeremiah Mason describes so graphically,[3] accentuated the widespread dissatis-

[1] Pound believes the history of a legal system can begin too far back. He says: "Pol-lock is well warranted in insisting that the history of the comman law, for practical pur-poses, begins at the end of the thirteenth century. For American purposes we might begin with the seventeenth century. For the common law which we received was Coke's common law. English case law and English legislation prior to Coke was summed up for and handed down to us by (Coke) in what we have chosen to consider an authoritative form; and we have looked at it through his spectacles ever since. In like manner the history of the common law in America begins, for practical purposes, after the Revolution and the century ending with 1876, sees an American law fully established and beginning to show the rigidity and the dogmatic inflexibility of a settled system." "Judge Story in the Making of American Law," *American Law Review,* vol. 48, p. 678.

[2] "In spite of the difficulties recited, law had made some progress in America at the outset of the Revolution. There had been a gradual evolution of a judicial system and in many places there was coming to be a well-trained bar. Doubtless this would have insured a reception and development of the common law, but it happened here, as in seven-teenth century England, that the common law became useful as a political weapon. As Coke had invoked the common law against James I and Charles I, the Continental Congress of 1774 invoked it against George III. Thus a tradition arose that the colonists had brought with them the common law, as a much-prized heritage, and had clung to it and asserted it in the new world. After unquestioned currency for more than half a century, that doctrine has been overthrown by a study of colonial records and of colonial legisla-tion." Pound, *ibid.,* p. 680.

[3] "As I have before stated, the time when I commenced the study of law was a period of intense depression and poverty throughout the country. The war of the Revolu-tion had exhausted all the resources of the country. For the want of an efficient National Government, trade and all other kinds of business remained stagnant. The profession of law felt this depression severely. The State of Connecticut was overstocked with lawyers;

faction with law and distrust of lawyers.[4] "The circumstances of the country, from the peace of 1783, to the adoption of the Federal Constitution, " says William Sullivan, President of the Suffolk Bar and leading member of the Massachusetts legal profession during this period, "were exceedingly oppressive. In such times, professional agency has a very direct relation to real or imaginary evils. The vice of the times or the unwelcome operations of government are referred to those whose duty it is to aid in coercing the performance of contracts or in furnishing a legal remedy for wrongs. Our profession was most reproachfully assailed by newspaper essayists; and even the legislature entertained projects of reform in practice . . ."[5] Indeed the trying days of Shays' Rebellion, in 1786-87, tested the strength of the legal and political institutions of Massachusetts to the full. "Nothing perhaps, but the firmness of the Senate of the state," remarks one pessimistic commentator, "preserved our whole system of land and government from being trampled under foot by the unprincipled Jack-Cades of that day."[6]

Under circumstances so trying and difficult, how could this period be so important for the adoption of English legal materials? The answer is that the needs of the day overcame all other considerations. "The United States," in the words of one commentator, "freed from the restrictions of colonial subjection, almost immediately sprang up into the full maturity of a commercial nation. With commerce came a host of contracts, maritime, and domestic; an increase of the value of land gave rise to greater nicety in the examination of titles, and all tended to produce important questions, frequently involving intricate points of legal science."[7] While this statement overlooks some of the immediate problems of the post-Revolutionary period, it does point to the general

---

most of them had but little business, with fees and compensation miserably small. The professional income of Pierpont Edwards, supposed to be the largest in the State was said not to amount to two thousand dollars a year. Very few obtained half that sum: my master Baldwin, with his utmost diligence, was scarcely able to maintain his small family, living in the most simple manner. Seeing the list of needy young lawyers, some with clever talents seeking business with little or no success, I soon became satisfied that my prospect was exceedingly unpromising." *Memoir and Correspondence of Jeremiah Mason* (1873), p. 17.

[4] Charles Warren, *History of the American Bar.*

[5] *An Address to the Members of the Bar of Suffolk, Massachusetts, at their Stated Meeting on the first Tuesday of March, 1824.* Boston, 1825, 8 vol., 63 pp. Reviewed in *The North American Review*, vol. 21, July, 1825, p. 228.

[6] *The North American Review*, vol. 29, October, 1929, p. 420. It is interesting to note, that during Shays' Rebellion, the demand was made in one of the towns that the inferior courts and lawyers should be "entirely eliminated." See William D. Herrick, *History of the Town of Gardner*, p. 78. See also Minot's *History of the Insurrection*, 25, 36; see also Andrew M. Davis, *"The Shays Rebellion: A Political Aftermath,"* A Reprint from the *Proceedings of the American Antiquarian Society for April, 1911,* Worcester, Massachusetts, 1911, at p. 5.

[7] *Ibid.*, p. 420.

direction of the country's growth and indicate the fundamental necessities for the adoption of English legal materials. Whereas opposition to the common law and its technicalities might be given some practical effect in the sometimes rude and sparsely settled periods of colonial society, when lawyers were few and far between and the role of common sense and scriptural precept was sometimes emphasized, this sentiment could not control when the social order grew more complex.[8] The truth of this statement is evidenced, toward the end of the colonial period, as the increasing number of lawyers and the popularity of Blackstone indicates. The increasing needs of that period gave rise to a very definite movement toward the common law, a movement which was stimulated by the stirring events which characterized the period immediately preceding the war.

Chief Justice Isaac Parker further writes:

The first period in which jurisprudence seems to have taken an exalted rank and demanded of its professors elevated character and respectable learning, was that which immediately preceded the revolution. *Without doubt, the approaching dismemberment of the colonies from the parent country, had enlarged the minds and invigorated the faculties of the lawyers of that day, for we always find that a great political crisis produces extraordinary efforts of the human understanding.* The constant claim of prerogative on one side, and privilege on the other, required a knowledge of the rights and duties of the subject in those who presented themselves for royal patronage or popular favor. Profound discussions of the principles of free governments, the duty of submission and the right of resistance, sharpened the faculties and exercised the wits of the most distinguished lawyers, to which class of the community these discussions were almost entirely left. The nature of the social compact, the extent and true object of political power, the inalienable rights of man, the questionable authority of kings, and the before unquestioned supremacy of Parliament had become fashionable topics of debate. Learning of all kind, especially political, moral, and juridical, was necessary, in order to support with reputation, the conflict between contending parties. The public mind was strained to an unnatural avidity for learned essays, and profound disquisitions, and the Gazettes of that day contain abundant proof of the historical,

---

[8] "It is true," writes Chief Justice Isaac Parker, "that our ancestors brought with them that complex mass of juridical wisdom, the common law of England, which to understand required no little diligence and research, but they seem to have brought it rather as a store for future use than immediate application. They legislated for themselves, and their minute attention to the existing wants of a young and poor community almost superseded the use of the common law. It was only when property became separate and valuable, and commerce had begun to polish the rough face of affairs or when their civil and political rights were brought into jeopardy, that the invaluable principles of that venerable code excited attention and commanded the reverence of the community. But when this favorable change had taken place, although jurisprudence undoubtedly assumed a higher rank, yet, from the silence of history, and utter want of biographical notice of eminent jurists, we may conclude, that until a few years before the revolution, law was considered rather as a trade than a science, and its professors viewed as cunning artificers rather than as profound jurists." *The North American Review*, vol. 3, May, 1816, pp. 16-17.

political, and professional knowledge of the popular and prerogative lawyers. Otis, Adams, the Sewalls, Trowbridge, the Quincys, honoured the profession of which they were distinguished members; and it cannot be doubted that the law was then deemed a science, worthy of the most enlightened minds to learn, and honourable for the most dignified institution to teach.[9]

While the war for Independence checked the movement toward the common law it could not stop it completely. The fact of the matter is, that law was needed and a great systematic source was available. Moreover, it must be remembered that the English common law had been in one of its great growing periods, in the era between the middle of the seventeenth century and the time of the American Revolution. This fact was not unknown or without influence in the new world. Indeed the developments taking place in the common law during those years were closely related to the political developments in the colonies, and could not be ignored. Peter Du Ponceau wrote in 1825:

The true era of the common law is the period which followed the Revolution of 1648 to the time of our own emancipation. It was then that it assumed that bold and majestic shape, those commanding features which have made it the pride of the nations who possess it, and the envy of those who do not. During that period, the rights of man have been acknowledged and defined, and limits have been set to sovereign authority. The prerogatives of the crown (I am speaking here of England) have been ascertained, and restricted within proper bounds; the legislative, executive, and judicial authorities, have taken their respective stations, and know the extent of their several powers; judges, have been rendered independent, and juries have been freed from ignoble shackles. The writ of *habeas corpus* has been made effectual, a fair and unexceptional mode of trial has been provided for cases of high treason. The press has been freed from the unhallowed touch of state licensers. Religious toleration has been established. The hand of arbitrary power has been paralysed; and man has been taught to walk erect, and to feel the dignity of his nature; civil jurisprudence has also been considerably improved, and it is in a progressive state of further amendment.[10]

Some system of legal principles applicable to existing conditions had to be adopted and some system of courts established as well. Since colonial reports and precedents were virtually lacking, as Chancellor Kent points out, no help from that source was available.[11] English legal materials were at hand. They were received in due course and made over by men learned in the English law "sitting on the bench, making law in the legislature and lecturing and writing as law teachers."[12] In a very short time a perfectly bewildering array of reported decisions

[9] *Ibid.*, pp. 17-18.
[10] Quoted from his address before Law Academy of Philadelphia. See *The North American Review*, vol. 21, July, 1825, pp. 132-133.
[11] Roscoe Pound, *The Spirit of the Common Law*, p. 115.
[12] *Ibid.*, p. 118.

was established. It has been estimated that by 1822 there were about "one hundred and forty volumes of American Reports, all published since the organization of the federal government."[13] The rate of increase was so rapid that by 1824, complaints were being made concerning the "vast and increasing multiplication of reports as well as law treatises."[14] "It is not a matter of little surprise," asserts one observer, writing in 1826, "that twenty-five years ago, the best library of American reports that could be summoned by money or magic, within the circumference of the Union, might have been borne on the circuits in a portfolio, while now there are hardly less than two hundred within our territories."[15]

Defenders of this rapid increase in our reports came quickly to the front. As they viewed it, the common law grew naturally and became more extensive as progress was made. To assist its growth, able reports of well-investigated cases were necessary.[16] The rapid multiplication of law reports, they said, should be "regarded with a feeling of unmingled satisfaction," since it indicated clearly "the increasing demand, and the more general diffusion of intelligence, on a subject, of all others, the

[13] See "A Collection of Cases Overruled, Doubted, or Limited in their Application. Taken from American and English Reports," by Simon Greenleaf, Counsellor at Law, Portland, 1821. *The North American Review*, vol. 15, July, 1822, p. 65.

[14] "Previous to the year 1804, but eight volumes of indigenous reported cases had been printed in America; and the lapse of only one-fifth of a century has added to the number *one hundred and ninety* volumes, exclusive of any valuable reports of single cases. Of these eighty-nine volumes and part of a few others are occupied with the decision of the state courts of Virginia, Massachusetts, New York and Pennsylvania. Reports have been purchased in fifteen states, and in eight of them there is a reporter appointed and commissioned by public authority in addition to the reporter of the decisions in the Supreme Court of the United States. (Griffith's Law Register). Whither is this rapid increase of reports to lead us, and what are to be the ends and consequences of it? If year after year is to be thus prolific of its annual harvest of reports, we do not ask what fortunes will ere long be capable of compassing the purchase of a complete law library, but we ask what mind will be adequate to the task of storing up the infinite multiplicity of decided case?" *The North American Review*, vol. 9, April, 1924, p. 377. "Is there no means, then," the same writer asks, "of checking the progress of the multitude of 'flying reports' to use the words of Sir Harbottle Grimston, which daily creep abroad; no means of withstanding the tide of 'undigested crudities' which threatens ere this age passes away to deluge and overwhelm the ancient landmarks of the law?" *Ibid.*, p. 377.

[15] *Reports of Cases Argued and Determined in the Supreme Judicial Court of Maine*, by Simon Greenleaf, vol. II, Containing cases of the years 1822 and 1823. Hallowell, 1824. Reviewed in *The North American Review*, vol. 22, Jan., 1826, p. 27.

[16] It is by the publication of printed reports, said one of these early writers, "that the Common Law like all other sciences is destined perpetually to improve. The system is becoming better, as well as more generally known. On the hearing of a question of controversy, the object is looked upon from every possible point of view. All the various and seemingly conflicting decisions upon the subject, are brought before the court and canvassed. The postulates and arguments on which they rest, are severly scrutinized; the valuable truths selected and the material errors discarded, from each. And there is every reason for believing that by his mode of proceeding, the really sound principles of law will inevitably be reached at. This is precisely the way by which all sciences improve; and it is the only way which our courts of judicature can take on the settlement of a litigated question." *The North American Review*, vol. 27, July, 1828, p. 181.

most important to the peace and good order of society." "The publication of such reports," remarked one writer of the time "is the promulgation of the laws. They are promulgated, too, with the principle on which they are founded. In no other way is it possible to make them generally known; and as they arise out of the actual demands for justice, they are likely to be peculiarly well suited to the existing want and condition of society."[17] It was also argued that the "prompt and full publication of law reports" was of inestimable importance to personal rights.

Another argument which received wide consideration was the allegation that printed reports secured the judiciary, by every possible motive, to the faithful administration of justice. "What wrongs from this service may we not look for, in a community where the decrees of the courts of judicature are suppressed and kept from public view?" enquired one advocate of printed reports, who argued that judges cannot do their best work, unless they are required to write out the reports of their decisions. When they know that their decisions will go unreported, he says, "although they feel the sense of duty in all its purity, yet want the consciousness of being narrowly and extensively observed, which is a powerful incentive to great and generous efforts, even among the most elevated minds," their work will naturally suffer. But "when they know, that their opinions may be severely scrutinized by the ablest men of their own, and perhaps of coming ages; when they reflect that these opinions will be either made the basis of farther adjudications or rejected as inconclusive and false; above all, when from fear or error they are led, as in this country they almost universally are, to write their opinions at length, and themselves prepare them for the press, they have every inducement, interested and disinterested, which can possibly be crowded upon the mind to be laborious, accurate and impartial." In short, it was contended that our legal decisions should be brought before the public; "for nothing can tend more unerringly to the faithful administration of justice."[18] This is a strong argument for adequate decisions. Chancellor Kent in his *Commentaries*[19] made an equally powerful one. Other writers of the day did likewise[20] and the case for the printed report would not be denied. While the growth of the

[17] This is part of an able review of the *Reports of Cases Argued and Determined in the Circuit Court of the United States for the Second Circuit, comprising the Districts of New York, Connecticut, and Vermont,* by Elijah Paine Jr., Counsellor-at-Law. Vol. I, 800, pp. 718, New York, 1827, found in *The North American Review,* vol. 27, July, 1928, p. 179.

[18] *Ibid.,* pp. 179-180.

[19] Pp. 455, 462, 463.

[20] A splendid argument for the necessity of adequate reporting is set forth in *The North American Review* of January, 1825, at pages 180-191, in a review of Octavius Pickering's *Reports of the Cases argued and determined in the Supreme Judicial Court of Massachusetts.*

reporter system could not be held back, there was a growing recognition of the defects which arose out of its unmanageable proportions and many prominent jurists including Justice Story suggested remedial measures of one kind or another.[21]

The state of Connecticut was one of the first of our commonwealths to become active in establishing a system of regularly printed reported cases. This was due largely to the efforts of men like Zephaniah Swift,[22] to whom Connecticut owes her simple and orderly system of private law; Jesse Root,[23] one of her earliest reporters; and Tapping

[21] "The mass of the law is, to be sure, accumulating with an almost incredible rapidity," said Justice Story in 1829, "and with the accumulation, the labor of students, as well as professors, is seriously augmented. It is impossible to look without some discouragement upon the ponderous volumes which the next half century will add to the groaning shelves of our jurists. The habits of generalization which will be acquired and perfected by the liberal studies which I have ventured to recommend, will do something to avert the fearful calamity which threatens us of being buried alive, not in the catacombs but in the labyrinths of the law. I know indeed of but one adequate remedy, and that is, by a gradual digest, under legislative authority, of those portions of our jurisprudence which under the forming hand of the judiciary, shall from time to time acquire scientific accuracy. By thus reducing to a text the exact principles of the law, we shall, in a great measure, get rid of the necessity of appealing to volumes which contain jarring and discordant opinions; and thus we may pave the way to a general code, which will present in its positive and authoritative text, the most material rules to guide the lawyer, the statesman, and the private citizen. It is obvious, that such a digest can apply only to the law, as it has been applied to human concerns, in past times; but by revision, at distant periods, it may be made to reflect all the light which intermediate decisions may have thrown upon our jurisprudence. To attempt any more than this would be a hopeless labor, if not an absurd project. We ought not to permit ourselves to indulge in the theoretical extravagances of some well meaning philosophical jurists who believe that all human concerns for the future can be provided for in a code speaking a definite language. Sufficient for us will be the achievement to reduce the past to order and certainty; and that this is within our reach cannot be matter of doubtful speculation." "Address delivered before the Members of the Suffolk Bar in 1829," *The American Jurist, No. 1*, January, 1829, p. 31. Reviewed in *The North American Review*, vol. 29, Oct., 1829, 418-426.

[22] The career of Zephaniah Swift (1759-1823) is of special interest because he also published the first American law text. This was *A System of the Law of the State of Connecticut* which was published in two volumes in 1795 and 1796. His career as a jurist was interrupted by political factors and he consequently directed more of his time to his legal studies. In 1810 he published a *Digest of the Law of Evidence, in Civil and Criminal Cases; And a Treatise on Bills of Exchange, and Promissory Notes*. In 1816, he published *A Vindication of the Calling of the Special Superior Court, at Middleton, . . . for the trial of Peter Lung*. This treatise arraigned legislative interference with the judiciary and defended his own conduct as chief justice. In 1822-23, he published a *Digest of the Laws of the State of Connecticut*. The second volume of this work came out after his death. This work came to be widely used throughout the country both in legal instruction and as guide to the courts. It was invaluable in Connecticut; where it was said "no other individual has done so much towards reducing the laws to an intelligible system adapted to our habits and condition." Simeon E. Baldwin, "Zephaniah Swift," *Great American Lawyers*, vol. II, 1907; F. B. Dexter, *Biographical Sketches of the Graduates of Yale College*, vol. IV, 1907; E. D. Larned, *History of Windham County, Conn.*, vol. II, (1880); *Proc. Am. Antiquarian Society*, April, 1887; memoir in Swift's *Digest of the Laws of the State of Conn.*, vol. II, 1823; R. J. Purcell, *Connecticut in Transition*, (1918); *Encyclopedia of Connecticut Biography*, vol. 1; *American Historical Review*, July, 1834.

[23] Jesse Root (1736-1822) was admitted to the bar in 1763. In 1789 he was

Reeve, the founder of the Litchfield Law School.[24] In 1789, another Connecticut man, Ephraim Kirby (1757-1804),[25] made a permanent place for himself in the annals of American law when he published in Litchfield, his *Reports of Cases Adjudged in the Superior Court and Court of Errors of the State of Connecticut from the year 1785 to May, 1788* (1789). This work was the first fully developed volume of law reports published in the United States. In some respects it holds a place in American legal literature comparable to Plowden's *Commentaries* in English legal literature. In a preface to this work, Kirby contended that a system of reporting was necessary to the development of American law. Kirby's task of putting these Connecticut cases into book form,[26] was made possible by a statute passed in 1784 on the recommendation of Roger Sherman and Richard Law which required the Judges of the Supreme and Superior Courts to file written opinions, in disposing of cases on points of law, in order that they might be properly reported and "thereby a foundation laid for a more perfect and permanent system of common law in this state."[27] Under the influence of Swift, a systematic scheme of reporting was made permanent.

In 1790, Alexander Dallas[28] issued his first collection of Pennsylvania decisions. This collection of cases it should be pointed out,

---

appointed assistant judge of the superior court of Connecticut and in 1798 succeeded to the duties of chief justice. In the same year he published *Reports of Cases Adjudged in the Superior Court and Supreme Court of Errors . . . 1789 to 1793*. In 1799, he added a second volume. See J. P. Root, *Root Genealogical Records*, 1870; J. H. Trumbull, *The Memorial History of Hartford County, Connecticut*, 1886, vol. I, Connecticut, 1904, vols. II, III, ed. by Forrest Morgan; Thomas Day, *Reports of Cases . . . in the Supreme Court of Errors . . . Conn.*, vol. I, 1817, p. xxxii.

[24] W. D. Lewis, ed., *Great American Lawyers*, vol. 2, (1907), 469-71; A. C. White (ed.), *The Bi-Centennial Celebration of the Settlement of Litchfield* (1920), 49-58; T. D. Woolsey, *Hist. Discourse . . . Pronounced Before the Alumni of the Law Department of Yale College at the Fiftieth Anniversary of the Foundation of the Department*, 1874; A. C. White, *The History of the Town of Litchfield* (1920), pp. 98-109; D. C. Kilbourn, *The Bench and Bar of Litchfield County, Conn., 1709-1909* (1909), 181-214; D. S. Boardman, *Sketches of the Early Lights of the Litchfield Bar*, 1860, pp. 7-10.

[25] D. C. Kilbourn, *The Bench and Bar of Litchfield, Connecticut, 1709-1909*, (1909); M. E. Dwight, *The Kirby's of New England*, 1898; P. K. Kilbourne, *A Biographical History of the County of Litchfield*, 1851, and *Sketches and Chronicles of the Town of Litchfield, Connecticut*, 1859; Dunbar Rowland, *Courts, Judges, and Lawyers of Mississippi, 1783-1935*, vol. 1, 1935, pp. 8, 11, 20, 21.

[26] Charles Warren, *History of the American Bar*, p. 324.

[27] *Statutes of Connecticut*, Revision of 1784, p. 207; see also J. H. Boutell, *The Life of Roger Sherman*.

[28] Alexander J. Dallas (1759-1817), secretary of the treasury under James Madison and United States district attorney for the Eastern District of Pennsylvania for thirteen years, not only brought out the *Reports of Cases Ruled and Adjudged in the Several Courts of the United States and Pennsylvania, etc.*, (4 vols., 1790-1807), but also the *Laws of the Commonwealth of Pennsylvania*, (4 vols., 1793-1801). See Geo. M. Dallas, *The Life and Writings of A. J. Dallas*, 1871; James Dallas, *The Hisory of the Family of Dallas*, 1921.

began as far back as 1754. In 1793, Chipman's Reports were started in Vermont.[29] In 1790, the United States Supreme Court Reports were instituted.[30] In 1804 a regular and systematic series of Reports was commenced in Massachusetts. Previous to that time many points were mooted and opinions delivered which would have been well worth receiving, "still the minutes of them were so few and loose" that no reliance could be placed upon them.[31] In 1804 Caines became the first official reporter in New York State.[32] While Connecticut was the first

[29] In 1793, Nathaniel Chipman (1752-1843), published his *Reports and Dissertations*, which consisted mainly of reports of cases before the Supreme Court of Vermont. In 1787, he had been appointed justice of that court, the first lawyer to hold that post in Vermont. In 1796 and again in 1813, he was to sit in the same court, but on these occasions as chief justice. A thorough student of the law, he was one of the ablest men in early Vermont. His *Sketches of the Principles of Government* (revised ed., 1833), still remains well known. See Daniel Chipman, *Life of the Honourable Nathaniel Chipman*, 1846, and *Vermont Historical Collections*, (2 volumes, 1870-71). It was his brother, Daniel Chipman (1765-1850), however, who served as the first official reporter of Vermont. In 1823, the legislature appointed him to that post and he prepared volume I of *Reports of Cases Argued and Determined in the Supreme Court of . . . Vermont*, covering the years 1789-1824. This volume was published in 1824. He also wrote *An Essay on the Law of Contracts for the Payment of Specifick Articles*, 1822, referred to elsewhere; the life of his brother previously mentioned; and *A Memoir of Thomas Chittenden, the First Governor of Vermont, with a History of the Constitution, during his Administration*, 1849. See *Vermont Historical Gazeteer*, vol. I, 1868, p. 87.

[30] These reports were named for the official reporters until 1874. They include: Dallas (1790-1800); Cranch (1801-1815); Wheaton (1816-1827); Peters (1827-1842); Howard (1843-1860); Black (1861-1862); Wallace (1863-1874).

[31] *The North American Review*, vol. 29, p. 421, Oct., 1929.

[32] In 1802, George Caines (1771-1825), published anonymously the first volume of *An Enquiry into the Law Merchant of the United States; or Lex Mercatoria Americana on Several Heads of Commercial Importance*. See J. G. Marvin, *Legal Bibliography*, 1847. Although somewhat indifferently received it called attention to his capacities and when the New York legislature in 1804 provided for the appointment by the state supreme court of a reporter of its decisions, Caines was immediately considered for the post. He received the appointment and became the first official reporter in this country. Prior to his appointment all legal reports in the United States had been private ventures. In due course he issued *New York Term Reports of Cases Argued and Determined in the Supreme Court of that State*, in three volumes, covering the period May, 1803-November, 1805 (1804-06). In 1813-14, a second edition of this work was issued with corrections and additions. During the same period he compiled his *Cases Argued and Determined in the Court for the Trial of Impeachments and Correction of Errors in the State of New York*, (two volumes, 1805-07), commonly cited as *Caines' Cases in Error*. In 1808 he edited a second edition of William Coleman's *Reports of Cases of Practice Determined in the Supreme Court of Judicature of the State of New York, 1794 to 1800*, adding cases up to November, 1805. This work is usually cited as *Coleman and Caines' Cases*. A later edition appeared in 1883. Retaining his position of reporter for less than three years, his work was extremely useful. His reports were brief but accurate and long enjoyed a high reputation with bench and bar. Subsequent statutory amendments have, of course, deprived them of much of their original utility. In addition to his work as a reporter, Caines was the author of a practical manual, *Summary of the Practice in the Supreme Court of New York* (1808), and *Practical Forms of the Supreme Court (of New York) Taken from Tidd's Appendix*, 1808. See D. McAdam, *et al.*, ed., *History of the Bench and Bar of New York*, vol. 1, 1897; B. V. Abbott and A. Abbott, *Digest of New York Statutes and Reports*, 1860, I, XIV, XVI; Charles Warren, *History of the American Bar*, 1911, p. 331; *New York Spectator*, July 15, 1825.

American state to print judicial decisions, this work was done, as we have seen, as a private venture. New York and Massachusetts were the first states to order official publication of decisions. New Jersey followed this practice in 1806 and South Carolina in 1811.[33] Connecticut did not attempt to print judicial decisions as a state enterprise until 1814 and Kentucky in 1815.[34]

In short, it may be said that while the movement toward the common law was greatly retarded by the strains and stresses of war and the bitter hatreds engendered by war psychology, it could not be held

[33] South Carolina's experience with reporting cases is of interest. During the colonial period important or controversial decisions were preserved in full, in the records of the court or the journals of the Assembly. In 1799, a law provided that every judge in the Constitutional Court of Appeals (which was the name given for the Circuit Judges en banc) "should give for preservation in writing his opinion and reason." In 1809, Judge E. H. Day published the first volume of his reports of South Carolina cases and in 1811 his second volume. In 1811, an act was passed, requiring the opinions of the Appeal Court to be recorded and indexed in books. In 1819, two volumes of Appeal Court cases for 1817 and 1818, were privately published by John Mill. In 1816, an act was passed, requiring one judge to write the court opinion and directing the court to select the most important opinions for publication. In 1820, the first two volumes were presented. These volumes were edited by Nott and McCord. In 1823, an official reporter was provided for, to report both equity and law cases. This step was part of the judicial reform movement culminating in 1824. After this time, few private reports applied. Wallace, *History of South Carolina*, vol. II, 1934, p. 471.

[34] A provision in the first constitution of Kentucky in 1792 required judges of the appellate court "to state in their opinions such facts and authorities as should be necessary to expose the principle of each decision." No method of reporting the decision was provided by the legislature until 1815, however, when the governor was authorized to appoint a reporter. Previous to that time, writes Lewis Collins, "James Hughes, an eminent 'land lawyer' had, at his own expense, published a volume of the decisions of the old District Court of Kentucky, whilst an integral portion of Virginia, and of the Court of Appeals of Kentucky, rendered in suits for land—commencing in 1785 and ending in 1801: Achilles Sneed, clerk of the Court of Appeals, had, in 1805, under the authority of that court, published a small volume of miscellaneous opinions, copied from the court's order book; and Martin D. Hardin, a distinguished lawyer, had, in 1810, published a volume of the decisions from 1805 to 1808, at the instance of the court in execution of a legislative injunction of 1807, requiring the judges to select a reporter. George M. Bibb was the first reporter appointed by the Governor. His reports, in four volumes, include opinions from 18— to 18—. Alexander K. Marshall, William Littell, Thomas B. Munroe, John J. Marshall, James Dana, and Benjamin Monroe were successively appointed, and reported, afterwards. The reports of the first, are in three volumes—of the second, in six—of the third, in seven—of the fourth, in seven—of the fifth, in nine—and the last, who is yet the reporter, has published seven volumes. Consequently there are now forty-six volumes of reported decisions of the Court of Appeals of Kentucky, of these reports, Hardin's, Bibb's, and Dana's are most accurate—Littell's, Thomas B. Moore's, and Ben Monroe's next. Those of both the Marshall's are signally incorrect and deficient in execution. Dana's in execution and in the character of the cases, are generally deemed the best, of the decisions in Dana, it has been reported of Judge Story that he said they were the best in the Union—and of Chancellor Kent, that he said he knew no state decisions superior to them. And that eminent jurist, in the last edition of his commentaries, has made frequent references to opinions of Chief Justice Robertson, and has commended them in very flattering terms." *Historical Sketches of Kentucky* (1848), pp. 106-107.

back completely.[35] This fact becomes increasingly clear, in the years immediately following the war, which were marked by a vastly expanding population, a rapidly developing commerce, and a greatly increasing wealth. It was also reflected in the increased business and fees of the legal profession.[36]

The growth of the trans-Allegheny regions which were almost unsettled at the close of the Revolution can be used to throw light on the nature and scope of this remarkable expansion. In the year 1800, the entire population of the Northwest territory, which included the present states of Ohio, Indiana, Illinois, Michigan, Wisconsin and a portion of Minnesota, numbered a scant 45,365. In 1810, Ohio alone had a population of 230,760. This was a tremendous increase. In the years that followed, this amazing growth in numbers continued. In 1820, the population of Ohio was 581,295; in 1830, 937,903; in 1840, 1,519,467; in 1850, 1,980,329. A society in this phase of development had need for a legal order which would provide uniformity, equality, and certainty.[37] These qualities could be secured only through

[35] "After the war had been closed, by the peace of 1783," writes Chancellor James Kent, "the landmarks of our ancient jurisprudence reappeared. They had, fortunately, not been obliterated or disturbed by the tempest. Almost the entire system of the English law recognized by our Constitution was put into operation. The profession was called into the most active business; and as the principles applicable to our Constitution were unsettled, and the rules of law unknown, except through the distant and dim vision of English reports, the claims of real property opened at once a large field of forensic legislation. Everything in the law seemed, at that day, to be new; we had no domestic precedents to guide us. English books of practice as well as English decisions were resorted to, and followed with the implicit obedience and reverence due to oracles. Our judges were not remarkable for law learning. Almost every point of practice had to be investigated and tested. Even Mr. Hamilton thought it necessary, at a circuit at which I was present, in 1784, to produce authorities to demonstrate and guide the powers of the court in the familiar case of putting off a cause at a circuit. A few gentlemen of the colonial school resumed their ancient practice, but the bar was chiefly supplied by a number of ambitious and high spirited young men, who had returned from the field of arms with honourable distinction, and by extraordinary application, they soon became qualified to commence their careers at the bar with distinguished reputation," *Address to Law Association of New York in 1836*.

[36] Whereas the income of Pierpont Edwards practicing in New England in the period following the Revolution might be extremely limited, though the largest in that vicinity, it is reported that the earnings of the South Carolina bar in the years between 1793 and 1815 were enormous. Charles Fraser in his *Reminiscences*, 71, states that four of the leading members of the Charleston bar during that period earned annually between $18,000 and $23,000 and that eight or ten others earned between $10,000 and $12,000 a year. Wallace, *History of South Carolina*, vol. II, 1934, p. 456.

[37] The situation in the "Western Reserve" in Ohio is of interest in this connection. In 1800, acts of Congress and of the Connecticut legislature confirmed the title of Connecticut to the soil of the Reserve on the one hand and released jurisdiction to the United States on the other. From 1795 to 1800 there were no laws nor government of any kind. There were no courts, no laws, no records, no magistrates or police and no methods of enforcing or protecting land titles or personal rights. Nevertheless "lands were bought and sold, personal contracts made, marriages solemnized and personal rights respected as in the best governed societies, and all without government and without law." This was largely due to the fact that these settlers who were largely from New England were long

rules and system. A system, in which lay justice with its crude, unequal, and partisan administration, would be given large consideration could supply none of these things. The English legal system could provide some of them.[38] In consequence rules were developed which were predicated on the traditional legal materials made over partially by legislation and partly by judicial decision. While legislative activity was important,[39] it was the courts who reshaped the received materials of the English law to "the conditions of an individualistic economic order in an era of enterprise and of exploitation of natural resources." This action was taken with the conditions of a pioneer, agricultural society in mind. England in reshaping seventeenth and eighteenth century legal materials, did so with the needs of an urban and industrial society in mind.[40] This placed her at a great advantage in the days to come.

In the immediate post-war years the struggle between the need for law and hostility to the source of law was extremely intense. For example, in New Jersey, Delaware, Pennsylvania, and Kentucky laws were enacted forbidding the citations of English decisions which were made after Independence.[41] In New Hampshire a rule was adopted forbidding such citations and judges and legislators everywhere were influenced by the popular feeling.[42] As late as 1808, Henry Clay was prohibited from citing an English authority by the Supreme Court of Kentucky,[43] and Ralph Waldo Emerson in his "Essay on Power" writes

accustomed to the discipline of self-government. This condition could not continue indefinitely, however, and when in 1800, the United States took the Western Reserve, it became a part of the Northwest Territory and was organized into a county for governmental purposes. This action brought the people of the Western Reserve within the protecting folds of a civil jurisdiction for the first time. See E. O. Randall, "Tallmadge County," *Ohio Archaeological and Historical Publications*, vol. 17, 1908, p. 279.

[38] See *Reports of Cases Argued and Determined in the English Courts of Common Law.* Edited by Thomas Sergeant and John C. Lowber, Sqrs. of the Philadelphia Bar. Reviewed in *The North American Review*, vol. 21, October, 1825, pp. 377-388.

[39] The period between 1776 and 1873 witnesses a remarkable legislative reform movement. See Pound, *Criminal Justice in America*, pp. 119-1020.

[40] *Ibid.*, pp. 119-120.

[41] Some of these measures may have been influenced by other considerations. It is interesting to note, that Thomas Jefferson, who favored a rule prohibiting the citation of English authorities after George III, explained that such a rule would eliminate all of "Mansfield's innovations." Tyler, *Letters and Times of the Tylers*, I, 265.

[42] Many of the untrained magistrates of the time encouraged this feeling. The justice of the court of New Hampshire who stopped the reading of an English law-book because the court understood "the principles of justice as well as the old wigged justices of the dark ages did" is a good example of this tendency. See Baldwin, *The American Judiciary*, pp. 14-15; also Plumer, *The Life of William Plumer*.

[43] *Hickman* v. *Hoffman*, Hardin's Reports, 348, 364; Baldwin, *op. cit.*, p. 14. "A statute of 1816," writes Lewis Collins, the Kentucky historian, in 1847, "enacted, that 'all reports of cases decided in England since the 4th of July, 1776, should not be read in court or cited by the court.' The object of this strange enactment was to interdict the use of any British decision since the declaration of American independence. The statute, however, literally imports, not that no such decision shall be read, but that 'all' shall not be. And this self-destructive phraseology harmonizes with the purpose of the act—that is,

that "a Western lawyer of eminence said to me, he wished it were a penal offense to bring an English law book into a court in this country, so pernicious had he found in his experience, our deference to English precedents."[44] In Pennsylvania opposition to the common law led to the impeachment of the Chief Justice and two Associate Justices of the Supreme Court for sentencing one Thomas Passmore to jail for "contempt of court." The ground of the impeachment was that punishment for "contempt" was a piece of English common law barbarism, unsuited to this country.[45] Many lawyers of the day, as Chancellor Kent points out, came from the Revolutionary armies, or from the halls of Congress. They brought with them "many bitter feelings and often but scant knowledge of the law."[46] Some opposition to English precedents may be explained as an effort on their part "to palliate this lack of information by a show of patriotism."[47] The opposition of some of the untrained magistrates of the time may be similarly explained.[48]

Public sentiment was also influenced by the radical elements who excoriated English precedents as the "rags of despotism" and the judges who rendered them as "tyrants, sycophants, oppressors of the people and enemies of liberty."[49] This was a direct survival of war time thinking. At the time of the Revolution, it will be remembered, many eminent members of bench and bar were loyalists although not all of them by any means.[50] Indeed Lorenzo Sabine asserts that a "majority

---

to smother the light of science and stop the growth of jurisprudence. But for many years, the Court of Appeals inflexibly enforced the statute—not in its letter, but in its aim. In the reports, however, of J. J. Marshall, and Dana, and Ben. Moore, copious references are made (without regard to this interdict) to post-revolutionary cases and treatises in England, and now that statute may be considered dead." *Historical Sketches of Kentucky*, 1848, p. 107.

[44] *Conduct of Life*, (ed. 1893), p. 63.

[45] *University of Pennsylvania Law Review*, vol. LVI, 1908.

[46] Pound, *The Spirit of the Common Law*, pp. 116-117.

[47] *Ibid.*, p. 116. Alexander Hamilton's preparation for the bar, it will be recalled, was four month's reading.

[48] Baldwin, *op. cit.*, pp. 114-115.

[49] Pound, *op. cit.*, pp. 116-117.

[50] "Of the barristers in Boston and its immediate vicinity . . . five were loyalists, and John Adams alone lived through the Revolution as the advocate of American independence. Twenty-four of the principal barristers and attorneys in the colony, and one hundred and twenty-three merchants and traders, including others, in Boston, signed the address to Governor Hutchinson, 30 May, 1774; and similar addresses to Governor Gage, as late as 14 October, 1775, were signed by the same class of people, and in still larger proportion to population in Salem and Marblehead. Plymouth Colony was the stronghold of the loyalists. . . .

"Many of these who finally adhered to the Crown were among the most earnest denunciators of the Stamp Act. . . . Not that the tories were fonder of paying taxes than were the patriots, but they were content when the obnoxious tax was repealed, and were disinclined to (follow John Adams and) make an issue on the Declaratory Act of the parliamentary right to tax." Mellen Chamberlain, *John Adams*, (1884), cited by Frank W. Grinnell in "The Bench and Bar in Colony and Province (1630-1776)," *Commonwealth History of Massachusetts*, vol. II, 1928, pp. 181-182.

of the lawyers were Whigs." At least in his researches, he found "but comparatively few who adhered to the crown," whereas "a large part of the speakers and advocates on the popular side were educated to the law." Moreover, one of the objects of the "Stamp Act" was "to drive from the profession those members of it who annoyed the loyal governors and other officials, and who, as a member of the House of Commons said, were 'pettifoggers.'" He also points out that "many gentlemen of the bar, on being retained by the merchants, became impressed with the enormities of the commercial side, and in advocating the cause of clients who claimed to continue their contraband trade on the ground of usage and prescription. . . . were impelled to follow the example of Otis, and to take the lofty stand that commerce should be, and on principles of justice really was as open and as free to British subjects in the New World as it was in the Old."[51] He knew, of course, that "the ministry had their partisans among the barristers at law" and that some of them were persons "of great professional eminence." Indeed he admits that "the giants of the law" in the colonies "were nearly all loyalists." "As in the case of the clergy," he writes, "many of them were driven into exile. Several entered the military service of the crown and raised and commanded companies, battalions, and even regiments. At the peace, a few returned to their former abodes and pursuits, but the greater number passed the remainder of their lives in England, or in her present possessions in America.[52] The anti-revolutionary bar in Massachusetts and New York, furnished the admiralty and common law courts of New Brunswick, Nova Scotia, Canada, and the Bermudas, with many of their most distinguished judges."[53]

[51] Lorenzo Sabine, *The American Loyalists*, Boston, 1847, pp. 52-53.

[52] George A. Ward, *Journal and Letters of the late Samuel Curwen, Judge of Admiralty, etc., an American Refugee in England from 1755 to 1784, Comprising Remarks on the Prominent Men and Measures of that Period. To which are added Biographical Notices of many American Loyalists and other eminent persons*, 1842. Reviewed in *The North American Review*, vol. 56, Jan., 1843, pp. 89-108. See also *The North American Review*, vol. 55, pp. 97ff.

[53] Many of the Loyalists gained official berths in other parts of British America. "Thus, Smith, chief justice of New York, who wavered and doubted till the struggle was well-nigh half over, attained to the same dignity in Canada. Jonathan Bliss, Daniel Bliss, Ward Chipman, Jonathan Sewall, Edward Winslow, James Putnam, and Joshua Upham, were all on the bench of New Brunswick. Foster Hutchinson (His sister Abigail died at Halifax, N. S., July, 1843, at the age of 74. Their father was a judge of the Supreme Court of Massachusetts, and brother of Governor Hutchinson) and Sampson Satter Blowers were on the bench of Nova Scotia. John Wentworth, the last royal governor of New Hampshire, received the executive power over Nova Scotia, a baronetcy, and a pension of £500 a year. Routh, collector of Salem, held the same post at Newfoundland and was also chief justice there. William Hutchinson was king's councillor at the Bahamas. Samuel Quincy was king's attorney at Antigua. Daniel Leonard was chief justice of the Bermudas, and William Browne was governor of the same islands. Jonathan Stearns was attorney general of Nova Scotia. Sir John Johnson was governor of Canada. Of these it is of interest to add that Smith was educated at Yale College; and all the others, Routh and Johnson excepted, at Harvard University." See *A History of the Operations of*

Sabine mentions at least 130 lawyers who left the country as Tories and there were undoubtedly many more. The lot of those who remained at home was not pleasant and in some instances, direct punitive measures were taken against them. In New York, for example, an act was passed by the legislature on Oct. 9, 1779, "suspending from practice all attornies, solicitors, and counsellors at law, who had been licensed previous to April, 1777, to practice in any of the courts of law or equity of the former colony of New York." This suspension could only be removed by the inquisition of a jury of enquiry, establishing upon oath, that the applicant had been "a good and zealous friend of the American cause." In March, 1785, an attempt was made to procure a repeal of this law, so far as it respected certain prominent legal gentlemen of known integrity, but it proved unsuccessful; "and many men of talent were thereby excluded from the profession to which they had been educated, and which constituted their dependence for the support of their families." For example, Peter Van Schaack,[54] who had revised the statute laws of the colony of New York was excluded by this act of 1779 and was not readmitted to the New York bar until April, 1786.[55] It seems that a great many lawyers of loyalist persuasion did not wait for official acts of the foregoing character, but retired voluntarily from the profession.[56] Nevertheless opposition to the profession because of the war record of some of its members continued to follow it for a long time after the war was over.

It should be mentioned that a considerable body of opposition to the English common law sprung from sources which were not patriotic or political in character, or influenced by the dictates of some special interest. It was an opposition, which was derived from a somewhat different set of circumstances; and may be explained as being a part of the frontiersman's usual opposition to scientific law.[57] This sentiment, which was present during the colonial period, manifested itself in a striking way during the formative period of our institutions, during which period strenuous efforts were made to overcome it. It survives to the present day in many forms as William E. Dodd has pointed out,[58] as does also "individualism," "egalitarianism," "self-sufficiency" and numerous other thought-patterns of the frontier. This sentiment with

a Partisan Corps, called the Queen's Rangers commanded by Lieut. Col. J. G. Simcoe during the War of the American Revolution, with a memoir of the author, etc., 1844, pp. 328 ff. Reviewed in The North American Review, vol. 59, October, 1844, pp. 275-276.
[54] Henry Van Schaack, The Life of Peter Van Schaack, 1842, p. 400.
[55] Ibid., pp. 402-403.
[56] See Sabine, Loyalists of the American Revolution, 1864, and William Sullivan's Address to the Suffolk Bar, 1825.
[57] Pound, op. cit., pp. 117-118.
[58] W. E. Dodd, "Our Ingrowing Habit of Lawlessness," Century Magazine, October, 1928, vol. 116, pp. 691-698.

regards to law may have been accentuated in the immediate post-Revolutionary period by a growing popular resentment toward the aristocratic tendencies of many leaders of bench and bar.[59] When these tendencies were brought directly to the fore in the party battles between the silk-stocking forces of Federalism and the rising tide of Jeffersonian democracy, the law and its practitioners came into disfavor in some quarters since many prominent lawyers and judges followed Federalist principles. This is illustrated by conditions in New York where practically all of the leading members of bench and bar, except Aaron Burr and the Livingstons, followed Alexander Hamilton,[60] Rufus King,[61] and Gouverneur Morris,[62] the leaders of the aristocratic tradition. "The lawyers," says Dixon Ryan Fox, "formed a numerous order—President Dwight, of Yale, estimated that there were more than twice as many in New York as in Connecticut for each thousand of population, and their aristocratic tendencies were resented by the popular party."[63] Professor Fox's study leaves little doubt that many of the leaders of the New York bar of that early period were decidedly sympathetic to the aristocratic principle.[64] Studies of conditions in early Connecticut by Richard J. Purcell[65] and Jarvis M. Morse[66] also indicate the close

[59] "The influence which gave the English bar an exclusive and aristocratic character operated even more strongly in the new world. Here the absence of an aristocracy founded on hereditary privilege, and the absence of great wealth gained from the rapid development of commerce and industry during the later phase of our history gave to our bar an unquestioned social and political leadership to which perhaps it could not under other conditions have obtained. These influences made the bar the most English of our institutions and during the early part of the nineteenth century it had a more highly developed class-consciousness than at probably any other time in its history." Stone, *op. cit.*, p. 176.

[60] Hamilton's frequently repeated description of the public as "a great beast" indicates his point of view in the matter. Dixon Ryan Fox, "New York becomes a Democracy," *History of the State of New York*, (Alex. Flick, ed.) vol. 6, 1934, p. 6.

[61] Rufus King "had the manner as well as the mental outlook of the old ruling class, preserving its formal courtesy and, long after it had generally disappeared, the old costume of prestige and dignity, silk-stockings and silver buckles, small clothes and lace." *Ibid.*, p. 6.

[62] In Gouverneur Morris' opinion "there never was and never will be a civilized society without an aristocracy." *Ibid.*, p. 6.

[63] "Beware of lawyers (warned the *New York Daily Advertiser*, on March 4, 1789). Of the men who framed the monarchial, tyrannical, diabolical system of slavery, the *New Constitution*, one half were lawyers. Of the men who represented, or rather misrepresented, this city and county in the late convention of this state, to whose wicked arts we may chiefly attribute the adoption of the abominable system, seven out of nine were lawyers." *Ibid.*, p 607.

[64] "Old Tory lawyers in the city, like Richard Hanson, Josiah Ogden Hoffman and Cadwallader D. Colden, found the principles of Hamilton and Jay the best now practicable, and were welcomed to the party by conservative Whigs in the profession—Col. Robert Troup, now a powerful land agent in the Genesee country and one who did 'not admire . . . the republican system'; Col. Richard Varick, the high-toned and austere mayor of New York for many years; Egbert Benson, the state's first attorney general, John Wells, the Laurences, the Ogdens, and others." *Ibid.*, pp. 6-7.

[65] Purcell, *Connecticut in Transition, 1775-1818*, pp. 208, 303, 306.

[66] Morse, *A Neglected Period in Connecticut's History, 1815-1850.*

relationship between many members of the bar and the aristocratic principle. In New York the position taken by such luminaries as Chancellor James Kent, Chief Justice Ambrose Spencer, Jonas Platt, and William W. Van Ness, is of interest. In the New York Constitutional Convention of 1821, Chancellor Kent, who fought throughout his life "for the rights of the individual, as distinguished from those of the people" delivered his oft-quoted speech on the dangers of universal suffrage[67] and Chief Justice Ambrose Spencer who shared Kent's views concerning the dangers of popular government spoke along similar lines.

These views certainly could not have been lost upon the common man, and were undoubtedly responsible in some degree for the attitude which frequently manifested itself in somewhat crude expressions of disregard for the dignity of the courts and their membership. We get a suggestion of this attitude, during the immediate post-Revolutionary period from the Duc De La Rochefoucauld, who travelled in the United States during the years 1795, 1796, and 1797. In describing one phase of his journey, he says:

> One of my fellow passengers was Mr. Ellsworth of Connecticut, recently appointed Chief Justice of the United States. All the Americans who were with us, and they were almost all young people, showed him no more regard than if he had been one of the negroes, though he be, next after the president, the first person in the United States, or perhaps indeed, the very first. Disrespect to their seniors and to persons in public office, seems to be strongly affected among the Americans; such at least is the humour of the rude and ill-bred among them. This, surely proceeds from mistaken notions of liberty;

[67] In this speech Chancellor Kent described the dire results which democracy had produced in the republics of the old world. "By the report before us," he said, "we propose to annihilate, at one stroke, all property qualifications, and to bow before the idol of universal suffrage. That extreme democratic principle has been regarded with terror by the wise men of every age, because in every European republic, ancient and modern, in which it has been tried it has terminated disastrously, and been productive of corruption, injustice, violence and tyranny. And dare we flatter ourselves that we are a peculiar people who can run the career of history exempt from the passions which have disturbed and corrupted the rest of mankind? The men of property, together with crowds of dependents connected with the great manufacturing and commercial establishments, and the motley and indefinable population of the crowded ports, may, perhaps, at some future day, under skillful management, predominate in the assembly, and yet we should be perfectly safe if no laws could pass without the free consent of the owners of the soil. That security we at present enjoy, and it is that security which I wish to retain. The apprehended danger from the experiment of universal suffrage applied to the whole legislative department, is no dream of the imagination. It is too mighty an excitement for the moral condition of men to endure. The tendency of universal suffrage is to jeopardize the rights of property and the principles of liberty. There is a constant tendency in human society—and the history of every society proves it—there is a constant tendency in the poor to covet and share the plunder of the rich; in the debtor to relax or avoid the obligations of contract; in the majority to tyrannize over the minority, and trample down their rights; in the indolent and profligate to cast the whole burden of society upon the industrious and virtuous; and there is a tendency in ambitious and wicked men to inflame those combustible materials. . . . " See Jabez D. Hammond, *Political History of New York*, vol. I, pp. 301-302; Dixon R. Fox, *op. cit.*, pp. 23-24.

for, if ever the public office holders have a right to general respect, it must be, above all, in those free governments in which they hold their authorities in consequence of the election of the people. It is even astonishing to see how disrespectfully the people carry themselves in regards to the courts of justice. They appear at the bar with their hats on their heads, talk, make a noise, smoke their pipes, and cry out against the sentences pronounced. This last piece of conduct is universal; and there are, perhaps, some petty instances of injustice in the courts, which make it to be not without its use. However, this deficiency in respect to the state officers who discharge the public functions, and administer justice—one of the greatest blessings of social life—is actually seditious, and is utterly incompatible with the idea of a people living under a stable government.[68]

It is interesting to note that the popular disregard for the legal process, which is manifested so frequently during this early period, did not lack the encouragement and support of an active political leadership. The writings of Benjamin Austin (1752-1820) demonstrate this fact. An able pamphleteer of Anti-Federalist sympathies, Austin condemned the law and inveighed against the lawyers as well. He believed that the problem of law and law administration would be best worked out in the young republic by a plan which involved: (1) an American code of law; (2) parties to appear in person or by any friend whether attorney or not; (3) referees to take the place of courts; and (4) a State Advocate General to appear for all persons indicted.[69] Instead of adopting the English law, he favored the establishment of some "concise system, calculated upon the plainest principles and agreeable to our Republican government."[70] This step, he asserted, would render useless hundreds of volumes "which only serve to make practice mysterious." In introducing the whole body of English law into our courts,

[68] *Travels through the United States of North America, the country of the Iroquois and upper Canada, in the years 1795, 1796, and 1797, with an authentic account of Lower Canada,* 1799, p. 533.

[69] See *Observations on the Pernicious Practice of the Laws* by *Honestus* (Benjamin Austin) as *Published occasionally in Independent Chronicle in Boston, of April 20, 1786,* (1819). Austin's "Honestus" articles of 1786, ran in the *Boston Independent Chronicle* from March 9 to June 15. A digest was then made of them which was published in 1786 as his "Observations on the Pernicious Practice of Law" and in a second edition in 1819.

[70] Charles Warren, *History of the American Bar,* 211 ff. These proposals were assailed by the lawyers and Austin was accused of fomenting Shays' Rebellion which broke out in 1786. Resentful of these charges he became more extreme in his expressions and actions. His views were well received by the Boston masses, however, and John Quincy Adams describes a town meeting over-run by some seven hundred of his followers "who looked as if they had been collected from all the jails on the continent, with Ben. Austin like another Jack Cade at their head." *Proceedings of the Massachusetts Historical Society,* 2nd. ser., IV, 63. For Austin's political views see *Constitutional Republicanism, in Opposition to Fallacious Federalism; as Published Occasionally in the Independent Chronicle,* Boston, 1803. See also J. S. F. Gardiner, *Remarks on the Jacobiniad* (Boston, 1795, 1798); A. E. Morse, *Federalist Party in Massachusetts* (1909); B. Austin, *Memorial on the Grounds of Excusable Homicide to the Legislature of Massachusetts* (1806); T. O. Selfridge, *Correct Statement of the Whole Preliminary Controversy between Tho. O. Selfridge and Benjamin Austin* (Charleston, 1807); *The Democratiad* (Phil., 1795).

he said, we were simply borrowing trouble. "Why should these States be governed by English laws?"[71] Like Duane and many another he thought that the answer was decidedly in the negative.[72] "We may as well adopt the laws of the Medes and the Persians," he asserted. "The numerous precedents brought from old English authorities," in his view "serve to embarrass all our judiciary causes and answer no other purpose than to increase the number of lawyers."[73]

These views of Benjamin Austin reflect the opinion of many Anti-Federalists, who were not only hostile toward England and English institutions, but also interested in reforming existing practice and procedure as well. In 1800, the Anti-Federalists under able political leadership became the Jeffersonian Republican party which swept into power. For some time many of its members were inclined to urge the reception of the French law. Gratitude to France for her timely assistance during the Revolution was at a high point during these years and great interest was displayed in the language, literature, fashions, and manners of the French.[74] In South Carolina, for example, public opinion which had been greatly exercised with the problems of internal organization in the new Federal and State Constitutions, was diverted into the excitement and dangers of foreign affairs, by the spectacular activities of Citizen Genêt, who was appointed minister to the United States on the eve of the long war between France and England. Landing in Charleston in April 1793, Genêt aroused a storm of pro-French enthusiasm, which, stimulated by republican ideas and commercial interests, lasted for years. By the end of 1793, the population was divided into Francophile and Francophobe. There were at least two Jacobin Clubs organized in Charleston. The term "Citoyen" became a common term of address and interest in French politics manifested itself in parades and demonstrations.[75]

When the Revolution started in France, it had strong support in many parts of this country. It is no wonder that French legal authorities were given high standing in many quarters, and frequently found

---

[71] Austin, *op. cit.*

[72] Duane, *Samson against the Philistines.*

[73] Austin, *op. cit.*

[74] In 1779, the College of William and Mary established a chair of French. In 1780, Harvard did the same. In this connection see Howard Mumford Jones, *American and French Culture*, pp. 524-526; 527-572; also McMasters, *History of the American People*, V, 278-280.

[75] David D. Wallace, *The History of South Carolina*, vol. 2, 1934, pp. 352-353. It is interesting to note that when Henry Wheaton was a student at Rhode Island College, now Brown University, he was addressed by his school mates as "Citizen" Wheaton because of his interest in and zeal for the French political cause. For criticism of the so-called "French mania" of the country during these years see a review of the *Works of Fisher Ames, with a Selection of his Speeches and Correspondence* edited by his son, Seth Ames, which appeared in *The North American Review*, vol. 80, Jan., 1855, pp. 216-217.

their way into the older American reports. "In our courts of justice," asserts a commentator of that time, "the writings of the civilians are referred to freely and fearlessly. The Institutes of Justinian, and the commercial treatises of Pothier, Emerigon and Roccus, are naturalised among us; and in many libraries, Bynkershoek, Heineccius, and Valin, have taken their place by the side of the Blackstone and Coke. Our printed reports show the fruits of this liberal study."[76] In New York an unusual number of references to the authorities and writers of the civil law are to be found. Dean Pound points out that in the first volume of Johnson's *Reports* of decisions in the New York Supreme Court and Court of Error for the year 1806, the Institutes of Justinian were cited once, Pothier was cited four times, Emerigon five times, Valin five times, Casaregis twice, and Azuni twice. In arguments of counsel before the courts the French civilians were also repeatedly cited. In the seventh volume of the same reports for 1810 and 1811 the French civil code was cited once, Pothier was cited twice, Huberus twice, and Emerigon once. The Digest and the Institute were also cited. While these citations occurred most frequently in cases involving mercantile law, they were not confined exclusively to that field. In fact the civil law was turned to in connection with questions of conflict of laws, damages on a covenant of title, original acquisition of title to property, of rights as between owners of property and quasi-contract.[77]

"What indeed, should we think in the present times," asks a reviewer of Willard Phillips' *A Treatise on the Law of Insurance*, which was published in 1823, "of men who affect to be indifferent to the writings of such authorities as D'Aguesseau, Domat, Valin, Pothier, and Emerigon?"[78] To neglect Pothier, he suggests, would be a disgrace to the learning and literature of a nation. "Who," he continues, "has written with so much purity of principle, such sound sense, such exact judgment, such practical propriety on all the leading divisions of contracts? Who has treated the whole subject of maritime law so fully, so profoundly, so truly with a view to its equity and advancement, as Valin? Who has equalled Emerigon as a theoretical and practical writer on the law of insurance? He has exhausted every topic so far as materials were within his reach; and upon all new questions his work for illustration and authorities and usages is still unrivalled."[79]

Gratitude to the French people and admiration for their great civilian jurists were not the only features which encouraged a tendency in these early nineteenth century years to turn to French legal materials.

[76] *The North American Review*, vol. 21, October, 1825, pp. 387-388.
[77] Pound, "Judge Story in the Making of American Law," *American Law Review*, vol. 48, p. 685.
[78] *The North American Review*, vol. 20, Jan. 1825, p. 63.
[79] *Ibid.*, pp. 63-64.

Imperfections in the common law of that day, particularly as it related to commercial subjects, was also an important factor. "Almost all the principles that regulate our commercial concerns," remarks a writer of that day, "are of modern growth, and have been engrafted into the old stock of the law by the skill of philosophical as well as practical jurists."[80] Lord Mansfield's great efforts to incorporate the law merchant into the common law were not completed at the time of the Revolution. While his work was to have a controlling effect in America in due course, American judges were required to depend upon their own efforts in this field for some time to come.[81] Naturally they turned to French treatises on the civil law for assistance, and in many cases cited and approved them.

Even when English authorities might be available there were reasons for turning to French sources. One of the legal writers of that day makes this apparent. "The law merchant and marine, of this country have been formed," he said, "by the union of our own statutes and decisions with all the decisions above enumerated. The common, civil, and customary law of Europe have each precisely the same force with us in this branch, that is, our courts study them all and adopt from them whatever is most applicable to our situation, and whatever is on the whole just and expedient, without considering either of course obligatory. If Mansfield, Scott, or Ellenborough, is cited with deference or praise, so likewise are Bynkershoek, Valin, Cheirac, Pothier, and Emerigon. The authority of a decision or opinion, emanating from either of these sources, is rested on exactly the same foundation, viz: its intrinsic excellence. And if we seek instruction on mercantile law from jurists in England why not seek it from their masters on the continent of Europe? Why do we not go to the fountain-head? Why do we content ourselves with second-hand information? In fact all eminent lawyers in this country sooner or later find it necessary to study the law books of the continent, but such a course ought to be more early and universal, the continental law ought to be made an important, it might also be said the most important, branch of elementary legal education."[82]

In short the American people were favorably disposed to the direct reception of law from other lands than "old England" and the opportunity for widening the base of American law was a great one.[83]

[80] *The North American Review*, vol. 20, Jan., 1825, p. 56.

[81] Pound, *op. cit.*, p. 681.

[82] *The North American Review*, vol. 11, October, 1820, p. 412.

[83] "In adopting new rules it is indispensable to look to public convenience, mutual equities, the course of trade, and even foreign intercourse. It is plain, that in such inquiries, the customary and positive law of foreign countries as the result of extensive experience, must be of very great utility. No nation can be so vain as to imagine that she possesses all wisdom and all excellence. No civilized nation is so humble that her usages, laws,

Among others who took advantage of this opportunity for development was the scholarly Chancellor James Kent of New York who came on the bench in 1804. Depending upon what he called his "mysterious wand of French and civil law," he greatly expanded the law of New York. "The judges," he said, "were Republicans and very kindly disposed to every thing that was French, and this enabled one, without exciting claim or jealousy to make a fair use of such authorities and thus enrich our commercial law."[84]

The admiration held by many Americans for Robert Joseph Pothier, the great civilian jurist, which has been described, was heightened with the publication of his *A Treatise on Maritime Contracts of Letting to Hire*, which was translated from the French with notes and a life of the author by Caleb Cushing.[85] High regard for the art of other civilians was expressed in many ways. When Mr. David Hoffman brought out his admirable *Course of Legal Study* in 1817, one commentator, after giving high praise to the course of study, went on to say that the *civil law side* of the course had perhaps not been given adequate consideration.[86] "To Mr. Hoffman's list of books on these subjects," he says, "we beg leave to add Heineccius' Elements of the Civil Law according to the order of the Institutes and the Pandects, whom Sir James Mackintosh has not scrupled to call the best writer of elementary books, with whom he is acquainted on any subject. We also recommend Ferrieve's Dictionaire de Droit et du Pratique, Calvinus' Lexicon Juridicum, M. Dessaules' Dictionaire du Digeste, Exton

and regulations, do not present many things for instruction, and some for imitation. In respect to the general principles of jurisprudence, those which are applicable to the ordinary concerns of human life in all countries, . . . it is undeniable, that much light may arise from the investigations of foreign jurists. Genius and learning can never fail to illustrate the principles of universal law, even when the primary object is merely to expound municipal institutions. The Dutch, the German, the Italian, the Spanish, or the French civilian is not less a master of equity and rational jurisprudence, when he deals with the Roman law, colored, and it may be shaded, by his own local customs and ordinances, than the Lord Chancellor on the woolsack enforcing trusts in *foro conscientiae* or the lord Chief Justice, when expounding commercial contracts at the Guildhall of London. The truth is, that the common law, however reluctant it may be to make the acknowledgment, and however boastful it may be of its own perfection, owes to the civil law and its elegant and indefatigable commentators (as has already been listed), almost all its valuable doctrines and expositions of the law of contract. The very action of assumpsit, in its modern refinements, breathes the spirit of its origin. It is altogether Roman and Pretorian. And there never has been a period in which the common lawyers, with all their hostility to the civil law, have not been compelled to borrow its precepts. The early work of Bracton shows how solicitous some of the sages were even in that rude age to infuse into their own code some of that masculine sense, which found favor in the day of Justinian." *The North American Review*, vol. 20, Jan., 1825, pp. 62-63.

[84] Pound, *op. cit.*, pp. 686-687; see *The North American Review*, vol. 6, 1817-18, p. 55.

[85] An interesting and informing review of this book is found in *The North American Review*, vol. 13, July, 1821. pp. 1-20.

[86] *The North American Review*, vol. 6, November, 1817, at p. 76.

and Zonch and Spelmen on the Admiralty Jurisdiction; Cleiraac's Us et Coutumes de la Mer, Emerigon's Traite des Assurances, Pothier's works and particularly his Treatise on Maritime Contracts, Boucher's Translation of the Consolato del mare, Peckins ad rem nauticum, D'Abreu sur les Prisas, and 'though last, not least, Caseregis' Discursus de Commercio."[87]

If Mr. Hoffman gave inadequate consideration to the Civil Law, it was not due to lack of appreciation. On the contrary he had a very real admiration for the Civil Law. "English jurisprudence," he remarked in a later work, "has been copiously supplied from the purest stream of the Civil Law, though but little, and a very reluctant acknowledgement has ever been made for the heavy debt thus contracted."[88] "Though the Roman Law," he added, "has not been extensively studied by the legal scholars of England, there have not been wanting those who perceived the narrow and technical features of the Common Law and the expansive and equitable character of its rival."[89] "Some," he continued, "who are now engaged in the laudable exertion of abrogating the rigid and feudal refinements, so unsuited to the present age, and of supplying their place by doctrines found in other codes, have resorted mainly to the writings of the civilians; and even before this; several of their judges, as Hale, Holt and especially Mansfield, had shown a liberal willingness to appeal authoritatively in some cases, and with due respect, in others, to the Justinian Code."[90]

Mr. Hoffman's admiration for the civil law was shared by many a distinguished member of the profession during this period, including Peter S. DuPonceau,[91] a scholarly member of the Philadelphia bar. In

[87] Ibid.

[88] The North American Review, vol. 36, April, 1833, p. 399.

[89] Ibid., p. 400.

[90] Ibid.

[91] When Peter Stephen DuPonceau (1760-1844) commenced the practice of law in Philadelphia in 1785 the international situation was extremely complicated. The United States was neutral, and questions involving international law and practice were frequent. DuPonceau's acquaintance with foreign law and language brought him quickly to the fore in this field where he soon became recognized as an authority. A diligent student of the law, he published, among other things: a translation of Bynkershoek's, A Treatise on the Law of War . . . Being the First Book of his Quaestiones Juris Public (1810) (This was a translation from the original Latin with notes); A Dissertation on the Nature and Extent of the Jurisdiction of the Courts of the United States, 1824; and A Brief View of the Constitution of the United States, 1834. See American Law Magazine, April, 1845; Law Rep., vol. 7, p. 62; Western Law Journal, May, 1844; W. W. Story, Life and Letters of Joseph Story, 1851. He was instrumental in establishing the Law Academy of Philadelphia in 1821. At the outset this institution was designed to be "a national law school" both for students in law offices and for younger members of the bar. In fact, it set out to be a competitor of the Harvard Law School. DuPonceau's plan was to supplement practical office work with moot court work and lectures. In his inaugural address he advised his hearers "to show yourselves worthy of the honor of being considered as the Founders of a National Law School in the United States." This attempt to establish a law school that would supplement rather than supplant the law office as a training

an address[92] delivered on April 22, 1824, at the opening of the Law Academy in Philadelphia, Mr. DuPonceau, who was a thorough student of, and admirer of, the common law, urged the practical importance of the Civil Law in this country, "where the administration of the Civil and the Common Law is committed to the same judges, and the same body of judges is called upon to practice both."[93]   Another distinguished lawyer, who became greatly interested in the Civil Law during this period was Hugh Swinton Legare of South Carolina. Legare who was later to become Attorney General of the United States in John Tyler's administration developed an interest in the Civil Law during his early life.[94] He maintained this interest throughout his brilliant career. Like Edward Livingston he believed that it "was practicable and desirable to infuse a larger portion of the spirit and philosophy of the Civil Law and even of its forms and process into our system of jurisprudence." His writings, which were brought together in two volumes,[95] include articles which reflect Mr. Legare's desire to expand the common law by infusing into it some of the principles of the civil law.[96] They were on a scholarly plane and were highly commended by such competent students of the law as Justice Story.[97]

---

medium did not succeed, however. In 1832, the plan was abandoned and the Academy addressed a petition to the University of Pennsylvania to enter the field of legal education. The Academy was reorganized as a moot court society and was incorporated in 1838. It still survives in this form. See George Sharswood, *The Origin, History, and Objects of the Law Academy of Philadelphia*, 1883; Margaret Klingelsmith, "History of the Department of Law," *University of Pennsylvania Proceedings at the Dedication of the New Building of Law*, 1900, pp. 213 ff; A. Z. Reed, *op. cit.*, pp. 205, 432.

[92] See *A Dissertation on the Nature and Extent of the Jurisdiction of the Courts of the United States, being a Valedictory Address, delivered to the Students of the Law Academy, at Philadelphia, at the close of the Academical Year, on the 22nd of April, 1824*, by Peter S. DuPonceau. *To which are added a Brief Sketch of the National Judiciary Powers Exercised in the United States, prior to the Adoption of the Present Federal Constitution*. By Thomas Sargeant, Esq., Vice Provost, *and the Author's Discourse on Legal Education, delivered at the opening of the Law Academy, in February, 1821, with an Appendix and Notes*. 254 pp. Philadelphia, Abraham Small, 1824. Reviewed in *The North American Review*, vol. 21, July, 1825, pp. 104-141.

[93] *The North American Review*, vol. 36, April, 1833, p. 400.

[94] After graduating from South Carolina College in 1814, he spent three years in the study of law. In 1818 he went to Europe, where he studied Roman law for a time. In 1832, he was appointed charge d'affairs in Belgium by Edward Livingston, then secretary of state. During this four-year period in Europe, he once more studied the Roman and Civil Law, this time under the great Savigney.

[95] *Writings of Hugh Swinton Legare* (2 vols. 1845-46), ed., with a memoir, by his sister, Mary S. L. Buller; W. C. Preston, *Eulogy on Hugh Swinton Legare* (1843); B. J. Ramage, *Sewanee Rev.*, Jan., April, 1902, reviewed in *S. C. Historical and Genealogical Magazine*, April, July, 1902; *Official Opinions of the Attorney General of the United States*, vol. IV, 1852; L. G. Tyler, *The Letters and Times of the Tylers*, vol. II, 1885.

[96] *The Origin, History and Influence of Roman Legislation*, I, 502; Kent's *Commentaries*, II, 102; *Codification*, II, 559.

[97] Legare's essays were said to have been "characterized by a brilliance and breadth of scholarship that are hardly paralleled by the writings of any other American jurist." Judge Story, in an address to the Dane Law School students, eulogized Legare's essay on

Despite the favorable attitude manifested toward French law in this country, there were a number of practical difficulties which stood in the way of its ready adoption. The linguistic barrier was particularly difficult to overcome. Some incomplete translations of Pothier were made, including, as noted before,[98] the one on Maritime Contracts. Translations of this kind did not become available however, until it was too late for them to exert a great deal of influence.[99] In consequence few judges or lawyers were able to make effective use of French legal materials. Scholars like Kent and Story were prepared to draw heavily upon the Civil Law, but they were the exceptions.[100] Another vastly important factor which militated against the reception of the French law was the unexpected vitality which was displayed by the legal profession in developing Anglo-American legal materials.[101] Starting with Kent, Story, and Marshall at the beginning of the nineteenth century, the growth of American law went forward rapidly and well until the close of the Civil War period. The advancement made during this brief span of seventy-five years, says Dean Pound, will compare favorably with that of any period of growth and development in legal

the Roman Law in fulsome terms. So highly did he regard Legaré's scholarship that he is said to have remarked that "to me, had my own career closed before his, a single word of praise from his lips, could I have looked back to know it, would have been as valuable a tribute as from any other human being." Moore, "The Law Writers of the South," *The South in the Building of the Nation*, vol. 7, p. 330.

[98] In 1818 a 636-page book on the *Laws of the Sea with Reference to Maritime Commerce during Peace and War*, written by Frederick J. Jacobsen in 1815, was translated from the German by William Frick and published in Baltimore by E. J. Coale. A review of this book appears in *The North American Review*, vol. 7, Sept., 1818, pp. 323-347. This review discusses at great length the influence of civilian authors and principles upon the Anglo-American system, particularly in the field of commercial law where Lord Mansfield's great contributions were made.

[99] *The North American Review*, vol. 13, July, 1821, pp. 1-20.

[100] The influence of civilian writing is also seen in Gulian C. Verplanck's *An Essay on the Doctrine of Contracts; being an Inquiry into how Contracts are affected in Law and Morals, by Concealment, Error, or Inadequate Price*, New York, 1825, 234 pp. Reviewed in *The North American Review*, vol. 22, April, 1826, pp. 232-273.

[101] Writing in 1838, one commentator says: "Our own country, too, which twenty years ago, had done little more than adapt a few English textbooks to our meridian, with just enough of editorial matter to make a decent apology for a copyright, has since vied with the mother country in the number and value of its works on legal subjects. In proof of this, we need only mention (among others) the learned treatises of Mr. Willard Phillip on Insurance and on Patents, and of Judge Gould on Pleading, Mr. Laussat's Essay on Equity . . . the treatises of Mr. Stearns and Judge Jackson on Real Law, the various legal publications of Mr. Angell, Mr. Cushing's Essay on the Trustee Process in Massachusetts, . . . Dunlap's Treatise on Admiralty Practice, (in which . . . the editorial labors of Mr. Sumner constitute much the most valuable portion) and above all, the Commentaries of Chancellor Kent on American law in general, and of Mr. Justice Story on Bailments, Constitutional Law, the Conflicts of Law, and Equity Jurisprudence, all of which have acquired an European reputation; and earned, for these eminent jurists, in other countries that meed of applause which is like the calm, unbiased judgment of posterity. Nor . . . should we omit the name of Mr. Theron Metcalf. . . . " *The North American Review*, Jan., 1838, pp. 72-73.

history. "The closest analogy," he says, "both in the time taken and the amount and character of work accomplished is the classical period in England—the Age of Coke."[102] The making over of the civil law in France, culminating in Pothier's writings and the Civil Code, he points out, took at least a hundred years; while a century and a half elapsed between the first draft of a Prussian Code, under Frederick the Great and the establishment of the Civil Code for the German Empire. Moreover, he points out, there was an abundance of modern material at hand in both France and Germany which had been "long studied and thoroughly expanded."[103] In this country, he adds, there was no such material at hand. When the illustrious Kent went on the bench in New York, he found that "there were no reports or state precedents. The opinions from the bench were *ore temus*." "We had," he said, "no law of our own and nobody knew what the law was." Commenting on his experiences as Chancellor which commenced in 1814 he said, ". . . for the nine years I was in that office there was not a single decision, opinion, or dictum of either of my predecessors . . . from 1777 to 1814 cited to me or ever suggested."[104] In short, American judicial authorities had few materials immediately at hand when they started in upon their great period of law building. They were confronted with numerous other obstacles at the outset.

[102] Pound, *op. cit.*, p. 683.
[103] *Ibid.*, p. 683.
[104] *Ibid.*

CHAPTER V

THE PROBLEM OF ESTABLISHING PROFESSIONAL STANDARDS AMONG THE BUILDERS OF THE AMERICAN LEGAL SYSTEM

We have already considered some of the unfavorable circumstances which attended the development of the legal system in the immediate post-Revolutionary period. There were many others. Not only was legal learning at a low tide in this period but, as Jeremiah Mason pointed out,[1] the unfavorable social and economic situation held little promise of improvement for the immediate future. Conditions certainly were not favorable for the establishment of a learned profession of the law. Recruitment of the legal profession was largely effected by the hit or miss methods of apprenticeship or through an outgrowth of this method in the so-called "private law school." Throughout this early period the practitioners of the law were likely to put considerable store by their legal monopoly in the field of instruction. Many of these early lawyers would receive all the students they could get and their law offices practically became private law schools. For example, after the able Tory lawyer, Peter Van Schaack, was readmitted to the bar in 1786 he turned his attention to the educational process and is said to have instructed "nearly a hundred young gentlemen."[2] Jesse Root and Charles Chauncey of Connecticut were also exceedingly active in the closing years of the eighteenth century. Charles Chauncey who retired from the bench in 1793 is said to have been "a lecturer on jurisprudence" for forty years.[3] There were any number of private law schools scattered throughout the country during this early period.[4]

As time passed, considerable dissatisfaction with this method developed and some law schools appeared to supplement the apprenticeship

[1] *Memoir and Correspondence of Jeremiah Mason,* 1873, p. 17.

[2] See A. Z. Reed, *op. cit.,* p. 431.

[3] One of Chauncey's students was David Daggett, who was appointed to a professorship of law at Yale University in 1824, *ibid.,* p. 129.

[4] A. Z. Reed, *op. cit.,* pp. 431-432. Chancellor James Kent, for example, studied law in the office of Judge Benson of Poughkeepsie with five other students. A notable array of early New England lawyers, including Chief Justice Smith of New Hampshire, Chief Justice Mellen of Maine, and Judge Davis of the Federal Court, studied law in the office of Shearjashub Bourne of Barnstable, Massachusetts. *The Centennial History of the Harvard Law School,* 1918, p. 1.

system and the private law school.[5] Writing in 1833, one analyst of contemporary legal problems remarked:

The mode in which, until of late, the rising generation of lawyers in this country were initiated in the mysteries of their profession sufficiently accounts for their want of acquaintanceship with general jurisprudence. The lawyer's office was considered not only as the training ground, where the young soldier of Themis is to be fitted for active service by the direction and example of a veteran in his profession; but it was resorted to, both as the primary school and the university, in which the student's education was to be begun and completed. Now it is true that the office is the best, nay the only fit place for acquiring that practical information, without which the most learned general jurist makes no figure in the arena of professional labor and competition. But this nursery of practical skill is not and cannot be a complete seminary of jurisprudence. It is vain to expect, that the most able and faithful student should gain in the office that fundamental and comprehensive knowledge of the law, without which the most consummate practical discernment still retains the character of instinct, which is useful chiefly in cases of common occurrence, but never conducts to a thorough understanding of the science. The scientific student on the other hand, never rests, until he has entered into the inmost nature of the law, as well as the general character of the cases to which it is applicable, and on this account is never at loss to discern, in any case, the accidental accompaniments and the essentials; and to distinguish between those circumstances which afford ground for argument, and those which predetermine the decision. Such a knowledge of the law, which distinguished the scientific lawyer from the empiric, cannot be derived from the office of a successful practitioner, but it requires an ample and judicious collection of men and books, such as a well organized law school, or law academy, is intended to comprise.[6]

In the spirit of these observations and purposes, far-seeing men lent their energies to the organization of law schools in different parts of the country, and their efforts have had a most important effect on the course of American legal development. At first, these schools were likely to be confined to professorships after the fashion of Blackstone's Vinerian chair at Oxford. The Harvard law school began in this fashion. Isaac Royal, who died in 1781, provided in his will for such a professorship. In 1815 this professorship was established and Chief Justice Isaac Parker was appointed the first professor of law,[7] although his chair was not a

---

[5] Thomas Jefferson was always critical of the apprenticeship system. In setting up a course of study for a young relative in 1790, he said: "It is a general practice to study the law in the office of some lawyer. This indeed gives to the student the advantage of his instruction. But I have ever seen that the services expected in return have been more than the instructions have been worth." *Writings*, V, 180. Chief Justice Isaac Parker also criticized the inadequacy of office training. Warren, *History of the Harvard Law School*, vol. I, 1908, pp. 299-302.

[6] *The North American Review*, vol. 36, April, 1833, p. 396.

[7] See Inaugural Address delivered in the chapel of Harvard University by the Hon. Isaac Parker, Chief Justice of Massachusetts, and Royall Professor of Law. *The North*

teaching one. Instead, he lectured to college seniors, residents, and occasional members of the bar. In other words, he followed the practice of Chancellor Wythe who was delivering lectures at William and Mary College as early as 1779, of James Wilson who lectured at the College of Philadelphia in 1790, and James Kent who lectured at Columbia in 1793. In his inaugural address, Professor Parker expressed the hope that sometime in the near future "a school for the instruction of resident graduates in jurisprudence" might be added to the professorship.[8] May 17, 1817, he laid before the corporation a plan for a law school. The plan was adopted and Asahel Stearns was appointed "University Professor of Law." He was to live in Cambridge, open and keep a school, prescribe a course of study, read appropriate lectures, act as tutor, and confer with and examine students.[9]

In laying the groundwork for his course of instruction, the new professor followed the practice of Tapping Reeve's great pioneer law school at Litchfield, Connecticut, which began about 1784.[10] Since the Litchfield experiment developed by slow stages from a law office to a

---

American Review, vol. 3, May, 1816, pp. 11-27. It is interesting to note that in 1663, Jonathan Mitchell, Senior Fellow of the college, composed a document called a "Modell for the maintaining of students, and fellows of choice abilities at the College of Cambridge, tending to advance Learning among us, and to supply the publike with fit Instruments, principally, for the work of the Ministry," which displayed some interest in legal training. See *Publications of the Colonial Society of Massachusetts*, Boston, 1895, XXXI, pp. 308-322. While the chief emphasis of the document was placed on the need for trained ministers, Mitchell also took cognizance of the need for trained grammar school masters and magistrates. "It sufficeth not," the document reads, "to Have supplyes for the ministry, for time will shew that unless we Have the Help of Learning and education to accomplish persons for the magistracy and other civill offices, things will goe to decay among us." Accordingly his scheme of endowed fellowships provided for a "Linguist"; an "Historian and Antiquary"; a "polemicall Divine"; a *Civilian well-studyed in the Law and especially in the Laws of the English nation;* and for "Choice and Able Schoolmasters," etc. President Dunster as early as 1647 displayed a similar interest when he petitioned the New England confederation for funds to purchase suitable books "in law, phisicke, philosophy, and mathematickes." *Plymouth Colony Records*, IX, p. 95. Samuel Eliot Morison, *The Founding of Harvard College*, 1935, p. 249.

[8] Samuel E. Morison, *Development of Harvard University, 1869-1929*, 1930, pp. 472-473.

[9] *Ibid.*, p. 473.

[10] The Litchfield school was opened in 1784. For some time before that Reeve had been giving regular instruction in law in a methodical way in his office. He apparently followed a somewhat similar method in his school. Reeve worked alone for some fifteen years. During this time some two hundred students attended the school. In 1798 he was appointed a judge of the superior court. Accordingly he selected James Gould, a former pupil and a recent graduate of his school, to carry on the work. Gould was quite successful. He devoted practically full time to the school until 1816, when he, too, was appointed to the bench. Gould was an able administrator. He undoubtedly deserves the major credit for developing "an institution that in the early years of the nineteenth century brought to Litchfield hundreds of young men from almost every state in the Union and numbered among its graduates some of the most prominent men in the public life of the next generation." See *Dictionary of American Biography*, vol. 15, p. 469; W. D. Lewis, *Great American Lawyers*, vol. II, 1907, pp. 469-471.

law school, the exact date of its beginning is uncertain; in fact, it retained some of the characteristics of an expanded law office to the end,[11] with the students copying precedents of pleadings and of conveyances, and reading such books as were at hand, in the same fashion as the apprentices in lawyers' offices.[12] There was, of course, a greater number of students and there were dictated lectures which in a day when printed textbooks were few, served as a partial substitute. While Asahel Stearns' school followed the methods of Tapping Reeve, the possibilities of the Cambridge school were much greater. In the past, "there had been professorships of law in colleges without law teaching, and teaching of law in schools which in spirit and method were but law offices."[13] The Cambridge school united the two methods, "combining the English idea of apprenticeship training with the continental idea of academic law teaching."[14] In so doing, it established "the first university school of law in any common law land."[15] It supplemented the Litchfield method by adding a moot-court, after the fashion of the Inns of Court, and lectures by a university professor. It moved "in the direction of an academic professional school, as contrasted with the purely academic law schools of continental Europe, and the purely professional legal education which

[11] The influence of the Litchfield School upon the political and juristic history of the country is incalculable. It was powerful, however, if we consider it only in the light of its effect in the trans-Allegheny region. In early Ohio when institutional patterns were being shaped, for a long period of time men influenced directly or indirectly by the Litchfield School, were directly to the fore. Among its prominent graduates who achieved distinction in widely separated parts of the country were John C. Calhoun of South Carolina, Horace Mann of Massachusetts, George Y. Mason of Virginia, and Levi Woodbury of New Hampshire. The influence of the Litchfield School in the field of legal education alone is of the utmost importance. Among its graduates who were active in the field of legal instruction were Samuel Howe of Northampton, Massachusetts; Theron Metcalf of Dedham, Massachusetts; Edward King of the Cincinnati Law School; William Gould of Augusta, Georgia; and Amasa Parker of the Albany Law School. See A. Z. Read, *Training for the Public Profession of the Law*, 1921, pp. 130-131, Bulletin No. 15, Carnegie Foundation.

[12] Before the Litchfield School closed its doors in 1833, it had sent out over a thousand graduates. From the time of the war until the advent of James Gould in 1798, the number of graduates is said to have been two hundred and ten, or an annual average of some ten or fifteen. During the next ten years the school did not grow very rapidly. Its attendance varied from nine students in one year to twenty-one in another. In 1809, the attendance rose to thirty-three students and in 1813 to fifty-five. This figure remained for twenty years, a record attendance for American law schools. In 1835 the University of Virginia established a new record with sixty-seven students and in 1838 Harvard established another record, with seventy-eight students. Litchfield continued to have a good attendance as late as 1826. After that it declined rapidly. This was due, among other things, to the rise of new schools with younger men and greater resources; to the general lowering of educational standards throughout the country in the wake of the democratic movement, and to political reasons. See A. Z. Reed, *Training for the Public Profession of the Law*, 1921, p. 130, Bulletin No. 15, Carnegie Foundation.

[13] Pound, *op. cit.*, p. 473.

[14] For comments on these two types of training see *The North American Review*, vol. 36, April, 1833, pp. 396-397.

[15] Pound, *op. cit.*, p. 473.

prevailed in England."[16] In other words, it marked the beginning of what Dean Pound calls "a distinctively American type of legal education."[17]

At the end of ten years, Stearns was of the opinion that the Cambridge school had raised "the general standard of professional education by introducing a more methodical and thorough course of instruction."[18] The school's course of study and instruction was certainly widely adopted by other schools and by private preceptors. Of course, the chief need of the time was to provide competent practitioners in the courts since the chief work of the lawyer was in the trial of causes and knowledge of "local procedure and ability to move jurists were sufficient professional equipment."[19] Later on, it became necessary to have lawyers who could play their part in developing a system of law which would meet the exacting requirements of a rapidly growing country whose commercial activities were moving forward by leaps and bounds. A bar trained by the apprenticeship-method, which thought in local terms and chiefly concerning the mechanics of procedure could not fill this need.

This fact is well brought out by President Josiah Quincy of Harvard University in his address delivered at the dedication of Dane Law College in Harvard University on October 23, 1832. "Commerce, as well internal as external," said President Quincy, "is ever, from its very nature, expansive and varying, in accordance with which the principles of this branch of law necessarily vary and expand. That they may be well understood, and be diffused through the nation with a rightly grounded uniformity, nothing seems more important than that the education of legal students should, in this respect, have the supervision and aid of some of the great lights of the law, whose exclusive duty it should be to lead their minds to take comprehensive and practical views of this complex subject, and to teach them, among its fluctuating interests, how to fix upon its sound and immutable principles."[20] In the light of these facts, President Quincy urged the importance of adding instruction in Commercial Law to Harvard's legal curriculum.

Nathan Dane, whose abridgment has already been referred to was another who recognized this fact and his endowment of the Dane Professorship for Joseph Story, who took up his duties in 1829, has been described as "a turning point in American law."[21] Since Story was trained in the common law, there could be no doubt that the school

[16] *Ibid.*, p. 473.
[17] *Ibid.*
[18] *Ibid.*, p. 474.
[19] Pound, *ibid.*, p. 474.
[20] *An Address delivered at the Dedication of Dane Law College in Harvard University*, October 23, 1832, by Josiah Quincy, LL.D., President of the University, 1832. Reviewed in *The North American Review*, vol. 36, April, 1833, p. 398.
[21] Pound, *op cit.*, p. 475.

would remain a professional school under his guidance. On the other hand he was widely versed in the philosophical background of the law, and it was equally certain that the institution he directed "would be a school of law, not a lawyer's office teaching rules of thumb." And so it was. Story not only taught the doctrines of the common law "in the light of a natural law philosophy and of comparative law," but produced a series of outstanding leading works, which greatly assisted the development of equity and commercial law as well. This task was accomplished with "the help of comparative law and rational philosophical speculation" while retaining a common law basis. In short, Story safeguarded the common law in the law school[22] and in the country at large, as we shall see. He also built a law school that continued to be a great force in the development of American law.

In both of these tasks, he received the able assistance of Simon Greenleaf (1783-1853)[23] who had succeeded to the Royall Professorship of Law in 1833 upon the death of Ashmun. Associated with Story in the law school for thirteen years, Greenleaf succeeded to the Dane Professorship upon his death. While altogether unlike Story, he, too, gave great strength and leadership to the law school in this early period. Where Story was quick, brilliant, and inspiring, Greenleaf was deliberate, thorough, and awakened a deep desire for learning. "Story prepared the soil," says Theophilus Parsons, "and Greenleaf sowed the seed."[24] A tower of strength as a teacher, Greenleaf made his presence felt in the field of legal writing as well. His greatest work is his *Treatise on the Law of Evidence* which was published in 1842. It was immediately acclaimed the ablest work on the subject, "distinguished alike for its deep learning, clarity of style, and practical utility." In 1846 he added a second volume, and in 1853 a third. In its completed form, this work

[22] That Story's efforts in behalf of the common law were not unrecognized by those who were also interested in the Civil Law may be seen from the following passage from *The American Jurist*, a legal journal which flourished during this early period. "While endeavoring to advance the *science* of the law in our own country, particularly by means of law-schools and lectures on the *Common Law*," the article says, "we ought at the same time to take care that the *Civil Law* should not be wholly neglected. We have just had an illustrious example of professional liberality in the donation made by our learned countryman, Dr. Dane, to the University of Cambridge, for the advancement of *American* law. And we earnestly hope, that some benefactor of equal liberality will soon be found, who will devote a portion of the well-earned fruits of an honourable life to a chair for the *Civil Law* in that ever-cherished institution. This would complete the department of jurisprudence in our university law-school and at once give it preference over every other." "*Remarks on the Study of the Civil Law.*" From the *American Jurist*, No. III, Boston, July, 1829. Reviewed in *The North American Review*, vol. 36, April, 1833, pp. 398-399.
[23] William Willis, *A History of the Law, the Courts, and the Lawyers of Maine*, 1863, p. 522; W. T. Davis, *Bench and Bar of the Commonwealth of Massachusetts*, 1895; *Law Reporter*, November, 1853.
[24] *Law Reporter*, November, 1853, p. 414; *Centennial History of the Harvard Law School*, 1817-1917, (1918), pp. 216, 215-219.

came to be viewed as the foremost American authority in this field. It passed through numerous editions under successive editors.

After this monumental work was completed, he published *Cruise's Digest of the Law of Real Property, Revised and Abridged for the Use of American Students* (7 vols. in 5, 1849-50). In the United States, this work entirely superseded the English original. He also published *A Discourse Commemorative of the Life and Character of the Hon. Joseph Story* in 1845, and a *Brief Memoir of the Life and Character of the Honourable Prentiss Mellon, LL.D., late Chief Justice of Maine*, 17 Maine Reports, 467, in addition to numerous speeches and articles. Before entering the academic field, he had prepared and published his *Reports of Cases Argued and Determined by the Supreme Judicial Court of the State of Maine*, vols. 1-9 (1820-1832). These reports are notable for their clear yet concise captions and admirable abstracts of the arguments. Their accuracy has never been impugned, and they have always been highly valued by the profession. He also compiled *A Collection of Cases, Overruled, Denied, Doubted, or Limited in Their Application*, which was published in 1821. In short, Greenleaf was a learned and indefatigable worker in many phases of the law and could not help but assist Story in his great enterprise. As time passed, a distinguished company of legal scholars were to follow in the footsteps of these pioneers in legal education.

"From Story and Greenleaf to Parsons and Washburn, thence to Langdell and Ames, and thence to the American law schools of today," says that other great teacher of the Harvard Law School, Dean Pound, "is a continuous evolution. It has given us a system of legal education which grows out of and expresses the spirit of our law as completely as the continental system expressed the spirit of the modern Roman law, and as the English system expressed the spirit of medieval common law."[25] The work of Parsons, Parker, and Washburn during the period between 1848 and 1870 "carried on and in a sense completed the work of the Story-Greenleaf period."[26] The writings of Theophilus Parsons (1797-1882)[27] in the field of Contracts, and of Emory Washburn (1800-1877)[28] in the field of Real Property, took their place with the

[25] Pound, *op. cit.*, p. 475.

[26] *Ibid.*, p. 475.

[27] Theophilus Parsons was appointed professor of law in 1848. He was succeeded by Langdell in 1869 who promptly introduced the case method of instruction. The son of Theophilus Parsons, the jurist who did so much to shape the jurisprudence of Massachusetts and the nation, he was one of the most prolific legal writers of his day. Charles Warren, *History of the Harvard Law School*, 1908, vol. II; *The Centennial History of the Harvard Law School*, 1918; *The Albany Law Journal*, April 10, 1880.

[28] Emory Washburn, one time governor of Massachusetts and acknowledged leader of the bar of western Massachusetts, was probably the best loved teacher in the history of Harvard's law college. He served between 1855 and 1876. Batchelder, "Old Times at

writings of Story.[29] While the writings of Joel Parker (1795-1875), the third member of this memorable triumvirate, were not so extensive, he more than compensated for this lack in other regards.[30]

Parsons' *The Law of Contracts* (2 vols., 1853-55) ran through nine editions. In preparing this volume, he was greatly assisted by the notes of Christopher Columbus Langdell, who was at that time a student. In addition to his work on *Contracts*, he published: *The Elements of Mercantile Law* (1856, 1862); *The Laws of Business* (1857); *A Treatise on Maritime Law* (2 vols., 1859); *The Constitution* (1861); *A Treatise on the Law of Promissory Notes and Bills of Exchange* (2 vols., 1863, 1876); *A Treatise on the Law of Partnership* (1867 and later editions); *A Treatise on the Law of Marine Insurance and General Average* (2 vols., 1868); *A Treatise on the Law of Shipping* (2 vols., 1869); *The Political, Personal, and Property Rights of a Citizen* (1874); *A Memoir Commemorative of Theophilus Parsons* (1859); *An Address Commemorative of Rufus Choate* (1859). Emory Washburn was not so prolific a writer as Parsons, but his work was quite important. His *A Treatise on the American Law of Real Property* (2 vols.), which was published in 1860-62, was quickly received "as the most satisfactory and trustworthy American book on the subject." In 1863, he published *A Treatise on the American Law of Easements and Servitudes*. His *Sketches of the Judicial History of Massachusetts from 1630 to 1775* which was published in

---

the Law School," *Atlantic Monthly*, November, 1902. See Charles Warren, *History of the Harvard Law School*, (1908); *The Centennial History of the Harvard Law School*, 1918; W. P. Peabody, *Proceedings*, Massachusetts Historical Society, vol. XVII, 1880; J. C. Washburn, *General Notes of the Washburn Family*, 1898; *Central Law Journal*, March 30, 1877; *American Law Review*, April, 1877; *Albany Law Journal*, March 24, 1877.

[29] Pound, *op. cit.*, p. 475.

[30] Joel Parker was appointed Royall Professor of Law at Harvard in November, 1847, after a noteworthy career as a jurist in New Hampshire, including a period as chief justice of the state. His career was characterized by his great independence, which received wide attention in a clash with Justice Story over the interpretation of the Bankruptcy Act of 1841. (See 14 N. H., 509 and 48 U. S., 612.) He taught in the Harvard Law School until 1868. His teaching was thoroughly sound (S. F. Batchelder, *Bits of Harvard History*, 1924). He was highly regarded by such students as Joseph Choate, Henry Billings Brown, and Oliver Wendell Holmes, Jr. His writings included: *Daniel Webster as a Jurist* (1852); *Non-Extension of Slavery and Constitutional Representation*, 1856; *Personal Liberty Laws (Statutes of Massachusetts) and Slavery in the Temtone's*, 1861; *Habeas Corpus and Martial Law*, 1862; *International Law*, 1862; *The War Powers of Congress, and of the President*, 1863; *Constitutional Law and Unconstitutional Divinity*, 1863; *Revolution and Reconstruction*, 1866; *The Three Powers of Government . . . The Origin of the United States and the Status of Southern States*, 1869. See G. S. Hale, "Joel Parker" *American Law Review*, Jan., 1876; Emory Washburn, Memoir in *Proceedings*, Massachusetts Historical Society, vol. XIV, 1876, and in *Albany Law Journal*, Aug. 28, 1875; C. H. Bell, *The Bench and Bar of New Hampshire*, 1894; Charles Warren, *History of the Harvard Law School*, 1908, vol. II; *Centennial History of the Harvard Law School*, 1918; *New England Magazine*, July, 1912.

1840 has been referred to before. The effect of the teaching and writing of this notable group of Harvard Law School men upon the course of American legal development is of the greatest importance. The writing of Story alone had a tremendous effect on the growth of our law. In the country at large, as mentioned elsewhere, Story's writings greatly assisted many of our growing young American commonwealths "to receive and adopt a general Anglo-American legal system instead of experimenting with codes."

The work done at the Harvard Law School in this early period was bound to encourage the establishment of similar institutions throughout the country, and so it did. In discussing this point a writer in *The North American Review*, in 1833, says:

Law schools have been established, in different States, and considering the little time that they have been in existence, the number of students who resort to them is sufficient to prove that, the usefulness of these institutions begins to be more and more acknowledged. As yet, however, their funds are too small to make provision for instruction in every important part of the law. Teachers have been employed and books collected, in order to give the students of the law a more scientific acquaintance at least with those parts of jurisprudence, which are of more immediate and frequent practical application. These most practical parts of the law should indeed be the chief, but by no means the only subject of a system of instruction, that would deserve the name of a liberal law-education. In our law-schools, there is generally some provision made for other branches besides the common law of England, and that of the United States. But owing to the infancy of these establishments, there are still so many departments, each of which requires the labor of an individual, compressed within the appointment of one professor, that it is impossible he should do more than give the bare outlines of each, such as form the substance of that course of lectures, which in German Universities is called the "Encyclopedia of Jurisprudence."[31]

The character of some of the work done may be ascertained by a glance at the *Course of Legal Study Respectfully Addressed to the Students of Law in the United States*,[32] which was prepared by David Hoffman, Professor of Law in the University of Maryland[33] and published

[31] *The North American Review*, vol. 36, April, 1833, pp. 397-398.

[32] This publication of some 383 pages is reviewed at length in *The North American Review*, vol. 6, Nov., 1817, pp. 45-47. In addition to his *Course of Legal Study* and his *Syllabus of Law Lectures in the University of Maryland*, Mr. Hoffman prepared a work of 626 pages entitled *Legal Outlines: being the Substance of a Course of Lectures now delivering in the University of Maryland*. See *The North American Review*, vol. 30, Jan., 1830, pp. 135-160.

[33] After actively assisting in the establishment of the University of Maryland, David Hoffman (1784-1854) was appointed professor of law in 1816. He did not begin to lecture until 1823, however. In the meantime he published his *Course of Legal Study*. Justice Joseph Story deemed it "the most perfect system for the study of law which has ever been offered the publick." *The North American Review*, November, 1817, p. 76. He followed this plan in his university lectures which continued until 1832. His views on legal education were far in advance of his time. He disparaged dependence upon

in Baltimore in 1817.[34] The general course of study proposed by Mr. Hoffman was summed up in a general syllabus, which included: (1) moral and political philosophy; (2) the elementary and constitutional principles of the Municipal Law of England, including a study of (*a*) the Feudal Law, (*b*) the Institutes of the Municipal Law generally, and (*c*) the origin and progress of the Common Law; (3) the Law of Real Rights and Real Remedies; (4) the Law of Personal Rights and Personal Remedies; (5) the Law of Equity; (6) the Lex Mercatoria; (7) the Law of Crimes and Punishments; (8) the Law of Nations; (9) the Maritime and Admiralty Law; (10) the Civil or Roman Law; (11) the Constitution and Laws of the United States of America; (12) the Constitution and Laws of the several states of the Union; and (13) political economy. This was followed by a particular syllabus under every title of the general syllabus, in which were collected the best works on every successive subject belonging to the heads under which they were arranged. Connected with these heads was a series of notes "or perpetual Commentary upon the character and relative value of the authors whose works are cited, or the history and relative importance of the topics which they discuss, etc. . . ."[35]

The work in legal education at Columbia during this period is of particular interest because it is directly connected with the work of Story's great co-builder of American law, Chancellor James Kent, who taught and wrote at Columbia on two different occasions.[36] Although the law school proper was not established at Columbia until 1857,[37] King's College, which emerged from the Revolution with the name of Columbia,[38] "a word and name then for the first time recognized anywhere

memory despite his concern with "reading and knowledge," and emphasized "the general and pervading principles of the science." He possessed a rich background in the legal field and was noteworthy for his appreciation of Bentham and codification and for his advocacy of careful study of statutes and of legal forms and pleading. His bibliographies, which were designed to promote systematic reading, indicate a wide knowledge of foreign literature. It is interesting to note in this connection that he, like Legare, spent considerable time in Europe, where he received honorary degrees from Oxford and Göttengen. Deeply interested in the ethics of the legal profession, his "Resolutions in Regard to Professional Deportment" anticipated most of the present canons of conduct of the American Bar Association. See *Legal Hints*, 1846. See also *Address of the Treatise of the University of Maryland to the Public*, 1823; B. C. Steiner, *History of Education in Maryland*, 1894; E. F. Cordell, *University of Maryland, 1807-1907*, I, 1907, 338-48; *The Centennial Celebration of the Foundation of the University of Maryland*, 1908; *Maryland Hist. Magazine*, Dec., 1906, pp. 358-362.

[34] *The North American Review*, vol. 6, 1817, pp. 45-47.

[35] *Ibid.*; for a valuable analysis of early law school curriculum see A. Z. Reed, *Training for the Public Profession of the Law*, 1921, pp. 453-455, Bulletin No. 15, The Carnegie Foundation.

[36] *Ibid.*, p. 342.

[37] Reed, *ibid.*, p. 342.

[38] *Ibid.*, pp. 60-61. The New York legislature, on May 1, 1784, passed "an act for granting certain privileges to the college heretofore called King's College, for altering the name and charter thereof, and erecting a University within this State." Reed, *ibid.*, p. 59.

in law or history," was the first institution of learning in the United States to establish a professorship of law. This was done in 1773 and the Rev. John Vardill, A.M., was appointed to this post. This was an interesting appointment, since Mr. Vardill was a Tory while the legal theories of the time were decidedly revolutionary in character. It is not clear that his professorship was ever actually put into operation and with the coming of the War it was discontinued in 1776. In 1784, when King's College was reorganized as Columbia University, her Trustees, among whom we find John Jay and Alexander Hamilton, voted to establish a law school with three professorships, including: "A professorship in the law of Nature and Nations, a professorship in the Roman Civil Law, a professorship in the Municipal Law." This project failed of realization for financial reasons.

In 1792, however, with the assistance of the legislature, one professorship of law was established by the Trustees. In 1793, James Kent was appointed to the chair,[39] which he prepared for by reading "Bynkerschoeck, Quintilian, and Cicero's rhetorical works besides English reports and digests." A prospectus published in 1794 indicates that this course, like Parker's first course at Harvard, was not designed primarily for professional students. In fact, it seems to have been a part of the work of the Arts faculty.[40] On November 17, 1794, the opening lecture was delivered. It was published by the college Trustees for private distribution[41] and was favorably received by a large body of readers including John Adams who was much pleased with Kent's methods and treatment.[42] Kent's course consisted of twenty-six lectures,[43] and was at-

[39] He received the modest stipend of £200 a year for his efforts. He thought, however, that the post would "aid my professional practice at the bar" and prove "not only honourable but profitable." Reed, *ibid.*, p. 336.

[40] In the prospectus referred to it says: "Mr. Kent having been so recently appointed, has not as yet entered upon a course of lectures; but this professorship is intended to comprise a brief review of the history, the nature, the several forms, and the just ends of civil government—a sketch of the origin, purpose, and final settlement of the United States—a particular detail of the organization and duties of the several departments of the general government together with an examination of such parts of the civil and criminal codes of the federal jurisprudence as shall be the most susceptible of illustration and most conclusive to public utility. The courts of the several states and the connection they bear to the general government will then be considered, and the more particular examination of the constitution of this state. The whole detail of our municipal law, with relation to the rights of property and of persons, and the forms of administering justice, both civil and criminal, will then be treated fully and at large." See "The State of Learning in the College of New York," quoted in Reed, *ibid.*, p. 337.

[41] See *Columbia Law Review*, Vol. III, p. 330.

[42] *A History of Columbia University*, 1904, p. 337.

[43] These lectures, he wrote his brother on March 1, 1795, extended "not only through the Constitution of this and the other states, but our doctrine of real property. My first plan was to examine the law of personal property, including the commercial branches, and the system of our criminal code. But I found myself absolutely unable to complete the whole, and was obliged to leave this first course incomplete. It will be an easy thing to make these additions and review and improve the whole thing by next

tended by "seven students and thirty-six gentlemen, chiefly lawyers and law students who did not belong to the college."[44]

During his second course which commenced in November, 1795, he reports that he "read thirty-one lectures in my office, and had only two students besides my clerk."[45] During the next year no students presented themselves and on May 2, 1797, he resigned.[46] His resignation was not accepted by the Trustees, however, until April, 1798, when he was appointed a judge of the Superior Court. After his retirement, the professorship of law remained vacant until his retirement from the chancellorship in 1823, at the age of sixty, when he was reappointed to his old professorship.

Accepting with some reluctance, he soon became thoroughly interested in the project,[47] and his second attempt at legal instruction was productive of some remarkable results, although not on the strictly instructional side which he gave up in the spring of 1826, "having got heartily tired of lecturing," although his name was carried in the Columbia catalogues as a professor until his death in 1847.[48] The results referred to were the writing and publication of his *Commentaries on American Law* in eight volumes which became an authoritative exposition of the English common law in this country, as well as a standard interpretation of the constitution. Any loss to legal education in the formative period of American law that may have been suffered from his withdrawal from the classroom was certainly compensated for by his

---

November. I am satisfied that my lectures have been well received and that my expectations are answered." *Ibid.*, p. 338.

[44] *Ibid.*, p. 338.

[45] In the second year, he published his three preliminary lectures and a summary of the entire course. His writing was cited in Brown's "Treatise on Civil and Admiralty Law," published shortly thereafter, in what is believed to be the first citation ever made of an American law book by an English writer. See *ibid.*, p. 339.

[46] The unhappy ending of Kent's first course was shared by similar courses in other parts of the country at that time. For example the extremely able and distinguished Associate Justice James Wilson of the United States Supreme Court, who became professor of law in the College of Philadelphia in 1790, was unable to carry on his work successfully after the first year. Chief Justice Isaac Parker's initial efforts at Harvard were also subject to the same discouraging conditions. *Ibid.*, p. 340.

[47] *Ibid.*, p. 340.

[48] The success which met the publication of the first volume of his Commentaries and the tremendous labor required by his writing undoubtedly influenced his decision to withdraw from the class-room. At any rate, in the preface to his first volume, he expresses satisfaction with his academic work. "In the performance of my collegiate duty," he says, "I had the satisfaction to meet a collection of interesting young gentlemen of fine talents and pure character, who placed themselves under my instruction, and in whose welfare a deep interest is felt. Having been encouraged to suppose that the publication of the lectures might render them more extensively useful, I have been induced to submit the present volume to the notice of students, and of the junior members of the profession, for whose use they were originally compiled. Another volume is wanting to embrace all the material parts of the lectures which have been composed." The additional volume proved insufficient, however, so a third volume was published in 1828 and a fourth in 1830. *Ibid.*, p. 341. See William Kent, *Memoirs and letters of James Kent*, 1898.

written work which Abram Hewitt described as having "had a deeper and more lasting influence in the formation of national character than any other secular book of the century."[49] In short, Columbia's experience with her first great teacher of law terminated in the writing of a great legal classic rather than in the founding of a law school. In 1848, William Betts was chosen to fill the professorship made vacant by Chancellor Kent's death. He lectured intermittently until 1854, when the professorship remained vacant for some years.

In 1857, a school of jurisprudence was finally established. It was not intended as a professional school, however, and its course of study included History, Political Economy, Political Philosophy, the Principles of National and International Law, Civil and Common Law, the writings of the Greeks and the Romans and of such modern civilians and jurists as would be appropriate to the last three subjects. In the fall of 1857, the school of jurisprudence had six students. Shortly afterwards, it was decided that the school would be more likely to succeed if it were organized with "a view of actual admission to the bar" and "that instruction in other and higher branches, not absolutely necessary for such admission, may be superadded to the course and placed within the reach of students." This policy was adopted. It was also decided to give the control of the new department to one man. This policy was also adopted and Theodore W. Dwight who had organized and maintained a flourishing law school at Hamilton College was appointed Professor of Municipal Law in 1858. Dwight, whom Professor Dicey described "as one of the ablest professors of law that any school of law ever possessed,"[50] soon had the new venture on the road to successful achievement.[51]

The work done in legal education at the University of Pennsylvania also has its beginning at an early date. In 1789, Benjamin Franklin's College of Philadelphia was revived and in 1791 it was merged with the new University of Pennsylvania.[52] In 1790, a year before the merger took place a three year law course was inaugurated at the College of Philadelphia. Philadelphia was at that time the national capital, and James Wilson (1742-1798),[53] Associate Justice of the

[49] Reed, op. cit., p. 341.

[50] Professor Dicey in his article on "Legal Education" in Macmillan's Magazine, XXV, p. 127, in 1871, asserted that Dwight had "a reputation throughout the whole Union as the greatest living American teacher of law, who has in substance founded and keeps alive, simply by his own capacity as a teacher, one of the best schools of law." Lord Bryce held Professor Dwight in equally high regard. See "The Legal Profession in America," Macmillan's Magazine, vol. 25, 1871, p. 209.

[51] A History of Columbia University, 1904; Dwight, "Columbia College Law School, New York," The Green Bag, vol. I, 1889, 14.

[52] George B. Wood, "History of the University of Pennsylvania from its Origin to the Year 1827," Memoirs of the Historical Society of Pennsylvania, vol. 3, 1834, p. 109.

[53] Educated at the University of Edinburgh, Wilson studied law in the office of

United States Supreme Court, was appointed to the new professorship. The course contemplated three lectures weekly, with additional law exercises every Saturday. The lectures started out brilliantly, the first one of the series being attended by President and Mrs. Washington, many members of Congress, and various other persons of distinction. The object of the course was non-vocational. It proposed, instead, "to furnish a rational and useful entertainment to gentlemen of all professions and in particular to assist in informing the legislator, the magistrate, and the lawyer." In working out the course, Associate Justice Wilson attempted the ambitious project of restating Blackstone in American terms. The first year of the course was largely devoted to general legal principles, of an introductory character—including some aspects of international law. The second year of the course was devoted to the field of governmental organization in the United States, as a sub-division of the Law of Persons. In this connection, he followed the method and plan of Blackstone. A start was also made in Criminal Law but was not finished, as Wilson abandoned the course before the year was up. In 1804, Wilson's lectures so far as completed were published and are to be found in James D. Andrews' *Works of James Wilson*, published in 1896. Wilson was keenly aware of his opportunity to lay the foundation of an American system of jurisprudence. Departing from the Blackstonian definition of law· as the rule of a sovereign superior, he discovered the residence of sovereignty in the individual, and instituted therefor "the consent of those whose obedience the law requires." He justified the American Revolution on this basis while challenging Blackstone's denial of the legal right of revolution.[54] Despite his very real ability, Wilson's interest in practical affairs precluded him from realizing his ambition of becoming the American Blackstone, and left to Kent and Story the task of establishing the basis for an enduring American jurisprudence.

John Dickinson for two years and was admitted to the bar in 1767. His greatest achievement in public life was his part in the establishment of the federal constitution. Indeed James Bryce thought him "one of the deepest thinkers and most exact reasoners" in the convention. He also thought that Wilson's speeches displayed "an amplitude and profundity of view in matters of constitutional theory which place him in the front rank of the political thinkers of our age." *The American Commonwealth*, 1888, vol. I, 250, N., 665N; see also Sanderson, *op. cit.*, VI, p. 154. While serving as an Associate Justice of the Supreme Court to which post he was appointed by President Washington on Sept. 29, 1789, he was one of the first justices to declare an act of Congress unconstitutional. See Max Farrand, "The First Hayburn Case," *American Historical Review*, Jan., 1908. He served on the bench until his death in 1798 despite criticism and talk of impeachment. See G. J. McRee, *Life and Correspondence of James Iredell*, vol. II, 1857, p. 532. See Bird Wilson, *The Works of the Honourable James Wilson*, (3 vols., 1804); D. J. Andrews, *The Works of James Wilson*, (2 vols., 1896); R. G. Adams, *Political Ideas of the American Revolution*, 1922; R. G. Adams, *Selected Political Essays of James Wilson*, 1930.

[54] *Selected Political Essays*, p. 251.

In 1817, Charles W. Hare, grandfather of John James Clark Hare, one of Pennsylvania's greatest jurists,[55] revived the course as a three-year project. The first year was to be devoted to "Natural Jurisprudence," the second to "International Jurisprudence," and the third to "Jurisprudence of the United States and Pennsylvania." Mr. Hare was compelled to give up the work after the first year, however, and by 1834 the chair of law had been formally abolished.[56] In 1850, the law department was revived by George Sharswood. Judge Sharswood (1810-1883)[57] who served on the bench in Pennsylvania for thirty-seven years, including a period as chief justice, was appointed professor of law in the University of Pennsylvania in 1850. He reorganized the plan of legal education and served steadily for eighteen years. An able jurist and a distinguished legal writer, he gave great strength to the university's course of legal instruction. A voluminous writer, Judge Sharswood is perhaps best known for his *A Compendium of Lectures on the Aims and Duties of the Profession of Law* (1854), also known by the half-title, *Professional Ethics*. This work was several times republished as *An Essay on Professional Ethics*. He also wrote *Popular Lectures on Commercial Law* (1856); *Lectures Introductory to the Study of Law* (1870); and numerous other articles including *The Common Law of Pennsylvania* (1855). In addition to editing the *American Law Magazine* for three years (1843-1846), he engaged in editing the American issues of eight English law textbooks, of some twenty-nine volumes of the collected English cases, and of two volumes of United States statutes.[58]

The work done at the University of Maryland during this early period is also noteworthy. In 1784, an attempt was made to create a state university which would embrace the colleges recently established on the western and eastern shores of the state. This plan which was modelled somewhat on the basis of the "University of the State of New

[55] John J. C. Hare served on the bench in Pennsylvania for forty-five years. Although kept in subordinate courts because of political conditions, he was one of the greatest jurists produced in Pennsylvania. He was particularly effective in the establishment of equity in Pennsylvania and as a law writer. See W. D. Lewis, *American Law Register*, Dec., 1906; J. H. Martin, *Martin's Bench and Bar of Philadelphia*, 1883.

[56] Margaret C. Klingelsmith, "History of the Department of Law," *University of Pa. Proc. at the Dedication of the New Building of the Dept. of Law*, 1900, pp. 213 ff.

[57] Samuel Dickson, "George Sharswood," *Great American Lawyers*, vol. VI, 1909, pp. 123-61; C. H. Hart, *Memoir of George Sharswood*, 1884; G. W. Biddle, *A Sketch of the Professional and Judicial Character of the late George Sharswood*, 1883, printed in *Pennsylvania State Reports*, vol. 102, pp. 601-30; H. L. Carson, "Historical Sketch of the Law Department," *Catalogue of the Alumni of the Law Department of the University of Pennsylvania . . . 1790-1882* (1882), pp. 23-28; *Legal Intelligencer*, June 1, 1883, vol. XL, 220; *Legal Intelligencer*, June 8, 1883; vol. XL, pp. 230-232.

[58] See S. A. Allibone, *A Critical Dictionary of English Literature and American Authors*, vol. II, 1870. His opinions are in the *Philadelphia Reports*, vols. I, VI (covering 1850-1868) and the *Pennsylvania State Reports*, vols. LVII-CII.

York" was abandoned in 1806. In 1807, an incorporated College of Medicine of Maryland was started in Baltimore. In 1812, an attempt was made to expand this into a university. A charter was secured for the University of Maryland and the school was organized. While the plan involved the addition of three traditional faculties to the Medical Faculty, the attempts to build up Faculties of Theology and of Arts came to nothing. A Law Faculty of six was promptly appointed, however, and one of their number, Mr. David Hoffman, assumed the task of organizing the prospective curriculum.

Devoting four years to this task, he published his results in 1817, under the title of a "Course of Legal Study," that admirable course of study which has already been described and which Justice Story estimated would take seven years to complete. Inadequate financial resources did not permit the establishment of this course until 1823, however. The competition of "the large and successful" private school of Judge Walter Dorsey of the Court of Appeals had something to do with its somewhat inauspicious beginnings. In 1821, Hoffman published a modified revision of his original course, which he proposed to cover in two years of ten months each, lecturing one hour daily. He planned to start instruction in the fall of 1822, but actually did not deliver his first lecture until after Dorsey's death in 1823. It took him much longer to cover the "Maryland Law Institute," a quiz body; the "Rota," a debating society; and an elaborate system of moot courts.[59]

His plans did not succeed. At the end of the year, difficulties arose. The state stepped in, took over the university property, and ousted the faculty. Hoffman accepted appointment from the new trustees but new difficulties arose. In 1832, he ceased lecturing and went to Europe. In 1836, he published a revised and expanded *Course of Study* for the profession at large. In 1844, he attempted to start a private law school in Philadelphia but in 1847 returned to Europe. Failing in his impossible attempt to reform American legal education single handed, Hoffman nevertheless had a wide influence on the course of American legal development.[60] His attempt to approach American laws systematically was rendered difficult by the fact that American law was "expanding at such a rate that a systematic survey of the entire field became antiquated almost as soon as it was published."

The work done in legal education at Yale University may be said to have begun in 1823 with the thirteen students of Judge David Dag-

[59] E. F. Cordell, *Historical Sketch of the University of Maryland*, 1891.

[60] A. Z. Reed, *op. cit.*, pp. 124-126. The failure of a law school in this early period was not unique. For example, the school opened in Washington, D. C., in 1826, by Judge William Cranch and W. T. Carroll was abandoned during the next year. See C. H. Stockton, "Historical Sketch," *Records of the Columbia Historical Society*, vol. 19, 1916, pp. 99, 124.

gett.[61] In 1825, the establishment of the "Law School" as such was formally announced. In some ways it resembled the school at Harvard.[62] In both schools a distinguished judge gave to the school such portions of his time as he could afford. In both schools, a distinguished judge lectured to seniors in the college and to professional students in the school. In both schools, the attempt to combine instruction of college seniors with that of professional students was soon abandoned. In both schools, the principal duties of administering the school was entrusted to a younger practitioner. The Harvard school, however, attempted to expand the broader, more scholarly aspects of its work, whereas the Yale school followed more closely the type of work pursued at the private law school of the day. In this respect, it resembled the Northampton school, established in 1823 by Judge Samuel Howe, a Litchfield graduate, in which John Hooker Ashmun taught for two years.[63] In fact, it continued to give a practitioner's course for some time, requiring two years of work and including practice in drafting written instruments and in the more "important duties of an attorney's clerk."[64] While no degrees were given for this work until 1842,[65] the attendance was quite satisfactory as compared with contemporary schools.[66] In 1835, however, the attendance figures at Harvard permanently passed those of Yale and continued to increase as the Harvard Law School went on to play its commanding role in the field of legal education and in the development of American law.

The work in legal education in Virginia during this formative

[61] David Daggett, who became Chief Justice of the Supreme Court of Connecticut, was a student of Charles Chauncey, who as noted previously, was a "lecturer on jurisprudence" for "fifty years" prior to his retirement in 1793. A. Z. Reed, *op. cit.*, p. 129. Daggett also prepared young men for the legal profession. One of his students was Seth P. Staples. Staples was admitted to the bar in 1799. In 1800 he secured a good library and many young men undertook to take advantage of it as law students. One of this number was Samuel Hitchcock. Hitchcock was admitted to the bar in 1815. In 1817, he was taken into Staples' law firm as a partner. In 1824, Daggett succeeded Staples as senior partner in the now established "school of law" maintained by Staples and Hitchcock. A. Z. Reed, *op. cit.*, p. 431. Daggett then took a professorship at Yale, as mentioned, and the names of his thirteen pupils were included in the catalogue list of Yale students. In 1826 the catalogue formally announced the establishment of the Law School, as such. In 1833, an endowment was secured for Daggett's chair and the title of "Kent Professor of Law" was established after the fashion of the "Royall Professorship at Harvard." See A. Z. Reed, *op. cit.*, p. 141.

[62] A. Z. Reed, *op. cit.*, pp. 450, 451, 452.

[63] A. Z. Reed, *op. cit.*, pp. 141, 431.

[64] Leonard M. Daggett, "The Yale Law School," *The Green Bag*, vol. I, 1889, p. 239; Thomas Thacher, "Yale in Its Relation to the Law" in *The Yale Bicentennial Celebration, 1901*, (1902), pp. 174-198; Theodore D. Woolsey, *Historical Discourse pronounced before the Alumni of the Law Department*, 1874; Francis Wayland's "Law Department," in W. L. Kingsley's *Yale College: a Sketch of Its History*, 1879, pp. 90-99; Henry Wade Rogers, "Historical Statement" *Yale Shingle*, 1911.

[65] Thomas Thacher, *op. cit.*, p. 185.

[66] A. Z. Reed, *op. cit.*, pp. 142, 450, 451.

period is of the greatest importance. On December 4, 1779, the board of visitors of William and Mary College which included Thomas Jefferson who was at that time governor of Virginia established a "Professorship of Law and Police." This has been said to be the first chair of law in an American college and came but twenty-one years after the establishment of the Vinerian professorship of English law at Oxford. It was continued until 1861. The great Chancellor Wythe,[67] who had been Jefferson's preceptor, was entrusted with the difficult task of charting this new course in American jurisprudence. He formulated a series of lectures which followed Blackstone in some regards,[68] in which he contrasted English and Virginia law.[69] This work was supplemented by moot courts and legislatures in which he trained the forty young men under his care in judicial and parliamentary procedure.[70] In 1789 he was elected sole chancellor of Virginia and in 1791 he resigned his professorship and moved to Richmond. He was succeeded by St. George Tucker, a judge of the general court, who had a distinguished record at bench and bar.[71] St. George Tucker was the first member of that distinguished family which was to play such an important role in the legal life of Virginia and the nation over a long period of years.[72] His annotated edition of *Blackstone's Commentaries* (5 vols.) published in 1803 was one of the important law books of its day.[73] The appendix to the first book contained a discussion of the origin and nature of the Federal constitution, which received wide attention.[74] Some of his

[67] L. G. Tyler in *Great American Lawyers*, vol. 1, 1907, (ed. W. D. Lewis); John Sanderson, *Biography of the Signers of the Declaration of Independence*, vol. II, 1822; *Dictionary of American Biography*, vol. 20, pp. 586-588.

[68] In 1780 when John Marshall attended the school, the lectures seem to have been a mere running commentary upon legal heads arranged in alphabetical order. See digest of Marshall's notes in Beveridge, *Life of John Marshall*, vol. I, 1916, p. 174.

[69] L. G. Tyler, *The College of William and Mary in Virginia, Its History and Work, 1693-1907*, pp. 60-61.

[70] See *William and Mary Quarterly*, vol. 9, 1900, p. 80; L. G. Tyler, *Early Courses and Professors at William and Mary College*, 1904; Charles Warren, *op. cit.*, pp. 343 ff; "Laws and Regulations, 1837," *Bulletin of the College of William and Mary*, vol. XI, No. 2, 1917.

[71] M. Herndon Moore, "The Law Writers of the South," in *The South in the Building of the Nation*, vol. 7, p. 328.

[72] Daniel Call, "Memoir," *Call's Reports*, (Va.) vol. 4; J. R. Tucker, "The Judges Tucker of the Court of Appeals of Virginia," *Virginia Law Register*, Mar., 1896; S. S. P. Patterson, "The Supreme Court of Appeals of Virginia," *The Green Bag*, July, 1893; S. E. M. Hardy, "Some Virginia Lawyers," *ibid.*, Jan., 1898; H. St. George Tucker, "Patrick Henry and St. George Tucker," *University of Pennsylvania Law Review*, Jan., 1919.

[73] *William and Mary College Quarterly*, VI, 182; IX, 80.

[74] "It has been said that it is a tribute to the originality as well as the ability of the author that all subsequent controversial disquisitions on the subjects treated in this work 'have appealed to him as authority, or have attempted to overthrow his doctrines.'" M. H. Moore, *op. cit.*, p. 328.

other writings were also given wide attention but his *Blackstone* remained his outstanding piece of work.[75]

In 1804, St. George Tucker resigned his professorship at William and Mary College.[76] He was succeeded by Judge Hugh Nelson, who followed the system established by Wythe and Tucker. The work was apparently well presented. At any rate, it was claimed by some that the course was better developed than the one given at the Litchfield school during this same period.[77] In 1811, Judge Hugh Nelson resigned and was succeeded by his brother, Chancellor Robert Nelson who died in July, 1818. He was succeeded by Judge James Semple, who served from 1819 to 1833, when he was followed by Nathaniel Beverly Tucker. Judge Tucker served from 1833 to 1852, when he was succeeded by George P. Scarburgh.[78] Scarburgh served until 1855 when Lucien Minor took over his duties. Minor was a man of capacity. His younger brother John Barbee Minor thought that he was capable of rivaling Story or Tucker. Actually he wrote very little; his principal contribution being a one volume edition of Hening and Mumford's *Reports* (1857), and an edition of the first three volumes of Call's *Reports* (1854).[79]

This younger brother, John Barbee Minor, (1803-1895),[80] had a

[75] He wrote a *Dissertation on Slavery; with a Proposal for its Gradual Abolition in Virginia.* This pamphlet, which appeared in 1796, advocated the emancipation of children born to slave mothers. It was widely read and acclaimed, in fact it was reprinted in Philadelphia in 1861. He also published an essay entitled "How Far the Common Law of England is the Common Law of the United States." Mr. Lyon Tyler asserts that Tucker's lectures at the college which were printed in 1803, constitutes "the first distinctive textbook of the law published by any professor in the United States." *Op. cit.,* p. 68.

[76] William Taylor Barry, who was Postmaster General in Andrew Jackson's cabinet, was a student at William and Mary in 1804. Concerning the legal instruction given, he says, in a letter written Feb. 6, 1804: "Mr. Tucker is a man more profoundly read in the Law perhaps than any lawyer of the present time. No person can with more ease and facility clear up or elucidate a knotty or abstruse point of law, and he not only possesses the capacity of doing so, but does it with willingness, and appears solicitous to communicate every information that he is possessed of. . . . I'll tell you how I employ my time generally. I rise about sun up, read until 11 o'c, then go to the lecture room, the examinations almost always detain me until 2 o'c in the evening. I then return and dine about 3 o'c. The rest of the evening I devote to exercise and company, until about 7 o'c at night when I commence reading again and continue at it until 11 o'c which is good bedtime." Quoted by Lyon G. Tyler, *op. cit.,* p. 71.

[77] In a letter from Bishop Madison to C. H. Todd, such a statement appears. See Sprague, *Annals of the American Church,* vol. 323. Quoted by Tyler, *op. cit.,* p. 68.

[78] Lyon G. Tyler, *op. cit.,* p. 88.

[79] J. B. Minor, *The Minor Family of Virginia* (1923). It is interesting to note that another Virginian of the name of Minor had a part in preparing an edition of Hening and Mumford's Virginia Reports. This man was Benjamin Blake Minor (1818-1895), the well-known editor of the *Southern Literary Messenger,* who also edited *Decisions of Cases in Virginia by the High Court, by George Wythe, with a Memoir of the Author, (1852).* See L. G. Tyler, *Encyclopedia of Virginia Biography,* vol. III, 1915.

[80] P. A. Bruce, *History of the University of Virginia, 1819-1919* (5 vols., 1920-1922); P. B. Barringer and J. M. Garnett, eds., *University of Virginia,* 1904, vol. 1; *Virginia Law Register,* November, 1895; *The Green Bag,* September, 1895; *Report of*

much greater influence on the course of legal education in Virginia and in the country at large. Indeed his efforts raised the law-school of the University of Virginia, which was established in the year 1826,[81] to an extremely high plane. Appointed Professor of Law at the University of Virginia in 1845, at the age of 32, he held the chair for fifty years. He was the fourth to occupy that chair, his predecessors being Lomax, Davis, and Tucker. John Tayloe Lomax[82] was the first professor of

the Virginia State Bar Association, vol. IX, 1896; *The Alumni Bulletin of the University of Virginia,* July, 1895, Feb. 1, 1896; *University of Virginia Magazine,* November, 1895.

[81] Though the University of Virginia was granted a charter in 1819, it was not until 1826 that the Law School was opened. Thomas Jefferson was actively interested in the establishment of this school, and in the selection of its first professor. He considered this matter to be of the greatest importance. "In the selection of our Law Professor," he wrote James Madison, "we must be vigorously attentive to our political principles. You will recollect that before the Revolution, Coke-Littleton was the universal elementary book of law students, and a sounder Whig never wrote, nor of profounder learning in the orthodox doctrines of the British constitution, or in what were called English liberties. You remember also that our lawyers were then all Whigs. But when his black letter text and uncouth but cunning learning got out of fashion, and the honeyed Mansfieldism of Blackstone became the students' law book, from that moment the profession (the nursery of our Congress) began to slide into Toryism, and nearly all the young brood of lawyers now are of that line. They suppose themselves, indeed, to be Whigs, because they no longer know what Whiggism or republicanism means. It is in our seminary that that vestal flame is to be kept alive; it is thence that it is to be spread anew over our own and the sister States." Quoted by Dean William Minor Lile, "The Law School of the University of Virginia," *The Centennial of the University of Virginia,* 1921, p. 153, see also Herbert B. Adams, *Thomas Jefferson and the University of Virginia,* 1888, pp. 137-140; also *Writings of Thomas Jefferson,* ed. P. L. Ford, 1892-99, vol. 5, pp. 172, 180.

[82] The first efforts in legal education under Lomax were designed to afford the students the broadest education possible rather than a mere professional knowledge along practical lines. In 1829, however, a demand arose that the work be reorganized to more immediately meet the needs of students preparing for active practice. It was said that while other schools were able to present the bare vocational needs in the studies of one session, the courses at Charlottesville were so extensive that two sessions were required to master them. As a result of this reorganization, the course of the first session was made an epitome of all the important branches of municipal law. During the second year, a more comprehensive treatment was made. Since many of the students could only stay one year, the second part of the course was prone to be given less emphasis. "The day has gone by," wrote Lomax in 1830, "when any person was ashamed to appear at the bar under a period of less than three years study. The necessities of some, and the impatience of others, urge most students into their profession after a year's study, or at most, two years. They are eager that the period shall be devoted to such instruction as may practically fit them for their profession. Their demand for the law is as for a trade—the means, the most expeditious and convenient, for their future livelihood. I found myself irresistibly compelled to labor for the satisfaction of this demand, or that the University would have no students of law. . . . I have selected what after much deliberation, I deemed the most approved and suitable English text-books." This selection consisted of Blackstone's *Commentaries;* Cruise's *Law of Real Property;* Selwyn's *Abstract of the Law of Nisi Prius,* and Muddock's *Chancery.* He supplemented his lectures with materials from the appellate courts of Virginia and other states. To complement the professional course, he recommended the establishment of an "academic course of law" which should study American jurisprudence in its broadest aspects. P. A. Bruce, *History of the University of Virginia, 1819-1919,* vol. 2, pp. 102-103.

law appointed after Francis Walker Gilmer[83] had been originally chosen but was unable to take the post. Lomax taught for four years "on a little oatmeal," as he described it; then his inadequate salary forced him to resign and go on the bench. He was succeeded in 1830 by John A. G. Davis who served until 1840.[84] During the next year, the chair was filled by N. P. Howard on a temporary appointment. He was succeeded in 1841 by Henry St. George Tucker, who served until 1845. In 1845, Tucker was succeeded, as mentioned before, by John B. Minor, who served longer than any other man.[85]

Under his direction the law school standards were immediately raised and graduation was made more difficult. The enrollment steadily increased under his direction. Like Dwight he was one of the great law teachers. His teaching method was that of searching analysis, based on the system of Hale and Blackstone. He was an ardent admirer of the common law and prone to oppose change. His greatest work is his *Institutes of Common and Statute Law* (1875-1895) which he began publication of in 1875. This monumental contribution to American jurisprudence, which grew out of his courses in common and statute law, went through many editions. It was cited in all American courts and still remains an authority. He also wrote *The Virginia Report,*

[83] The difficulties of securing a satisfactory man to fill the first professorship were great. At that time, the College of William and Mary was the only local institution to maintain a regular lecturer in this department of study; and "in 1824, there were probably not more than three or four private law schools in Virginia." Bruce, *op. cit.*, p. 25. Among others who were considered and approached were Francis Walker Gilmer, Chancellor James Kent, Henry St. George Tucker, P. P. Barbour, William Wirt, and Judges Carr and Dade. Bruce, *op. cit.*, pp. 26-31. Gilmer seems to have been the choice of Jefferson. Bruce, *op. cit.*, p. 29.

[84] Davis was inclined to put considerable emphasis on the several aspects of public law that were deemed important at that time. In the junior course were included such subjects as the law of nature and nations, the science of government, constitutional law, the history of the common law and the elementary principles of criminal and municipal law. The textbooks used were Blackstone's *Commentaries*, Vattel, *The Federalist*, *Resolutions of 1798-99*, and a treatise that Davis himself had prepared. In the senior course, attention was given to the theory and practice of law as a profession, as illustrated in different works on common statute law, equity, maritime and commercial law. Bruce, *op. cit.*, p. 105; see *A Discourse on the Life and Character of the late John A. G. Davis, Professor of Law in the University of Virginia, delivered before the Society of Alumni, June 29, 1847,* by Lucian Minor, Esq., Richmond, 1847, 8 vol., 32 pp. Reviewed in *The North American Review*, vol. 65, Oct., 1847, pp. 507-508.

[85] In 1851, the Department of Law, then known as the "School of Law," was divided into two schools. James P. Holcombe was appointed to the second chair, and taught until 1861. After the Civil War, Stephan O. Southall succeeded to Holcombe's chair. Upon his death in 1883, James H. Gilmore was named as his successor, resigning in 1897. In 1893, another professorship was added and the work of the law school equally divided among these three—Minor, Gilmore, and the new professor, Lile. In 1895, Walter T. Dabney was appointed to succeed J. B. Minor, with R. C. Minor as Adjunct. In 1899, Charles A. Graves succeeded Professor Dabney. In 1909-10 more courses were established and the staff was increased. *The Centennial History of the University of Virginia,* 1921, pp. 154-155.

1799-1800 (1850), and an *Exposition of the Law of Crimes and Punishments* (1894). His son, Raleigh Colston Minor (1869-1923),[86] followed closely in his footsteps, teaching in the University of Virginia Law School for 30 years. The overlapping teaching careers of father and son covered a period of 78 years. The contributions of the son were outstanding in the field of private international law, where he did important work. His *Conflict of Laws*, published in 1901, became an American legal classic and greatly clarified the problems in this difficult field.[87]

In many ways the history of the Minor family is remindful of the Tucker family in its influence upon the law of Virginia and the nation. We have already noted the work of St. George Tucker. The work of Henry St. George Tucker[88] is also important. The eldest son of St. George Tucker, he followed closely in his father's footsteps. Appointed chancellor of the state in 1824, he served until 1831, when he was made president-judge of the Virginia Court of Appeals. He resigned this position in 1841, upon being elected professor of law at the University of Virginia where he taught with vigor until 1845. During the seven years of his chancellorship, he organized and conducted a private law school at Winchester, which was a great success. During this period he wrote his *Commentaries on the Laws of Virginia* (2 vols., 1836-37). Later on he published his *Lectures on Constitutional Law* (1843) and his *A Few Lectures on Natural Law* (1844). These works established him firmly in the field of legal authorship.

A second son of St. George Tucker who achieved distinction in the legal field was Nathaniel Beverly Tucker.[89] Like his brother Henry St. George Tucker and his half-brother John Randolph he was educated in the law. Elected professor of law at William and Mary College in 1834, he taught and wrote there for 15 years. His writings included his *Lectures Intended to Prepare the Student for the Study of the Constitution*, published in 1845 and his *Principles of Pleading*, published in

---

[86] J. B. Minor, *The Minor Family of Virginia*, 1923; P. A. Bruce, *History of the University of Virginia, 1818-1919*, vol. IV, V, 1921-22; P. H. Barringer and J. M. Garnett, *University of Virginia*, vol. II, 1904; *Univ. of Virginia Alumni News*, June, 1923; *Virginia Law Review*, Dec., 1923, Feb., 1926; *Proceeding of the Virginia Bar Association*, vol. XXXV, 1923.

[87] He was also the author of *The Law of Tax Titles in Virginia*, 1898; *The Law of Real Property*, 1908; and *Notes on the Science of Government and the Relations of the States to the United States*, 1913.

[88] J. R. Tucker, "The Judges Tucker of the Court of Appeals of Va.," *Virginia Law Register*, March, 1896; S. S. P. Patteson, "The Supreme Court of Appeals of Virginia," *The Green Bag*, July, 1893; S. E. M. Hardy, "Some Virginia Lawyers," *ibid.*, Jan., 1898; P. A. Bruce, *History of the University of Virginia*, vols. I, IV, 1920-21.

[89] "Nathaniel Beverly Tucker," *Richmond College Hist. Papers*, vol. 2, No. 1 (1917); W. C. Bruce, *John Randolph of Roanoke*, (2 vols., 1922); L. G. Tyler, *Letters and Times of the Tylers*, (2 vols., 1884-1885).

1846.[90] His nephew, John Randolph Tucker,[91] the son of Henry St. George Tucker, carried on the same tradition as a lawyer, teacher, and writer. He taught law at Washington and Lee University between 1870 and 1874 and again from 1884 to 1897. His writings were chiefly in the constitutional field and include *The History of the Federal Convention of 1787* published in 1887 and his *The Constitution of the United States,* published in 1899. In brief, legal education in Virginia, during the formative period of American life was greatly assisted by a brilliant galaxy of legal scholars starting with Chancellor Wythe and continuing down through the years. The chief centers of legal education during this time were William and Mary College and the University of Virginia[92] and the great teaching influence of the day was frequently found in some member of the remarkable Tucker family, or later in the equally remarkable Minor family.

In the trans-Allegheny region the problem of legal education did not remain neglected. It is interesting to note that the course of legal instruction set up at Harvard University had a direct effect upon pioneer legal educational experiments in the new lands of the west. Timothy Walker (1802-1856)[93] was one of the important connecting links in this transplanting of legal education. After several years of teaching in the Massachusetts schools, Walker entered the Harvard Law School in 1829. After studying under Justice Story and his colleagues for one year he moved to Cincinnati, Ohio, where he continued his legal training in the law office of Storer and Fox. In 1831 he was admitted to the bar. In 1833, with Judge John C. Wright, a former justice of the Ohio Supreme Court and Edward King of New York, a former student of the Litchfield school, he organized a private law school. This institution had but a few students and was not authorized to confer degrees. In 1835 it became a part of Cincinnati College, founded in 1818. It

---

[90] He also published numerous writings on political economy and law, including *A Discourse on the Importance of the Study of Political Science as a Branch of Academic Education in the United States,* 1840.

[91] Alexander Hamilton, *Memorial of John Randolph Tucker,* 1897, and *Virginia State Bar Association Reports,* 1897; R. T. Barton, "John Randolph Tucker," *Virginia Law Register,* May, 1897.

[92] The Law School of the University of Virginia opened in 1826 with 26 students. The average attendance down to the Civil War was around 60. Between 1825 and 1842, there were 705 young men enrolled in Law. P. A. Bruce, *History of the University of Virginia, 1819-1919,* vol. 2, 1920, p. 80. During the four years of the war, 31 students were enrolled. From the close of the war until 1895, the average was around 110 per session. Since then it has increased. From the earliest days its students have been drawn from all parts of the country. Lile, *op. cit.,* p. 155.

[93] C. T. Marshall, *A History of the Courts and Lawyers of Ohio,* 1934, vols. I, III; H. P. Farnham, (ed.) *Ohio Jurisprudence,* vol. 1, 1928, p. CVI; A. G. W. Carter, *The Old Court House,* 1880, pp. 122-24; Clara L. Chambrun, *The Making of Nicholas Longworth,* 1933, which contains part of Walker's diary; *Cincinnati Gazette,* Jan. 16, 1856; *Cincinnati Daily Enquirer,* Jan. 16, 1856.

continued to be known as the Law School of the College of Cincinnati until 1896, when it became a part of the University of Cincinnati.

The role of Timothy Walker in the legal developments of the Middle West was an important one. The influence of the institution which he founded spread through this entire section and continued on down through the years. The graduates of the Cincinnati Law School like the graduates of the Litchfield Law School a little earlier, had an influence upon the legal and political developments of the middle West, that is beyond measurement. Walker not only built a great law school, whose graduates found their ways into high places throughout the country; he also served as a jurist and in 1843 he became editor of the *Western Law Journal*. He was greatly interested in improving the law; and gave much time and energy in working for simplification of the rules of pleading and practice, as well as for changes in the laws having to do with crime and with the status of married women. Many of his suggestions were incorporated into the law of Ohio. As early as 1835, he wrote an article in favor of codification. His greatest work, however, was a series of lectures delivered in the law school which he had established which were published in 1837 as *An Introduction to American Law*. This book which undertook to provide facilities for studying "the elementary principles of American jurisprudence" was given almost immediate approval by the legal profession of the day. It continued to enjoy this same approval for many years. Indeed it went through eleven editions in all, the last one being published in 1905.

Another highly influential legal center in the trans-Allegheny region was established long before the Cincinnati School, however. That was the law professorship at Transylvania University which was founded in 1779, when George Nichols, a graduate of the College of William and Mary was appointed "Professor of Law and Politics." This professorship was apparently continued with more or less popularity until 1879. Starting out with nineteen students, Transylvania had a larger enrollment than the Litchfield school in 1821-22.[94] Under the direction of George Robertson in 1842-43, it was just behind Harvard in size, having 75 students.[95] For a generation it maintained the only organized center of legal education west of the Alleghenies. One of the outstanding figures connected with the school during its earlier history was Henry Clay.

At a much later date another legal institution was established in this part of the country, which in the years immediately preceding the Civil War had a larger enrollment than that of Harvard.[96] This

[94] It had 49 students, as compared with Litchfield's 26.

[95] Robert and Johanna Peter, *Transylvania University, Its Origin, Rise, Decline, and Fall*, 1896; A. F. Lewis, *History of Higher Education in Kentucky*, 1899.

[96] In 1859 Cumberland had 180 students, as compared with Harvard's 159.

institution was the law school of Cumberland University which was established in 1847 at Lebanon, Tennessee.[97] Cumberland continued to graduate large numbers[98] and to make its influence felt over a long period of time,[99] particularly in the South and Southwest. The Cumberland Law School officially began when Judge Abraham Caruthers met seven students, in Lebanon, in the office of his brother, Robert L. Caruthers. "During the first term," writes Joshua W. Caldwell the historian of the Tennessee bar, "the number increased to thirteen. The first lesson recited was in the *History of a Lawsuit*, a little book of forty pages which Judge Caruthers had published and which he called the 'Primer.' He did not adopt the lecture system, but assigned lessons in textbooks, and upon each of these rapidly examined the students, holding that this was the only proper way to teach the law. He adopted also a system of moot courts, thereby making his students practicing lawyers from the first. His plan was popular, and was satisfactory to the management."[100] In the second year of the Law School, Judge Caruthers was joined by Judge Nathan L. Green of the Supreme Court and Bromfield L. Ridley, Chancellor of the Lebanon Division. Judge Ridley gave little time to this work but Judge Green quickly became absorbed in the work of the law school and resigned from the bench in 1852 to give full time to this work. In 1856, his son Nathan Green, Jr., afterwards head of the school, became an active member of the faculty.[101]

While the number of lawyers trained in the law schools remained pitifully small during the early years of the nineteenth century, their influence was considerable in a profession which tended to gain rapidly in importance as the trying war years receded.[102] The complete effect of the early American law school is difficult to ascertain. There can be no doubt, however, that their efforts to establish professional standards in this period of democratic egalitarianism and frontier self-sufficiency was of the greatest importance in building a system of scientific law.

[97] See Nathan Green, "The Law School of Cumberland University," *The Green Bag,* vol. 2, p. 63; see also William G. Hammond, "American Law Schools, Past and Future," *Southern Law Review,* N. S., 1881, vol. 7, pp. 400-429.

[98] A. Z. Reed, *op. cit.,* p. 451. On p. 451 Mr. Reed has a table indicating the attendance at individual law schools prior to the Civil War. On p. 450 he has a table showing the enrollment at Litchfield, Harvard, Yale, Virginia, and Pennsylvania in the years between 1817 and 1840. On p. 452, he has a table showing the attendance at the six largest schools since the Civil War.

[99] Cumberland maintained a law school from 1847 to 1861 and then again from 1866 on. See A. Z. Reed, *op. cit.,* pp. 478, 154.

[100] *Sketches of The Bench and Bar of Tennessee,* 1898, p. 148.

[101] *Ibid.*

[102] When the Litchfield school closed in 1833, Max Radin estimates there were about 150 law school students in the United States. See *Social Science Encyclopedia,* vol. 9, p. 338.

Their graduates were scattered to the four corners of the country and among their number were men who exercised a lasting influence upon the legal structure of their own and other states. The early law school undoubtedly did much to establish professional standards among the members of the bar and bench in the period when the American legal system was being built.

CHAPTER VI

THE INFLUENCE OF JUDGE, LEGISLATOR, AND COMMENTATOR ON THE DEVELOPMENT OF AMERICAN LEGAL PATTERNS

It is interesting to note that as the profession in general increased in strength, "the citation of French authorities" which occurred so frequently in the earlier period "dwindled and finally vanished." This did not take place overnight, however, and as late as 1857 Sir Henry Maine believed that a reception of French law was taking place in America.[1] While the possibilities of a complete and successful reception were over long before this, the years between 1820 and 1850 witnessed numerous efforts to revive interest in its possibilities. For this period is marked not only by a movement to adjust the common law to changing conditions in the new world but by a widespread movement toward statute law making[2] in which French influence was not without effect.[3] Indeed new conditions made statutory additions necessary. "So many new subjects of legislation had arisen, so many changes from the old

[1] "In 1871 he reprinted a lecture containing the statement that the French code, as adopted in Louisiana, and not the common law, was becoming the susbtratum of the law in the newest states. I have never been sure what he had in mind. Possibly the adoption of the Field Codes in California and in the territory of Dakota may have mislead him. At any rate, all danger of a reception of the French law was over some time before 1856; but at one time it was a real danger." Pound, *op. cit.*, p. 682.

[2] "At the end of the eighteenth century transition from the stage of equity or natural law to the stage of maturity of law was complete. On the continent, codification had begun with the draft code of Frederick the Great in 1794 and in 1804 the French Civil Code summed up the work of the eighteenth century jurists and they furnished the model for practically all the codes of the Roman law world until the Germans set a new model in 1896. In the common law world Mansfield had incorporated the law merchant in English law, equity had crystallized so that in 1818 Lord Coke could say that the principles of equity were almost as fixed and uniform as the rules of the common law and bills of right were codifying the natural rights of man. The completion of this rigidifying process, which had been going on for more than a century, coincided with an epoch-making change in the philosophy of law. The theory of natural law had done its work of liberalization and modernization and had become for the time an agency of stabilization. Men thought it possible to discover a body of fixed and immutable principles, from which a complete system, perfect in every detail, might be deduced by purely logical operations, and held it the duty of the jurist to find them and of the legislators to promulgate the deductions in the form of a code." Pound, *The Spirit of the Common Law*, pp. 145-146.

[3] Dean Pound points out that when the movement to reform common law pleading and procedure arose in this country it took the form of "pretentious codes of civil procedure and ambitious attempts to produce a civil code along French lines," whereas in England it resulted in procedure acts and rules of court. "Judge Story in the Making of American Law," *American Law Review*, vol. 48, p. 685.

common law had been made necessary by the new economic and social conditions," says Charles Warren, "that the statute books of most of the older states contained an accumulation of resolves and statutes, contradictory, illogical, unnecessary, partly repealed, and partly obsolete."[4] All of this gave strength to the codification movement,[5] which was particularly strong in the years following the adoption of the Napoleonic code, when the lack "of formal congruity in the common law was contrasted with the order of the systematic treatise of civil law writers."[6]

Of course, the idea of codification was not introduced into the country at this time as a novelty. The colonies and the states which succeeded them had had something in the nature of codes for nearly two centuries. As early as 1592 Lord Bacon had proposed in the House of Commons to codify the laws of England. During the commonwealth period the task was actually begun under the leadership of Sir Matthew Hale. In the light of these circumstances, it is clear that the colonists were quite familiar with the thought of a "complete and orderly arrangement of the law to which they might be subject." The codes formulated by them, however, were but "partial and fragmentary." They were often arranged in alphabetical order, as in the case of the Connecticut Code of 1650.[7] In time, as statutes multiplied, the American codes became mere compilations, and the need for order and coherence was given renewed attention.[8]

Some light may be thrown upon the varying emphases that have been placed upon codification in this country by observing the experiences of one state, South Carolina, particularly during the earlier phases of its history. A movement toward codification in South Carolina was stopped by the Revolution. On Feb. 3, 1784, a resolution was passed by the Representatives, providing that a code be drawn up to relieve the confusion and multiplicity of the laws. On March 1, 1784, the Senate resolved that if John Rutledge had done the work, he be required

---

[4] *History of the American Bar*, 1911, p. 508.

[5] "The popular trend toward codification was the result of five intermingling factors: first, the old underlying antagonism of the American public toward the common law, as being of English origin; second, the ever-active jealousy, entertained by laymen in a democracy toward lawyers, as a privileged class and a monopoly, and the consequent desire to make the law a laymen's law; third, the increase in the number of law reports deemed, even then, to be 'vast and unwieldy'; fourth, the success of the *Code Napoleon* in Europe; fifth, the influence of Jeremy Bentham." *Ibid.*, p. 508.

[6] Pound, *op. cit.*, p. 688.

[7] This code which was drawn by Roger Ludlow, a skilled barrister, was one of the best passed by any of the colonies. After a general declaration of rights, taken from the Massachusetts Body of Liberties of 1641, the first titles concerned themselves with "Ability, Actions, Age, Arrests, Attachments, Ballast, Barratry, Bills, Bounds of Townes and Particular Lands, Burglary and Theft," *Colonial Records of Connecticut*, I, 511.

[8] A. Z. Reed, *Training for the Public Profession of the Law*, 1921, Bulletin No. 15, *The Carnegie Foundation*, pp. 110-111.

to deliver it and that he be paid the amount promised in the commons resolution of April 13, 1768. On March 8, 1785, an act was passed providing for the election of three commissioners to make a digest of the laws. A committee was appointed composed of Judges Pendleton, Burke, and J. F. Grimké. In 1789, this committee, which was assisted in its labors by the previous work of John and Hugh Rutledge, submitted its report.[9] The laws, one of the commissioners said, "now lie concealed," so that the ablest lawyers could not know the law in force without expending great time and energy. The law was condemned to remain "mingled in a confused chaos," however, for this digest failed of adoption although many improvements recommended were adopted soon afterwards. The commission's recommendation that the circuit courts be given equity jurisdiction was hotly argued in 1836, but did not come into the Constitution until 1868. Grimké's *Laws* which were published in 1789 probably drew largely upon the work of the commission, on which he labored. Five hundred copies of this book were published. Grimké supplemented this work with two other books, *The South Carolina Justice of the Peace*, published in 1788, and *The Duty of Executors and Administrators*, published in 1797. In 1814, Brevard's *Digest* was published in three volumes[10] In 1822, James' *Digest of the Laws of South Carolina* was published. In 1836, William Rice added an index through that year to Judge Grimké's index.

The greatest work of this character consisted of editing and publishing ten volumes containing every law, with few exceptions, enacted in South Carolina from her founding through 1838. The first five volumes of this monumental work were prepared by Dr. Thomas Cooper after his enforced withdrawal from the presidency of South Carolina College. David J. McCord was responsible for the rest of the work. In 1848, B. C. Pressley was paid by the State to digest the law relating to magistrates. In the same year a *Digest of the Negro Law* was passed and in 1850 Judge Evans' *Road Law* was passed. In the year 1824, judicial reform received considerable attention and codification of the common law was strongly urged by many, including Thomas S. Grimké. H. S. Legaré was among those who opposed the movement.[11] In 1859 the legislature recognized "the growing necessity for a code, eliminating obsolete, contradictory, or duplicated enactments, and arranging the existing statute law in one systematic whole by topics." James L. Pettigru was appointed to undertake this difficult

[9] See *House Journal*, March 12, 16, 1785; *Senate Journal*, March 23, 1785; *Treas. Accounts*, 1783-85.

[10] See *Dictionary of American Biography*, VII, 634.

[11] See T. S. Grimké, *South Carolina Bar Association*, 1827; Legaré, *Works*, II, 482; *Southern Review*, Aug., 1831. See also *The Annual Message of Governor Wilson*, 1824; R. I. Manning, 1826; Taylor, 1828; Miller, 1829.

task.[12] Pettigru revised so freely, that his great work was rejected, when it was presented in 1862. He had been employed, it was stated by critics of his work, to codify and not to remake the law. His efforts were not without results, however, and "his magnificent reduction of chaos to order, on Blackstone's method, became largely the basis of the work" of the commission which presented in 1872, in one large volume, the first code of South Carolina, the "Revised Statutes of South Carolina." Since then the code of statute law has been kept up to date by frequent action.[13]

The chief exponent of codification during the earlier phases of the formative period was Jeremy Bentham (1748-1832), one of the "great seminal minds" of Anglo-American law. He likewise advocated the complete abolition of the common law. "So long as there remains any of the smallest scrap of unwritten law unextirpated," he wrote President James Madison, "it suffices to taint with its own corruption—its own inbred and incurable corruption—whatever portion of statute law has ever been, or can ever be, applied to it."[14] The influence of Bentham was first felt in America through the works of Edward Livingston, another genius of the law.[15] After reading Bentham's *Legislation, Civil and Criminal* (1802), Livingston drafted a Code of Procedure which became the first real code in America. It was adopted by the Louisiana legislature in 1805. Livingston later prepared a complete code of Crimes and Punishments, Criminal Procedure, Evidence and Prison Discipline.[16] This code was never enacted into law as a complete whole,

[12] James Louis Pettigru (1789-1863), was the undisputed head of the South Carolina state bar for forty years. It has been said of him that while "he never occupied a high public station" yet "he was a statesman"; and that while "he never held judicial positions," nevertheless "he was a great jurist." J. D. Pope, "James Louis Pettigru," *Great American Lawyers*, W. D. Lewis (ed.) IV, 1908, pp. 30-31. A practicing lawyer throughout his active life, he has been called "the greatest private citizen that South Carolina has ever produced." Profoundly learned in the law, he was also noted for the clarity and simplicity of his legal reasoning. Indeed it is said that he "turnpiked the legal pathway out of the most complicated labyrinths of law and fact." "Memorial of the Late James L. Pettigru," *Proc. of the Bar of Charleston, S. C., March 25, 1863* (1866).

[13] See David D. Wallace, *The History of South Carolina*, vol. II, 1934, pp. 468-471.

[14] *Bentham's Works*, vol. V, p. 460.

[15] Charles H. Hunt, *Life of Edward Livingston*, 1864; "Edward Livingston and the Louisiana Codes." *Columbia Law Review*, vol. 2; Carleton Hunt, *Life and Services of Edward Livingston*, in *Proc. of the La. Bar Association*, May 9, 1903; S. Lewis, *Strictures on Dr. Livingston's System of Penal Laws*, 1825, and *Remarks on the Hon. Edward Livingston's Introductory Report to His System of Penal Law*, 1831; "Two Letters of Chancellor Kent," *American Law Review*, April, 1878, pp. 478-490; Eugene Smith, "Edward Livingston and the La. Codes," *Columbia Law Review*, 1902, pp. 25-26; E. H. Moore, "The Livingston Code," *Journal of the American Institute of Criminal Law and Criminology*, Nov., 1928, pp. 344-63, including a bibliography.

[16] Livingston began his complete code in 1820 at the request of the Louisiana legislature. He made a report in 1822, and the entire work was finished in 1824, although not in full until 1833. For a comprehensive review of this criminal code see *The North American Review*, vol. 17, October, 1833, pp. 242-268.

but nevertheless it proved "an unfailing fountain of reforms" and Livingston's contribution was a continuing one.[17]

In New York, a revision of the statute law of the state was made in 1827. This revision went far beyond the usual attempt to condense the law, improve its phraseology and correct a few of the most obvious and dangerous defects. Indeed it "revolutionized the laws of that State as to the tenure of real property, and was a long step forward in the direction of full codification," an achievement attempted at a later date.[18] In Georgia, the legislature gave serious consideration to codification in 1858. Out of the resulting labors came a code, sometimes called the code of 1861, although it did not go into effect until 1862. "This code was remarkable," says E. M. Coulter, the Georgia historian, "in that here for the first time in any state or country appeared the substantive common law reduced to writing."[19] Thomas R. R. Cobb, "one of the ablest men in the state's history," was largely instrumental in carrying out "this exacting and difficult task."[20]

In Massachusetts, interest in codification was also present from an early date. In 1812, Governor Gerry, in a message to the legislature spoke strongly in favor of codification. The importation of English law books had been stopped by the War of 1812 and Dane's *Abridgment and Digest of American Law*, which was started in 1800, was not finished until 1826, although the first volume appeared in 1823, at which time a revised edition of the General Law of Massachusetts prepared by Asahel Stearns and Lemuel Shaw was published in two volumes by authority of the legislature.[21] While various compilations had been made, no adequate consolidated version of the Massachusetts statutes had been effected. In short, the inaccessibility of the "sources of the law" encouraged the movement toward codification.

Starting in 1815, *The North American Review* published a number of articles in favor of general codification and during the next twenty years it continued to publish such articles. It is interesting to note that some of these articles are said to have been written anonymously by Judge Story, who was for some time greatly interested in codification although his later books were destined to check the movement. In 1829,

[17] Warren, *op. cit.*, p. 518.

[18] See *Remarks on the Projected Revision of the Laws of New York,* first published in the *Atlantic Magazine* for April, 1825, 8 vol., 19 pp., New York. Reviewed in *The North American Review,* vol. 21, July, 1825, pp. 249-250.

[19] *A Short History of Georgia,* p. 276; see also Stephen F. Miller, *The Bench and Bar of Georgia,* vol. 2, 1858, pp. 25-26.

[20] *Ibid.*

[21] For a review of this work see *The North American Review,* July, 1823, pp. 69-91. The reviewer was an admirer of Mr. Dane and looked forward to the publication of his *Digest of American Laws,* as ushering in "a new era in our judicial history." *Ibid.,* p. 90.

The American Jurist, one of our first law magazines was founded.[22] It was edited by Willard Phillips, Charles Sumner, George S. Hillard and Luther Cushing, in succession. Sumner was particularly active in advocating codification.[23] Apparently his fellow editors were also favorably inclined to the idea, although the bar in general and Chief Justice Isaac Parker, in particular, were opposed to it.

In 1832, a commission composed of Charles Jackson, Ashur Stearns, and George Ashmun, was appointed by Governor Levi Lincoln to prepare the first general revision of the Massachusetts statutes. Upon the death of George Ashmun, John Pickering, a strong proponent of codification was appointed to his place. In 1835, this commission reported a revision which was accepted in substance; and "it forms a landmark in the history of Massachusetts law."[24] In 1836 Governor Edward Everett advocated codification of the common law in his inaugural address and the legislative committee to whom the subject was referred was greatly sympathetic to the idea. In 1836, a special commission, headed by Justice Joseph Story was established. In 1837 this body reported in favor of codification of the criminal law and Governor Everett felt that Massachusetts would certainly lead the world along the pathway of codification.

In the meantime forces were at work which tended to offset this movement. For one thing Lemuel Shaw was appointed Chief Justice of the Supreme Judicial Court in 1830; for another thing the common law was rendered more accessible by the writings of Story and Kent. The appointment of Chief Justice Shaw was important, since "he had the ability to explain the common law in such a way as to counteract the enthusiasm for codification," and it is said that Daniel Webster[25] among others urged him that it was his duty to do so. The writings of

[22] *The United States Law Manual and Civilian's Magazine* was founded earlier. See *The North American Review,* vol. 16, Jan., 1823, pp. 181-188.

[23] See Edward L. Pierce, *Memoir and Letters of Charles Sumner,* vol. I, 1878, pp. 153, 186, 188, 189, 195, 288; vol. II, pp. 135, 170, 272, 299.

[24] The commissioners did not attempt to embody the principles of the common law into their revision to any greater extent than had been previously done, since they deemed "it of questionable utility" to put into "the form of a positive and unbending text, numerous principles of the common law which are definitely settled and well known." "It has been remarked by distinguished American jurists," they said, "that the common law is peculiarly well fitted to the rapidly advancing state of our country, because it possesses in an eminent degree the capacity of adapting itself to the gradual progress of improvement among us; and that this accommodating principles which pervades it, will adjust itself to every degree and species of improvement that may be suggested by practice, commerce, observation, study, or refinement." For such reasons they deemed it expedient "to leave those important principles as they at present exist rather than to attempt to incorporate them into the inflexible text of a written code." See F. W. Grinnell, "The Judicial System and the Bar, (1820-1861)," *Commonwealth History of Massachusetts,* (Hart ed.), vol. 4, 1930, pp. 48-49.

[25] *Ibid.,* pp. 48-49; see *Commonwealth* v. *Temple,* 14 Gray, 14.

Justice Story[26] also tended to counteract the codification movement, as mentioned elsewhere.[27]

Many prominent legalists took up the argument for codification and during these years the matter was widely discussed.[28] In some quarters support for codification was enthusiastic and intense.[29] This was likely to be the case among the younger lawyers who were not so sure that the common law was "the perfection of human reason" as were their older colleagues who had taken their views from Blackstone. A spirit of reform actuated this younger group which looked askance upon anything that savoured of the misty past and determined to clear away many of the law's archaisms.[30] This spirit led to a critical movement which scrutinized all legal rules and doctrines with a skeptical eye. It was part and parcel of a general movement which was concerned with improving political and social institutions as well as legal practices. In England it was encouraged by both Bentham and Austin. But whereas Bentham criticized all systems of law with equal force, Austin was prone to commend the Roman law and recommend its study; and as the movement for reform in the common law advanced in England, the revival of the study of Roman law progressed as well.

In America the movement to reform the common law was encouraged by the inclination toward the French law already referred to.

---

[26] Between 1832 and 1845, Story published the following textbooks: *Commentaries on the Law of Bailments*, 1832; *Commentaries on the Constitution*, 1833; *Conflict of Laws*, 1834; *Equity Pleading*, 1838; *Commentaries on the Law of Agency*, 1839; *The Law of Partnership*, 1841; *Bills of Exchange*, 1843; *Promissory Notes*, 1845. This was made possible by the generosity of Nathan Dane, who, as noted before, used the proceeds of his "Abridgment of American Law" to secure Justice Story as a Professor at Harvard with an opportunity to lecture and write. Dane was greatly influenced in this connection by Viner, the great English lawyer. It will be remembered that Dane's *Abridgment* was begun in 1800 and finished in 1826. In preparing this work he followed the example of Viner, whose *Abridgment* was yet authoritative. He followed Viner still further when he fostered legal learning with his professorship; for Viner had founded the Vinerian Professorship of English Law at Oxford from the royalties of his book. The published lecture of the first Vinerian professor, Blackstone, had become a legal classic. Dane had this in mind when he devoted the proceeds of his *Abridgment* to the establishment of a professorship of American law. Desirous of stimulating legal authorship as Viner did, he provided that the lectures delivered on the foundation should be published. He devoted ten thousand dollars to the foundation. The success of his plans may be seen when we recall that Story's series of Commentaries, Greenleaf's Evidence, Parson's well known works, and Langdell's published writings were all made possible by the provisions of his grant. Story was the first one to take advantage of this opportunity to write, and like Blackstone, the first professor working on the Vinerian foundation, he more than justified the experiment. *The Centennial History of the Harvard Law School, 1817-1917*, (1918), pp. 9-10.

[27] *Ibid.*, p. 49.

[28] Warren, *op. cit.*, pp. 518-519. For criticism of codification see *The North American Review*, vol. 8, Dec., 1818, pp. 63-71; *The North American Review*, vol. 7, July, 1818, pp. 184-198; *The North American Review*, May, 1816, pp. 21 ff.

[29] Pound, *op. cit.*, p. 688.

[30] See *The North American Review*, October, 1824, pp. 411-439.

This tendency as we have seen, had been stimulated by the adoption of the *Code Napoleon*, and in New York as far back as 1809, there was agitation for a civil code similar to the French code.[31] In the minds of the reformers the lack of system in the common law "was contrasted with the order of the systematic treatises of civil-law writers, and they were led to think and speak far worse of their own system than the substance of either body of law warranted. More or less attempt was made to incorporate doctrines of the civil law in projected codes, and here and there a court professed to adopt doctrines of the civilian on some point instead of the common law rule."[32]

Although New York, Pennsylvania, and Massachusetts took steps during the late twenties and early thirties toward codification in a limited sense,[33] it was not until the time of David Dudley Field that a Code in the broad and correct sense of the term was prepared in this country.[34] It failed of adoption in New York, but in 1865 this Field Code was adopted by the territory of Dakota, and in a modified form was adopted still later by the states of North Dakota, South Dakota, Montana, and Idaho.[35] While the movement for complete codification was not successful in the period between the Revolution and the Civil War, limited reforms of the old systems of pleading and practice made decided progress during this time. In 1836 Massachusetts initiated a few minor procedural reforms. In 1848, New York passed a code of Civil Procedure, which was of far-reaching effect. Within a few years codes based on the New York reforms were passed in many states.[36]

The most important factor influencing the earlier phases of the codification movement as mentioned before was the work of James Kent[37] and Joseph Story.[38] The writings of these great American

---

[31] For discussion of the Napoleonic code during these earlier years see *The North American Review*, vol. 20, April, 1825, pp. 393-417.

[32] Pound, *op. cit.*, p. 688.

[33] Warren, *op. cit.*, pp. 524-526.

[34] *Ibid.*, p. 533.

[35] *Ibid.*

[36] Civil Procedure Codes based on the New York model were adopted in Missouri in 1849; in California in 1850; in Iowa, Kentucky, and Minnesota in 1851; in Indiana in 1852; and in Ohio in 1853. It greatly influenced Codes adopted in Oregon and Washington in 1854; in Nebraska in 1855; in Wisconsin in 1856; in Kansas in 1859; in Nevada in 1861; in Dakota in 1862; in Montana in 1863; in Arizona and Idaho in 1864; in North Carolina, Arkansas, 1868; in Wyoming in 1869; in South Carolina, Florida, and Utah, in 1870. See Charles M. Hepburn, *The Historical Development of Code Pleading* 1897.

[37] See James Kent, *Memoirs and Letters*, ed. by William Kent, Boston, 1898; John Duer, *Discourse on the Life, Character, and Public Services of James Kent* (New York, 1848); F. C. Hicks, *Men and Books Famous in the Law*, (Rochester, 1921), ch. VI; M. Coxe, "Chancellor Kent at Yale," *Yale Law Journal*, vol. XVII, 1907-08, 311-37, 553-72; James Brown Scott, "James Kent, 1763-1847" in *Great American Lawyers*, ed. by William Lewis, 8 vol. (Phil. 1907-09), vol. II, pp. 491-533; Thomas Thacher, "Yale in Relation to Law," *The Yale Bicentennial*, 1901, pp. 182-184.

[38] W. W. Story, *Life and Letters of Joseph Story*, 2 vol. (Boston, 1851); William

jurists not only had the effect of bringing English legal institutions into new prominence, but also discouraged the possibilities of a reception of the French law, since they presented in a systematic, orderly, reasoned fashion what was in substance sound common law. Their service to the common law was particularly effective since their generous citations of French law seemed to be favorable to its adoption. It is perhaps not too much to say that their writings saved the common law.[39] They certainly provided well-written guides for American judges and lawyers to turn to. These guides not only stated the common law as worked out in the English courts but seemed to exhaust the resources of the civil law as well. "Thus," says Dean Pound, "at this critical time the common law was so presented as to make the reception easy, and the energies of our judges were turned to the right channels of applying common law principles to concrete cases. Until our case-law was to stand by itself such aid was indispensable. Without it I doubt if we should live under the common law today. As Coke summed up the development prior to his time and thus furnished the basis for a juristic new start, so these text-writers summed up English case-law of the seventeenth and eighteenth centuries and made it available as the basis of a new start in America."[40]

Story's work is particularly interesting in this connection. Starting with his *Commentaries on the Law of Bailments,* published in 1832, he continued to work vigorously until 1845 when his book on *Promissory Notes* was published. His books, turned out in rapid succession, had a decisive effect in this critical period in American legal history. Of them, Dean Pound writes:

In quantity, in timeliness, and in its relation to the law that went before and came after, this body of legal writing is in many ways comparable to that of Coke. In each case the judge-made law of the past was restated and was made conveniently, and, as it were, authoritatively available for the future. If in each case there is much to criticise in the details of the performance, the answer is, after all, that this body of writing must be judged as a whole and appraised by its results. So judged, it must be counted one of the controlling factors in the shaping of American law. Moreover, Story's writings may

---

Schofield in *Great American Lawyers,* ed. by William Lewis (Phil., 1907-09), vol. III, pp. 123-185; Roscoe Pound, "The Place of Judge Story in the Making of American Law," *American Law Review,* vol. 48, 1914, pp. 676-97.

[39] "Lay discussions of American law in the first quarter of the nineteenth century abounds in demands for an American code. Had such men as Kent and Story allowed their good sense to be overcome by the continental philosophers of law in the eighteenth century, whom they undoubtedly admired, the future of American law might have been very different. I doubt if our judges would have been strong enough to withstand the movement. But when the movement did gather strength in the draft codes of David Dudley Field, the common law was thoroughly received and well established and was able to resist it." Pound, *op. cit.,* p. 691.

[40] Pound, *op. cit.,* p. 691.

deceive the casual reader by the apparent weight which is given to the authorities of the civil law. Great as is the use which he seems to make of them, it is in fact almost wholly by way of reenforcement or illustration or example. When he goes further, as, for instance, in his treatise on bailments, he has had little permanent effect. In substance, his books are treatises upon the common law. Moreover, their relation to the civil law happily is to that part of the law where the Romans were at their best and the common law was least developed.[41]

Summing up the English case-law from the seventeenth to the early nineteenth century in these books, Story worked it over on a philosophical basis and made it available for the bench and bar of the new commonwealths which were springing up west of the Alleghenies. In his *Commentaries on the Constitution,* published in 1833, he departed from eighteenth century ideas concerning the contract basis of government and emphasized the idea of historical approach. Like Kent he tended to give natural law a historical content and to shift the theoretical basis of positive law from natural law to history, from reason to experience.

This work on the Constitution, it is interesting to note, continued to be the only authoritative and extensive treatise on the subject over a long period of time. For over fifty years it furnished students of the law with the principles which John Marshall with Story's assistance had done so much to establish. It undoubtedly had great influence on the bench and bar for two generations. Passing through various editions, it was given new life and utility by Thomas McIntyre Cooley when he prepared the fourth edition with copious annotations. "It would be difficult," says Andrew McLaughlin "to overestimate the importance of such volumes in the days when the critical case system was not used by beginners, when texts were comparatively few, and when practicing attorneys and judges were not provided with long series of reports, in days also when the layman was interested in problems concerning the nature of the Union and the powers of government."[42]

His *Conflicts of Law* and his *Equity Jurisprudence* were also of paramount importance in shaping the course of American legal development, inasmuch as they took the judge-made law of the past in these two important fields and restated it in convenient and usable form for American purposes. His work on *Equity Jurisprudence* had an almost immediate effect on American legal practices. "It forthwith systematized, one might almost say created," writes Dean Pound, "a whole branch of the law of England."[43] While the decisions of Kent, as

[41] *Ibid.*
[42] *The Cambridge History of American Literature,* vol. II, p. 76.
[43] "The Place of Judge Story in the Making of American Law," *Proceedings of the Cambridge Historical Society,* vol. VII, 1914, p. 39.

Chancellor of New York, were of the utmost importance in fashioning and making applicable in America the principles of equity, Story's writings had an equal or even greater influence in the establishment of the American system of equity.

The work of Kent was also of the utmost service in "the recreation of American law in the image of Blackstone." As previously noted, his lectures at Columbia which followed the plan of Blackstone were published as the *Commentaries on American Law*, becoming an authoritative exposition of the English common law from the American point of view as well as a valuable interpretation of the American constitution. The twelfth edition of this great work was edited by Oliver Wendell Holmes, Jr., in Boston in 1873, bringing its influence on American law directly into the present century. Justice Story called Kent's *Commentaries* "our first judicial classic." Kent's work on the bench was also of great assistance in the development of American law during this period.[44] He was very fortunate in that his decisions were extremely well reported by William Johnson, another Yale graduate, who was reporter of the Court of Chancery from 1814 to 1825.[45] In the field of equity, the work of Kent is of striking importance[46] In some respects it is remindful of the work of Eldon, the Great Chancellor, who during these same years was completing the historic system of equity as distinct from the common-law system.[47] With twelve more years to serve when Kent came upon the bench, Eldon was concluding his great task of revising equity and reducing its main rules and principles "to a coherent and orderly system capable of further development at the hands of later judges and yet in general unalterable in its main structure, save by the action of Parliament." While the work of Kent and Eldon may not be altogether comparable, it must be recognized that the New York chancellor with the help of Story did give the American legal profession a better knowledge of equity, and developed judges trained in the

[44] Thacher, *op. cit.*, pp. 182-183.

[45] "Without such reporting the influence of Kent's decisions would not have been such as to entitle Judge Dillon to call him, 'more than any other person, the creator of the equity system of this country.' Judge Story said 'no lawyer can ever express a better wish for his country's jurisprudence than that it may possess such a chancellor [Kent] and such a reporter' [Johnson]." Thacher, *op. cit.*, p. 184.

[46] Putnam, "The Early Administration of Equity in this Country," *Central Law Journal*, vol. 90, 1920, p. 423.

[47] John Scott, First Earl of Eldon and brother of Lord Stowell, was born in 1751 and died in 1839. During a long career as Lord Chancellor he reviewed in the Court of Chancery practically the whole range of equity, deciding many cases which are now regarded as constituting the judicial foundations of the system. Highly conservative he devised no new equitable doctrines but did strengthen it by his activity. He was an able successor to Lord Ellesmere who had vindicated the independence of Chancery, and of Lord Nottingham and Hardwicke who had expanded and systematized it. See Horace Twiss, *The Public and Private Life of Lord Chancellor Eldon, with Selections from his Correspondence*, 2 vols., London, 1846.

twofold system. At the same time, the organization of American courts and the procedural reform movement which appeared toward mid-century tended to make for a "fusion" of law and equity[48] and this movement would not be denied as subsequent events demonstrated.[49]

At this point it should be remarked that some observers, including Professor Andrew A. McLaughlin the distinguished historian of the American constitution, are of the opinion that the names of John Marshall and Henry Wheaton should be joined with those of Story and Kent in any consideration of this building period of American law. "In jurisprudence," he says, "Marshall and Kent and Story and Wheaton, by judicial opinion or by written test, laid the foundations of American public and private law, and ably performed a creative task such as rarely, if ever, before fell to the lot of the jurist."[50] There is much to be said for Professor McLaughlin's observation. The contributions of John Marshall (1755-1835) were certainly unparalleled in the field of constitutional law[51] and the work of Henry Wheaton (1785-1848) in the field of international law was of the utmost importance.

[48] "The Federal Judiciary Act of 1789, committed law and equity to the same tribunal, and that tribunal was set up in the image of a court of law. The newer states, especially those in the North, were not inclined to set up or keep up separate courts of equity. Then came the constitution of 1847 in New York, abolishing the court of equity, and soon after the code of civil procedure and its one 'civil action.'" Pound, *Harvard Law Review*, vol. 37, 1928, pp. 397-398.

[49] The experience of South Carolina is of interest in this connection. In that state, equity was administered by special judges until 1868. Until 1784, these were the Governor (or Lieutenant Governor) and Council, who were usually laymen. In 1784, three equity judges were provided for, to be elected and removed by mere address of legislature. In 1808, an equity appeal court of all equity judges was created. These equity courts were then and until 1824 exceedingly unpopular in South Carolina as in some of the other states because of their freedom in making law and in overruling even the constitutional Court of Appeals. In this respect they repeated the history of English equity courts. Just prior to 1800, the legislature indicated its dislike for equity courts by refusing to fill vacancies for two years. Even the legal profession could not know the law, Governor John L. Wilson charged, in a bitter attack upon equity courts. He advocated a separate Supreme Court over all and in 1824 his request was granted. In that year a Court of Appeals with three judges was created, with complete powers in all appeals in law or equity, and with the right to order separate courts. The number of equity judges was also reduced and the title of Chancellor given them. A larger use was also made of Masters (O'Neill, I, 280, and Statutes by years). After 1824, the Chancellors were never again allowed their old uncharted freedom. In 1868, the office of Chancellor was eliminated by the Constitution of that year—which provided for uniting the administration of law and equity—a change which had been long advocated. In passing it should be remarked that not all of the Chancellors were held in disregard. Henry W. De Saussure, chancellor from 1808 to 1839, who was the most influential man in establishing the South Carolina courts of equity, was an outstanding exception. He is said to have been "to South Carolina what Kent was to New York" and he was held in high regard. Wallace, *History of South Carolina*, vol. II, pp. 460-461.

[50] *The Cambridge History of American Literature*, vol. II, 1918, p 71.

[51] "He was not the commentator upon American constitutional law; he was the author; the creator of it. . . . The field was absolutely untried. Never before had there been such a science in the world as the law of a written constitution of government. There were no precedents. . . . An original field of judicial exertion very rarely offers

The influence of Marshall overshadows everything in these formative years. His efforts were apparently untiring. During the first ten
years of his service, he delivered practically all of the opinions of the
court to which any name is attached. In the thirty volumes of reports
from the *1st Cranch* to the 9th period, which covered Marshall's 34
years of service on the Supreme Court, 1215 cases are reported. In
94 of these cases, no opinions were given and 15 of them were *per
curiam*. Of the remaining 1106 cases, Marshall delivered the opinion
of the court in 519. In the constitutional field 62 judgments were
recorded. In 36 of these cases, Marshall spoke for the court. The
remainder of the cases were apportioned among seven judges, as follows:
Story, 11; William Johnson, six; Bushrod Washington, five; Paterson,
Cushing, Baldwin and Thompson, one each. In 23 of Marshall's 36
opinions on constitutional questions, there was no dissent.[52] The difference between a Marshall on the bench in these early days and someone
else—says Spencer Roane of Virginia who was Jefferson's choice—is
almost impossible to measure.[53] The effect of Marshall's personality
on the development of American public law is powerful, however
viewed.

Marshall's work was in many respects more that of a statesman
than a judge. Compelled to consider public question of far-reaching
importance and to formulate fundamental principles for a new form of
political order, he was unable to go to a well-furnished armory of legal
learning, such as jurists in the domain of ordinary private law may
draw upon. Indeed, as Andrew McLaughlin suggests "one may question whether, had his mind been stored with vast legal lore, he could
have entered on his work without falling into traps of pedantry or
finding himself clogged by precedent and technicality." However that
may be, it is true that Marshall did not usually predicate his opinions

itself. To no other judge has it ever been presented, except to Mansfield in the establish-
ment of the commercial field; unless perhaps the remark may be extended to the labors
of Lord Stowell, in the department of English consistorial law, and to those of Lord
Hardwicke in equity." *Address of Edward J. Phelps*, Am. Bar Assoc., 1893; see also
A. J. Beveridge, *The Life of John Marshall* (4 vols.) (1916-19); Edward S. Corwin,
John Marshall and the Constitution, 1919; Joseph Story, *A Discourse upon the Life,
Character and Services of the Honourable John Marshall, LL.D.*, 1835; J. F. Dillon,
John Marshall, Life, Character and Judicial Services, 3 vols., 1903; J. F. Dillon, ed.,
John Marshall: Complete Constitutional Decisions, 1903; J. P. Cotton, ed., *The Con-
stitutional Decisions of John Marshall*, 2 vols., 1905; J. W. Brockenbrough, ed., *Reports
of Cases Decided by the Honourable John Marshall in the Circuit Court of U. S., for the
Dist. of Va. and N. C., from 1802 to 1833*, inclusive, 2 vols., 1837; Charles Warren,
The Supreme Court in U. S. History, 3 vols., 1922.

[52] Van Vechten Veeder, "A Century of Federal Judicature," *The Green Bag*, vol.
15, 1903, p. 24.

[53] Charles Kerr, "If Spencer Roane Had Been Appointed Chief Justice Instead of
John Marshall," *American Bar Association Journal*, vol. XX, No. 3, March, 1934, pp.
167-172.

on a long line of precedents or "seek refuge behind the thoughts and words of others." In some of his greatest cases, there is not a single citation of authority.[54] At all times the details of the immediate problem are viewed in the light of a body of principles which were formulated as though they were to endure for the ages. With a prophetic eye on the future growth of the nation, he laid the basis for our American constitutional law.[55]

While the work of Henry Wheaton is in no way comparable with that of Marshall he was an indefatigable and important worker in this formative period of American jurisprudence. The work for which he is chiefly known, *The Elements of International Law*, appeared in 1836. This book was immediately successful. It passed through nine editions and was translated into many foreign languages including the French, Italian, Spanish and Chinese.[56] It has been considered to be one of the most valuable contributions to the science of international law made during the nineteenth century.[57] In his first edition, a sketch of the history of international law was included. Later on this preparatory historical sketch was expanded into a separate work. This historical sketch was originally written in French. After publication in Leipzig in 1844 it was brought out in New York in 1845 with the title, *History of the Law of Nations in Europe and America, from the Earliest Times to the Treaty of Washington, 1842*. In 1842 he published his *Enquiry into the Validity of the British Claim to a Right of Visitation and Search of American Vessels Suspected to be Engaged in the African Slave Trade* (2nd ed., London), 1858.

[54] "He began," says Andrew McLaughlin, "with simple statements, founded, one is led to think, in common sense, and then, with a careful but not overwrought analysis, he leads one directly to his conclusions, always with a directness and a simplicity which are characteristic of strong mental grasp but conceal the cleverness with which the road has been chosen or the arguments exposed. By his very statement of the issues involved in a case he could quietly disclose to the litigants against whom he was ruling the far-reaching and perhaps destructive consequences of their own contentions. And, as we have said, he did this, as he must needs do it in constitutional decisions, not by an elaborate dissecting of precedent and legal authority, but by a calm outlook upon the field and a searching analysis of the elements involved in the discussion." *The Cambridge History of American Literature*, vol. II, 1918, p. 73.

[55] "Though Marshall's best known decisions were in the field of constitutional law where he was easily master, his work was by no means confined to that subject, for many problems besides those involving constitutional construction came before the court. During his term as chief justice he rendered over five hundred opinions, dealing with almost every one of the main divisions of modern jurisprudence. But he did even more; he placed the court itself in a position of authority and influence, dignified and made potent the whole Federal judicial system, and thus helped to build up that respect for the Federal courts which has been of such tremendous importance in the development of American life. This in fact was no easy task; the Supreme Court was often fiercely attacked; it often went counter to the intense prejudice of parties, states, and sections. But by virtue of his own integrity and inherent power he compelled respect and overcame prejudice." *Ibid.*, p. 76.

[56] F. C. Hicks, *Men and Books Famous in the Law*, 1921, pp. 222-223.

[57] McLaughlin, *op. cit.*, p. 78.

In addition to his work as an expounder and historian of international law, Wheaton is remembered as an able reporter of the decisions of the United States Supreme Court. Starting in 1816, Wheaton published annually a volume of such decisions. In 1828, he was succeeded by Richard Peters (1779-1848) who compiled the *Reports of Cases in the Supreme Court of the United States, 1828 to 1842*, 16 vols., 1828-42.[58] Wheaton's efforts as reporter were without reward at the outset and he depended upon the sale of the *Reports* for his compensation.[59] Beginning in 1817, however, an annual salary of $1000 was established to assist these services. Wheaton's reportorial work was characterized by the extent and excellence of his notes, a fact which has been frequently commented upon by those familiar with his work. Daniel Webster who was closely associated with Wheaton in a number of cases, was of the opinion that "no reporter in modern times has inserted so much and so valuable matter of his own."[60]

In addition to his work as a reporter and in the international field, Wheaton found time to play an active role in other ways as well. In 1815, he framed a national bankruptcy law and urged its passage by Congress. In 1829 he served with Benjamin F. Butler and John Duer as a commissioner to revise the laws of New York. While the part he played in this revision is not altogether clear, there is some evidence to believe that he drew up the general plan which was followed by his colleagues.[61] Starting out as a journalist he continued to write throughout his career. In 1815 he published *A Digest of the Law of*

---

[58] Richard Peters was the son of Richard Peters (1744-1828) the distinguished Pennsylvania jurist to whom Justice Story declared himself indebted "for his rich contributions to the maritime jurisprudence of our country" (W. W. Story, *Life and Letters of Joseph Story*, 1851, I. p. 540). The elder Peters published *Admiralty Decisions in the District Court of the United States for the Pennsylvania District, 1780-1807* (1807). His reporter son, in addition to his sixteen volumes of United States Supreme Court reports published *Reports of Cases in the Circuit Court of the United States for the Third Circuit . . . District of New Jersey, 1803 to 1818, and in the District of Pennsylvania, 1815 to 1818*, (1819); *Reports of Cases . . . in the Circuit Court of the United States for the Third Circuit . . . from the manuscripts of Bushrod Washington*, 4 vols., 1826-1829; *Condensed Reports of Cases in the Supreme Court of the United States . . . from its Organization to the Commencement of Peters' Reports*, 6 vols., 1830-34; *The Public Statutes at Large of the United States . . . 1789 to Mar. 3, 1845*, (1848); and a *Practical Treatise on the Criminal Law*, 3 vols., 1847, an edition of the work of Joseph Chitty. See N. P. Black, *Richard Peters: His Ancestors and Descendants, 1810-1889* (1904); J. W. Stinson, "Opinions of Richard Peters, (1781-1817)," *University of Pennsylvania Law Review*, March, 1922; A. J. Dallas, *Reports of Cases Ruled and Adjudged in the Several Courts of the U. S.* (4 vols., 1790-1807); *Pennsylvania Magazine of History and Biography*, July, 1899, July, 1916, October, 1920. See also Octavius Pickering and C. W. Upham, *The Life of Timothy Pickering*, 4 vols., 1867-73.

[59] In *Wheaton v. Peters*, Peters, vol. 8, p. 591, it was decided that "no reporter has or can have any copyright in the written opinions delivered by the court."

[60] W. B. Lawrence, "Introductory Remarks" in Wheaton's *Elements of International Law*, 6th ed., 1885, p. xliv.

[61] *The North American Review*, vol. 21, July, 1825, pp. 249-250.

Maritime Captures and Prizes; in 1821 he published *A Digest of the Decisions of the Supreme Court of the United States;* in 1823 he edited William Selwyn's *Abridgment of the Law of Nisi Prius;* and in 1826 he published *Some Account of the Life, Writings and Speeches of William Pinckney.*[62]

In all of his writing and in all of his work, Wheaton shows the influence of his European training and experience.[63] Acquainted with the civil law from his studies and observations at Poitiers as early as 1805, when he translated the new *Code Napoleon* into English, he maintained an interest in codification and uniformity throughout his life.[64] Indeed his unique experience gave him a better opportunity than most Americans of his day to understand the strengths and weakness of a system of codification.[65] "A witness," writes W. B. Lawrence, "of the transition from the *droit coutumier,* and from a system composed of the Roman civil law and of royal ordinances and local regulations, to a uniform written law, he was preparing himself to exercise an enlightened judgment on codification—a subject, which, as a commissioner of New York, under the first law passed by any State of the Union for the liberal revision of its statutes he had twenty years afterwards occasion to discuss with a view to its practical application." In short Henry Wheaton had the opportunity, the ability, and the

[62] A second edition of this study is included in Jared Sparks, *Library of American Biography,* vol. VI, 1836.

[63] Commenting upon his breadth of experience, one British critic of the time remarked that "no American ever had about him less of the peculiar stamp which marks the citizen of a new state" than Henry Wheaton. *Littel's Living Age,* Dec. 5, 1857. A thorough going student all of his life, he was particularly adept as a linguist. Indeed in 1828, after a year's stay in Denmark, we find him publishing an article on a Danish study of the public law of Denmark. See *The North American Review,* October, 1828.

[64] He made the acquaintance of Jeremy Bentham in 1827.

[65] After reading law in a Providence law office, Wheaton went to Europe in 1805 and stayed four years. During this period events of the greatest importance took place in the political system of France, and extraordinary changes were also attempted in the theory and administration of the public law. Upon arriving in France, writes William Beach Lawrence, Wheaton's biographer, the diligent young law student "took up his abode in the quiet rural city of Poitiers, where, besides the French language, the mastery of which contributed so much to the success of his career, he acquired the foundations of that knowledge of the French law, which was not less useful to him as a publicist. His residence in France took place at an important period in the history of French jurisprudence. He witnessed the formation of the imperial codes and the reduction of the written and unwritten law of France to a uniform text—a work in which Napoleon I took not only a deep interest, but an active part, frequently attending the meetings of the commission charged with the preparation of the codes, and mingling in the debates. (See *The North American Review,* vol. XX, p. 393.) Mr. Wheaton fully appreciated the importance of this great revision of the law of France, and prepared a translation of the codes for publication in this country, which was prevented from taking place only by the accidental destruction of the manuscript." See *The North American Review,* vol. 82, June, 1856, p. 8. This volume contains a book review of Wheaton's *The Elements of International Law With the Last Corrections of the Author, Additional Notes, and Introductory Remarks, containing a Notice of Mr. Wheaton's Diplomatic career and of the Antecedents of his Life.* By William Beach Lawrence, Boston; 1855.

disposition to render exceptional services to the American legal order during its growing period and he labored diligently and effectively to meet this responsibility.[66]

While the work of Marshall and Wheaton was of tremendous importance in the field of public law, the contributions of Story and Kent are probably of greater weight in the other branches of American jurisprudence. Beginning work at a time when very little was written upon American law, and some considerable antagonism to the English common law remained, they nevertheless successfully seized upon these principles of the common law and adapted them to the American environment and experience. When their efforts were completed the foundations of a coherent and usable system of American law had been laid. With their writings Dean Pound observes, the age of reason came to an end and the age of history began. This is significant since any efforts to supplant the common law as the basis of the American legal system was bound to conflict directly with this emphasis on historical continuity. When they started to write it was not settled that we should receive the common law. As a result of their writings, however, the question did not remain unsettled for long, and the legal system which took form and shape during these years and which was expanded as the century advanced, was the common law system of Hale, Holt, Mansfield and Ellenborough, and of Coke, Blackstone and Fortescue.[67]

The common law was very definitely adjusted to American conditions, however, and could not be mistaken for its English counterpart in any regard.[68] It was not, nor could it be identified with, the English common law, and, many adjustments to American conditions were effected. Mr. Peter DuPonceau, speaking in 1825, described the progressive state of improvement of the common law whereby it became more and more "dignified with American features." There were a number of noteworthy changes. Our landed states, for example, had become allodial; and the traits of the feudal system were practically

---

[66] W. B. Lawrence, "Introductory Remarks" in Wheaton's *Elements of International Law* (6th ed., 1855); Edward, "Life, Services, and Works of Henry Wheaton," *The North American Review*, Jan., 1856; Charles Sumner, "The Late Henry Wheaton," *Boston Daily Advertiser*, March 16, 1848; George Shea, "Henry Wheaton and the Epoch to Which He Belonged," *N. Y. State Bar Assn. Reports*, vol. II, 1879; W. V. Keller, *Henry Wheaton, An Appreciation*, 1902; F. R. Jones, "Henry Wheaton," *The Green Bag*, Dec., 1904; James Brown Scott, "Henry Wheaton," in W. D. Lewis, *Great American Lawyers*, vol. III, 1907; F. C. Hicks, "Henry Wheaton" in *Men and Books Famous in the Law*, 1921; A. B. Benson, "Henry Wheaton's Writings on Scandinavia," *Jour. of English and Germanic Philology*, October, 1930.

[67] Pound, *The Spirit of the Common Law*, p. 118.

[68] See O. W. Holmes, *The Common Law*; H. T. Terry, *Some Leading Principles of Anglo-American Law*; J. F. Dillon, *The Laws and Jurisprudence of England and America*; R. Pound, "Place of Judge Story in the Making of American Law," *American Law Review*, vol. XLVIII, 1914, pp. 676-697. See particularly *The North American Review*, vol. 17, July, 1823, p. 72.

effaced, save for few forms and phases, among which was the *fee simple*. The principles of conveyancing were simplified, and registries were established to supersede the ancient form of livery and seizin. Where entails were not abolished, they were easily destroyed. The laws of descent were assimilated to the rules of succession, established by the Roman law, and the rule of primogeniture was abolished. The intricate peculiarities of English practice in general were less observed, legal proceedings rendered less expensive, and legal rights were made more easily understood. Most of these changes, it should be observed, "were in operation, and the whole impulse communicated before the Revolution." Nevertheless, the spirit of change continued to manifest itself, and Mr. DuPonceau might very well predict that the United States would eventually come to have a common law, which would be "not that of England, nor of Rome, nor of France, but the common law of the United States."[69]

[69] *The North American Review,* vol. 21, July, 1825, p. 139.

CHAPTER VII

THE SHAPING OF LEGAL MATERIALS IN THE EVENTFUL FORMATIVE PERIOD

The years between 1830 and 1860 were busy ones on all sides.[1] During this time far-reaching legal developments took place, as old common law doctrines were worked over with great effect. It will be remembered that this was a period of great ferment on all sides, as ideas which were set loose by the French Revolution and repressed in the Age of Metternich, reappeared in different form during the restless thirties and forties and made their presence felt.[2] In Europe, this ferment manifested itself in widespread legal stirrings. In America a similar excitement was experienced as Andrew Jackson and his followers ushered in a new day. One highly important change effected by the Jacksonian movement was the abolition of the property qualifications for the suffrage. This action was not only responsible for the development of the new democratic party with its liberalizing policies but "was also unquestionably a factor in the liberal and progressive, sometimes radical, decisions for which the courts (especially in Massachusetts, New York, and Pennsylvania) were noted during this era."[3]

During this same period, American law was moving toward that stage of maturity, which was to characterize the nineteenth century.[4] Equality of opportunity and security of transactions came to be emphasized. These developments are remindful in many ways of England's era of strict law, which commenced in the Norman period and extended to the sixteenth century. During that long period, security was the

---

[1] "Our classical period from the Revolution to the Civil War, is not so much a period of growth as one of adaptation; it was not a creative period, but instead was a period in which received materials were worked over into better form and were developed into a consistent legal system. Hence with all its appearance of growth, it was a period of stability, and in common with the maturity of law everywhere is comparable to the stage of the strict law." Pound, *The Spirit of the Common Law*, pp. 148-149.

[2] Gilbert Seldes, *The Stammering Century*, 1928.

[3] Charles Warren, *History of the American Bar*, p. 447. See Justice Joseph Story's lament at the passing of the "old court" of Marshall's day and the ascendancy of the new Jacksonian crowd with Roger Brooke Taney as Chief Justice. The reactions to Taney's opinion in the Charles River Bridge case are of interest in this connection. See Carl B. Swisher, *Roger B. Taney*, pp. 347-379, 361-374.

[4] Dean Pound describes five historical periods in the development of Anglo-American law. They are: (1) The Period of Archaic Law; (2) the Period of Strict Law; (3) the Period of Equity or Natural Law; (4) the Period of the Maturity of Our Law; (5) the Period of the Socialization of Our Law. See Hugh E. Willis, "Historic Periods in Development of Our Law," *Amer. Bar. Assn. Jour.*, vol. 9, 1923, p. 187.

chief end of the law. It was effected by supplanting primitive self-help, so far as individuals were concerned, by a system of law, which employed its own processes and remedies. This system of law was characterized by its rigid formality, since the men of those days would not relinquish what they regarded as their right to attain their own redress unless they were granted the assurance of a system of formal law, in its place. In time, they found that they had succeeded in establishing a greater tyrant than any against which they were trying to protect themselves and valiant and successful efforts were made to mitigate the excess formality and technicality which had been created.[5]

American legal developments during the formative period under consideration followed a somewhat similar pattern. Form and technicality began to play an increasingly large role as a growing emphasis was placed on the need for certainty and for uniformity.[6] In 1933, at the one hundredth anniversary of the founding of the Cincinnati Law School Dean Pound stated:

We may say that one hundred years ago . . . American law had entered upon the era of maturity which was to characterize the nineteenth century. Through the efforts of Eldon in England and of Kent in America, equity had been crystallized. The chancellor would say: "The doctrine of this court ought to be as well settled and made as uniform almost as those of the common law . . . I cannot agree that the doctrines of this court are to change with every succeeding judge. Nothing would inflict on me greater pain, in quitting this place than the recollection that I had done anything to justify the reproach that the equity of this court varies like the chancellor's foot." The whole spirit of nineteenth century is in this passage. If Walker's account of American case law in the newer parts of the country in 1833 was less sure of the supreme importance of certainty and uniformity, the time was not far distant when they were to be worshipped in Ohio no less than at Westminster.[7]

As rules tended to become hard and fast the liberalizing effect that accompanied the process of absorbing the law merchant tended to disappear and the influence of equity was not felt with complete effect. The process of absorbing the law merchant, which began in the seventeenth century, was carried on vigorously in the eighteenth century under the leadership of Lord Mansfield. This process, which was already finished in England, was substantially completed in this country with the work of Story and Kent. "In the hands of Kent and Story and the great judges of the first part of the nineteenth century," says

[5] In the field of substantive law the formality and technicality of the strict period was satisfactorily eliminated in due course; "but in the field of adjective law, or procedure, at least in the United States, the law is to a great extent still where it was in the early period of strict law, and some parts of our substantive law, like real property and consideration in contracts, still has the mark of strict law." Willis, *op. cit.*, p. 187.

[6] "The Future of the Common Law," *Cincinnati Law Review*, vol. 7, 1833, p. 346.

[7] *Ibid.*

Dean Pound, "the ascertainment of the law merchant, as an element in the received common law, involved creative use of comparative law as well as rational speculation on the basis of established precepts."[8] As American law advanced toward maturity, however, this liberalizing process ceased and "the supervening reform of procedure and merger of law and equity in codes and practice acts, with all its good qualities, had the unhappy influence of leading to a decadence of equity" and to an application of equitable rules as though they were legal.[9]

This was to be expected, however, as the emphasis on strict law would not be denied. Equity with its informality and discretion, its tendency to identify law and morals, and its emphasis upon duties could not be expected to flourish in a period when the emphasis was upon the *rights* and *rules* and *formalities* of the strict law. The increasing emphasis upon *individual rights* under law had some ameliorating influences, however, which were manifested in, "the emancipation of married women; the safeguards thrown around infants, the insane, and criminals; prison reforms; milder forms of criminal punishment; abolition of imprisonments for debt; the treatment of bankruptcy as a misfortune and not a crime; the removal of the bars against the testimony of witnesses and parties in civil and criminal cases; the recognition of labor unions; and the simplification of the law by codes and statutory revisions for the benefit of laymen as well as lawyers."[10] The tendency of the day toward freedom of contract and individualism encouraged the philosophy which put "individual rights at the foundation of our legal system."[11] Since men continued to think in terms of the "natural rights of men," of "laissez faire," of the "law of supply and demand," of "individualism," of "constitutional safeguards," for some time to come it is not strange that legal rights come to be overemphasized.[12]

As social and economic changes took place many phases of the common law required adjustment.[13] When new agencies of transportation and communication were introduced, problems were forced upon the court which required an extensive degree of creative efforts upon their part. With the coming of the railroads it became necessary for them to develop the law of torts to meet the varied problems which arose out of their relations to the public and to their employees. Other

[8] Pound, *op. cit.*, p. 345.

[9] *Ibid.*

[10] Charles Warren, *op. cit.*, p. 146. See also Joseph C. Beale, Jr., "Jurisprudence— Its Development During the Past Century," *Congress of Arts and Sciences*, vol. III, 1906.

[11] Pound, *The Spirit of the Common Law*, p. 145.

[12] Hugh E. Willis, *op. cit.*, p. 188.

[13] "The second characteristic of the era was the remarkable modernization of old legal doctrines. The inventions that so thronged it were a severe test of the malleability of the old Common Law; and of its capability of adaptation to fit the new economic, commercial and social conditions." Charles Warren, *History of the American Bar*, p. 447.

inventions brought similar problems.[14] One of the outstanding changes in common law doctrine took place in the law of evidence. Throughout the period between 1830 and 1860, many important changes were made in this field.[15] Indeed the courts were hard at work in all fields adapting the old materials to new conditions, in this, the classical period of American law.

Just as John Marshall devised constitutional doctrines which enabled his countrymen to build a nation,[16] so the judges sitting in the state courts were shaping common law materials to fit the conditions peculiar to their particular jurisdiction. A remarkable group of pioneer jurists participated in this movement. In Massachusetts, for example, a substantial record of judicial accomplishment was instituted at an early date by Chief Justices Theophilus Parsons (1750-1814)[17] and Lemuel Shaw (1781-1861).[18] When Theophilus Parsons became Chief Justice of Massachusetts in 1806, few changes had been made in the cumbersome judicial system that had existed in the colonial period. Procedural abuses still bore heavily upon the community and caused dissatisfaction with courts and lawyers as it did in 1786, at the time of Shays' Rebellion. Parsons succeeded in correcting many of these difficulties. He was equally effective in the settlement and development of the common law. When commercial law, which was little known in his day, became important, he studied and mastered it. In his decisions as Chief Justice are found

. . . clearly and concisely stated, the common law in relation to real estate and to commercial and marine contracts, as well as lucid explanations of the law merchant. In his varied and important experience of over thirty years at the bar he had become familiar with the course and usages of trade and

[14] Charles Warren, *op. cit.*, pp. 451, 452, 454, 456, 461.

[15] *Ibid.*, pp. 472, 473, 474.

[16] Address of Edward J. Phelps, *Am. Bar Assn.*, 1893.

[17] Lewis, *op. cit.*, vol. 2, 1907, pp. 91-92; *Memoir of Theophilus Parsons*, 1859, by his son, Theophilus Parsons. This memoir contains the obituary address of Chief Justice Isaac Parker (also in 10 Mass. Reports, 521); S. E. Morison, *The Life and Letters of Harrison Gray Otis, Federalist, 1765-1848*, 2 vols., 1913; *A History of the Constitution of Massachusetts*, 1917, and "The Struggle over the Adoption of the Constitution of Massachusetts, 1780," *Proc. Mass. Hist. Soc.*, vol. L, 1917; S. L. Morse, *The Federalist Party in Massachusetts to the Year 1800*, (1909). Parson's opinions appear in 2-10 Mass. Reports.

[18] "It was the task of those who went before you, to show that the principles of the common and the commercial law were available to the wants of communities which were far more recent than the origin of those systems. It was for you to adopt those systems to still newer and greater exigencies; to extend them and the solution of questions, which it required profound sagacity to foresee, and for which an intimate knowledge of law often enables you to provide, before they had even fully risen for judgment. Thus it has been, that in your hands the law has met the demands of a period of unexampled activity and enterprise; while over all its varied and conflicting interests you have held the strong, conservative sway of a judge, who molds the rule for the present and the future out of the principles and precedents of the past." Address to Ch. J. Lemuel Shaw, by the bar of Massachusetts in 1860; quoted by Warren, *op. cit.*, p. 448.

commerce and with New England life in its varied domestic, religious, social and political aspects; and combining these commercial usages and popular customs with the fundamental principles of English common law, he determined and stated, with great originality, boldness and wisdom, a common law of New England that had a strong and beneficent influence in the development of law throughout the United States.[19]

Lemuel Shaw was a worthy successor to Chief Justice Parsons. He served as Chief Justice of Massachusetts from 1830 to 1860.[20] During these years Massachusetts was transformed from an agricultural to an industrial community. Shaw's great task was to adapt the principles of the common law, developed in an agricultural era, to the needs of an industrial urban civilization. He performed this task with "an appreciation of the requirements of the community whose officer he was." While his technical knowledge was surpassed by many, his understanding of public policy was not. "It was this which made him, in the language of the late Judge Curtis, the greatest magistrate which this country has produced."[21] He took the position that private interest must give way before public interest, in the drive for industrial expansion. As the industrial movement advanced, courts throughout the country turned to his decisions for the solution of new problems.[22] His contributions in the development of railroad and public utility law were particularly valuable.[23]

In Pennsylvania a great piece of creative judicial work was done by John B. Gibson (1780-1853)[24] who was a member of the Supreme

[19] Lewis, *op. cit.*, vol. 2, pp. 91-92.

[20] Joseph H. Beale, Jr., in *Great American Lawyers*, ed. by W. D. Lewis, vol. III, (Phil., 1908), pp. 455-90; Frederic H. Chase, *Lemuel Shaw*, (Boston, 1918); Walter Nelles, "Commonwealth v. Hunt," *Columbia Law Review*, vol. 32, 1932, pp. 1128-69; *Lemuel Shaw, Chief Justice of the Supreme Court of Massachusetts*, (Cambridge, 1885).

[21] O. W. Holmes, *The Common Law*, 1881, p. 106.

[22] "In questions of social policy Shaw was a conservative; and when the interests of business conflicted with those of the workers, he resurrected the fellow servant rule (*Farwell* v. *Boston and Worcester R. R. Co.*, 45 Mass. 49, 1842), holding that when an employee was injured by the negligence of another employee the company which they both served was not liable, a doctrine which put a heavy burden on American workers. Nevertheless, Shaw understood the forces in the nascent struggle between capital and labor; in *Commonwealth* v. *Hunt* (45 Mass. 111, 1842), he handed down the first liberal decision in the United States on labor disputes, which settled that a combination of workers is not illegal, if activities are carried on by fair means even though they tend to impoverish others, and that peaceable coercion may be used to effect a lawful object." A. H. Feller, *Social Science Encyclopedia*, vol. 14, 1934, p. 18.

[23] See *Norway Plains Co.* v. *Boston & Maine R. Co.* (67 Mass., 263, 1854); and *Lombard* v. *Stearns* (53 Mass., 60, 1849).

[24] T. P. Roberts, *Memoir of John Bannister Gibson*, (Pittsburgh, 1890); W. A. Porter, *An Essay on the Life, Character, and Writings of John B. Gibson* (Philadelphia, 1855); S. D. Matlock, "John Bannister Gibson" in *Great American Lawyers*, ed. by W. D. Lewis, 8 vol., (Phil., 1907-1909) vol. 3, pp. 351-404; J. W. Appel, "Gibson and Progressive Jurisprudence," Pennsylvania Bar Association, *Reports*, vol. 15, 1909, pp. 356-370; Owen Wister, "The Supreme Court of Pennsylvania," *The Green Bag*, vol. 3, 1891, pp. 72-87.

Court for thirty-seven years, and Chief Justice during a large part of this time. Serving in the constructive period of the law, when many of its parts were first laid and all were given shape and developed, it would be hard to overstate the influence of his clear intellect playing over these difficult legal materials in their plastic, formative condition. His opinions which run through seventy volumes of reports, have had a powerful effect on the development of the law of Pennsylvania.[25] When Gibson started out the law of real property and pleading were the most important branches of the law. Commercial law was as yet undeveloped; railroads were unknown, and corporations of any sort unusual. Gibson was trained in the fundamentals of the common law as furnished by Coke and Bacon. His understanding of fundamental principles enabled him to meet the various new problems arising out of the great developments in commerce and industry, which presented themselves during his fifty years of legal activity.[26] Speaking of his influence upon the law of Pennsylvania, one commentator says:

To his profound knowledge of the common law, to his appreciation of its spirit, and above all to his treatment of it, not as a fixed and lifeless system but as an organism capable of adaptation to its environment and therefore alive —Pennsylvania owes, in a great degree, the framework of her jurisprudence. With an unsurpassed learning in the old precedents, Gibson never joined a blind following of them. From well grounded premises, he reasoned with masterly logic, strong common sense and striking independence, always realizing that this commonwealth had a judicial system of her own rooted deeply in the ancient customs of the English people, but growing and spreading in its own way and along its own lines.[27]

In Ohio the difficult task of laying the groundwork of an adequate body of law was greatly assisted by the efforts of Peter Hitchcock (1781-1852) who served on the supreme court for twenty-one years, between 1826 and 1852. Indeed the work of Hitchcock has been compared with the work of John Marshall in the national field. When he came upon the bench, the law of Ohio was in a formative process; books were scarce; and the judges had access to only a few elementary works, as a general thing. In the words of one commentator:

[25] "Judge Gibson's name is signed to more than 1500 opinions; and it is not only in these that his influence appears. Many *per curiam* opinions bear unmistakable indication of his style; and his domination in the consultations of the court may be seen in countless opinions bearing the name of his associates. No name among them ranks higher than Black's and his reverence for the learning and wisdom of Gibson has already been shown." Lewis, *op. cit.*, vol. 3, pp. 370-371.

[26] "The tendency of the common law to adapt itself to the feelings and habits of men, as they actually exist in society, instead of molding their transactions into forced and artificial forms by inflexible rules, is one of its most estimable qualities, and one which gives it as a practical system, preeminence over every other that has prevailed." *Shapley* v. *Garey*, 6 Sergeant and Rawle's Repts., 539.

[27] Lewis, *op. cit.*, vol. 3, pp. 370-371.

In making up a decision, it was not a question of ranging numberless authorities on both sides, and sifting out a rational conclusion from the tossing wave of conflicting opinions, but the work set before him and his compeers was to adapt the common law to the conditions of a new country and to a people rapidly becoming imbued with the fervid heat of nineteenth century life; a people largely sprung from New England ancestry but mixed with the blood of many other states and nations, endowed with gigantic vigor and energy, and having small respect for forms and precedents; regardful of the law in an uncertain, vague way but inclined at times to be turbulent and disorderly. Judge Hitchcock brought to the supreme bench just the endow-ments necessary to meet the conditions confronting him.[28]

His work was marked by a singular capacity for maintaining the general principles of the common law, while giving full realization to the needs of the rapidly expanding frontier society of early Ohio.[29]

In Kentucky, John Boyle (1774-1835), sitting on the supreme bench for sixteen years during the formative period of Kentucky juris-prudence, had an outstanding influence in directing its lines of growth. His biographer says:

The mere printed record of his work is to be found in the fifteen vol-umes of Kentucky reports beginning with first Bibb and ending with third Monroe; but a more enduring record exists in the jurisprudence of his state and the honorable traditions of its bench and bar. Such an opportunity comes to few men. Robertson, perhaps the greatest of his successors, suggested that the criticism had been made that he adhered more rigidly to the ancient principles of the common law than was consistent with its improvements and its adaptation to the genius of American institutions—that he was not a Mansfield nor a Hardwicke, but more like Hale and Kenyon—but concluded that if he did not improve, he did not mar the law. But in a better sense, Boyle was a pioneer of the law. He applied established principles to new facts and adjusted new conditions to the fixed rules of justice. More than any other man in Kentucky, he established the authority and dignity of judicial decision, and was to the jurisprudence of Kentucky what Marshall was to that of the United States.[30]

[28] Lewis, *op. cit.*, vol. 3, pp. 340-341, *Pioneer and General History of Geauga County*, 1880; *Ohio Archaeological and Historical Quarterly*, Jan., 1923; Henry Howe, *Historical Collections of Ohio*, I, 1908, p. 687; C. H. Galbreath, *History of Ohio*, vol. II; E. O. Randall and D. J. Ryan, *History of Ohio*, vols. IV and V, 1912.

[29] "If the application of a strict rule of common law worked injustice under the changed conditions of life in a new country, he (Judge Hitchcock) did not hesitate to modify it to meet existing conditions. Thus it early became a rule in Ohio that 'the common law is a part of our law so far as its principles are reasonable and consistent with the letter and spirit of our constitution and suitable to the condition and business of our people, and the state of our society, but if wanting in any of these we will depart from it.' It must not be imagined that in applying this rule the judges acted solely upon their individual convictions of right and wrong unguided by authority or precedent, or that they attempted to make a new and distinct system of 'judge-made law.' On the contrary the well-established principles of the common-law were consistently followed and judiciously interpreted into a concrete system conforming to its spirit." *Op. cit.*, pp. 344-345.

[30] Lewis, *op. cit.*, vol. 2, pp. 233, 234; Richard H. and Lewis Collins, *History of*

In Indiana, the name of Isaac Blackford (1776-1859) is mentioned, when the history of the application of the common law to that state is reviewed. Sitting as a judge of the Supreme Court of Indiana for more than thirty-five years, he had an exceptional opportunity to influence the development of law in that state. Evidence of his judicial labors and his influence upon the common law of Indiana are to be found in the eight Blackford's Reports and in the first, second, and third volumes of Indiana Reports and in Smith's Reports; 655 of his opinions are contained in the eight Blackford's Reports; 192 in the first, second, and third Indiana Reports; 50 in Smith's Reports; and eight more in the second edition of the first volume of his reports. It has been said of these reports that while many judges in England and America have written more opinions and longer ones in a much shorter period, no judge in either country has delivered so many opinions with so few misstatements of the law, or inaccuracies of expression as are contained in these 900 opinions of Judge Blackford. These decisions developed the common law in Indiana "in as pure a state as it was ever administered at Westminster Hall." Of Blackford, a contemporary remarked: "He has done more than any other man to build up a jurisprudence on the broad foundation of the common law."[31] As a result of his labors, the common law remained firmly established in Indiana until "the wave of legal reforms swept over the western country, impelled by the movement for reform started in the state of New York by the adoption of a Civil Code of procedure."[32]

In the state of Mississippi, Chief Justice William Lewis Sharkey (1798-1873) assumed a most important role during the formative years of its jurisprudence. Appointed circuit judge in 1832, he served only a few months when he was elected one of the three judges of the high court of errors and appeals, despite the fact that he opposed that part of the constitution of 1832 which subjected the judiciary to popular election. He was re-elected without fail until November, 1851, when financial pressure caused him to resign. His continued support by the electorate is surprising since he refused to adopt a popular course of action throughout his career. For example, before one election, he resisted the popular demand for the repudiation of the Union Bank bonds although his opponents had promised the voters a decision against the validity of the bond issue.[33] In addition to his judicial labors he

Kentucky, 1874; Biog. Encycl. of Ky., 1877; H. Levin (ed.) Lawyers and Lawmakers of Kentucky, 1897. His decisions in the Kentucky court of appeals are published in Bibbs (4 vols.), Marshall's (3 vols.), Littel's (5 vols.) and Monroe's (7 vols.) Reports.

[31] Lewis, op. cit., vol. 3, 302-203.

[32] Ibid., pp. 202-203.

[33] Dunbar Rowland, Courts, Judges, and Lawyers of Mississippi, 1798-1935, vol. I, 1935, p. 88.

served as a member of a commission to compile *The Revised Code of the Statute Laws of Mississippi* (1857).[34] Tennessee also produced some jurists of note in its early period and the work of Judges Haywood, Overton, and White left a lasting mark on the jurisprudence of that commonwealth.[35]

North Carolina was also represented by a great creative jurist during the formative period in the person of Thomas Ruffin (1787-1870) who served on the bench of that state for a quarter of a century. The name of Ruffin is known wherever the English common law is known. He wrote some 1460 opinions embracing almost every type of civil and criminal law, many of which are cited in an authoritative way.[36] In the constitutional field his work has been compared with John Marshall and Lemuel Shaw while his work in the common law and equity is equally noteworthy. His opinions are said to have been characterized by "breadth of view, fullness of discussion, force of reasoning, strength and simplicity of language, lack of citation of authorities, and the almost inevitable character of their conclusions."[37] While prone to respect 'precedent, he did not permit himself to be enslaved by it. His independence of thought was responsible for two important departures from English precedents in the equitable field. One had to do with the rejection of the doctrine of past performance as a basis for decreeing the specific execution of a verbal contract for sale of land; the other the discarding of the doctrine of vendor's lien upon land sold upon credit. An indefatigable worker, Ruffin left a lasting impression upon the law of North Carolina as well as the nation.

Another creative jurist during this formative period was Francois Xavier Martin (1762-1846), the "father of jurisprudence in Louisi-

[34] H. S. Foote, *The Bench and Bar of Mississippi*, 1881; Dunbar Rowland, *Courts, Judges, and Lawyers of Mississippi, 1798-1935*, vol. I, 1935, pp. 87-94; J. F. H. Claiborne, *Mississippi* (1880); J. W. Garner, *Reconstruction in Mississippi* (1901); "Judge Sharkey Papers," ed. by F. G. Davenport, *Miss. Valley Hist. Rev.*, June, 1933. Miss. Hist. Soc. *Pubs.*, vol. IV, XIV, 1901-14; J. S. Morris, *Miss. State Cases*, vol. I, 1872, pp. iii, v.

[35] "The times that tried judges' souls were not those after 1834, when Tennessee was becoming a commercial and manufacturing state, and when Green and Reese and Turley and McKinney and others were wisely and skillfully rounding out and finishing the fabric of our jurisprudence, but when mighty John Haywood and Overton and White were clearing the ground and laying the foundations. The one great source of litigation in the ancient period was land titles. In that time the soil of Tennessee was as prolific of land claims almost, as of its natural products. English precedents could not in many cases furnish a guide. Conditions were new, and the court was compelled to make the law. It did make the land law." Joshua Caldwell, *Sketches of the Bench and Bar of Tennessee*, 1898, p. 137.

[36] J. M. Vanfleet, *The Law of Collateral Attack*, 1892, Sections, 634; *Steel* v. *Dixon*, 17 Chancery Division, 825.

[37] Walter Clark, "Thomas Ruffin" in *Great American Lawyers*, vol. IV, 1908, ed. by W. D. Lewis; W. A. Graham, *Life and Character of Hon. Thomas Ruffin*, 1871; *The Papers of Thomas Ruffin*, 1918-20, ed. by J. G. de R. Hamilton. See also 13-43, 51, 57, *North Carolina Reports*.

ana."[38] Born in France, Martin was admitted to the bar in North Carolina in 1789, where he wrote and published several volumes dealing with the duties of executors and administrators which had a wide sale. In 1792, the legislature employed him to collect the Parliamentary statutes in force in the state and in 1794 to collect the private laws of North Carolina. Later on he was employed to make his well-known "Revisal" of the *Laws of the State of North Carolina.* During this same period he published reprints of North Carolina statutes, translations of the *Latches Reports* in 1793; *Cases in the Court of King's Bench during the Reign of Charles I* in 1797; *Notes of a Few Decisions of the Superior Courts of the State of North Carolina* in the same year; and Pothier's *A Treatise on Obligations* in 1802. He practiced for twenty years in North Carolina. During this time he acquired command of the English language, became a master of common and statute law, and acquired a familiar acquaintance with Roman and French law as well. In 1890 he was appointed to a federal judgeship in the Mississippi territory by President Madison. In 1810, he was transferred to the territory of Orleans, where his knowledge of the French language and law was of great assistance to him. In 1815, he became a judge of the state supreme court. In 1836, he became chief justice. In 1846, when the new constitution abolished the court, he resigned.

His judicial career was a highly useful one. When he came upon the supreme court in 1815, Louisiana law was in hopeless confusion. Indeed, both French and Spanish law was in operation and the introduction of English-American law tended to add to the confusion. The common law was made the basis of criminal jurisprudence by virtue of an act of Congress, and in 1808, a civil code had been adopted which did not repeal other law not in conflict with it. In consequence, the courts were required to study and compare Spanish and French codes, to know the Roman law and the essentials of the English common law as well. Martin's unique background made it possible for him to play a notable part in reconciling the conflicting systems and bringing order out of chaos. In the creation of the new jurisprudence of Louisiana, Martin's indefatigable labors were outstanding, and he won a great name "in constructive jurisprudence, particularly for his skillful blending of the English and Roman law." His opinions run through fifty-one volumes of Louisiana Reports.[39] In addition to his heavy judicial labors,

[38] Dunbar Rowland, *Courts, Judges, and Lawyers of Mississippi, 1798-1935,* vol. 1, 1935, pp. 28-29.
[39] His first opinion, *Johnson v. Duncan* (3 *Martin's Reports,* Old Series, 530), was written during the War of 1812. It is noteworthy in that it held that neither the executive nor any subordinate had the power to suspend the regular operation of the laws or the writ of habeas corpus. Such suspension he declared to be a legislative power. Moreover, the legislative power could not be used to impair the obligation of private contracts.

Martin published reports of cases decided by the courts from 1811 until 1830. His total output amounted to some thirty-four volumes in all, including his *A General Digest of the Acts of the Legislature of the Late Territory of Orleans and of the State of Louisiana and the Ordinances of the Governor under the Territorial Government* which was published in 1816 and his *History of Louisiana* which appeared in 1827, and his *History of North Carolina* which appeared in 1829.[40]

In New Hampshire, William Richardson (1774-1838)[41] who served on the Supreme Court from 1812 to 1838, and Joel Parker (1816-1888)[42] who served from 1838 to 1847 were performing equally important roles in the development of the early American legal system. In New Jersey, Henry Woodhull Green (1804-1876)[43] who served on the bench from 1846 to 1860 was doing important work. In Connecticut, Thomas S. Williams (1777-1861),[44] said by Tapping Reeve to be the best scholar ever sent from the Litchfield Law School,

[40] Memoirs by W. W. Howe in Martin's *History of Louisiana*, 2nd ed., 1882, and in Lewis, *Great American Lawyers*, vol. II, 1907; S. A. Ashe, *Biog. History of North Carolina*, vol. I, 1906; Charles Gayane, *Ferando de Lemos*, 1872; Dunbar Rowland, *op. cit.*, pp. 28-29.

[41] When Richardson came upon the bench in New Hampshire in 1816, "no printed reports of cases previously adjudicated in the state were in existence, there was little uniformity of practice, and great uncertainty about branches of the law, more especially in regard to the construction of statutes. At the close of his long, diligent, and efficient service, the rules of practice had become well established, and the decisions of his court had been published to the profession and were recognized as of value and authority in this state and elsewhere." C. H. Bell, *The Bench and Bar of New Hampshire*, 1894, p. 72. Among the important cases Richardson took part in was the case of *Trustees of Dartmouth College* v. *Woodward*, 1 N. H. 111, in which he wrote the opinion of nearly thirty printed pages, holding that the charter of the college was not a contract and that the legislature might add new members without consulting the old corporation. This opinion was reversed by Marshall, but many lawyers have looked with approval upon Richardson's views. (His opinions appear in *1-9 N. H. Reports*.) It is interesting to note that Richardson "read the best Italian, French, and Spanish authors in the original tongue," had "a thorough knowledge of botany," and was interested in all the natural sciences and "kept up his knowledge of the classics" throughout his life. Bell, *op. cit.*, p. 75; see also J. A. Vinton, *The Richardson Memorial*, 1876; *Biog. Dir. Am. Cong.* (1928).

[42] Parker, who served as Royall Professor at Harvard between 1847 and 1868, was a jurist of great independence. Justice Oliver Wendell Holmes, a pupil of his, referred to him as "one of the greatest of American judges . . . who showed in the chair the same qualities that made him famous on the bench." *Speeches by Oliver Wendell Holmes, Jr.*, 1891, p. 35; G. S. Hale, "Joel Parker," *American Law Review*, Jan., 1876; Emory Washburn, memoir in *Proc. Mass. Hist. Soc.*, vol. XIV, 1876; and in *Albany Law Journal*, Aug. 28, 1875; C. H. Bell, *The Bench and Bar of New Hampshire*, 1894; Charles Warren, *History of the Harvard Law School*, vol. II, 1908; *The Centennial History of the Harvard Law School*, 1918; S. F. Batchelder, *Bits of Harvard History*, 1924.

[43] He held judicial office for nearly twenty years. Although his record as chancellor was good, his reputation rested mainly upon his work as chief justice. E. I. Keasbey, *Great American Lawyers*, vol. IV, 1908, ed. by W. D. Lewis; *N. J. State Bar Assn. Year Book*, 1904-05; *Proc. N. J. Hist. Soc.*, 2 ser., vol. IV, 1877.

[44] *Dict. of Am. Biog.*, vol. 20, p. 293; John Hooker, 29 *Connecticut Reports*, 611-614; "Memoranda," 18 *Conn.* 254; William's Judicial Opinions appear in 7-18 *Connecticut Reports*.

who was on the Supreme Court from 1834 to 1847, was identified with equally important legal developments.

In fact, able jurists were laboring earnestly and effectively throughout the whole of this period adapting old materials to new conditions. As they labored, the law which had been fluid and uncertain tended to crystallize, as the condition of maturity and stability which was to characterize the last quarter of the nineteenth century came upon it.[45] The task of examining the details of English decisions and pre-Revolutionary statutes with regards to their applicability to American conditions was still taking place, but it was just about finished. The problem as to whether the common law should be received as a common law for the whole land was about settled. The uncertainty which was inevitable in the creative or formative period had become unpopular and was being diminished by judicial effort, although creative activity continued during the nineteenth century period of maturity in the form of legislative activity.[46] But legislation "was resorted to chiefly to do away with accumulated anachronisms. Judicial creative work was confined to logical unfolding of established conceptions and choice between competing starting points for legal reasoning in the traditional legal materials."[47] In short, the American legal system was approaching maturity.

It is interesting to examine some of the forces which are involved in this movement toward maturity. The need of an expanding society for certainty and uniformity was of outstanding importance in this connection. It was supplemented by the demands of a people who feared power and hoped to protect themselves against its undue exercise through a system of rules which would limit governmental activity. These factors awakened a deep-seated interest in scientific law and its place in organized society as an infallible instrumentality of control and protection. In the view of some commentators, this interest was stimulated in part, at least, by ideas advanced to the effect that legal certainty could be secured by employing the methods of mathematics and that governmental powers could be held down by employing a system of mechanical

[45] By 1832, John Austin had published his *Province of Jurisprudence Determined*. This laid the foundation for the analytical jurisprudence which was to reign in the English speaking world for the rest of the century. This work very obviously formulates a science of law for matured or developed systems. "It postulated," says Dean Pound, "a separation of powers in which creative effort was left to the legislature. It postulated a complete and thereby completed body of logically interdependent authoritative grounds of judicial action, with perhaps some interstices to be filled by logical development of established premises, but in the main equal by the aid of an established technique to the solution of any problem with assurance in advance of a predetermined result. Soon its method was to be complementary to that of historical jurisprudence, the latter giving conceptions and the former providing the means of developing and applying them." "The Future of the Common Law," *American Law Review*, vol. 7, 1933, pp. 348-349.

[46] The legislative reform movement in both England and America, was in full tide at least fifty years.

[47] Pound, *op. cit.*, p. 349.

checks and balances, similar to the system discovered by the great Sir Isaac Newton which ordered the positions and movements of the solar system.

In the seventeenth century, it will be remembered, great advances were made in mathematical knowledge. This new knowledge had a tremendous effect on all the social sciences including the law. The methods of mathematics, it was said, would make legal certainty attainable. "It was believed," says John Dickinson, "that the one and only rule for every possible legal situation could be written off in advance by a proper combination of axiomatic first principles with the same accuracy as the answers to all the problems in the Euclidean geometry. Law ceased to be an instrument working for certainty; it became certainty."[48] In the eighteenth century, these ideas were further advanced in the writings of Montesquieu, Leibitz, Richard Cumberland, Samuel Clarke, John Fortescue-Aland, and David Hume.[49] The "force of laws and of particular forms of government is so great," writes David Hume, "and so little dependence have they on the humors and tempers of man, that consequences almost as general and certain may be deduced from them, as any which mathematics affords us."[50]

Encouraging the belief that law could be reduced to a perfect system of rules and precedents, this type of thinking was partially responsible for the widespread attempts at codification which took place during this period. In France, Napoleon's belief in legal logarithm tables undoubtedly led to the Civil Code.[51] In this country, it stimulated the threat of codification over a long period of time. While it is difficult to measure the exact effect of this mathematical influence on the increasing interest in scientific law during this period, it is certainly not negligible. In the opinion of some observers, the influence of Isaac Newton's scientific contributions upon the form of the American system of government and the place of law in that system is beyond question. As Woodrow Wilson saw it, the American system was predicated on "a theory of political dynamics which was basically Newtonian in its assumptions."[52] The builders of this system were apprehensive of unlimited power in any form. "Misers there be but not of power" was a favorite expression during the building period. Influenced by Hobbes and Harrington, an attempt was made to reduce arbitrary power to a minimum by establish-

[48] *Administrative Justice and Supremacy of Law in the United States*, p. 115.

[49] *Spirit of Laws*, Book I, ch. I; Dickinson, *op. cit.*, p. 116.

[50] David Hume, *Essays: Moral and Political*, 1742; Dickinson, *op. cit.*, p. 116; Robson, *Civilization and the Growth of Law*, pp. 315-316.

[51] Napoleon at one time believed that law could be reduced to single geometrical demonstrations, simply and easily pronounced upon. This early belief led to the Civil Code which bears his name. This code was completed in 1804.

[52] *Constitutional Government in the United States*, 1908, pp. 54-56.

ing a "government of laws and not of men."[53] With this thought in mind, faith was placed in "written constitutions" and "parchment barriers." The same influence led to the adoption of the "separation of powers" philosophy of Montesquieu and an involved system of "checks and balances." It is interesting to note that there were at least eight of these checks in the federal system if John Adams has estimated correctly,[54] and that their establishment is held by some observers to represent a direct application of the Newtonian interpretations of heavenly bodies to political institutions.[55]

"It is jealousy and not confidence," writes Thomas Jefferson, "which prescribed limited constitutions to bind down these whom we are obliged to trust with power," and it was in that spirit that we approached the establishment of our political and legal institutions. This spirit was reenforced on the American frontier where the greatest possible freedom of activity for the individual was demanded and a maximum of restraint quickly became irksome. Paradoxically, these very tendencies placed emphasis on a "regime of law" and stimulated the development of a system of detailed rules which rigidly bound the servants of the people.[56] In other words, our liberty-loving, restraint-hating forefathers devised rules not only for the purpose of providing for the needs of a developing society, but also to protect themselves against arbitrary power in their officials.[57] Unlike their ancestors of the colonial

[53] Corwin, *The Twilight of the Supreme Court*, 1934, p. 102; Haines, *The American Doctrine of Judicial Supremacy*, pp. 500-512.

[54] John Adams mentions: (1) the state and territories against the federal government; (2) the House against the Senate; (3) the Executive against the Legislative; (4) the Judiciary against the House, the Senate, the Executive, and the state governments; (5) the Senate against the President in respect to appointments and treaties; (6) the people against their representatives; (7) the state legislatures against the Senate; (8) the electors against the people. *Works of John Adams*, 1814, p. 467.

[55] The discovery of the solar system by Isaac Newton was one of the most important scientific events of the seventeenth century. It is thought by some students that the discovery had a strong influence on American government. Like the Whigs in England who sought to limit the arbitrary power of the King and balance the powers of the executive, legislative, and judicial branches, the founding fathers fell back upon a system of checks and balances for protection. Robson, *Civilization and the Growth of the Law*, 1935, pp. 316-317.

[56] "The theory of our system," says Justice Miller of the Supreme Court, "is opposed to the deposit of unlimited power anywhere. The executive, the legislative, and the judicial branches of these governments are all of limited and defined powers. . . . A government which held the lives, the liberty and the property of its citizens subject at all times to the absolute disposition and unlimited control of even the most democratic repository of power is, after all, but a despotism. It is true that it is a despotism of the many—of the majority, if you choose to call it so. But it is none the less a despotism." *Loan Association* v. *Topeka*, 1875, 20 *Wall.* 655.

[57] Throughout the period when our first state governments were being established, great emphasis was placed on the reign of law, to which public officials as well as ordinary citizens were to be subservient. The sovereignty of the people was to be secured through a reign of law. "It is the essence of a free republic," it is stated in the Massachusetts convention of 1780, "that the people be governed by fixed laws, of their own making."

period, they demanded rules which would provide for the future as well as decide the instant case. These requirements made the establishment of an effective judiciary a very important matter; for it involved a system of rules through case-law. In applying the principles of the common law, the courts applied a system which emphasized the individualism which the new country demanded.[58]

This same spirit of individualism and fear of restraint was made an effective barrier of opposition to the codification movement. "There have been, in times past," said Chief Justice Isaac Parker in his inaugural address as Royall Professor of Law delivered in Harvard Chapel, "attempts by great and enlightened minds to establish perfect and perpetual codes, which should relieve the labor of research and limit the necessity of legislation, but they have generally proved abortive; and it seems now to be received as a political axiom, that *complexity of laws is the price of freedom, and that despotism alone is equal to the task of establishing a simple and invariable standard for the regulation* of the infinitely varied concerns of man."[59]

Looking upon that "vast amalgamation of principles, axioms, and precedents," the common law, as the best defense of civil liberty and political rights, Chief Justice Parker urged its retention and warned against any attempts to substitute a completely codified system in its place.[60] "Let the legislature," he said, "from time to time, as they have

---

[58] "Seven factors of the first importance have contributed to shape our American Common Law. These are: (1) An original substratum of Germanic legal institutions and jural ideas; (2) the feudal law; (3) Puritanism; (4) the contests between the courts and crown in the seventeenth century; (5) eighteenth century political ideas; (6) the conditions of pioneer or agricultural communities in America in the first half of the nineteenth century; and (7) the philosophical ideas with respect to justice, law, and the state that prevailed in the formative period in which the common law was made for us by American courts. All but one of these made strongly for the individualism that made the classical common-law tradition so out of accord with popular feeling in the first decade of the present century." Pound, *The Spirit of the Common Law*, p. 15.

[59] *The North American Review*, vol. 3, May, 1816, p. 21.

[60] Justice Parker eulogized the common law as "the recorded wisdom of times which are past, drawn from every civilized country in ancient and modern times, and modified to the circumstances of our country, having the sanction of immemorial usage for its authority." "It is in truth," he continued, "common sense and sound reason, reduced to system and practice, the result of the researches and profound meditations of the wisest sages of every civilized nation. It is that body of rules, principles, and maxims, which are not to be found in any formal legislative act, but exist in the records of the courts, in the treasured opinions of wise and learned judges, in the writings and essays of reverend sages. It contains the fundamental principles of civil liberty, the rules by which property is acquired, transferred and transmitted, those by which our persons are secured from outrage, our reputations from reproach and our memories from dishonor. It provides punishments for the guilty, and protection for the innocent, prescribes limits to the judge, gives authority to the jury, and suggests principles to the legislature. It contains, in short, remedies for all wrongs, determines the competency of witnesses, settles the form and force of deeds and other instruments, the nature and true construction of contracts, and finally is the basis and security of all the objects, for which civil government was instituted, and is supported and preserved." *Ibid.*, pp. 22-23.

heretofore done, repeal such parts as change of circumstances may render inconvenient, or simplify those which may be obscure; but the venerable mass ought to stand forever, to provide for unseen emergencies, and even to correct defective legislation."[61] In short, Chief Justice Parker made the common law synonymous with freedom, and codification synonymous with restraint. This point of view was expressed frequently throughout this early period and undoubtedly gave strength to the triumphant march of the common law just as it retarded the movement toward codification.[62]

[61] *Ibid.*, p. 23.

[62] This point of view is found in a review in *The North American Review* of July, 1818, of Dudley A. Tyng's *Reports of the Cases Argued and Determined in the Supreme Judicial Court of the Commonwealth of Massachusetts for the year 1817,* which was published by Cummings and Hilliard in Boston in 1818. "About thirty years ago," writes the author of this review, "the Russian code of laws was reprinted in this country, in the compass of a common spelling book. Many visionary men, at that time, exclaimed with wonder at the comparatively massy bulk of our statutes, and seriously talked of simplifying our jurisprudence and reducing all of our laws into a narrow, elementary compound. Reformers sprang up, like locusts, in the time of Shays' Insurrection—and our statute book now bears witness to their folly. These crude notions had their day and disappeared. The lessons of a long experience were confirmed by more correct and enlarged views of the principles of civil liberty and our jurisprudence was suffered to remain without further attack, and to be gradually improved by the wisdom of enlightened and practical men. The discussions of the principles of government, which were called forth by our secession from Great Britain and the establishment of new constitutions, convinced all rational minds that there can be no security for property or liberty, where the laws are as short and few as in the Russian code. In a despotism, it is of little importance whether the preestablished edicts are few or many, or whether there are any at all. The reigning monarch cannot be controlled by them. If he refuses to adhere to them after they are promulgated, no earthly power can call him to account, or arrest the course of a new and different command. But where every action and word of a man's life when called in question are to be decided upon by fixed principles and rules—where nothing is left to caprice, or even to the conscience of the judge—it is manifest to the meanest capacity that no collection of legislative wisdom is competent to embody into a system the rules which are to govern the multifarious, the infinitely diversified affairs of men. And yet it is clear, that without a fixed rule of some sort, existing before the case to which it is applied, there can be no liberty and security. The judge must decide arbitrarily, or he must refuse cognizance because no remedy is provided. It would be of very little consequence to the suitor or to the public, which of these courses the judge might pursue. These suggestions justify, we think, our zealous attachment to the common law—our father's birthright and boast—our own glory and defence." *The North American Review,* vol. 7, July, 1818, pp. 184-185.

CHAPTER VIII

THE PROBLEM OF THE COURTS DURING THE FORMATIVE PERIOD OF AMERICAN LEGAL DEVELOPMENT

A problem which assumed a large importance in the beginnings of our legal system had to do with the organization of other courts. With independence a fact, the establishment of a judicial system became an important and difficult problem. In setting up the judiciary, English experience was again consulted, although the English court system of this period was far from a desirable model to follow.[1] In the eighteenth century, it was characterized by a multiplicity of courts. It had undergone little change since the days of Edward III, and it was to undergo little further change until 1873 when it was reorganized to fit the needs of an industrial age. While it was too involved to be followed in detail in this country, it nevertheless served as a model for our system. Conditions prevailing in the rude, frontier society of the new world determined its application. When our first court systems were established in the late eighteenth century, travel was difficult and communication was slow. To set up a centralized system under these conditions would have entailed intolerable hardships to litigants. The primary task was to establish a system which would bring justice to every man's door.

The manner in which this task was accomplished may be seen from an examination of the system set up in Ohio shortly after the turn of the century.[2] The first constitution of Ohio was drawn up in 1802. By its terms, a Supreme Court was established which was required to hold a term once a year in each county. This requirement kept the judges on horseback half the year and compelled them to give opinions in frontier towns where no law books were available. Judge Moses Granger writes:

Every lawyer-judge traveled many hundreds of miles each year upon a circuit in which the best roads were very poor, and most of them almost

[1] "Independence necessarily brought about a reconstitution of the judicial system of every state, and at the close of the Revolution, Georgia was the only one which was found without a supreme tribunal of last resort. (Hildreth, *History of the United States*, 373.) In some, as, for example, New York and New Jersey, the ancient system was preserved of making it half a judicial and half a political body, in most, it was now made strictly judicial in its composition and its function." *Two Centuries Growth of American Law, 1701-1901*, p. 22.

[2] F. R. Aumann, "The Development of the Judicial System of Ohio," *Jour. Ohio Arch. and Hist. Society*, April, 1932, p. 202.

impassable on wheels. The president-judge of the third (then the Eastern) Circuit, began at Warren, Trumbull County, on the second Tuesday in March, and ended at Zanesville, Muskingum County, as soon after the fourth Tuesday in December as the docket there would permit, but next before going to Zanesville, he had to sit at Marietta. If you look at the map you can trace him from Warren in Trumbull via New Lisbon in Columbiana, Steubenville in Jefferson, St. Clairsville in Belmont, and Marietta in Washington to Zanesville in Muskingum. Although the Ohio river bounded four of his counties, and a passage by boat was sometimes had, the navigation was too irregular to be relied on. The president-judge in the First and Second Circuits rode about equal distances. . . . Members of the county bar traveled with, or met, the judges and lodged with or near them during term. The saddle-bags carried Ohio Statutes, then small in bulk, Blackstone's *Commentaries*, sometimes Coke on Littleton, sometimes a volume or two of an English law or equity report, and a small "vade mecum" legal treatise the name of which is now known to few of our profession.

The court of general jurisdiction was the Court of Common Pleas. For the purposes of this court the state was divided into three Common Pleas circuits. In each circuit there was a president of the court and in each county there were two or three associate judges. Three terms of this court were held annually in each county.[3] This system, which was adopted from Pennsylvania and used from April, 1803, to February, 1852, carried with it remnants of lay administration. The president-judge of Common Pleas in each county was usually a lawyer, but the associate justices were frequently laymen. In addition to the Common Pleas Court, the Constitution provided for a number of justices of the peace in the townships of the state. In this fashion, justice was brought to every man's door in frontier Ohio.

The systems of other states were established along similar lines. The formula employed contemplated a number of local courts of general jurisdiction, and our policy has been one of multiplication of courts ever since.[4] If one word were used to characterize the judicial systems set up at the time, that word would be "decentralized."[5] These systems, with the exception of some important changes in the method of selection and in the tenure of judges, have continued down to the present day

[3] See Randall and Ryan, *History of Ohio*, vol. 5, pp. 114-115.

[4] " . . . A general outline might be perceived which was the model of American judicial systems. To begin at the bottom this was: (1) local peace magistrates and local inferior courts for petty causes, (2) a central court of general jurisdiction at law and over crimes, with provision for local trial of causes at circuit and review of civil trials in bank in the central court, (3) a central court of equity in which causes were heard in one place, though testimony was taken in the locality, (4) a separate court with probate jurisdiction, and (5) a supreme court of review. In the United States all but five or six jurisdictions merged the second and third." Pound, *The Spirit of the Common Law*, 1921, p. 121, "Organization of Courts," Bulletin VI, *Publications of the American Judicature Society*, pp. 11-12.

[5] Pound, *op. cit.*, p. 121.

with very little modification.[6] While the details of the judicial organization adopted in the several states present the greatest variety, they involved for the most part: (1) a series of local peace magistrates and local inferior courts for petty cases, (2) a series of courts with general jurisdiction in law and in equity over crimes, (3) a series of courts with jurisdiction in probate matter, and (4) a supreme court of review.

The court system of Georgia, which did not follow this plan, is of interest. Georgia for a long time remained the only state in the American Union which did not have a Supreme Court. There were several reasons for this state of affairs. For one thing, she feared the power of judges who might be beyond the reach of the people, and the decision of the United States Supreme Court against Georgians in *Chisholm* v. *Georgia* made her apprehensive of her own courts as well. Then, too, it has been said that the lawyers were not in favor of a Supreme Court since they undoubtedly "found it easier to win their cases where no printed decisions of the past could be brought up to refute them." In consequence, a system was maintained wherein the verdict of the superior court was final in each county "and under whatever circumstances errors might be corrected, the local judicial autonomy of the county was preserved."

To establish uniformity in the application of state law, the superior court judges adopted the custom of holding a yearly conference, at which they discussed difficult points of law and constitutional questions. In one such conference of judges to make uniform various points of law, Judge John M. Berrien and three associates declared certain laws of the legislature unconstitutional. The state legislature immediately reprimanded them for this action, hopeful that this mild rebuke would prevent a more harsh procedure in the future. These events took place in 1815, and it was not until 1835 that the necessity of a state Supreme Court was officially recognized. In that year the constitution was amended to set up a Supreme Court, but it was not until ten years later that the legislature passed the legislation necessary to put it into operation, so jealous was it of its own prerogatives. In 1848, the court was finally put into operation, with Joseph H. Lumpkin,[7] Eugenius A. Nisbet,[8] and Hiram

---

[6] J. M. Matthews, *American State Government,* 1924, pp. 431-438.

[7] Joseph Henry Lumpkin, 1799-1867, the first chief justice of Georgia, had studied law under Thomas W. Cobb. He presided over the court for more than a score of years and died in office. To him the scientific application of legal principles meant less than deciding a case on its merits. This attitude was almost necessary in a state which had gone for more than seventy years without a final court of review. The first supreme court under Lumpkin attempted to pronounce judgments the inherent justice of which would be apparent. They also attempted to harmonize and make uniform the administration of law throughout the state. Lumpkin's strong conviction against permitting technical rule of practice to defeat justice made him an ideal chief justice during the beginning years. Despite his attitude toward technicalities, many of his decisions became widely accepted precedents. This is a remarkable fact when it is recalled that many of his more than

Warner[9] as judges.[10] These pioneer jurists of Georgia quickly established the court on a firm basis.[11] Indeed, they won the confidence of the state so thoroughly that in 1858 the legislature declared that a decision of the court should have the same effect as if it were a law of the state.[12]

In addition to the state courts, a separate system of federal courts was also established. In creating this dual system, a course was pursued which is quite different from that followed by other countries employing a federal system.[13] The Dominion of Canada is organized on a federal

---

two thousand opinions in volumes 1-35, Georgia reports, were reduced to writing after having been given orally. Shortly after becoming chief justice, a School of Law was added to the University of Georgia, and Lumpkin lectured there until the outbreak of the Civil War. See J. R. Lamar, "History of the Establishment of the Supreme Court of Georgia," *Report of the Twenty-fourth Annual Session of the Georgia Bar Association,* 1907; W. J. Northern, *Men of Mark in Georgia,* vol. II, 1910; memorial in 36 *Georgia Reports,* pp. 1-42.

[8] Nisbet, who served between 1845 and 1853, was a student of the Litchfield School in Connecticut for a short time. During the difficult beginning years of Georgia's Supreme Court, he contributed all the force of his vigorous mind, writing a number of opinions which were notable. J. R. Lamar, "Eugenius Aristides Nisbet, 1803-1871," *Great American Lawyers* (W. D. Lewis, ed.), vol. IV, 1908; George White, *Historical Collections of Georgia,* 1854; I. W. Avery, *The History of the State of Georgia,* 1881; L. L. Knight, *Georgia's Landmarks,* 2 vols., 1913-1914.

[9] Hiram Warner (1802-1881) served on the Supreme Court of Georgia during its beginning years, resigning in 1853 to return to general practice. After the Civil War he served as a circuit judge until 1867 when he was appointed chief justice of the Supreme Court. In 1868 he was reduced to an associate justiceship when the Supreme Court was reorganized. In 1872 he again became chief justice and served as such until he resigned in 1880. He was widely read in the law and, like Lumpkin, was characterized by abundant common sense. George White, *Historical Collections of Georgia,* 1854; L. L. Knight, *Georgia's Landmarks,* vol. II, 1908; W. J. Northen, *Men of Mark in Georgia,* vol. III, 1911; memorial in 68 *Georgia Reports,* 845-855.

[10] For discussion of Georgia's experience without a Supreme Court see remarks by Justice Joseph R. Lamar in the *American Bar Association Journal,* vol. X, 1924, p. 513. See also Stephen Miller, *The Bench and Bar of Georgia,* vol. I, 1858, pp. 73-74.

[11] "When in 1845 the Court was actually organized, the task of bringing order out of confusion without unduly disturbing titles and affecting rights, and of bringing her jurisprudence into harmony with that of the other American states, was a new and delicate problem extremely difficult of solution. The task would indeed have been impossible had it not fallen to men of extraordinary ability. Lumpkin, Warner, and Nisbet, the first justices, were extremely capable men. Elsewhere the ablest judges have entered into the labor of others and have continued the development of a system which they found already existent and where, often, they had to follow what they felt was unsound. But the first justices of the Georgia Supreme Court found conditions plastic, with an opportunity for wise service." J. R. Lamar, "Life of Eugenius Aristides Nisbet (1803-1871)," in *Great American Lawyers* (W. D. Lewis, ed.), vol. IV, 1908.

[12] E. M. Coulter, *A Short History of Georgia,* pp. 277-278, 164-165.

[13] "The dual judicature of the United States is unique in the world. . . . In the increased cost of justice and in the grave loss of judicial efficiency that flows from the conflict of jurisdictions the nation pays keenly for retaining in the twentieth century an institution based on the petty jealousies of the eighteenth." Herbert A. Smith, *Federalism in North America: A Comparative Study of Institutions in the United States and Canada,* 1923, pp. 125-126.

basis,[14] as is the Commonwealth of Australia.[15] Neither country, how-ever, has adopted the dual judicature which characterizes the American system. In our system, the federal courts were provided with jurisdiction over parties and controversies in a limited and prescribed field, while the jurisdiction of the state courts was broadly inclusive.[16] Although federal jurisdiction has increased greatly in recent years,[17] the great bulk of every-day judicial activity remains with the states.[18] Varying in the nature and scope of jurisdiction, the two systems of courts were organized on a somewhat different basis as well. While federal judges are appointed, most state judges are elected by the people. While life tenure features the federal system, most of our state judges serve for a term of years.

Upon this bifurcated judicial system with its division of authority and multiplicity of courts fell the difficult task of developing an adequate law for the rapidly growing American society. Assuming this task with little preparation but with willing spirit, the courts which were set up devoted their chief energies during the rest of the century to the development of our case law. The burdens imposed upon them during this period were not light as a complex society developed which demanded more and more law. In undertaking these responsibilities they performed a very useful function for the young democratic society which was attempting to live under a rule of law.[19] As the nineteenth century ad-

[14] In the Dominion of Canada courts established in the separate provinces are the sole agencies employed to administer both the laws of the Dominion (exclusive of those dealing with patents and revenue) and the provincial laws, subject to review by a Dominion Supreme Court which is independent of the several provinces. Kennedy, *The Constitution of Canada*, 1922, pp. 393-395.

[15] In the Commonwealth of Australia the judicial power of the Commonwealth is vested in the High Court and in such other courts as it may invest with federal jurisdiction. In accordance with this provision (Const. Chap. III) the several courts of the states are vested with federal jurisdiction. The result is that all judicial power is placed in one system of state courts subject to final review by the High Court of the Commonwealth. Kennedy, *Law of the Australian Commonwealth*, 1925, p. 237, 254, 282.

[16] W. F. Willoughby, *Principles of Judicial Administration*, 1929, pp. 247-253.

[17] See Frankfurter and Landis, *The Business of the Supreme Court*, 1927. Walter F. Dodd points out that the United States Supreme Court disposed of more cases at its 1926 term than in the whole of the first thirty years of its history. *State Government*, 1928, p. 303.

[18] State courts are the most important legal agencies in the life of the citizen. They administer the laws of the state, which includes both law and equity, both civil and criminal law, both common and statute law.

[19] Some idea of the difficulties surrounding the tasks of our first courts may be obtained by viewing the operations of one court during its beginning years, or by observing the activities of one judge. The career of Jeremiah Smith (1759-1842), chief justice of New Hampshire and father of Jeremiah Smith (1837-1921), jurist and law teacher, is of interest in this connection. "In the spring of 1786, Mr. Smith was admitted to the bar in Amherst, New Hampshire. . . . The practice of the New Hampshire courts at this time was loose and irregular, for the judges often had not belonged to the profession, and would trust to their own vague notions of common equity, instead of bending down the case by the rigid principles of the law. In spite of the common prejudice on this score,

vanced, they moved far away from the simpler forms of justice of post-Revolutionary days and developed a complex system of justice according to law, judicially administered. Moreover, the system to which they gave form and shape, and which they gradually expanded, as the century advanced, was the common law system which goes back through Blackstone to Coke and Fortescue.[20]

Another exceedingly important development of the period between 1775 and 1860 was the gradual readjustment which took place between the legislative and judicial branches. When our system began, the idea of the separation of powers was looked upon as a basic principle.[21] This theory, as enumerated by Montesquieu, assumed three departments of government; the division of governmental powers among three departments in such a manner that each department would act as a check upon the other and the existence of certain functions that were particularly "legislative," "executive," and "judicial."[22] While this theory lies at the basis of our political organization, it has never been completely operative.[23] At any rate, our first state governments were largely

it may safely be said that no conduct is so short-sighted as this, or so likely to defeat the great ends of justice. When the rules, established, limited, and perfected by the experience of centuries are once shut out, passion, caprice, or accident will rule, and uncertainty, the mother of litigation, is sure to propagate and extend the evil. Mr. Smith saw the faults in the administration of justice in his native state at an early period and labored most zealously to correct them." See Review of *The Life of the Hon. Jeremiah Smith, LL.D., Member of Congress during Washington's Administration, Judge of the United States Circuit Court, Chief Justice of New Hampshire*, etc., by John H. Morison, in *The North American Review*, vol. 61, July, 1845, pp. 116-117. Becoming chief justice of New Hampshire in 1802, he rode the circuit for the next few years and worked indefatigably to raise the standards of New Hampshire justice. In Jeremiah Mason's opinion he succeeded in remedying the "most intolerable evil of a bad administration of justice" resulting from vague and uncertain judicial decisions, by "establishing and enforcing a more orderly practice, and by strenuous endeavors to conform all judicial decisions to known rules and principles of law." (Morison, *op. cit.*, p. 210). In the opinion of one able commentator, "he did more perhaps for the improvement of the jurisprudence of the State than any other man." C. H. Bell, *The Bench and Bar of New Hampshire*, 1894, p. 61; Albert Smith, *History of the Town of Exeter, N. H.*, 1876. Jeremiah Smith, Jr., *Decisions of the Superior and Supreme Courts of New Hampshire from 1802 to 1809 and from 1813 to 1816 . . . with Extracts from Judge Smith's Manuscript Treatise on Probate Law*, 1879.

[20] Pound, *The Spirit of the Common Law*, p. 118.

[21] Frank A. Goodnow, *Comparative Administrative Law*, pp. 25-30; R. Pound, *Introduction to the Philosophy of Law*, p. 105.

[22] Frederick Green, "Separation of Powers," *Yale Law Journal*, vol. XIX, p. 371.

[23] "If we look into the constitutions of the several states," writes James Madison, "we find that, notwithstanding the emphatical and in some instances the unqualified terms in which this axiom has been laid down, there is not a single instance in which the several departments of power have been kept absolutely separate and distinct. . . . It is but too obvious that in some instances the fundamental principles under consideration have been violated by too great a mixture, and even an actual consolidation of the different powers, and that in no instance has a competent provision been made for maintaining in practice the separation delineated on paper. . . . " *Federalist*, XLVII.

characterized by legislative supremacy.[24] In that early period, the popular will was considered omnipotent and the legislature was looked upon as the chief organ of the popular will. Constitutional theories could not cope with the legislature which, in the words of James Madison, drew "all powers into its voracious vortex."[25] On the other hand, the philosophy of the day demanded checks and limitations upon governmental power. The courts, as time passed, became the custodians of these limitations, which at the outset were confined to our legislative bodies.

The doctrines of legislative sovereignty which obtained when our first state constitutions were established were influenced in part by Blackstone. In the view of Blackstone, virtually all the powers of government should be placed at the disposal of the legislature. Moreover, all categories of "law" except positive law were to be ignored and the only real law was that which had the express or implied sanction of the sovereign legislative power. This theory reduced concepts of "higher law" and "law of nature" to a very meager role. This conception of law gave little basis for judicial interference with legislative acts.[26] When legislatures came to exercise their powers, not wisely but too well, a different view upon some of these matters developed. Commenting upon this development Roscoe Pound says:

> Legislative oppression of those politically opposed to the majority in control of the law-making machinery was rife after the Revolution and led to constitutional prohibition of bills of attainder, bills of pains and penalties, and ex post facto laws. Legislative attempts to relieve economic depression after the Revolution at the expense of creditors led to constitutional prohibition of state laws impairing the obligation of contracts. But the legislatures claimed to be the judges of the scope of these limitations and contests between courts and legislative assemblies over legislative high-handedness begin at the outset of our policy. Legislative disregard of the Jay Treaty, legislative disregard of the guarantees of the constitution by directing summary connections in order to force a depreciated currency into use, mark the beginning of our constitutional law.[27]

It was not until after the Civil War, however, that the doctrine of the legislatively declared will of the people gave way before the doctrine of the supremacy of the law judicially interpreted.[28] In the meantime, the legislative and judicial branches engaged in a struggle for power.[29]

[24] Holcombe, *State Government*, 1926, pp. 62, 63.

[25] *Federalist*, XLVIII.

[26] *Commentaries*, 91.

[27] Pound, *Criminal Justice in America*, pp. 132-134.

[28] "The doctrine of the supremacy of the law which was evolved to check the usurpations of a king ruling by paramount title," writes John Dickinson, "has thus been turned into an instrument to control the action of popularly chosen officials and legislators by the supposedly fixed and absolute standards of an abstract law." *Administrative Justice and the Supremacy of the Law in the United States*, pp. 98-99.

[29] A. N. Holcombe, *State Government*, 1926, pp. 109-143.

This contest largely revolved around the establishment and general acceptance of the doctrine of judicial review of legislation.[30] A growing dissatisfaction with legislative performance hastened this shift of power. The legislatures were held responsible for debts and deficits incurred in the thirties and forties, which the people insisted upon at the time. In Ohio, for example, a vast system of public improvements was carried on during the thirties and forties. The state subscribed for stock in railroads, turnpikes, plank roads, and private canals. The canals of the state cost over fifteen millions of dollars. While this far-flung system quickened the development of the state, it brought with it a burden of debt. The state owed nearly twenty millions of dollars, the interest of which, almost a million a year, was paid to foreign bond-holders and foreign creditors. The legislatures were blamed for many other policies as well. As legislative prestige declined, judicial power expanded rapidly. In the post– Civil War period, a new era began in which the courts become increasingly powerful.[31] This was an important development and "since the ruling principle of Anglo-Saxon jurisprudence is the supremacy of the law as made, interpreted, and applied by courts of justice," it was not an altogether unexpected one.[32]

During the year immediately following independence, however, the possibilities of such a development seemed quite remote as the courts labored against great odds to establish themselves. A brief examination of our original state governments will indicate the weak position held by the judiciary during this early period.[33] In Vermont, the courts

[30] "The control of courts over legislation, combined with the notion of law as an embodiment of Anglo-American jurisprudence constitutes the basis of the American doctrine of judicial supremacy." Haines, *The American Doctrine of Judicial Supremacy*, pp. 24-25.

[31] "The distinguishing characteristic of the American system of government is the extraordinary power and position of the judiciary. The people, it is maintained, established in the constitution written limitations upon the legislature; these limitations and the constitutions are superior to any legislative act; it is the function of the judiciary to say what the law is, and if legislative acts are to be found in conflict with the constitution, to declare such laws invalid. Thus the judiciary, a coordinate branch of the government, becomes the particular guardian of the terms of the written constitution. The legislative and executive departments are held within the bounds of authority as understood and interpreted by the judicial power and there is a well marked distinction between constitutional laws and ordinary statutes. Not only does the written constitution require an extraordinary power for its amendment, but there also has developed an elaborate series of precedents and judicial determinations which with the sanction of the highest court have the force and effect of the original provisions of the constitution. . . . The judiciary has the sole right to place an authoritative interpretation upon the fundamental written law.

"The practice of all department of government to defer to the courts and abide by their decisions when in a suit between private parties and the majority of justices hold that in their opinion a statute or executive order is unconstitutional and therefore null and void, is the most significant feature of constitutional law in the United States." Haines, *ibid.*, p. 23.

[32] Haines, *op. cit.*, p. 27.

[33] The governments of the original states, says Arthur Holcombe, were for the most part "governments characterized by the supremacy of the legislature, and if judicial inter-

were completely subordinated to the legislative body which made rules, granted new trials, and vacated and annulled judgments.[34] Apparently no one supposed that "an act of the legislature, however repugnant to the constitution, could be adjudged void and set aside by the judiciary which was considered by all a subordinate department of the government."[35] The courts asserted that any attempt upon their part to review the constitutionality of a legislative enactment would be an assumption of "arbitrary power not warranted by law."[36] In Rhode Island and Connecticut, little opportunity was given to the courts to interfere with state laws.[37] In New York, the courts accepted the Council of Revision's construction of the constitution, or in the last instance the Court of Errors, a court in which the judicial element was in the minority. In ten states the courts had the same right as the other departments to construe the constitution, with the advantage that they considered the question after the other departments had acted.[38] In Pennsylvania, the Council of Censors determined whether or not the constitution had been preserved inviolate in every part, and whether or not the executive and legislative branches had exercised other or greater powers than had been granted by the constitution.[39] The Vermont system worked to better advantage than the Pennsylvania system apparently.[40] In both states, the system probably delayed the development of judicial review.[41]

The experience of the people with these early judicial bodies was not at all a happy one. The Council of Revision in New York was criticized as a body which had become the guardian of old Federalist principles. While Chancellor Kent, Chief Justice Ambrose Spencer, Jonas Platt, and William W. Van Ness constituted a majority in that

---

ference with legislative acts was sometimes tolerated, the operation of the governmental system was not altered thereby." *State Government*, 1926, pp. 62-63.

[34] A critical review of the administration of justice in Vermont during this early period is found in *The North American Review*, vol. XVII, October, 1823, p. 376. The great defect in Vermont justice, it was alleged, was due to "the want of a provision for a permanent and independent judiciary. "To this," it is said, "they owe the instability in the administration of justice, which they have sometimes experienced; if indeed we must call by that name those strange decisions of causes, in which neither law nor justice seems to have been regarded or understood. . . . " *Ibid.*, p. 376.

[35] Chipman, *Memoirs of Thomas Chittenden*, p. 112.

[36] *Paine v. Ely*, Chipman's Reports, vol. 1, p. 37.

[37] Chipman, *Sketches of the Principles of State Government*, 1793, pp. 119-127.

[38] A. N. Holcombe, *State Government*, 1926, pp. 58, 59, 66, 77-80.

[39] The Pennsylvania Council lasted from 1776 to 1790, while the Vermont Council existed from 1777 to 1870.

[40] Allen Nevins, *The American States During and After the Revolution, 1775-1789,* 1924; L. H. Meader, "The Council of Censors," *Papers from Historical Seminary of Brown University,* 1895; A. N. Holcombe, *State Government*, 1926, p. 58; W. F. Dodd, *State Government*, 1928, pp. 115-116.

[41] W. F. Dodd, *Revision and Amendment of State Constitutions,* 1910, pp. 34-42; W. C. Mooney, "The Genesis of a Written Constitution," *Annals of the American Academy of Political and Social Science,* April, 1871; "The First State Constitution," *ibid.,* September, 1893.

body and "could veto any law, democracy might well complain," as a glance at the record will demonstrate. In 1809, the Council disallowed a bill for setting off new districts in the state; in 1812 the Council refused permission for the enlargement of the Supreme Court by a Democratic Council of Appointment. It checked the "War Hawks" in their measures for conscription and the treatment of deserters, and favored the interests of the old Federalists in many other ways, particularly in opposing the Constitutional Convention which met in 1821.[42] This opposition was actuated by a sense of self-preservation since in that convention it was urged that the "people's adversaries" be shorn of their power by eliminating the Council of Revision. "The judiciary," it was said, "must be separated from the other branches to supply the check demanded by the perfect scheme of Montesquieu." It was also said that "the old council had acted *ultra vires* when they vetoed laws as inexpedient," that they should have passed on constitutionality alone. But the chief criticisms were based on their Federalism and their arrogant attempts "to stay the march of progress." Their "opposition to the will of the majority was hopeless," remarks Dixon Ryan Fox, "and the council was abolished without a dissenting vote, though not without protest."[43]

In a number of states the system of appellate jurisdiction subordinated the courts to the legislature.[44] In colonial days appellate jurisdiction was exercised by king and council. When the first state constitutions were established, courts of last resort were set up to accomplish this function in most states. In some states, however, appellate jurisdiction was vested in the governor or legislature. This feature which disregarded the views of Montesquieu,[45] Hamilton,[46] and others was a sur-

---

[42] Dixon Ryan Fox, "New York Becomes a Democracy," *History of the State of New York*, vol. II, 1934, p. 15.

[43] *Ibid.*, pp. 19-20.

[44] "The transition to the form of government of a republican state from the colonial form in our country, in which the legislature was the General Court and its members the Supreme Judiciary, was marked by many anomalies. Some of these were in consequence of the inability of the members of the legislature to divest themselves of the idea that the judicial system established by the new constitution was of such a nature that it could not stand alone as an independent department of government.

"Even up to the present time there are, in the country at large, frequent appeals to the legislature by one or another party in a litigation, demanding that a court be restrained, or ordering certain action out of the usual course, or petitions making vengeful charges against justices. Persons of a cast of mind apprehending imperfectly the principles of justice, and having but a meager conception of the political measures necessary to public safety and thrift, are greatly given to plans of having the courts so reconstructed that they will sustain the action of this class, however narrow and partial it may be.

" . . . When the legislature could not be induced to interfere with the courts, violent action was taken against them directly, as in Shays' Rebellion in Massachusetts, the Whiskey Insurrection in Pennsylvania, and the anti-rent disorders in Eastern New York." *The Green Bag*, vol. 12, October, 1900, p. 497.

[45] "There is no liberty if the power of judging is not separated from the executive

vival of the colonial practice of vesting judicial functions in legislative and executive bodies.[47] It was exercised in New York until 1846[48] and in Rhode Island until 1857.[49] In that year legislative appellate jurisdiction ends in this country. It was a practice which directly contravened the separation of powers idea,[50] no matter how broadly that doctrine be construed.[51] In a few states the legislature could award a new trial after judgment. This practice did not become general but there are at least four instances of such legislative action in New Hampshire between 1791

---

power. If it were joined to the legislative power, the power over the life and liberty of the citizens would be arbitrary, for the judge would be legislator. If it were joined to the executive power, the judge might have the force of an oppressor." *Spirit of the Law*, Book XI, ch. 6.

[46] "Liberty can have nothing to fear from the judiciary alone but would have everything to fear from the union with either of the other departments." *The Federalist*, LXXVIII.

[47] Matthews, *American State Government*, 1924, p. 430; see also Raper, *North Carolina: A Study in English Colonial Government*, 1904, pp. 148-168; E. P. Tanner, "The Province of New Jersey," *Columbia Studies in History and Politics*, vol. XXX, 1908, p. 460.

[48] Browne, "The New York Court of Appeals," *The Green Bag*, vol. 2, pp. 277, 278.

[49] Eaton, "The Development of the Judicial System of Rhode Island," *Yale Law Journal*, vol. 14, pp. 148, 153.

[50] The following extract from the "Essex Result" of 1778 is of interest in this connection: "Should the executive and judicial power be united, the subject would have no permanent security of his person and property. The executive power would interpret the laws and bend them to his will, and as he is the judge, he may leap over them by artful constructions, and gratify, with impunity, the most rapacious passions. Perhaps no cause in any state has contributed more to promote internal convulsions and to stain the scaffold with its best blood than this unhappy union. And it is a union which the executive power in all the states had attempted to form; if that could not be compassed, to make the judicial power dependent upon it." Theophilus Parsons, *Memoirs of Theophilus Parsons*, Boston, 1859, p. 374.

[51] John Dickinson points out that our ancestors particularly opposed "executive courts." They feared that 'the great political officers of government, i.e., the king and his ministers, or under a republican form of government, the chief executive, might come to control the machinery of justice rather than any theoretical objection to the union of administrative and judicial functions in the hands of minor officials. As a matter of fact, at least the more southern colonies borrowed the English system of local administration which embodied a wide construction of executive and judicial duties in the hands of justices of the peace and county courts. Thus in Maryland the county courts levied taxes (Acts of 1704) (*Archives of Maryland*, XXVI, 292), fixed the boundaries of parishes (Acts of 1713, *ibid.*, XXIX, 338), and appointed road supervisors (Acts of 1704, *ibid.*, XVI, 250) and other administrative officials. In Virginia they supervised the schools, levied taxes, voted expenditures, and appointed the sheriffs. (Phillip ·Alexander Bruce, *Institutional History of Virginia*, 1, 337, 11, 558.) In New York they had similar duties. (G. E. Howard, *Introduction to Local Constitutional History*, p. 363.) Thomas Jefferson wrote in 1816 of the Virginia county courts: 'I acknowledge the value of this institution, it is in truth our principal executive and judiciary.' (Washington, VII, 18.) In Kentucky and Tennessee the county courts still combine judicial and administrative functions. (Beard, *American Government and Politics*, 1925, p. 770; Fairlie, *Local Government in Counties, Towns, and Villages*, p. 98.) On the other hand, the kind of combination of judicial and executive functions to which our fathers objected is illustrated by the case of Magdalen College, *State Trials*, XII, 1-114." *Administrative Justice and the Supremacy of Law in the United States*, pp. 33-34.

and 1817.[52] The New Hampshire practice was given wide attention in 1792 and 1793, when the so-called "pig acts" produced a crisis which ended in laughter and brought Jeremiah Mason, one of the greatest of early New England lawyers, to the forefront.[53]

This case which involved the taking of two young pigs brought legislative intervention in litigation into widespread disrepute.[54] The legislature in this case, without notice to either party, had passed an act directing the original magistrate to cite the plaintiff before him, set aside the default and try the action. Both parties were to have an appeal under this set of circumstances. By taking this action the legislature, in one view, became guilty of inciting useless litigation and of debasing the judiciary. Mason appeared for the plaintiff, denying the power of the legislature to pass the act, and making an argument on the constitutional restraints of legislative power. The opposing counsel answered by an attack on the audacity of the attempt of an inferior magistrate to question the power of the legislature.

The justice of the peace, who had served in the Revolutionary Army, was desirous of sustaining his high reputation for courage and of protecting his official dignity, as well. In consequence he promptly pronounced the act utterly void, and refused to obey it. The claim for an appeal was also disallowed by the justice, who said that as the whole proceeding was void he had no rightful power to record a judgment, nor to grant an appeal. At the next session of the legislature another act was passed, directing the court of Common Pleas to try the defaulted action. The parties met in this court and after argument the court determined to have nothing to do with the matter. Mason's argument had prevailed.[55]

[52] *Merril* v. *Sherburne*, (1818), 1 *N. H.*, 198, 216; Plumer, *Life of William Plumer*, p. 170.

[53] Born in Connecticut in 1768, Mason was admitted to the bar in Vermont in 1791. Leaving Vermont in the same year he was admitted to the bar in New Hampshire where he practiced until 1832, when he moved to Boston, Massachusetts. In New Hampshire he was associated with Jeremiah Smith, Ichabod Bartlett, George Sullivan, Richard Fletcher, and Daniel Webster. Long before he moved to Boston he was recognized as the ablest lawyer in New England. In Boston his career came to a climax and commanded an unparalleled professional prestige. "If you asked me who is the greatest lawyer I have known," Daniel Webster once remarked, "I should say Chief Justice Marshall, but if you took me by the throat and pushed me to the wall, I should say Jeremiah Mason." Elaborating on this point on another occasion, he said: "If there be in the country a stronger intellect, if there be a vision that sees quicker, or goes deeper into whatever is intricate or whatsoever is profound—I must confess I have not known it." *The Green Bag*, vol. I, 1889, p. 462.

[54] *The Green Bag*, vol. 12, 1900, pp. 499-500.

[55] Mr. Mason's arguments prevailed with regularity in the cases in which he took part. "Mr. Mason," says Mr. George Hillard, "was a great lawyer, perhaps the greatest lawyer that ever practiced at the bar in New England. But when we call a man a great lawyer, we use language which has a certain degree of vagueness. Chief Justice Parsons, Judge Story, Mr. Webster, Chief Justice Shaw, Mr. Choate were all great lawyers, but not two of them were alike. Each had powers and faculties peculiar to himself. . . .

"Mr. Mason's superiority as a lawyer may be thus stated: that of all the men who

By this time the "pig action" and the "pig acts" had become the center of widespread attention in the state. It succeeded in bringing all such special acts of the legislature which interfered with the regular course of procedure of the courts of law into great ridicule and contempt. The result was that the practice was fairly laughed out of existence in New Hampshire.[56]

The foregoing incident represents one of the many interesting modifications of the colonial practice which vested judicial functions in the legislature. A somewhat different modification of colonial practice took place in New Jersey in 1844 when the offices of governor and chancellor were finally separated. Prior to 1844 the governors of New Jersey handled equity and "prerogative" cases as "chancellor and ordinary" although it is true that many of them slighted the work in equity to a very considerable extent. In 1817, however, one Isaac Halsted Williamson (1767-1844)[57] was elected to the governorship by the legislature. He continued to be reelected annually without opposition until 1829. During his twelve-year tenure he did much to strengthen the badly neglected office of chancellor.[58] In 1799 the legislature had authorized the chancellor to make, alter, and amend rules of practice "so as to obviate doubts, advance justice, and expedite suits in that court."[59] Williamson was the first governor to attempt to do anything about this legislative grant of power. In 1822, after an exhaustive study of the English court of chancery, he drew up a set of fifty-eight rules which continued in effect over a long period of time. His efforts were particularly effective in its clarification of the situation of mortgages. Presiding over the chancery court for twelve years with great ability and enthusiasm, Williamson increased the dignity and effectiveness of that court tremendously. Indeed it is not too much to say that he laid the foundation for the unique position which the court of chancery still holds in New Jersey. It is thought that Williamson's work was also responsible in part for the separation of the offices of governor and chan-

---

ever practiced law in New England, he was the most fully equipped with all the weapons of attack and defence needed in the trial of causes. It is but putting the thing in another form to say that, of all men who have ever been at the bar in New England, he was the most formidable opponent. And, of all lawyers, he was the most successful, that is, no other man has ever tried so many cases and lost so few, in proportion to the whole number." *The Green Bag*, vol. 1, 1889, p. 462.

[56] *The Green Bag*, vol. 12, 1900, pp. 499-500.

[57] O. C. Halsted, *Address Upon the Character of the Late Hon. Isaac H. Williamson*, 1844; John Whitehead, *The Judicial and Civil History of the Jersey*, 1897; S. G. Potts, *Precedents and Notes of Practice in the Court of Chancery of New Jersey*, 1841; F. B. Lee, *New Jersey as a Colony and as a State*, vol. III, 1902, p. 377; W. H. Shaw, *History of Essex and Hudson County, New Jersey*, 1884.

[58] Williamson also aided the repeal of the statute forbidding the citing of English precedents made after 1776 in a New Jersey court of law or equity.

[59] O. S. Halsted, *op. cit.*, p. 10.

cellor which took place in 1844. With the new dignity and usefulness which Williamson had brought to it, it was unthinkable that it should be dependent upon the fortunes of frequent elections.

One of the most important factors contributing to the weakness of the judicial branch of our first state governments was the existence of a widespread tendency to pay little or no salary to judicial officers. This tendency was present in practically all of our rising young commonwealths and in the national government as well. The situation in New England in this respect is well illustrated by the experiences of Jeremiah Smith. In 1802 Jeremiah Smith was appointed to the chief justiceship of New Hampshire by Governor Gilman. The salary attached to the office at that time was but $850 a year, so he refused to accept. The legislature then raised the salary to $1000 and he accepted. This was less than a third of the sum he had earned in one year by his practice at the bar. Since his expenses exceeded $1200 a year, "not including the cost of going on circuit, which amounted to three hundred more," he addressed a letter to the legislature in 1804, intimating that he would be required to resign, if his compensation was not increased. In this connection, he said:

One would think it would be the policy of the public to invite, by holding out suitable encouragements, the most eminent at the bar . . . to a seat on the bench. There were, at a late period, living, ten persons who had resigned, and two who had declined, the office of judge of the Superior Court. Three are lately deceased. Since the Revolution, the judges of the Superior Court, upon an average, have held the office less than five years. Can there be better evidence that the emoluments are not considered adequate to the duties? While a judge holds the office no more than five years, have we much reason to experience uniformity in decisions? Do we lose all the benefits flowing from experience?[60]

The legislature immediately passed a bill by a large vote, fixing the salary of the chief justice at $1500. This was unusual for that period. Nevertheless the salaries of judges remained inadequate during a great part of the formative period. Writing in 1845, a commentator says:

Within a few years the rage for retrenchment in the public expenditures has caused the salaries of the judges to be materially diminished in nearly every state in the union though they were before confessedly far below the yearly gains of a lawyer in full practice, and though the expenses of living within the same period have considerably increased. Quite recently, if newspaper accounts may be credited, New Hampshire herself has narrowly escaped losing the chief ornament of her supreme bench, because a private manufacturing corporation wished to have him become their agent with a salary of two or three times that received by the chief justice. Massachusetts has had the mortification of seeing four out of the five judges in one of her courts

[60] John H. Monson, "Life of the Hon. Jeremiah Smith, etc.," 1845, p. 162; in *The North American Review*, vol. LXI, 1845, pp. 26-27.

resign their office within one year, because two political parties in her legislature were running a race with each other to see which should curry the most favor with the people by diminishing the public expense. Ohio has just lost her chief justice from a similar cause, and it is rumored that the whole bench are about to follow his example, while in Pennsylvania an important judgeship has recently gone begging among the members of the bar on the same grounds. If this unwise, parsimonious spirit continues to govern our legislative assemblies we may expect to see the character of the bench committed to judges who will dishonor it by their ignorance, or stain it by their corruption, or else that the aristocratic and monarchial principle will prevail of conferring high public office, as is now the case with a seat in the British parliament, only upon men whose great wealth enables them to serve without pay, and therefore without any sense of responsibility or obligation to their constitutions.[61]

In Massachusetts the limited salary scale for judges which prevailed during the greater part of the early period gave rise to several circumstances which are of interest. When Theophilus Parsons (1750-1813) was appointed by Governor Strong in 1806 to succeed Francis Dana as Chief Justice of the Supreme Judicial Court of Massachusetts, he took the post at a very great financial sacrifice. At the time of his appointment Theophilus Parsons undoubtedly stood at the head of his profession in the state of Massachusetts. The dockets of the state were three years behind schedule. A strong man was needed to clear the dockets. Parsons was looked upon as the proper man for the place, if he could be prevailed upon to accept. Parsons did accept, and he immediately cleared up the docket. He did more than that. He rendered outstanding service, as we have noted elsewhere, in forming the law of the new commonwealth of Massachusetts and indirectly the law of other states as well. When Parsons took this post in 1806 there were almost no American reports of judicial decisions. Moreover, very few English reports were available to American lawyers. In bringing order out of this chaotic condition, Parsons not only took the opportunity afforded to decide the instant case—but established a rule of general application as well. Drawing his rules from the English law, he combined the English doctrines with his profound knowledge of the unwritten colonial law, for he also had a strong desire to establish a system of law in Massachusetts, based upon the institutions and usages of the state. Extremely active in "shaping the older English and colonial law to meet the new problems presented by a rapidly growing commerce," his decisions were particularly valuable in the field of shipping and insurance. Following Lord Mansfield's example, he went to the merchants for their usages and established the principles embodied in those usages as rules of law. While his opinions lacked "philosophical insight or far-reaching analysis

---

[61] *Ibid.*, pp. 127-128. In June, 1809, Smith resigned his seat upon the bench and became Governor. *Ibid.*, p. 129.

of legal principles," they served an extremely useful purpose at the time and during that critical period when English institutions were under attack, Parsons, like Story, labored valiantly "to carry on the common law and restate it in intelligible form to suit American needs."[62] Like Story, also, his services were carried on under the decided handicap of a meager salary.

This condition of limited judicial salaries continued in Massachusetts for some time to come. It was brought to public attention once again in 1830 when the very able Lemuel Shaw (1781-1861) was appointed Chief Justice of the Massachusetts Supreme Court by Governor Levi Lincoln (1782-1868) to succeed Chief Justice Isaac Parker. Although the appointment of Shaw meant that he had to give up a practice with an income estimated from $15,000 to $20,000 a year, for a salary of $3500, he nevertheless accepted and served as mentioned elsewhere for thirty years. For a time, however, he was in doubt as to what course he could rightfully pursue. When one considers his creative efforts during an exceptionally long judicial career, one is impressed with the loss that might have resulted to the developing law of Massachusetts and the nation, because of the troublesome salary problem. Chief Justice Shaw's judicial career, as noted elsewhere, paralleled the development of many important industries. Consequently his great capacities "had full scope for making the law on such matters as water power, railroads, and other public utilities." Indeed it is said that Lemuel Shaw has influenced the development of commercial and constitutional law through the nation probably more than any other state judge. Moreover, most of the principles laid down by him proved sound, although his exposition of the fellow-servant rule undoubtedly delayed the replacement of that rule by workmen's compensation devices.[63]

The sacrifice made by Chief Justice Shaw in accepting the responsibilities of the judicial office was not unique. A similar condition prevailed when Joseph Story of Massachusetts was appointed to an associate justiceship of the United States Supreme Court. Story was appointed to that post by James Madison, on November 18, 1811. President Madison had already tried to honor three men with that position and failed. Levi Lincoln, formerly in Jefferson's cabinet, was the first man to be tendered this post and he declined to accept. Alexander

---

[62] E. G. Cook, "Theophilus Parsons," *Great American Lawyers* (Lewis, ed), vol. 2, 1907.

[63] F. H. Chase, *Lemuel Shaw, Chief Justice of the Supreme Judicial Court of Massachusetts, 1830-1860*, (1918), reviewed by E. H. Abbot, *Harvard Law Review*, December, 1918, see also *Lemuel Shaw, Chief Justice of the Supreme Judicial Court of Massachusetts*, 1865, a pamphlet which reprints articles by S. S. Shaw and P. E. Aldrich in *Memorial Biogs. New England Hist. Soc.*, vol. IV, 1885, and B. F. Thomas in *American Law Review*, Oct., 1867; see also J. H. Beale, in *Great American Lawyers*, vol. 3, 1907, ed. by W. D. Lewis.

Wolcott of Connecticut was then appointed but the Senate refused to confirm his appointment. John Quincy Adams was then selected but he preferred to remain as minister at St. Petersburg. At the suggestion of Congressman Ezekiel Bacon, President Madison then turned to Joseph Story, who had just recently passed his thirty-second birthday. Although the salary of $3500 was only slightly more than half of his professional income, Story accepted the post. While he did not overlook the permanence of tenure which went with the office he was motivated largely, he says, by the honor of the position and particularly by "the opportunity it will allow me to pursue, what of all things I admire, judicial studies."[64] The sincerity of Story's position is borne out by a circumstance which took place in 1816. In that year William Pinkney (1764-1822) was considering the request of the government that he go as minister to Russia. To facilitate his leaving he offered Joseph Story his law practice in Baltimore. Pinkney was one of the ablest if not the outstanding lawyer of his day in the view of many of his contemporaries.[65] His practice which has been described as the most extensive and lucrative of that time, is estimated to have been worth $20,000 a year. Although Congress had just refused to raise the salaries of the federal judges, Story, who was in very moderate financial circumstances, declined Pinkney's offer.

Meager judicial salaries were particularly marked in the more recently settled parts of the country. The situation which existed in Kentucky in the Court of Appeals during the early period illustrates this fact. When first organized, the Court of Appeals consisted of three judges, one of whom was commissioned "chief justice of Kentucky." In 1801, the number was increased to four. Thomas Todd who had been clerk of that court and who was appointed a judge of the United States Supreme Court in 1807, was made the fourth judge. In 1813 the number was reduced to three, where it has remained. The salary of each judge was $666.66 when this court was established. In 1801, it was increased to $833.33; in 1806 to $1000; in 1815 to $1500; in 1837

[64] *Life and Letters,* vol. I, p. 201.

[65] Most commentators of that day assert with very little reservation that William Pinkney was the most talented and versatile advocate of his time. In the seventy-two Supreme Court cases in which he appeared his efforts were outstanding. Chief Justice John Marshall called him "The greatest man I ever saw in a court of justice." (Samuel Tyler, *Memoir of Roger Brooke Taney,* 1876, p. 141.) Chief Justice Roger Taney, writing thirty years after Pinkney's death, said: "I have heard almost all the great advocates of the United States, both of the past and present generations, but I have seen none equal to Pinkney." *Ibid.,* p. 17. See also Henry Wheaton, *Some Accounts of the Life, Writing, and Speeches of William Pinkney,* 1826; Rev. William Pinkney, *The Life of William Pinkney,* 1853; H. H. Hagan, *Eight Great American Lawyers,* 1923; A. S. Niles in vol. 2, 1907, of *Great American Lawyers,* ed. by W. D. Lewis, *Law Reporter,* Sept., 1846, *Albany Law Journal,* August 20, 1870; *New Jersey State Bar Association Year Book,* 1906-07; *U. S. Law Intelligencer,* August, 1830; *American Lawyer,* July, 1905; *The North American Review,* Jan., 1827.

to $2000; and in 1843, it was reduced to $1500. During one period, salaries were paid in the paper of the Bank of the Commonwealth, which was so greatly depreciated that it reduced the value of each salary to about $750. It is interesting to note that this meager return did not deter some of the judges from serving for long terms. Indeed, of the eleven chief justices[66] who served between 1792 and 1847, three of them, Muter, Boyle, and Robertson, served some forty-one years, collectively. Of this group, Muter served for eleven years, Boyle for sixteen years, and Robertson for nearly fourteen. Justices Logan, Mills, and Owsley held their posts for a long period also. In 1803, Chief Justice George Muter, who was very poor and somewhat superannuated, was induced to resign by a promise of an annuity of $300. This promise was guaranteed by an act of the legislature in good faith, but was complained of as an odious and unconstitutional "provision" and was taken away by a repealing act of the next year.[67]

In the deep South, the courts also worked under the handicap of an inadequate salary scale. Indeed the state of Mississippi was able to retain an able judiciary only so long as its judges were able to put up with the slender income granted them. When they were unable to continue their personal sacrifices, the courts of Mississippi suffered. The case of William Lewis Sharkey, who served as Chief Justice of Mississippi between the years 1832 and 1850 is in point. Chief Justice Sharkey was undoubtedly one of Mississippi's greatest jurists. But when he resigned from the bench on October 1, 1850, it has been said "that he was moved to that step by pecuniary embarrassment growing out of the insufficient salaries at that time allowed the judiciary of the state."[68]

In addition to the handicap of poor salaries, the judicial branch of our early state governments was weakened by a number of other circumstances as well. One such factor was the general tendency during this early period to vest large powers in the legislature, in connection with the selection, removal, and compensation of judges, and in the organization of the judiciary generally.[69] The first constitutions, it will be remembered, provided for the main outlines of judicial organization, while the details of organization and procedure were left to the legislature. With judicial procedure, judicial organization and judicial personnel largely controlled by the legislature, the hope for three coordinate

[66] The list of chief justices during this early period included Harry Innis, George Muter, Thomas Todd, Felix Grundy, Ninian Edwards, George M. Bibb, John Boyle, George Robertson, E. M. Ewing, and Thomas A. Marshall. Collins, *op. cit.*, p. 106.

[67] Collins, *op. cit.*, p. 106.

[68] Dunbar Rowland, *op. cit.*, pp. 90-93.

[69] In Connecticut, Rhode Island, New Jersey, Virginia, North Carolina, South Carolina, and Georgia, the selection of judges was entirely in the hands of the legislature, while in Delaware and Pennsylvania the legislature participated with the executive in the choice. In New York judges were appointed by a special "Council of Appointment," and in Massachusetts, New Hampshire, and Maryland by the governor and council.

branches was not realized. When the legislature for political or other reasons chose to exercise its supremacy, it could do so. The situation in Ohio illustrates this condition. The Ohio constitution of 1802 was framed by follqwers of Thomas Jefferson. They were extremely hostile to the courts for partisan reasons. The Federalists had entrenched themselves in the judiciary and the Republicans were engaged in a "judge-breaking" movement.[70] It is not surprising that the Jeffersonians established a system of selection, whereby all judges, except the justices of the peace, were appointed for a term of seven years, "if so long they behave well."[71] This followed the practice of Connecticut, Rhode Island, New Jersey, North Carolina, and South Carolina.[72] This method was followed in Ohio until the constitution was revised in 1851, when a system of popular election was established.

Legislative control in Ohio was strikingly asserted in 1809 by the so-called "sweeping resolution" which removed from office three supreme court judges, three president judges of the common pleas courts, all the associate judges of that court (more than a hundred in number), and all of the justices of the peace.[73] Abuse of the removal power by the legislature was paralleled by an unsatisfactory use of the appointing power as well. In the constitutional convention of 1851, it was openly asserted that judicial office had become the spoils of party conflict and

[70] "The Republicans having become in the elections of 1800 the "dominant faction" the call to battle with their Federalist enemies who were still entrenched in the stronghold of the judiciary was sounded. Early in 1803, Jefferson directed Congress to make the first attack upon John Pickering, judge of the district court of New Hampshire. (*Annals*, 7th Congress, Second Session, p. 460.) The move was considered by the Federalists as the beginnings of a systematic attack upon the courts." Carpenter, *Judicial Tenure in the United States*, 1818, pp. 110-111.

[71] In the older states Jeffersonian principles were not accepted as readily as they were in frontier Ohio. In most of the older states tenure during good behavior was granted the judges, even before this plan was adopted by the federal government in 1787. In Pennsylvania the judges of the first state courts were chosen for a term of years. In 1790 this was changed to tenure during good behavior. Thorpe, *Charters and Constitutions*, p. 3079. In Vermont, Kentucky, and Tennessee, which were admitted soon after the ratification of the Federal Constitution, a similar tenure was provided. Thorpe, *ibid.*, pp. 1270, 3419, 2765. In Georgia, New Jersey, Rhode Island, and Connecticut, however, short term commissions were granted the judges. The most complete subordination of the courts to the legislature was in Ohio where Jeffersonian principles permeated the constitution. The people of Ohio gave their governor no veto power, entrusted him with no appointments of office, and limited the commission of all offices to a fixed term of years.

[72] Thorpe, *ibid.*, pp. 533, 2596, 2791, 3218, 3246, 4817. In Maryland, Massachusetts, New Hampshire, and Pennsylvania the appointments were made by the Governor and Council, while in New York the Governor acted with a special Council of Appointment. *Ibid.*, p. 2633. In Delaware appointments were made by the legislature and the executive. *Ibid.*, p. 564.

[73] See Rufus King, *Ohio, First Fruit of the Ordinance of 1787*, (1888), p. 314. For an interesting account of the rivalry between the legislature and judiciary in early Ohio, see William T. Utter, "Judicial Review in Early Ohio." *Mississippi Valley Historical Review*, vol. XIV, pp. 3-26; also "St. Tammany in Ohio: A Study in Frontier Politics," *ibid.*, vol. XV, pp. 321-40.

that appointment was not made on a basis of ability or fitness, but as a reward for party service.[74] Demands for change were made,[75] particularly during the time of the democratic popular election of judges.[76] Popular election was demanded also in the newer sections of the country by the debtor classes who were greatly aroused when the courts applied constitutional limitations to their favorite measures.[77]

These circumstances helped to raise the old cry that the courts were undemocratic.[78] This cry, which was heard so frequently during the party battle of the Jeffersonian period, became an important factor in circumscribing judicial power throughout the formative period of American life. During the early period of American life, the courts, it will be remembered, were a frequent object of attack. This was particularly true during the struggle between the Federalists and Jeffersonian Republicans. The Jeffersonians built their political and social philosophy upon the conception of human equality. While the Federalists did not ignore the principle of equality, they were prone to stress what seemed to them to be the dangers of this levelling principle. In their view, this principle tended to make all individuals the same, thereby ignoring "the mental, moral, and physical differences among men which were responsible for leaders and followers." Emphasizing the necessity of exceptional talents and virtues for positions of leadership and responsi-

[74] Statements were made in the convention to the effect that the legislature had become "a mere political arena, embittering the feeling of party spirit, and corrupting the pure foundation of justice." *Debates, Ohio Convention*, vol. I, 1850, p. 86. In Tennessee, a similar opinion existed. See Phelan, *History of Tennessee*, pp. 201, 301.

[75] "In many of the States where the governor was associated with the legislature in the appointment, nominations were made by caucus of the dominant party and no nominations thus made ever failed to receive the approval of the selecting authority. (Proceedings, *New York Convention*, 1846, pp. 103-104; Debates, *Kentucky Convention*, 1850, p. 168 et seq., Debates, *Maryland Convention*, 1851, 11 p. 490.) Thus not only were the judges removed from popular control but they were in the hands of those who sought to use the judicial office for partisan ends." W. S. Carpenter, *Judicial Tenure in the U. S.* 1918, p. 180.

[76] Frontier life was an important factor here. It emphasized the belief in popular sovereignty and the desirability of giving the people themselves a larger role in the direction of public affairs. See Charles A. Merriam, *American Political Theories*, ch. V. The Jacksonians believed there was no office to which the elective principle should not be applied.

[77] In Kentucky during the twenties, several acts favorable to the debtor class were annulled by the courts. Collins, *History of Kentucky*, vol. I, pp. 218 ff. A bitter attack on the courts resulted. See Charles G. Haines, *The American Doctrine of Judicial Supremacy*, pp. 257-258; McMasters, *History of the American People*, vol. 5, pp. 162-166; W. S. Carpenter, *op. cit.*, pp. 172-173. In Alabama and Maine a similar situation existed, *ibid.*, pp. 172-174.

[78] "Judges had for the most part ceased to exhibit the high handed and arrogant attitude which characterized the colonial judiciary and which a few judges like Addison had sought to adopt in the early state courts (p. 46). Yet there was a well defined feeling in many states that the courts were undemocratic and this was thought due to the long tenure which seemed to establish them as a privileged class." W. S. Carpenter, *op. cit.*, pp. 168-169; see also Sophonisbia Breckenridge, *Administration of Justice in Kentucky*, (Dissertation, University of Chicago, 1897), p. 36.

bility in society, they held that there was a close connection between these factors and the possession of property, of a family tradition, of a cultural inheritance, and an accepted intellectual and professional training. In turning against this self-proclaimed aristocracy of wealth, talent, and virtue the Jeffersonians brought the whole legal order, including both courts and lawyers, under fire.

The antipathy of the common man to the leadership of the lawyer in politics throughout this early period is an interesting phenomenon. There were good reasons for it, of course. When the common man came in contact with the legal profession, or the courts, his experience was not likely to be a happy one. Whether his contact with the law involved a disputed farm boundary, a tax collection case, a sheriff's sale, or a squabble over the payment of a personal note, he was likely to get less satisfaction than anticipated from his encounter, whereas the lawyer might reap a very rich harvest indeed.[79] Dependent upon the law but antagonistic to the pretensions of its servants, the common man, writes one historian of this period, became greatly exasperated at "the slow trials, heavy costs, and frequent misusages of justice."[80] When the lawyers, because of their training and experience, assumed an active role in the political life of the country, they were frequently attacked with great force and bitterness. This was true in the beginning years of the national period and continued to be true for a long time to come.[81] This

[79] The adverse attitude of the common man to the lawyer was of long standing. Writing upon the conditions which prevailed in Pennsylvania during Colonial times, Gabriel Thomas said: "Of Lawyers and Physicians, I shall say nothing, because this country is very peaceable and healthy, long may it so continue and never have occasion for the tongue of the one, nor the pen of the other, both equally destructive to men's estates and lives, besides forsooth, they hang men like they have a license to murder and make mischief." See *Historical and Geographical Account of Pennsylvania and of Western New Jersey*, by Gabriel Thomas, who resided there about fifteen years. London. Printed for, and Sold by A. Baldwin, at the Oxon Arms in Warwick Lane, 1698. *Narratives of Early Pennsylvania, West Jersey, and Delaware, 1630-1707. Original Narratives of Early American History*, edited by Albert Cook Myers, 1912, p. 328.

[80] Walter R. Fee, *The Transition from Aristocracy to Democracy in New Jersey, 1789-1829*, 1933, p. 107.

[81] "In the national period anti-lawyer feeling in New Jersey did not become prominent until near the close of Washington's administration. Among the first thrusts at the wearers of the black gown was one from a Morris County farmer. This gentleman was disturbed that lawyers should be "almost the sole dictators of all public measures," and he, with many others, appeared to believe that these men, now so important in affairs of State, were in earlier days cool-headed observers of a great struggle, Tories and refugees. (*Centinel of Freedom*, Dec. 14, 1796; *New Jersey Journal*, Jan. 25, 1797; *Journal of Legislative Council, Twenty-second Session, Second Sitting*, p. 54; *New Jersey Pamphlets*, vol. 107, no. 9; *Burlington Advertiser*, Nov. 2, 1790.) Just before the Congressional election of 1800, Moore Furman lamented that his small estate was governed "totally by the lawyers and the old Tories." (*Letters of Moore Furman*, p. 116.) The Republican committees of Essex County in December, 1800, called attention to the "improper and dangerous influence" which the lawyers possessed. They would warn the voters that the Federalist ticket for Congress included three lawyers and one aspirant to that dignity. And too, these men were recommended by a state meeting composed of lawyers, judges,

feeling naturally involved the courts and they too were bitterly attacked throughout this early period. These attacks, it should be noted, took place at different times and in different parts of the country and can be looked upon as one of the chief obstacles to the development of a strong judicial system during the formative period of American life.

A brief survey of some of the more important manifestations of a critical attitude toward the judiciary may be of interest in this connection. Such a survey might start in Massachusetts where violent action was taken directly against the courts during Shays' Rebellion.[82] It might also include the difficulties present in Pennsylvania at the time of the Whiskey Insurrection,[83] and during the party battles of McKean and Duane;[84] in eastern New York during the anti-rent disorders;[85] in Ohio during the same period when Tammany societies were being set up in the new commonwealth;[86] and in Kentucky during the bank controversy.[87]

The situation in Massachusetts which has come to be described as Shays' Rebellion grew out of the social and economic dislocations which followed the Revolutionary War.[88] Led by Daniel Shays (1747-1825), a former army officer, and others, it reached a high point in 1786, when armed conflict broke out between this group and the government of Massachusetts. Serious uprisings occurred in various

and late officers of the Adams personal army—all men "who wish to fatten themselves on the hard earnings of the industrious farmers and mechanics." (*Genius of Liberty*, Dec. 18, 1800.) An imaginative writer, "Marcus Brutus," from South Jersey, announced that he would not vote for any lawyer as these men were interested in fomenting disputes and belonged in a class with Tories, liars, drunkards, and adulterers. (*Ibid.*, Oct. 8, 1801.) Federalists dismissed these attacks by pointing out that they did not have a monopoly of legal minds in their party and that many of the prominent Federalist lawyers, instead of being unfriendly to American independence, were most active in its support. (*State Gazette and New Jersey Advertiser*, Dec. 27, 1796.)" Walter R. Fee, *op. cit.*, pp. 107-108.

[82] A. C. McLaughlin, *The Confederation and Constitution*, 1905, ch. X; J. B. McMaster, *History of the People of the United States*, vol. I, 1907, pp. 299-330; John Fiske, *Critical Period*, 1890, pp. 177-186.

[83] *Pennsylvania Archives*, 1876, 2nd Series, IV, H. H. Brackenridge, *Incidents of the Insurrection*, (1796); H. Adams, *Writings of Gallatin*, 1879; III, pp. 1-67. See also Myrl I. Eakin, "Hugh Henry Brackenridge, Lawyer," *Western Pennsylvania History Magazine*, July, 1927; Mildred Williams, "Hugh Henry Brackenridge as a Judge of the State Supreme Court, 1799-1816," *ibid.*, October, 1927.

[84] Wayland F. Dunaway, *A History of Pennsylvania*, 1935, pp. 420-424, 437.

[85] Edward P. Cheyney, "The Anti-Rent Movement and the Constitution of 1846," *History of the State of New York*, vol. VI, 1934, pp. 282-321 (Alex. Flick, ed.).

[86] W. T. Utter, "St. Tammany in Ohio: A Study in Frontier Politics," *Mississippi Valley Historical Review*, vol. XV, 1928-29, pp. 321-340.

[87] Lewis Collins, *Historical Sketches of Kentucky*, 1838, pp. 87-98, 104-105.

[88] "The disturbances in Massachusetts grew out of the sick and exhausted condition of the whole country at the close of the Revolutionary War. Public and private debts existed to an enormous amount, agriculture and commerce stagnated, taxation was heavy, and distress was universal. At this time Shays and his associates undertook to shut up the courts by violence. . . . " *The North American Review*, vol. 58, April, 1844, pp. 431-432.

parts of the state. The trouble lasted for some months, sorely trying the government of the new state. The Shays group was particularly bitter against the judiciary and they attempted to prevent the courts from sitting, in order to prevent the trial of cases against the debt-laden farmers of the state, whose interests they were supporting.[89] On August 29, 1786, Shays' insurgents prevented the sitting of the court of common pleas and general sessions. Their object was simply to prevent the court from giving judgments in debt cases before grievances were redressed. On September 26 they decided to prevent the sitting of the supreme court at Springfield, in order to prevent indictments from being brought against them. Major General Williams Shepard of the Hampshire militia, with some 800 men prepared to defend the court against an approximately equal number of insurgents. On this occasion, Shays acted as chairman of a committee which drew up resolutions that the court should be allowed to sit, if it dealt with no cases involving indictments of insurgents, or concerning debts. An agreement was then reached, both the militia and the insurgents disbanded, and the court adjourned. Armed outbreaks continued, however, and the legislature made no real effort to redress grievances. On the other hand it enraged the insurgents still further by suspending the writ of habeas corpus. As the winter advanced the insurgents gave up hope of peaceful adjustment of their difficulties and by January, 1787, it was apparent that the legislature intended to resort to strong measures, a course of action, that received the benedictions of George Washington of Virginia, who was

[89] It is interesting to note that the government at this time was enforcing the law against the majority of the people in many parts of Massachusetts. "It is certain," says one not too sympathetic commentator, "that their party had the majority in the whole state, for their great object was to postpone the decision of the whole matter till a new legislature should be chosen, when they were confident of obtaining the command of both branches. They held unlicensed conventions, in which more than fifty towns were represented [voted their own constitutionality], assumed the name of the people, demanded a revision of the constitution, arrayed themselves against the legislature, and demanded the redress of grievances with arms in their hands. Job Shattuck, one of their leaders, at the head of an armed force, took possession of the court house at Worcester, and sent a written message to the judges, that it is 'the *sense of the people* that the courts should not sit'." "They thought themselves," says Minot, the historian of the insurrection, "to be a majority of the people, as some pretended, and so vested with a supreme power of altering whatever appeared to them to be wrong in the policy of the country." *Ibid.*, pp. 431-432. Mr. Madison, in discussing this affair, said: "At first view, it might not seem to square with the republican theory, to suppose either that a majority have not the right, or that a minority will have the force, to subvert a government, and consequently, that the federal interposition can never be required, but when it would be improper. But theoretic reasoning in this, as in most cases, must be qualified by the lessons of practice. *Why may not illicit combinations for purposes of violence be formed or made by a majority of a State, especially of a small State, as by a majority of a county, or a district of the same State, and if the authority of the State ought, in the latter case, to protect the local magistracy, ought not the federal authority, in the former, to support the State authority?" Ibid.,* p. 432.

watching these various events in Massachusetts with an anxious eye.[90] In February, the superior force of the government prevailed and the ill-fated Shays' Rebellion was a thing of the past.[91]

The courts were also drawn into the conflicts arising in western Pennsylvania in 1794 in connection with the enforcement of the federal excise tax law on domestic spirits. This conflict which was called the Whiskey Insurrection reached its most acute condition in western Pennsylvania. It was not confined completely to this section, however. Indeed the legislatures of Maryland and Virginia, as well as of Pennsylvania, exhibited a strong dislike for the excise tax which was enacted by Congress in 1791. In the western Pennsylvania area grievance which was strongly voiced had to do with the fact that no action at law could be brought by the residents of that area in their own local courts for offenses against the Federal Government, but that they had to go to Philadelphia for trial. They also claimed that whiskey was the only valuable article in small bulk with which they could purchase commodities and that the law afforded them neither redress nor protection. Since their local courts which were likely to reflect their own sentiments more immediately were unable to exercise jurisdiction in the matter and the courts of a far-away seaboard center were used to implement the act of a far-away national government, the court entrusted with such a duty was necessarily looked upon with disfavor. When writs were issued against non-complying distillers, disturbances of a riotous nature ensued. On July 17, 1794, the home of General Neville, an inspector, was burned. The president immediately issued a proclamation and the governor of Pennsylvania and federal and state commissioners vainly attempted to bring order out of chaos. Shortly afterwards the president called out 17,000 militia although mass meetings were held and resolutions drawn up to the effect that the civil authorities could enforce

[90] When Washington was asked to use his influence in bringing about a peaceful solution of the Massachusetts difficulty, he is said to have replied: "You talk, my good sir, of employing *influence* to appease the present tumult in Massachusetts. I know not where that influence is to be found, nor, if attainable, that it would be a proper remedy for these disorders. Influence is not government. Let us have a government by which our lives, liberties, and properties will be secured, or let us know the worst at once. Let the reins of government then be braced, and held with a steady hand; and every violation of the constitution be reprehended. If defective let it be amended, but not suffered to be trampled upon while it has existence." *The North American Review*, vol. LVIII, April, 1844, p. 432.

[91] J. G. Holland, *History of Western Massachusetts*, 2 vols., 1855; G. R. Minot, *The History of the Insurrection in Massachusetts*, 1810; Jonathan Smith, "Features of Shays' Rebellion," 1903, *Historical Papers Read at Meetings of the Clinton Historical Society*, vol. I; Grindall Reynolds, "Concord during the Shays' Rebellion," *A Collection of Historical and Other Papers*; S. A. Green, "Groton during Shays' Rebellion," *Proc. Massachusetts Historical Society*, 2nd ser., 1, 1885; H. K. Sanderson, *Lynn in the Revolution*, 1909; C. O. Parmenter, *History of Pelham, Massachusetts*, 1898; J. P. Warren, "The Confederation and the Shays' Rebellion," *American Historical Review*, October, 1905.

the law. When the army actually went into action the people offered no resistance and after making a few arrests, the armed forces were withdrawn. While the net effect of the movement was to strengthen the national government, the resentment against the courts which served the national government did not subside completely for some time.

The feeling that the courts were undemocratic was also manifested in Pennsylvania in the days of the triumph of Jeffersonian Republicanism. It reached a high point in the gubernatorial election of 1802 when Thomas McKean (1734-1817) was reelected governor. The Federalist party was in the process of disintegration at this time and an intense struggle arose within the ranks of the victorious Jeffersonians. McKean became the leader of the conservative wing and William Duane (1760-1835) became the leader of the radicals. Duane was the editor of the *Aurora,* the organ of the Democratic-Republican party which had been founded by Benjamin Franklin Bache, and which continued in some ways the policy of Philip Freneau's *National Gazette,* which had ceased publication in 1793. Duane, with the assistance of Dr. Michael Leib, insisted upon a more democratic constitution, a curtailment of the powers of the executive, a reorganization of the judiciary, and a democratization of government in the interest of the masses.[92]

Duane was particularly critical of the judiciary and was instrumental in securing the removal from the bench of Judge Addison for misconduct. Under his influence impeachment proceedings were brought in 1804 in the Democratic assembly against the Chief Justice Edward Shippen, and two of his associates, Jasper Yeates and Thomas Smith. It is interesting to note that both Edward Shippen (1728-1806) and Jasper Yeates (1745-1817) had contributed largely to the jurisprudence of Pennsylvania, particularly to her system of legal reports. It is to Shippen that we owe the earliest published law reports of the supreme court of Pennsylvania[93] and some fair volumes of cases, covering the years 1791-1808, were reported by Yeates *(Yeates' Reports).* His opinions also appear in the six volumes of Binney's Reports and 1-2 Sergeant and Rawle. Indeed Jasper Yeates has frequently been called "the Father of the Law" in Pennsylvania, "because he was so habitually a record keeper and so influential in the establishment of Pennsylvania's system of state reports." Despite the strength of Duane's forces, these impeachment proceedings, under charges growing out of the Passmore case, were doomed to failure in

[92] See Wayland F. Dunaway, *A History of Pennsylvania,* 1935, pp. 421-422.
[93] See A. J. Dallas, "Reports of Cases . . . in Pennsylvania," printed in the first volumes of Dallas' *United States Reports,* II-IV.

the senate, when that body, by a 13 to 11 decision, voted for acquittal in January, 1805.[94]

Duane and his friends were also circumvented in their desires for a constitutional convention. McKean refused to sanction such a move and supported by Alexander J. Dallas and other conservatives he obstructed all such "giddy innovations" as he called them. He repeatedly vetoed bills for extending the jurisdiction of justices of the peace and similar measures, although some of these measures were badly needed. A measure establishing a system of compulsory arbitration for the trial of certain cases was passed over his veto. A measure giving justices of the peace jurisdiction over suits involving less than one hundred dollars was also passed over his veto. Laws simplifying legal practice and modifying the antiquated legal rules then in force were also passed. Violent political warfare now ensued. The Duane faction, which controlled the legislature, called a legislative caucus and nominated Simon Snyder for the governorship. Snyder, a farmer and archjacobin was the first candidate from the ranks of the new democracy to seek that office. Hitherto the governors and other high officials of the commonwealth had been men of education and property. In a campaign of great bitterness and abuse Snyder attacked the courts, judges, lawyers and all semblances of aristocracy. The friends of the existing constitution, including moderate Democrats and Federalists as well, united to defeat Snyder and re-elect McKean. His victory was hailed in state and nation as the triumph of law and order over the excesses of radicalism. During his third term (1805-1808) McKean undertook to place the judiciary upon a more effective basis.[95]

In New York the courts were also under fire during this early period. The series of disturbances in New York state (1839-1846) growing out of the opposition of the tenants, particularly upon Rensselaerwyck and Livingston Manor, to the payment of rent to the descendants of the original Dutch "Patroons" naturally placed the courts in a difficult position. Out of the general dissatisfaction arising from these disturbances, very definite proposals of change emerged, including

[94] See William Hamilton, *Report of the Trial and Acquittal of Edward Shippen, Jasper Yeates and Thomas Smith . . . on an Impeachment . . . 1805*; B. C. Atlee, "Jasper Yeates," *The Green Bag*, September, 1893; C. I. Landes, "Jasper Yeates and His Times," *Pennsylvania Magazine of History and Biography*, July, 1822; *Letters and Papers Relating Chiefly to the Provincial History of Pennsylvania*, 1855, ed. by Thomas Balch; Lawrence Lewis, Jr., *Pennsylvania Magazine of History and Biography*, April, 1883; *ibid.*, January, 1901, December, 1902.

[95] See James H. Peeling, "Governor McKean and the Pennsylvania Jacobine, 1799-1808," *Pennsylvania Magazine of History and Biography*, vol. LIV, pp. 320-354; Frank Eshelman, "Struggle and Rise of Popular Power in Pennsylvania's First Two Decades, 1682-1701," *ibid.*, vol. XXXIV, pp. 129-161; Elizabeth McWilliams, "Political Activities in Western Pennsylvania, 1800-1816," *Western Pennsylvania Historical Magazine*, vol. VII, pp. 225-234. See also Burton A. Konkle, *Benjamin Chew, 1722-1810*, (1932), pp. 277, 278, 279, 280-283.

suggestions for more popular elections, a reformed judiciary, and a modernization of the laws for the ownership and tenure of land. Indeed the sentiments awakened during the so-called anti-rent riots[96] which convulsed a large part of the state furnished the most conspicuous immediate occasion for the adoption of the constitution of 1846. In the constitutional convention of 1846 the reorganization of the judicial system of the state was recommended by a committee headed by Judge Ruggles.[97] While other suggestions were made, the recommendations of this committee, which involved the introduction of a popular method of selection, were accepted with little change. All judges were to be elected by the people, like other officers, and no longer appointed by governor and Senate.[98] Cases in law and equity were no longer to be settled in separate courts but were to be settled by the same court. Thirty-two judges of a superior court sitting in eight judicial districts were provided for also. A court of appeals consisting of eight judges, four of them chosen directly and four selected from supreme court justices, was established and legislative jurisdiction over appeals was abolished inasmuch as it was provided that the Senate should no longer have appellate jurisdiction as a court for the correction of errors. It

[96] For example, a group of farmers went to Stephan Van Rensselaer on May 22, 1839, to ascertain the course of action which the executors and heirs of his father intended to take towards such arrears of rent as had accumulated against them and which they had come to feel to be not only unjust but unbearable. "His answer came to them," says Edward B. Cheyney, "in a letter addressed to the chairman of the committee refusing any special terms. Anger spread among the farmers, while the executors of the old patroon secured writs of ejectment and *scire facias* from the supreme court of the state against those long in arrears, and placed them in the hands of the sheriffs for service." "Thereupon followed what is known locally as the Helderberg War. Deputies of the sheriff, and finally the sheriff himself, penetrated with their writs into the back country, only to be met by disorderly crowds of farmers, amounting sometimes to 75 or 100 men and eventually to many more, summoned together by the blowing of horns when anyone learned that the 'patroon's men' were out serving writs. They called the patroon's men 'scoundrels, traitors, villains,' blocked the roads, threatening and shaking their fists in the faces of the officers, seizing their horses' bridles and turning them back, setting tar barrels afire in the middle of the road, and for a long time effectually preventing any legal service. The sheriff, Michael Archer, who was a determined man, swore in a posse of 500 men early in the month of December, set out from Albany with his somewhat motley company, all unarmed, for the hills, only to be met by still larger crowds mostly mounted and armed with clubs, who filled the roads, peremptorily forbade them to pass or to serve their writs, and made it impossible for them to proceed. The sheriff hastened back to Albany, made his way to Governor Seward, although it was eight o'clock at night, and demanded military support. The governor was in a difficult position. He had long been opposed to the leasehold system, yet his duty to suppress disorder was clear. He secured corroboration of the sheriff's account of conditions, took advice from his staff, advised the sheriff to secure warrants of arrest for those who had opposed him both from the supreme court for their contempt in resisting its writs and from a justice of the peace for their disorder, and promised his adequate support in making the arrests." After a display of armed force and an appeal to orderliness, the authority of settled government was for a time successfully asserted. "The Anti-Rent Movement and the Constitution of 1846," *History of the State of New York* (Alex. C. Flick, ed.), vol. VI, pp. 297-299.

[97] Edward P. Cheyney, *op. cit.*, p. 315.
[98] *Ibid.*, p. 315.

was also provided that there should be one local judge in each county and that no judicial officers, excepting justices of the peace, should receive fees.[99]

The adoption of the elective principle in connection with the selection of the judiciary is the important change, however, and one that was to be expected. "Election instead of appointment of judges," says Edward L. Cheyney, "was typical of the general action. All officers, state and local, with the fewest exceptions, were now to be chosen by popular election. It was the "people's constitution" and the intention was to extend popular control as far as was in any way possible."[100] Although the burdensome land question had already been settled and improved by legal decisions and statutory enactments the convention nevertheless froze these corrections into the fundamental law.[101] The net result of the anti-rent movement was a court system made closely responsible to the people and a revised constitution which also reflected the democratic spirit of the day.[102]

The anti-court struggle in Kentucky was an exceedingly bitter one. The first constitution of Kentucky which commenced its operation on June 1, 1792, in the interest of judicial independence prohibited the legislature from reducing a judge's salary during his continuance in office. While the constitution which was adopted in 1799 contained no such provision, it did invest the supreme court with a large appellate jurisdiction, which was as permanent and inviolable as the constitution itself.[103] The "fundamental immutability" of the Supreme Court and

[99] *Ibid.*, p. 316.

[100] *Ibid.*

[101] *Ibid.*, p. 317.

[102] See D. S. Alexander, *A Political History of the State of New York*, 3 vols., 1906-1909; D. D. Bainard, "The Anti-Rent Movement and Outbreak in New York," *American Whig Review*, vol. 2, December, 1845, pp. 577-98; D. D. Bainard, *Discourse on the Life, Services, and Character of Stephan Van Rensselaer*, 1839; W. G. Bishop and W. H. Attree, *Report on the Debates and Proceedings of the Convention of the Revision of the Constitution of the State of New York*, 1846; Alden Chester, *Courts and Lawyers of New York*, 3 vols., 1925; E. P. Cheyney, *Anti-Rent Agitation in the State of New York, 1839-1846*, (1887); A. J. Colvin and Anson Bingham, *Slavery, or Involuntary Servitude: Does it Legally Exist in the State of New York?*, 1864; J. F. Cooper, *The Redskins, or Indian and Injin*, 1845; S. Croswell and R. Sutton, *Debates and Proceedings in the New York State Convention for the Revision of the Constitution*, 1846; Dixon R. Fox, *The Decline of Aristocracy in the Politics of New York*, 1919; J. D. Hammond, *A Political History of the State of New York*, 3 vols., 1852; J. S. Jenkins, *History of Political Parties in the State of New York*, 1846; C. Z. Lincoln, *Messages from the Governors*, 11 vols., 1909; J. B. McMaster, *History of the People of the United States*, 1883-1918, vol. VII, ch. LXXIV; David Murray, "The Anti-Rent Episode in the State of New York," *American Historical Association, Report for 1896*, vol. 1, 1897, 139-173; A. C. Niven, "A Chapter of Anti-Rent History," *Albany Law Journal*, vol. XXIV, 1881, pp. 125-127.

[103] "The great end of the constitution of Kentucky and of every good constitution," says Lewis Collins, "is to prescribe salutary limits to the inherent power of numerical majorities. Were the political omnipotence of every such majority either reasonable or

"the value of the durable tenure" by which the judges held their offices were challenged, however, by a series of events which grew out of the so-called "relief" laws. These laws were initiated in 1817-1818, by the retrospective prolongation of replevins, or judgments, and decrees and carried on further in 1820 by the establishment of the Bank of the Commonwealth, without either capital or the guaranty of state credit, and by additional laws which "extended replevins to two years in all cases in which the creditor should fail to endorse on his execution his consent to take at its nominal value local bank paper greatly depreciated." The purpose of the legislature in establishing the Bank of the Commonwealth and in enacting the supporting legislation, was "to enable debtors to pay their debts in much less than their value, by virtually compelling creditors to accept much less, or incur the hazards of indefinite and vexatious delays." When the constitutionality of this legislation was presented to the Supreme Court[104] of the state it "subjected to a severe, but decisive ordeal the personal integrity, firmness and intelligence of the judges, and the value of that degree of judicial independence and stability contemplated by the constitution." When the court held the "relief" legislation unconstitutional a great barrage of criticism was levelled against the judges. Their authority to disregard a legislative act as unconstitutional was denied by many and they were denounced bitterly as "usurpers, tyrants, kings."

At the next legislative session which was held in the fall of 1823, a preamble and resolutions for addressing them out of office were reported by John Rowan, to which the judges responded. After a vigorous debate, the preamble and resolutions were adopted by a majority of less than two-thirds. The judges refused to abdicate. At the next legislative session in 1824, a still larger majority voted against the judges and their decision. However, the vote was not quite two-thirds. The dominant party was now thoroughly aroused and passed "an act to reorganize the Court of Appeals." The object of this act was to

---

safe, no constitutional limitations or legislative *will* would be necessary or proper. But the whole tenor of the Kentucky constitution implies that liberty, justice, and security, (the ends of all just government) require many such fundamental restrictions. And not only to prescribe such as were deemed proper, but more especially to *secure their efficiency*, was the ultimate object of the people in adopting a constitution: And to assure the integrity and practical supremacy of these restrictions they determined that, as long as their constitution should last, there should be a tribunal, the judges of which should be entitled to hold their offices as long as the tribunal itself should exist and they should behave well and continue competent, in the judgment of as many as one-third of each branch of the legislature, on an address, or of one-third of the senate, on an impeachment. And to prevent evasion, they have provided that, whilst an incumbent judge of the Appellate Court may be removed from his office by a concurrent vote of two-thirds, neither the appellate tribunal, nor the office itself, shall be subject to legislative abolition." *Historical Sketches of Kentucky*, 1848, p. 102.

[104] This court was styled the Court of Appeals.

abolish the "old constitutional court" and substitute a "new legislative court." An active minority in the legislature opposed this act. Their protest to the house of representatives written by George Robertson was entered on the journal of that house without being read. When a copy of this protest was read in the senate, it was refused a place in the Journal of that body. Whereupon a reconsideration was moved in the lower house and this memorable document was eliminated from the record there also. The new court which was set up consisted of William T. Barry as Chief Justice, and James Haggin, John Trimble, and Rezin H. Davidge as associate justices. It took possession of the papers and records in the office of the Court of Appeals and appointed Francis P. Blair clerk. It immediately undertook to decide cases. The opinions rendered in these cases were published by Thomas B. Monroe, in a small volume which "has never been regarded or read as authority." The people were uncertain as to which body was the constitutional tribunal of revision. In consequence, some appealed to the one and some to the other.

"In this perplexing crisis of judicial anarchy," writes Lewis H. Collins, "the only authoritative arbiter was the ultimate sovereign— *the freemen of the State at the polls*. To that final and only tribunal, therefore, both parties appealed, and no period, in the history of Kentucky, was ever more pregnant, or marked with more excitement or able and pervading discussion, than that which immediately preceded the annual elections in the year 1825. This portentous agony resulted in the election to the house of representatives of a decisive majority in favor of the "old court," and against the constitutionality of the "new Court." But only one-third of the senators having passed the ordeal of that election, a small "new court" majority still remained in the senate, and disregarding the submission of the question to the votes of the people, that little majority refused to repeal the "reorganized act" or acknowledge the existence of the "old court." This unexpected and perilous contumacy brought the antagonist parties to the brink of a bloody revolution. For months the commonwealth was trembling on the crater of a heaving volcano. But the considerate prudence of the "old court party" prevented an eruption by forbearing to resort to force to restore to the "old court" its papers and records, which the minority guarded, in Blair's custody, by military means—and also by appealing once more to the constituent body in a printed manifesto prepared by George Robertson, signed by the members constituting a majority of the popular branch of the legislature. . . . The result of this last appeal was a majority in the senate, and an augmented majority in the house of representatives in favor of repealing as unconstitutional the "act to reorganize the Court of Appeals." That act was accordingly

repealed in the session of 1826-27, by "an act to remove the unconstitutional obstructions which have been thrown in the way of the
Court of Appeals," passed by both houses the 30th of December, 1826
—*the governor's objections notwithstanding.* The "new court" vanished and the "old court," redeemed and reinstated, proceeded without
further question or obstruction in the discharge of its accustomed
duties."[105]

When the controversy had subsided John Boyle "who had adhered
to the helm throughout the storm in a forlorn hope of saving the
constitution," resigned the chief-justiceship and George M. Bibb, an
advocate of "relief" and the "new court" plan, was appointed by a
"relief" governor to take his place. In the fall of 1828 Owsley and
Mills of the "old court" also resigned. They were renominated by
Governor Metcalfe who had just succeeded Governor Desha. The
"relief" senate rejected their nomination, however, and two "anti-
relief" and "old court" sympathizers, George M. Robertson and Joseph
R. Underwood, were appointed to succeed them. George M. Bibb
then resigned the Chief Justiceship and that post remained vacant until
near the close of the year 1829. In the meantime, Robertson and
Underwood constituted the court. During that year these two judges
not only disposed of about one thousand cases on the docket of the
court of appeals but declared all the acts and decisions of the "new
court" null and void. In December, 1829, Robertson was appointed
Chief Justice and another judge was added. And thus once more the
so-called "old court" was "complete, homogeneous and peaceful, and
the most important question that could engage the councils or agitate
the passions of a state was settled finally."[106]

While much of the popular criticism of the courts during the
formative period which tended to have a restrictive effect upon their
growth had to do with charges that they were undemocratic, there
were other sources of dissatisfaction as well. Most of their criticism
concerned the slowness with which they performed their duties. Complaints concerning this condition were made in Kentucky,[107] New
York,[108] Pennsylvania,[109] and Ohio.[110] These discontents effected ex-

[105] Lewis Collins, *Historical Sketches of Kentucky,* 1848, pp. 104-105.

[106] Collins, *op. cit.,* p. 105.

[107] See Collins, *History of Kentucky,* pp. 218 ff.

[108] An insufficient number of judges on the bench in New York caused the court to
fall two years behind in its docket. Proceeedings, *New York Convention,* 1846, pp. 370 ff.

[109] In Pennsylvania the judges were accused of indolence. This tendency was ascribed
to the unlimited tenure granted to them.

[110] At the legislative session of 1843-1844, Governor Shannon in his message to
the General Assembly urged upon that body the proposition of submitting to the people
the question of calling a constitutional convention for the purposes of correcting the evils
in the judicial system which prevented it from transacting the mass of business brought
before it. "The amount of costs," he said, "that are annually thrown upon litigants by

tensive alterations in the judicial system of the several states in the mid-century period, when terms were limited and popular election adopted in many states.[111] Changes in tenure were also effected. Between 1830 and the beginning of the Civil War the tenure of judges was limited to a period of years in twenty-one states. Many of these changes occurred in the newer, western states, where a short term of four or six years was preferred.[112] But many of the older states favored similar changes when they revised their constitutions. The states altering the tenure of their judges included Alabama in 1830; Mississippi, 1832; Tennessee, 1834; Michigan, 1835; Arkansas, 1836; Pennsylvania, 1838; Maine, 1839; Texas and Louisiana, 1845; New York and Iowa, 1846; Florida, Missouri, and Wisconsin, 1848; California, 1849; Kentucky and Virginia, 1850; Maryland, 1851; Kansas, 1855; and Oregon and Minnesota, 1857.

During these same years the theory of popular sovereignty and the principle of popular election of all public officials was given an increasingly wide acceptance. As the mid-century period approached, the unparalleled material development of the country made constitutional revision necessary in many states. Change was supported by those who believed that there should be some limitation placed on the power of the State to incur debts; those who believed that the power of the legislature in this matter as well as others should be definitely curbed; those who believed that all offices, legislative, judicial and executive should be elected directly by the people; and those who believed that the executive power should be increased and the judicial system im-

---

reason of the continuance of causes for the want of time to try them, would in the aggregate far exceed the amount paid in any state in this Union to maintain its entire judicial system. It is not only an expensive system but, in its practical bearings, produces, in most cases, a delay, and in many almost a denial of the administration of justice." *The New Constitution,* p. 74.

[111] Pound, *The Spirit of the Common Law,* pp. 7-8.

[112] When the Tennessee Constitutional Convention of 1834 met there was some considerable dissatisfaction with an unlimited tenure for judges. "Among the signs of the times," writes James Phelan, "were the impeachments of Judge Nathaniel W. Williams and Judge Joshua Haskell. Feeling secure in their seats, many of the judges had become so high-handed and overbearing and in many cases so neglectful of their duties, that a general protest went up from the people as well as the bar. The experiment of filling judicial seats with officers *quam diu bene se gesserint* was not a success in Tennessee." *History of Tennessee,* 1889, p. 301. Joshua W. Caldwell seems to agree with this statement. "The terms of all judges under the Constitution of 1796," he observes, "were during life or good behaviour, and this certain tenure of office seems in some cases to have produced very bad results. Impeachments were not uncommon and often the charges were well founded. It is said that impeachment was a favorite resort of defeated lawyers, who found it an easy means of shifting responsibility for failures, upon the courts. This, however, is an exaggerated statement. It is not insisted that life tenure alone was responsible for the unfortunate events in the history of our early judiciary, but it is beyond question that the responsibility rests largely upon it." *Sketches of the Bench and Bar of Tennessee,* 1898, pp. 70-71.

proved. Between 1848 and 1851, for example, no less than four states of the old Northwest found it necessary to revise their Constitutions. In 1848, Illinois led the way, overhauling her Constitution of 1818 in vigorous fashion. The state was heavily in debt due to unfortunate banking experience and internal improvement schemes. The legislature was blamed for much of this. Distrust of the legislature resulted in limitations on that branch in practically all of the constitutions adopted during the period. In 1850, Indiana and Michigan followed the Illinois precedent and Ohio did likewise in 1851. Constitutional change was not confined to these states. Conventions were also held for the purpose of effecting constitutional change in New York in 1846; Wisconsin, 1849; Kentucky, Missouri, Pennsylvania, Virginia, 1850; Maryland, 1851; Louisiana, 1852; Tennessee, 1853; Kansas, 1855; Iowa, Minnesota, and Oregon, 1857.

Throughout all of these constitutional changes ran the thread of the elective principle. It naturally affected the judiciary. In consequence, by the time of the Civil War an elective judicial system was provided for in nineteen of the thirty-four state constitutions. This included: Georgia, 1777; Mississippi, 1832; New York, 1845; Wisconsin, 1848; California, 1849; Kentucky, Michigan, Missouri, Pennsylvania, and Virginia, 1850; Indiana, Maryland, and Ohio, 1851; Louisiana, 1852; Tennessee, 1853; Kansas, 1855; Iowa, Minnesota, and Oregon, 1857. Mississippi,[113] it will be noted, provided for popular election of supreme court judges at an early date, but it was not until New York adopted the principle in 1846, that it received widespread acceptance.[114] Within the next eleven years, some seventeen states

[113] See Henry S. Foote, *The Bench and Bar of the South and Southwest*, 1876, p. 65; see also Dunbar Rowland, *Courts, Judges, and Lawyers of Mississippi, 1783-1935*, vol. 1, 1935, p. 88.

[114] For an interesting contemporary discussion in favor of periodical election of judges either by the people or by the legislature, see Frederick Grimké's *Consideration upon the Nature and Tendency of Free Institutions*, 1848, 544 pp. The author of this work had been a member of the Supreme Court of Ohio. This book is reviewed in *The North American Review*, Oct., 1849, pp. 440-469. The reviewer contends that Mr. Grimké's suggestions concerning the selection of judges are not well taken. As he viewed it, the judges should not be "chosen by the legislature; nor appointed by the Governor and His Council, or Senate; nor elected by the people." Instead, he argued, "all should unite in the choice; People, Legislature, and Executive." "We know not how else," he added, "to avoid the ignorance of the masses in relation to judicial qualification; the disposition of legislators to bargain away the bench for the United States Senate or some other equivalent; and the party bias for an Executive. Let every judge hold office till his successor is chosen, if the appointment is not for life; or rather, let the appointment be for life, and a successor be chosen while the incumbent is still alive. Let him be proposed by the Executive; confirmed by the legislature; and accepted by the people. He that shall be thus designated, and who shall look forward to a seat in the courts of his country, will assuredly be an able, just, and true man, and will have every inducement to prepare himself for his place. If this scheme is impracticable, and we fear it is, we have to decide which is the least of the three evils that we have enumerated as attendant respectively on

followed the lead of New York in establishing an elective judiciary. Legislative selection was in disfavor and the new method swept the country.[115] Politics had a great deal to do with this. The Jacksonian Democracy like the Jeffersonian Democracy viewed the judicial branch as a bulwark for the opposition group. The following brief passage from the debates in the Massachusetts Constitutional Convention of 1853, upon the problem of judicial selection, throws some light on the political angles involved:

Gentlemen seem to fear that if the judiciary is made elective, or the tenure of office limited, that political considerations will influence the choice of judges. Have not political influences controlled the choice of judges under our present system? How does it happen that only two judges of the supreme court were members of the Democratic party for more than half a century? Yes, sir, for more than fifty years, the judges of that court, with only two exceptions . . . were Federalists or Whigs. Many of these judges were not only politicians, but ultra politicians. Chief Justice Parsons was the brain of the famous Essex Junto. Chief Justice Parker was an ultra Federalist, and the present Chief Justice, I venture to say, entertains his political opinions with all the ardor and zeal of sincere conviction. Some of the more active, I may say violent politicians of the commonwealth have been appointed judges; and political considerations controlled their appointments. Every man of ordinary intelligence knows this to be so. Then why this extreme fear that politicians will be elected to the bench, or that politics will influence their appointment? It has ever been so, and I venture to say that it will continue to be so, in the future as in the past. It is said and I have reason to believe it to be so, that Judge Fletcher desired for several months to leave the bench until a Whig administration came into power. Then, in haste, he resigned, and a successor was appointed of the Whig school of politics, an able man, I know, and an able judge I am sure he will be; but a more violent political partisan it would be difficult to find in the State or in the Nation. Sir, I venture to say that the judges of our supreme court have been, and are now, strong, zealous politicians—as much so as any other class of public man. It has been so in other States. Chief Justice Spencer, in New York, played, while upon the bench, a leading part in the political history of that great state. He was the Warwick of New York politics and politicians, while on the bench. That great state has adopted the elective judicial system. Politics may now influence her judicial officers; but the judges under the present system will not influence so powerfully the political affairs of the state as they did

---

the three forms of election; and this decision, till we have more experience to guide us, is obviously a very difficult one." *Ibid.*, p. 465.

[115] The elective principle has survived in every state but one in which it was adopted. In 1865, Georgia abandoned popular election of judges in favor of their selection by a joint vote of the two houses of the legislature. Thorpe, *Charters and Constitutions*, p. 818. In 1868, Mississippi adopted the appointive system, but abandoned it in 1914. In 1864, Louisiana adopted the appointive system but returned to popular election in 1904. In 1868, Texas adopted the appointive system, but abandoned it in 1876.

from 1800 to 1825, especially while the judges were members of the Council of Appointment.

Sir, our history affords abundant evidence that the judges in this and other states have been men of as active and strong political feelings, prejudices, and opinions, as any other class of public men. And I am sure that our history shows that in the exercise of their judicial functions they have not been influenced, to any great extent, by their political opinions.[116]

While this revealing exposition was not without force, it did not have its desired effect in Massachusetts, which was one of the few states to remain unaffected by the strong movement throughout the country in favor of electing judges and shortening their terms. Perhaps one reason for this was the great rebuttal speech of Rufus Choate[117] before the same convention in 1853. This speech which was probably the supreme effort of that great advocate, remains one of the strongest expressions for an independent judiciary that can be found.

In his frequently quoted description of the qualities of a good judge, he says:

In the first place he must be profoundly learned in all the learning of the law, and he must be a man not merely upright, not merely honest and well-intentioned . . . but a man who will not respect persons in judgment . . . [in other words] he shall know nothing about the parties, everything about the case. He shall do everything for justice; nothing for his friends; nothing for his patron; nothing for his sovereign. If, on the one side, is the executive power and the legislature and the people—the sources of his honors, the givers of his daily bread; and on the other, an individual nameless and odious, his eye is to see neither, great nor small, attending only to the "trepidations of the balance." If a law is passed by a unanimous legislature, clamored for by the general voice of the public, and a cause is before him on it, in which the whole community is on one side, and an individual, nameless or odious, on the other, and he believes it to be against the Constitution, he must so declare it,—or there is no judge. If others come there to demand that the cup of hemlock be put to the lips of the wisest of men; and he believes that he has not corrupted the youth, nor omitted to worship the gods of the city, nor introduced new divinities of his own he must deliver him, although the thunder light on the untempted brow. . . . I would have him one who might look back from the venerable last years of Mansfield, or Marshall, and recall such testimonies as these to the great and good judge:

[116] Remarks of Henry Wilson of Natick in the Massachusetts Constitutional Convention of 1853. See *Debates and Proceedings*, vol. 2, pp. 706-707.

[117] Rufus Choate (1799-1859) was a leader of the Massachusetts bar at a time when it was graced by Jeremiah Mason, Franklin Dexter, Daniel Webster, Caleb Cushing, and Robert Rantoul. Although one of the greatest lawyers produced in this country, he, like Jeremiah Mason, William Pinkney, and Sergeant S. Prentiss, and several other great American advocates, has left little to recall his great personality and capacities. See *Works of Rufus Choate with a Memoir of His Life*, 2 vols., 1862, ed. by Samuel Gilman Brown; *Addresses and Orations of Rufus Choate*, 1878; Edward G. Parker, *Reminiscences of Rufus Choate*, 1860; Joseph Neilson, *Memories of Rufus Choate*, 1884; E. P. Whipple, *Some Recollections of Rufus Choate*, 1879; Claude M. Fuess, *Rufus Choate*, 1928.

"The young men saw me, and hid themselves; and the aged arose and stood up."

"The princes refrained talking, and laid their hand upon their mouth."

"When the Ear heard me, then it blessed me, and when the Eye saw me it gave witness to me."

"Because I delivered the poor that cried, and the fatherless, and him that had none to help him."

"The blessings of him that was ready to perish came upon me, and I caused the widow's heart to sing with joy."

"I put on righteousness and it clothed me. My judgment was as a robe and a diadem. I was eyes to the blind, and feet was I to the lame."

"I was a father to the poor, and the cause which I knew not, I searched out."

"And I broke the jaws of the wicked, and plucked the spoils out of his teeth."

"Give to the Community such a judge, and I care little who makes the rest of the Constitution, or what party administers it. It will be a free government I know. Let us repose, secure, under the shade of a learned, impartial, and trusted magistracy, and we need no more."[118]

Whatever may be thought of Choate's delineation of the judicial quality and its relationship to any particular method of selection, it is interesting to note that Massachusetts continued to appoint her judges and maintain them in office during good behavior. She was, of course, one of the few states to do so and today the elective principle is employed in whole or in part in thirty-eight states. In all of these thirty-eight states, the highest judges are elected by the people, while the trial judges are similarly selected in all but one of these states. In Florida, trial judges are appointed by the governor, although supreme court judges are popularly elected. In five states (Connecticut, Rhode Island, South Carolina, Vermont, and Virginia) the judges continue to be chosen by the legislature; and in one state they are appointed by the legislature upon the nomination of the governor. In five states (Maine, Massachusetts, New Hampshire, Delaware, and New Jersey) the highest judges are appointed by the governor, subject to confirmation by the executive council, or the senate.

Despite legislative advantages at the outset, and political, social and economic opposition throughout the period, the power of the judiciary grew by leaps and bounds, as the unique American doctrine of judicial review came to be accepted. Although the so-called doctrine of unconstitutionality is not expressly recognized nor sanctioned in either federal or state constitutions, it has been applied by both federal and state courts, apparently with the general consent of the people. This does not mean that the doctrine has been accepted from the beginning

[118] *Speech on Judicial Tenure delivered in the Massachusetts State Convention,* July 14, 1853. See *Addresses and Orations of Rufus Choate,* 1883, pp. 360-363.

of our system without question. As a matter of fact, it was some time before the doctrine was put into effect. Although it would be a difficult if not impossible task to set forth the exact time when the doctrine of judicial review was accepted by the American people, certain important steps can be noted.

The principle that an act of legislation which is contrary to the law under which a legislative body is organized is invalid, was familiar to Americans long before the constitution was adopted. Before the Revolution, colonial legislation was frequently subjected to review by the Privy Council,[119] and both before and after the adoption of the federal constitution, courts in a number of states had held statutes in conflict with state constitutions to be invalid.[120] The doctrine was set up as a national principle in 1803 in the case of *Marbury* v. *Madison*.[121]

[119] Before the Revolution, the validity of an act could be tested by an appeal to the King in Council to set aside the enactment of a colonial legislature, or by an appeal from the decision of a colonial court. These powers were not lightly considered. In fact, it has been estimated that some 8563 acts of the American colonies were submitted to the Privy Council, of which 469 were disallowed. Imperfect records of the Privy Council make it impossible to determine how many of these were set aside because of lack of authority on the part of the legislature to enact them, but enough is known to indicate that the proportion is large. (See Russell, *The Review of Colonial Legislation by the King in Council*; Andrews, *British Committees, Commissions, and Councils of Trade*.) In addition to appeals from the enactments of colonial legislatures to the Privy Council, there were also appeals from the decisions of colonial courts. Included in this group were three well-known cases: (1) *Winthrop* v. *Lechmere* (1727-1728). Thayer, *Cases on Constitutional Law*, I, 34; (2) *Philips* v. *Savage* (1738), *Acts of the Privy Council*, III, 432; (3) *Clark* v. *Tousey* (1745), *Acts of the Privy Council*, III, 540. The records of the Privy Council are imperfect in this connection also. In consequence it is almost impossible to determine how many of the cases appealed to it from the American colonies, aggregating more than 260 in number, were based on an alleged conflict between a legislative enactment and a colonial charter. See A. M. Schlesinger, "Colonial Appeals to the Privy Council," *Pol. Science Quarterly*, vol. 28, pp. 279, 433; Hazeltine, "Appeals from the Colonial Courts to the King in Council," *Annual Report of the American Historical Association for 1894*, p. 299. See Lawrence B. Evans, *Cases on Constitutional Law*, pp. 253-255.

[120] The rights of the courts to invalidate acts of the legislature had been exercised in at least five states before the constitutional convention assembled. As early as 1780, the highest court of New Jersey asserted the right of the courts to determine the validity of acts of the legislature in the case of *Holmes* v. *Walton*. (See *The American Historical Review*, vol. IV, p. 456.) In 1782, in the case of *Commonwealth* v. *Caton*, the same doctrine was asserted in Virginia; in 1784, in the case of *Rutgers* v. *Waddington* it was asserted in New York; in 1786, in the case of *Trevett* v. *Weeden*, decided in Rhode Island, a similar view was expressed (see Arnold, "History of Rhode Island," vol. II, ch. 24; Coxe, *Judicial Power and Unconstitutional Legislation*, pp. 234 ff; Kent, *Commentaries*, 12th ed., pp. 450-453); and in *Bayard* v. *Singleton*, decided in 1787 in North Carolina, the court asserted a similar principle. (All of these cases except *Holmes* v. *Walton* are printed in Thayer, *Cases*, I, 55-83.) See also B. F. Moore, *The Supreme Court and Unconstitutional Legislation* (1913), ch. I; C. C. Haines, *The Conflict Over Judicial Powers in the United States to 1870* (1909), p. 21; Lawrence B. Evans, *Cases on Constitutional Law*, pp. 255-256.

[121] 1 Cranch 137. In this case, Chief Justice John Marshall, in a classic statement, asserted the proposition that a Constitution is fundamental law, that legislative and executive powers are limited by this fundamental law, and that the courts as interpreters of the law must preserve and defend the Constitution. "The powers of the legislature," he said,

After that decision, the doctrine was accepted quite generally by state courts, state legislatures, and the people generally.[122] By 1818, the power of the courts to pass upon the constitutionality of legislation was recognized in every state but Rhode Island and the courts were largely following the lead of Marshall in proclaiming the power of the judiciary to pass upon the validity of legislative acts.[123] At the outset the courts moved slowly and with great caution. Of course, the amount of judicial business entrusted to it was not nearly as great as it came to be afterwards. Indeed during the first seventy-five years of the court's history the published reports did not average one a year. Of the reports published, five volumes were issued prior to Marshall's time; 27 were issued under Marshall, and 36 under Taney. During the first years of Taney's service the business of the court increased slowly, but from 1850 on, the increase became more rapid. Beginning with some 70 cases in 1850, the annual average increased to something over 400 during Waite's tenure of office. Whereas at mid-century, the court's calendar did not average 140 cases, and never reached 300 cases in any term; by 1890 it had reached 1500 cases. The work of the court during this time increased in volume, in importance, and in difficulty.[124]

"are defined and limited; and that these limits may not be mistaken or forgotten, the Constitution is written. To what purpose are powers limited and to what purpose is that limitation committed to writing, if these limits may at any time be passed by those intended to be restrained? The distinction between a government with limited and unlimited powers is abolished, if those limits do not confine the persons to whom they are imposed, and if acts prohibited and acts allowed are of equal obligation. . . . The Constitution is either a superior, paramount law, unchangeable by ordinary means, or it is on a level with ordinary legislative acts, and like other acts, is alterable when the legislature shall please to alter it. If the former part of the alternative be true, then a legislative act contrary to the Constitution is not law; if the latter part be true, then written constitutions are absurd attempts on the part of the people to limit a power, in its own nature illimitable." For a criticism of the decision in this case, see E. A. Corwin, *The Doctrine of Judicial Review and the Constitution*, ch. I, 1914; J. A. C. Grant, "Marbury v. Madison Today," *American Political Science Review*, vol. 23, pp. 673-681, August, 1929; A. C. McLaughlin, "Marbury v. Madison Again," *American Bar Association Journal*, vol. II, pp. 155-159, March, 1928; see also *Eakin* v. *Raub & R.* (Pa.) 330 (1825); also in Thayer, Cases, I, 133; Jackson's veto of the United States Bank Bill; Richardson, *Messages and Papers of the Presidents*, II, 581; also speech by Roscoe Conkling, April 16, 1860, *Congressional Globe*, 36th Congress, 1st Session, App. 233.

[122] In 1808, two judges of the Supreme Court of Ohio were impeached for declaring an act of the legislature unconstitutional and were removed from office. See F. R. Aumann, "The Course of Judicial Review in the State of Ohio," *Amer. Pol. Sci. Rev.*, vol. 25, May, 1931, pp. 36-38; William T. Utter, "Judicial Review in Early Ohio," *Mississippi Valley Historical Review*, vol. 15, pp. 3-26; William T. Utter, "Saint Tammany in Frontier Politics," *Ibid.*, vol. 15; pp. 321-340; T. M. Cooley, *Constitutional Limitations* (7th S.), p. 229, note; C. G. Haines, *The American Doctrine of Judicial Supremacy*, pp. 256-257

[123] The doctrine of judicial review, as stated by Justice Woodbury of New Hampshire in 1818, came to be the rule adopted in every state. See *Merril* v. *Sherburne*, 1 N. H. 204.

[124] Van Vechten Veeder, "A Century of Federal Judicature," *The Green Bag*, vol. 15, 1903, p. 230.

The slowness of the Supreme Court to exercise the practice of judicial review over acts of Congress is indicated by the fact that it held acts of Congress unconstitutional in only two cases before the Civil War,[125] although between 1803 and 1857 it heard arguments and passed upon the validity of a number of acts of Congress which it sustained.[126] It is interesting to observe that the state courts were moving with equal deliberation. Between 1776 and 1819, Charles G. Haines finds only eighteen cases in which state statutes are held invalid by state courts.[127] These figures are highly significant and indicate the general trend. The experience of one state may be used to throw further light on this tendency. Between 1802 and 1851 there are only seven officially reported cases in which the Ohio Supreme Court declared acts of the state legislature invalid, in whole or in part on constitutional grounds. In 1851, a new constitution was adopted which provided, among other things, for popular election of judges and stricter constitutional limitations. Encouraged to use their powers more freely, the courts proceeded to do so. Since 1851, it is safe to say, the Supreme Court of Ohio has declared acts of the legislature invalid in no less than two hundred cases.[128] The experience in the federal courts is much the same. Between 1789 and 1911, 279 state and federal acts were held invalid by the United States Supreme Court. Of this number, 32 measures were held invalid between 1789 and 1870; the rest were held invalid after that time.[129]

The process of judicial review does not really assume its present strength until after the Civil War.[130] But the principle of judicial review was established in the formative years and the developments which take place throughout that period perfect the idea of the separation of powers and make the system of checks and balances a workable system. The earlier practice of legislative supremacy falls by the wayside in the process. In the period after the Civil War when modern industrial

---

[125] Sometimes three cases are listed: (1) *United States* v. *Yale Todd*, 13 Howard, 52 (1793); (2) *Marbury* v. *Madison*, 1 Cranch, 137 (1803); and (3) *Scott* v. *Sandford*, 19 Howard, 393 (1857).

[126] See 17 *United States* 316 (1819); 19 *United States* 264 (1821); 22 *United States* 1 (1824); 22 *United States* 738 (1824).

[127] *The American Doctrine of Judicial Supremacy*, p. 228.

[128] F. R. Aumann, "The Course of Judicial Review in the State of Ohio," *Am. Pol. Sci. Rev.*, vol. 25, May, 1931, pp. 371-372; see also E. S. Corwin, "The Establishment of Judicial Review," *Michigan Law Review*, vol. 9, p. 314.

[129] Moore, "The Supreme Court and Unconstitutional Legislation," *Studies in History, Economics, and Public Law*, Columbia University, vol. LIV, App. III, 1913, pp. 139-141.

[130] From its institution in 1789 to May 17, 1937, the Supreme Court has disposed of about 40,000 cases. In seventy-seven of these, covering a period of one hundred and forty-eight years, it has held enactments of Congress unconstitutional: See Library of Congress (W. C. Gilbert), *Provisions of Federal Law Held Unconstitutional by the Supreme Court of the United States*, Government Printing Office, 1936. See also Warren, *Congress, the Constitution, and the Supreme Court*, 1925, ch. 9.

America was moving forward with powerful strides, the common law doctrine of the supremacy of the law and consequent judicial power over unconstitutional legislation gave the American judiciary a unique position in the political life of the country. It certainly gave the judiciary a relationship to the legislature which is quite different from that existing in the British system of government. Nevertheless, it is an achievement which is, in many respects, strictly in line with the history of the common law.[131] In fact it seems to entrench common law doctrine in our state and federal constitutions. This movement which reaches its climax in the Fourteenth Amendment places many of the fundamental and distinctive dogmas of the common law beyond the reach of ordinary State action. The judiciary becomes the special guardian and interpreter of these provisions which can be finally controlled in many cases only by a constitutional amendment.

This victory for the common law and the courts was not achieved easily. Many distinguished public men, including Thomas Jefferson, denounced the common law doctrine of supremacy of law, when applied by the courts in holding legislative acts unconstitutional. Such a course they claimed was an outright theft of jurisdiction. The states of Virginia, Kentucky, Pennsylvania, Georgia, and Wisconsin, successively denounced it, and Justice Gibson of Pennsylvania condemned the practice in a strong opinion. But despite strong and continuous objection, the common law principle became deeply rooted in our system,[132] as have "the common law dogmas of inviolability of person and property, of the local character of criminal jurisdiction, of due process of law— a phrase as old at least as the reign of Edward III, that private property cannot be taken for private use, nor for public use without just compensation, a doctrine as old as Magna Charta, that no one shall be compelled in any criminal prosecution to be a witness against himself, and of the right of trial by jury with all that was meant thereby at common law."[133] All of these dogmas, it is important to note, are protected in

---

[131] The three distinctive institutions of the Anglo-American legal system are: the doctrine of the rule of law, or "the supremacy of law," as it is frequently called; the doctrine of judicial precedent; and trial by jury.

[132] No state has departed from it and one of the states which formerly agitated for referring constitutional questions to a special, non-judicial tribunal, has since adopted a constitution in which the courts are expressly directed to declare the invalidity of unconstitutional legislation. See Judge Lurton, Proceedings, Bar Association of Tennessee, 1903, p. 125.

[133] Pound, The Spirit of the Common Law, vol. 18, 1906, pp. 18, 19, 20, 21. "If Coke were to come among us, he might miss the law of real property which he knew so minutely. Our law of contracts and our mercantile and corporation law would doubtless be unfamiliar, but he would be thoroughly at home in our common law. There he would see the development and fruition of his Second Institute. All that might surprise him would be that so much had been taken from him and made of his labors with so little recognition of the source." Ibid., p. 20.

federal and state constitutions so as to be substantially beyond the reach of legislation; and the courts are the special custodians and interpreters of our constitutions.

The triumph of the rule of law involved not only the powers of the courts to pass upon the validity of legislative action with reference to the constitution, but the validity of executive and administrative action as well, and the statutes governing such action. In the formative period, the importance and scope of executive and administrative action was not great. As time passed, however, and the field of public administration tended to become larger,[134] the application of the principle of the rule of law to this field placed the judiciary in a still more powerful position. A system of judicial interference with administrative action developed which sometimes resulted in a "paralysis of administration" by legal proceedings. On frequent occasions measures of police or administration were met with injunctions and with private suits by taxpayers to prevent alleged waste of public funds and misuse of the proceeds of taxation.[135] In consequence administration was held down to an inevitable minimum. Fearsome of control by administrative agencies, the American people permitted an increasing latitude and control to the courts. This tendency continued on to the end of the century, when new needs calling for a more continuing control and supervision, and for quicker enforcement led to the rapid development of administrative tribunals and agencies, and a consequent demand for the elimination of judicial review of administrative action wherever courts would hold it constitutional to do so, and in other cases to cut down such review to an unavoidable minimum.

[134] "In the earlier period of our history, government was a simple affair, but after the middle of the nineteenth century its functions broadened and the legislatures were unable to cope with the numerous problems that confronted them, many of which required expert knowledge. New agencies were created to collect and digest materials to serve as a basis for intelligent legislation. Some had their origin in the desire of the legislature to evade action on important questions; others were created to furnish spoils for the party in power; still others were the result of popular demands for agencies of social and industrial betterment. The growth of insurance, banking, railways, and other corporations, and the failure to control them by detailed legislation, led to the creation of boards of experts with large powers, legislative, administrative, and judicial combined." Gettel, *History of American Political Thought*, p. 542.

[135] "Coke's statement that the Court of King's Bench had jurisdiction to correct oppression of the subject or 'any other manner of misgovernment' was accepted by American courts down to the latter part of the nineteenth century, although as early as 1800 some courts began to desist from extreme assertion of the doctrine. But with the change from a rural, agricultural society to an urban, industrial one, a revival of administration and a reaction from the extreme development of the common law were inevitable." R. Pound, "Rule of Law," *Social Science Encyclopedia*, vol. 13, 1934, p. 465.

PART III

SOME PROBLEMS OF GROWTH AND DEVEL-
OPMENT DURING THE PERIOD OF
MATURITY OF AMERICAN
LAW, 1865-1900

CHAPTER IX

THE AMERICAN LEGAL SYSTEM IN THE PERIOD
OF INDUSTRIAL GROWTH

In the years that intervened between the Civil War and the turn of the century, the whole character of American life underwent a veritable transformation. The basis of the change was economic but it affected every aspect of life, including the legal order. During the early part of the nineteenth century, it has been noted, agriculture and commerce were the chief centers of interest. Energies were expended in supplying settlers for the new land to the westward, in shipping and in the production of staples for the European market. At the same time important revelations of science were making possible the application of the forces of steam and electricity to manufacture and transportation. As a result, modes of transportation which had been in use for generations gave way before the railway and steamboat and means of communication were revolutionized by the telegraph, telephone and wireless. Moreover, completely changed methods of manufacturing gave rise to large scale production, the factory system, and the movement to the cities. During this period group activity tended to supersede individual activity and combination of strength and resource, involving huge collections of capital, became necessary to make these changed activities of men effective.

The growth of large scale industry, the growing complexity of business relationships arising out of corporate organization and combination, the concentration of population in urban communities, the rapid increase and accumulation of personal property and the improved facilities for communication and transportation brought about remarkable changes in social conditions which demanded corresponding changes in the law. Ideas of liberty, liability, contract, and property based on earlier individualistic conceptions were made to yield to new interpretations based on new conceptions of social interdependence. Whereas the law of the first half of the nineteenth century was developed in the direction of strengthening and preserving individual rights, the law of the second half was developed in the direction of creating, reorganizing, and regulating the great combinations which were emerging.[1] In moving

[1] Brooks Adams, *Centralization and the Law*, pp. 46, 47, 53, 59, 61, 63, 100, 103, 108-11.

in this direction, American law, like English law, as Professor Dicey points out, was following a universal tendency.[2]

The early nineteenth century period in which American judges made over our system of law out of common law materials, represented, it will be remembered, a stage of legal development, which is sometimes called the strict law.[3] Resembling, as we have noted, that earlier classical period in which Coke and his contemporaries summed up and restated the law developed by the English courts from the thirteenth to the fifteenth century, it was characterized as are all periods of strict law by an extreme individualism.[4] While some elements in our inherited legal system emphasized the idea of "status" or "relation," Americans were prone to disregard them in the early nineteenth century.[5] They thought of legal problems in terms of individuals rather than of groups or relations.[6] The announcement and wide acceptance of Sir Henry Maine's theory that the evolution of law is a progress from status to contract encouraged this manner of thinking.[7] The doctrines of Herbert Spencer and the Manchester School of Economics encouraged it still further. In this view each individual knew his own interest best and any attempts to expand the functions of government, especially in relation to industrial conditions, were frowned upon. Law was looked upon as a slow and gradual creation arising out of past human experience and was not to be changed lightly, particularly with regard to industrial conditions. In this view, the courts were to discover and apply fixed rules of justice and rapid changes or extensive governmental interference was looked upon as undesirable.[8]

[2] Joseph C. Beale, Jr., "The Development of Jurisprudence during the Nineteenth Century," *Select Essays in Anglo-Saxon Legal History*, vol. 1, p. 537.

[3] Pound, "The End of Law as Developed in Legal Rules and Doctrines," *Harvard Law Review*, vol. 27, No. 3, Jan., 1914, pp. 195-235.

[4] Pound, *The Spirit of the Common Law*, pp. 18-20.

[5] "While the strict law insisted that every man should stand upon his own feet. . . the principal social and legal institution of the time in which the common law was formative, the feudal relation of lord and man, regarded men in quite another way. Here the question was not what a man had undertaken or done, but what he was." Pound, *The Spirit of the Common Law*, p. 20.

[6] "In the nineteenth century the feudal contribution to the common law was in disfavor. Puritanism, the attitudes of protecting the individual against government and society which the common law courts had taken in the contests with the crown, the eighteenth century theory of the natural rights of the abstract individual man, the insistence of the pioneer upon a minimum of interference with his freedom of action, and the nineteenth century deduction of law from a metaphysical principle of individual liberty— all these combined to make jurists and lawyers think of individuals rather than of groups or relations and to make jurists think ill of anything that had the look of the archaic institution of status." Pound, *ibid.*, pp. 27-28.

[7] Pound, *Interpretations of Legal History*, 1923, pp. 53-61.

[8] It should be remembered, however, that the humanitarian movement which took place in the early period brought about an increased recognition of industrial rights and protection of individuals. It led to successful efforts to abolish slavery and emancipate women. It gave a more favorable position to dependent individuals and liberalized the

When social and economic changes began to take place at a highly-accelerated rate, and a changed philosophy as to the nature and place of law in society became necessary, the courts were faced with the problem of reconciling these earlier thought-patterns with the realities of the new day. It was a trying time for the courts. A great many of the legal materials demanded by an industrial society collided violently with the traditional legal materials which had been developed for an agricultural society. The intense individualism which characterized the classical common law tradition was a stumbling block of huge proportions. Nevertheless a system of settled and stable jurisprudence was of fundamental importance to the rapidly developing industrial society.[9] The courts could not evade their duty. In consequence, the period between 1865 and 1900 is one of great labor for the legal order, as attempts were made to adjust law to a social order which was being rapidly altered by technological change.

Statute and common law expanded as public lands were opened to settlers and railroads were pushed far out into the West.[10] Great industrial corporations developed and population increased particularly in the industrial centers. In the next fifty years, the law of corporations,

---

harsh provisions of the criminal law. Imprisonment for debt was also abolished and bankruptcy came to be treated as a misfortune, not a crime. Beale, "The Development of Jurisprudence during the Nineteenth Century," *Select Essays in Anglo-Saxon Legal History*, vol. 1, p. 538.

[9] "But there is another group higher still in origin and in power, which being anterior in origin, and more out of sight, is still more commonly forgotten, or assumed as a matter of course. This group of causes on which the value of every man's work both to himself and others absolutely depends, is the group which is connected with the laws that protect all rights, and enforce all contracts, between man and man. It is these alone which create the industrial security without which no venture could possibly be undertaken or even thought of. A system of settled and stable jurisprudence, with an honest and firm executive—the paramount reign of law in all the relations of men—these are the indispensable, though the too often unseen and unthought of, foundations of every industrial society. All these are the imperative conditions, and the operative agencies in all production—the conditions and agencies of all enterprises—and so of all employment." The Duke of Argyll, *The Unseen Foundations of Society*, pp. 434-435.

[10] "A number of things conspired to introduce a new economic and social order into American life in the 60's and 70's. The high war tariffs caused men of capital to invest their money in manufacturing; and government contracts for war supplies gave impetus to this development. The state and national governments embarked on a policy of making vast grants of land and credit to railroad enterprises, thus laying the foundations for the modern era of railway development. The passage of the free homestead law of 1862 caused a rush of population toward the west, a movement that was vastly stimulated by the opening up of the less accessible regions to the railroads. These various factors reacted upon each other. . . . The unprecedented activity along all lines of economic behavior imposed fresh demands upon American inventive genius to which it responded with countless new appliances and machines for farm and factory." Schlesinger, *New Viewpoints in American History*, 248; Beard, *Contemporary American History*, 1914, p. 28); Emery, *Economic Development of the United States (Cambridge Modern History Series)*, vol. 7, ch. 22, pp. 696, 698; Rhodes, *History of the United States*, vol. 7, 1912, pp. 37-53.

railroads and public service companies and insurance developed rapidly. New and wide uses for the "police power" were also worked out. The burdens placed upon the courts by the increased use of the corporate form is of particular interest.[11] Although a few great trading companies had existed in the middle ages, the modern form of business association, the private corporation with limited ability, is a comparatively recent development. Such corporations were created by special act of the legislature all through the last century, but during the post–Civil War period general laws were provided under which they might be formed by mere agreement of the individuals. As large scale business became not only practical but necessary, the organization of corporate entities has engrossed the attention of the important industries of the country and has come to wield enormous powers upon the destiny of its people.[12]

The difficulties imposed upon the American legal system during this period began with the Civil War. The record of the United States Supreme Court graphically illustrates this point. Perhaps no more difficult and momentous questions were ever presented to any court than those which came before the Supreme Court during this period. Starting in the early sixties, when the country was straining every nerve and exerting every power to win the war, a veritable flood of difficult problems was forced upon the court for solution. Cases arising out of the war emergency involved the questions of jurisdiction of military tribunals; of the suspension of the writ of habeas corpus; of whether the confederacy was to be treated as a belligerent, and if so, its rights as such; of the rights of neutrals; of litigation concerning confiscation, prizes, blockade, and non-intercourse; of legislation to uphold the credit of the government and to sustain the armies of the government;

[11] "I found that in a recent volume of the reports of the Sup. Ct. of the U. S., sixty-one cases were reported, of which twenty-eight were between natural persons on both sides; twenty-seven were cases in which private corporations were concerned and six cases in which public corporations were concerned. In May, 1879, Chief Justice Waite wrote me that the court had at the recent term disposed of three hundred and seventy-nine cases, of which ninety-one related to the United States, one hundred and five were between private individuals. To ascertain whether the amount of corporate litigation in the Supreme Court was abnormal, I personally examined three volumes of the New York Court of Appeals Reports . . . that is, volumes LXIII, LXXIV, and CV . . . with the following result: Civil cases reported, four hundred and twenty-four; of which two hundred and thirty-four were between private persons, and one hundred and ninety were cases in which corporations, public or private, were concerned on one side or the other. I then examined volume I, Johnson's Reports, published in 1806. I found one hundred and thirty cases reported, of which only twenty related to any sort of corporations or involved corporation law.

"This change in the character of the litigation ought not, perhaps, to surprise us, since we know the business of banking, of manufacturing, of insurance, of railway and water transportation, of telepathy, and of nearly every branch of industry requiring considerable capital, prefers the safe and facile form of corporate organization and ownership to the inconvenience and liabilities of the co-partnership, or even joint stock relation." Dillon, *Laws and Jurisprudence of England and America*, 1894, pp. 376-377.

[12] Berle and Means, *The Modern Corporation and Private Property*, 1932.

questions of tax laws and of the rights of the government to declare its paper money legal tender for the payment of private debts; questions of personal liberty and of many other constitutional rights of primary importance. With the war terminated, still more important cases were presented, involving the reconstruction of the seceded states and the amendments to the constitution which had been adopted as a result of the struggle. The problems of the restoration of civil authority, the reconstruction of state governments and of proper amendments placed particularly heavy burdens upon the court. The Thirteenth, Fourteenth and Fifteenth Amendments, which were designed to give further security to personal rights, brought a train of highly important problems including the question of national supremacy with the question of the preservation of the rights of the state.

When the reconstruction period receded, the energies of the country were given over to the development of its natural resources and to the settlement of the more western states. It was then that industry and commerce expanded, that vast enterprises were undertaken, that wealth accumulated on a gigantic scale, and the struggle of competing interests in the political area was intensified. Out of these changed conditions arose a vast amount of litigation of vital consequence to the country. The application of the forces of steam and electricity to railway and steamship transportation and the transmission of intelligence by telegraph and telephone brought intricate problems of regulation before the court. The enlarged commerce on the seas, on the Great Lakes, and on the navigable waters of the country, greatly increased the number of admiralty cases and cases related thereto. Litigation was also increased by the unlimited facilities for the formation of contracts. Increased wealth and increased facilities for interstate commerce flooded the courts with controversies concerning state taxation and regulation. The development of the country's mineral resources and the distribution of vast grants of the public domain in aid of railroad building and for educational purposes brought further litigation to the court for settlement.[13]

The method in which the court met its grave responsibilities was to have a far-reaching effect on the judicial power and on the nation in the years to come. For it was in this period that the supremacy of the legislative departments gave way before the increased power of the courts. The new center of power was to remain unaltered throughout

[13] The court also considered important questions concerning the Indian wards of the nation, the status of polygamy among the Mormons, anti-Chinese legislation, the constitutionality of the Enforcement Act, the power of the President to remove from office, the extent of federal control over congressional elections, the Virginia land cases, the Coupon Tax cases, the power of the states to prohibit the liquor traffic, the repudiation of state debts, the meaning of the Eleventh Amendment, etc.

this period between 1865 and 1890 when the new industrialized America was building. When the twentieth century arrived, the leadership of the judiciary which was established in its full form in those post–Civil War days largely through the efforts of the Supreme Court was to be challenged by the advancing leadership of the executive. In the meantime the judiciary enjoyed a period of great power and great responsibility. It began in this period as the Supreme Court in epoch-making cases exercised the unique American doctrine of judicial review. This power, as we have previously noted, was seldom used before the Civil War.[14] In the troublesome post-war period it came into use with more frequency. In fact, some observers, including Louis Boudin,[15] argue that it was in this period that "government by judiciary,"[16] as they describe it, was fully set up for the first time.

During this period a number of strong men sat on the Supreme Court. Notable among this group were Justices Miller, Bradley, and Field. In the view of some observers, Justice Samuel Freeman Miller (1816-1890) dominated the court on constitutional questions,[17] with Stephen Johnson Field (1816-1899) a close second,[18] while Joseph B.

[14] "The frequency with which the court has been forced to exercise its solemn functions of nullifying unconstitutional acts of legislation affords a basis of comparison for estimating the extent and importance of the courts' labors during this period. Aside from the action of the judges with respect to the attempt of Congress to confer jurisdiction upon the Supreme Court in claims for pensions (2 Dallas, 409; 13 Howard, 32, n.) an act of Congress was declared invalid in *Marbury* v. *Madison,* 1 Cranch, 139, in 1803. From 1803 to 1864, there was only one instance of the exercise of such a power. (*U. S.* v. *Ferreira,* 13 Howard, 40, in 1851.) During the next twenty-five years, however, the power was exercised fifteen times. Prior to 1860, less than fifty statutes and ordinances of States and Territories had been declared unconstitutional by the Court. Between 1860 and 1889, the court nullified such acts in more than one hundred and thirty cases." Van Vechten Veeder, "A Century of Federal Judicature," *The Green Bag,* vol. 15, 1903, p. 223. This statement omits the Dred Scott case referred to earlier.
[15] Boudin, *Government by Judiciary,* 1932, pp. 1-2ff.
[16] The power of the courts has grown so rapidly since the Civil War that our system has been characterized by one French commentator as a "government by judges." (Edouard Lambert, *Le Gouvernement des juges, et la lutte contre la legislation sociale aux Etats-Unis* (Paris, 1921); W. F. Dodd, "The Growth of Judicial Power," *Pol. Sci. Q.,* vol. 24, p. 193). According to this observer, the final control of the social and economic policy of the country is vested in the courts. It is undoubtedly true that under such broad constitutional provisions as the "due process of law" clause, the courts do fix the limit of legislative power and accordingly determine policy in connection with social and economic legislation.
[17] " . . . During the period when Miller was a Supreme Court Justice—from his appointment in 1862 to his death in 1890—the Court under the successive leadership of Taney, Chase, Waite, and Fuller was called upon to decide problems, at first of political and later of industrial import, which were the gravest in the history of the country, second in importance to none, and ranking in that respect even with the questions of the nature and power of the Federal government to the shaping of which Marshall had devoted the talents of the greatest of American jurists." Lewis, *Great American Lawyers,* vol. 6, pp. 551-553.
[18] Stephen Johnson Field, brother of David Dudley Field and Cyrus West Field, served on the United States Supreme Court for a period of thirty-four years and seven

Bradley (1813-1892), was particularly concerned with strengthening the control of the Federal Government in the field of interstate commerce.[19] In matters of foreign and interstate Commerce, he said, there are no states. He looked upon all traffic crossing state lines as fully a national problem as were matters relating to the currency, the patent laws, or the regulation of the nation's army and navy. Inclined, as several of the justices of the Supreme Court at that time were, to a strengthening of the control of the National Government over interstate commerce, says one commentator, "their decisions are far from being as radical in this direction as were those of Bradley, and no one else has contributed so markedly as he toward the placing of commerce on an impregnable and uniform basis and the freeing of it from the obstacles of state interference, greed, and jealousy which had bound it in greater or less degree from the days of the Articles of Confederation to the Civil War and even beyond it."[20]

months. This exceeded the thirty-four years and five months of Chief Justice Marshall; the thirty-three years and ten months of Justice Story; the thirty-two years and six months of Justice Wayne; the thirty-two years and one month of Justice McLean; the thirty years and eleven months of Justice Washington; the thirty years and five months of Justice Johnson; and the twenty-nine years and one month of Justice Oliver Wendell Holmes. Field's greatest opinions were dissents and not expressions of the judgment of the Court. He acted principally as a curb upon the centralizing tendencies of his associates, by protecting state and local government as far as was consistent with national strength. His greatest influence was in his resistance to the impulse engendered by the War to make the central government an all-powerful agency, controlling not only broad questions of national policy but also the ordinary civil rights of citizens of the states. Despite his wish that the states retain full government power and that congress be prevented from exercising sweeping powers not delegated to it, his tendency in matters of interstate commerce was always toward the molding of a system by which Congress would be paramount and supreme where the question was one of more than local importance. He was more consistent in this attitude than any other judge save Bradley. "Indeed," says one commentator, "his dissenting opinions go to an extreme length in their denials to the states of the right to prohibit the introduction into their borders, or the exportation from their borders, of articles which were not recognized by them as legitimate subjects of commerce." Lewis, *Great American Lawyers*, vol. 7, p. 71.

[19] "The years of Bradley's career upon the bench, from 1870 to 1891, were characterized by a wonderful expansion of the country's commerce. In the decades following the Civil War, trade and commerce increased enormously, and no problems presented themselves to the judiciary so frequently as did those of commerce and navigation. In every volume of the Supreme Court reports for these years are to be found great numbers of decisions marking off the relative powers of state and nation to regulate transportation and interstate traffic. The attitude of Justice Bradley toward these problems is distinct, clearly defined, and usually consistent. No one was more aggressive than he in asserting the supremacy of the Federal Government in controlling interstate commerce. He looked upon his work on this subject as the most important of his activities upon the bench. . . . From his concurring opinion in *Ward* v. *Maryland*, 12 Wallace's Reports 418 (1870), decided in the first year of his judicial service, to his dissenting opinion in *Maine* v. *Grand Trunk Ry. Co.*, 142 *U. S. Reports* 217 (1891), almost the last decision of the court in which he participated, there is scarcely a break in the long line of cases in which he protests against the powers claimed by individual states to tax interstate commerce or the instrumentalities of interstate commerce under any form or guise whatsoever. (Some exceptions listed, p. 787)." Lewis, *Great American Lawyers*, vol. 6, pp. 382-388.

[20] Lewis, *Great American Lawyers*, vol. 6, pp. 387-388.

In 1868, the year the Fourteenth Amendment was adopted, a book appeared which was to have an immense effect upon American constitutional development and assist the movement well under way to enlarge judicial power at the expense of the legislature. This book which was called *A Treatise on the Constitutional Limitations which Rest upon the Legislative Powers of the States of the American Union* was to become the most frequently cited work in American constitutional law. It was written by Judge Thomas M. Cooley of Michigan[21] and lays the basis for the statement that is sometimes heard that Cooley is as important in American constitutional law as Coke is in English constitutional law.[22]

While much has been written upon American constitutional law before this time, it had been chiefly concerned with the interpretation of the national constitution. Judge Cooley approached the matter from the angle of the limitations imposed upon the legislative powers of the states. These limitations were apart from the provisions of their written constitutions. This theory was to have a wide influence upon the doctrine of judicial review in the days to come.[23] The present wide scope of that doctrine tends to obscure its narrower application in earlier years, when constitutional limitations upon the states, contained in such provisions as the contract clause, were few and of little effect. In earlier years, when Federalist influences still lingered on in the judiciary, attempts were made to find extra-constitutional limitations for the protection of vested rights by appealing to the "higher law" philosophy of the social compact and to natural and inalienable rights.[24] This movement was stopped for a time by the victories of the Jacksonian democracy. In consequence, state governments exercised wide powers and state legislative bodies, as noted before, remained supreme until

[21] Thomas McIntyre Cooley (1824-1898) served on the Supreme Court of Michigan from 1864 to 1885; taught in the law course of the University of Michigan for twenty-five years; and served as the first Chairman of the Interstate Commerce Commission which he helped to organize upon an effective basis. See Lewis, *Great American Lawyers*, vol. 7, pp. 431-491.

[22] In addition to his *Constitutional Limitations*, Judge Cooley published an edition of Blackstone's *Commentaries* which became one of the leading American editions of that work. In this work, he incorporated his *Suggestions upon the Study of Law*, which proved extremely helpful to thousands of young law students. In 1874, he prepared an edition of Story's *Commentaries on the Constitution of the United States*, adding greatly to the value of this work by notes and comments. In 1876, he published his well-known and widely used text book on the *Principles of Constitutional Law*. He also prepared the legal articles for the second edition of the *American Encyclopedia* and wrote many of the articles for the *Encyclopedia of Political Science*, in addition to numerous articles for legal periodicals and the leading magazines of the day.

[23] Cooley's doctrine of implied constitutional limitations has now "become assimilated under the 'rule of reason' in the extremely broad interpretation of the due process clause of the Fourteenth Amendment that now prevails."

[24] Justices Marshall, Paterson, Samuel Chase, Kent, and Story, made incursions into this field at one time or another.

about the middle of the nineteenth century. The enormous expenditures for public improvements demanded by the public and acceded to by state legislatures and the large subsidies to the railroads authorized by the same bodies were brought into question by the economic depressions of 1837 and 1857 and the state legislatures became a greatly discredited governmental agency.

After the Civil War, confidence in legislative bodies disappeared even more rapidly. In both state and nation, the calibre of their members declined and public approval of their activities dwindled as frequent instances of political corruption appeared. Legislative subservience to selfish interests and general disregard of the public led inevitably to corrective measures, in the form of constitutional provisions restricting the powers of the legislatures and taking many questions out of their hands. The decline in legislative power occurred as the power of the judiciary and executive tended to increase and as popular control over all three branches of the government became stronger.[25] The power of state governments was somewhat curtailed in the realignment. Their powers were greatly weakened by the Civil War and in the days to come their former powers were to continue to be diminished in many important respects.[26] Cooley's book, which was the first work to deal in a systematic fashion with the limitations resting upon the states, was to assist greatly in this process.

Cooley contended that written constitutions did not so much create new frames of government as embody the past political experience of a people. He worked out his implied constitutional limitations upon that basis. While he expressly repudiated any notions of higher law, he took the results of early higher law cases to support his own particular formula of control. His conception of implied constitutional limitations was predicated upon such ideas as the separation of powers, checks and balances and constitutional governments in general. The limitations he worked out were numerous and varied. Taxation could be lawful only for a public purpose and the power of eminent domain could be exercised only to take property for a public use; laws of special or discriminatory character could not be passed; legislatures could not interfere with a judicial function; nor could vested rights be divested, even apart from the due process clause of the state constitutions. His extended analysis of the idea of due process and his conception of it as a protection against any arbitrary interference of government, prepared the way for a similar construction of that provision of the

[25] Despite the decline in legislative prestige, the volume of legislation tended to increase and organized efforts to correct social and economic evils by law greatly modified the individualistic self-sufficiency of an earlier, simpler era.

[26] F. R. Aumann, "Whither the Sovereign State," *The South Atlantic Quarterly*, vol. 34, Oct., 1935, pp. 346-358.

Fourteenth Amendment by the Supreme Court during the eighties. He justified his conclusions by precedent, "but his creative role is evident from his insistence, among other doctrines that taxation must be for a public purpose, a rule clearly against the weight of existing authority but useful in checking the action of the state legislatures in favor of such private corporations as the railroads." Concerned for the most part with broad general principles he was true to his time and environment in emphasizing property rights more strongly than personal rights. The net result of his constitutional doctrine was to increase the power of the courts at the expense of the legislature.

Cooley's writings mark the beginning of a period of productive writing in the American legal field. The years between 1872 and 1882 were particularly important in this connection. Among other works published during this decade are Perry, *Trusts*, 1872; Dillon, *Municipal Corporations*, 1873; Freeman, *Judgments*, and High, *Injunctions*, 1873; Cooley, *Revised Edition of Story's Commentaries on the Constitution of the United States*, 1874; Cooley, *Taxation*, and Freeman, *Executions*, and *Remedies and Remedial Rights by the Civil Action According to the Reformed American Procedure*, all in 1876; Jones, *Mortgages*, 1878; Cooley, *Torts*, 1879; Cooley, *Principles of Constitutional Law*, 1880; Morawitz, *Corporations*, 1879; Pomeroy, *Equity Jurisprudence*, 1881-1883.[27] The influence of legal scholarship upon the development of the law which was to become even greater as the years passed, was anticipated by the work of the writers of this important decade.[28]

The work of John Norton Pomeroy[29] may be taken to illustrate

[27] In *American Law Review*, vol. 37, 1903, p. 312, it is stated that of the fifty textbooks which were most frequently cited by the courts during the late nineteenth century period, twenty of them were published in the decade, 1872-1882.

[28] Beale, "The Development of Jurisprudence During the Nineteenth Century," *Select Essays in Anglo-American Legal History*, 1907, pp. 558, 571.

[29] John N. Pomeroy (1828-1885) was perhaps the most important textbook writer of the last third of the nineteenth century. In his early law teaching at New York University, he is said to have anticipated, by several years, most of the essentials of the method introduced by Dean Langdell, into the Harvard Law School which did so much to shape the study of law in this country. *Great American Lawyers*, vol. 8, p. 99. A great part of his teaching career was spent at the University of California. While there he examined with care the Civil Code of California. This code of substantive law was substantially identical with the draft code reported to the legislature of New York in 1865, and for twenty years afterwards urged upon the legislature for adoption in that state. At the beginning of his career, he was skeptical of codification attempts; but his admiration for the Codes of Procedure, in their general principles and features, had made him quite sympathetic to the idea of a General Code, such as the one California has been experimenting with. His study of that code convinced him that it was filled with "errors, uncertainties, and inconsistencies" which demand a "judicial interpretation" for nearly every section. He concluded that the only salvation for the law of California lay in the "deliberate adoption of a method of interpretation different from that hitherto applied to statutory law." He wrote a series of papers on codification, both in New York and elsewhere. *Ibid.*, pp. 115-117.

the nature and extent of this influence. His work on *Remedies and Remedial Rights by the Civil Action According to the Reformed American Procedure* (1876), was highly useful in the procedural field;[30] and his work on *Equity Jurisprudence* exerted an influence upon our jurisprudence that was in many ways remarkable. "It is probably not too much to say," wrote Dean H. R. Hutchins of the University of Michigan Law School in 1906, "that during the past twenty years this work has exerted directly through the tribunals of last resort a greater influence upon our jurisprudence than any other single treatise."[31] Coming shortly after a period of brilliant work by English Chancery judges who in the third quarter of the nineteenth century had restated the principles and doctrines of equity with such effectiveness as to amount almost to a re-creation, Pomeroy welded the scattered labors of these men into a compact mass. This he did with great ingenuity and resource.[32] The most obvious way in which his book has exerted an influence has been in expressing in a definite and widely-accepted form many of the general

[30] This book was received with expressions of appreciation by such a widely assorted group as David Dudley Field, Stephen J. Field, Samuel L. Seldon, Theodore W. Dwight, John Dillon, Lord Chancellor Cairns, and Lord Chief Justice Coleridge; and by the judges of the New York Court of Appeals who joined in stating their appreciation. One commentator, in speaking of this work, said: "The judges and the lawyers had all been trained in the common law school; its system of pleadings, the most artificial the world has ever known, had come to be looked upon as the perfection of logical statement, its technicalities and even its fictions had so thoroughly taken possession of the mind as to be regarded as part of the law of remedy—they were always upon the tongue and were a guide to thought; the new terminology was strange, and seemed as barbarous as does that of the common law to the classical student before his tastes have been drowned; and it has not yet supplanted the old; the fact that all men travel more or less in grooves, that they feel lost and frightened when they find themselves out of the accustomed road, with all their pride, that they trust far less to reason than to tradition; these things made it impossible at once to understand and apply the new system in its full scope and with all its logical sequences. The bar looked eagerly to the courts, the courts clung timidly to the shore; some judges were hostile, some were friendly; the best were at a loss, and we should have gained more than we could have lost, had the decisions of the first ten years never been reported. . . . How many centuries were necessary to settle the old system, we do not fully know; the new is already assuming form and comeliness, but time will elapse before there will be perfect harmony in the construction and application of its rules. That time will be greatly hastened by such treatises as that of Mr. Pomeroy." Judge Phelamon Bliss of the Missouri Supreme Court, 2 *So. L. Rev.*, 1906, (n.s.), p. 339.

[31] *Michigan Law Review*, vol. 4, p. 248, cited in Lewis, *Great American Lawyers*, vol. 8, p. 130. Chief Justice McClellan of Alabama, writing on October 16, 1905, held Pomeroy's *Equity Jurisprudence*, to be one of the three greatest of law books that has been written in the English language. *Ibid.*, p. 130.

[32] "An important difference between the English system and the American system as to means and methods of legal growth and development, has sometimes escaped attention. . . . We profess to be ruled by precedent, but from the very vastness of their number we rely, rather—be it for weal or woe—on the rapid and constant interchange of opinion— of "persuasive authority"—from state to state, from text-writer to judge. The word dictum is not, with us, a word of opprobrium. In our composite system, the text-writer of high authority has a place of influence—unknown in the English law—nearly equal to that of the greatest judge; a dignity, realized or not, approaching that of the juristic writers in the Roman law. To few works, it is true, is such authority conceded; Pomeroy's Equity Jurisprudence at once took rank with them. . . . " *Ibid.*, p. 129.

rules and doctrines of equity.[33] Beyond this it illustrates the creative power "which under the American system, is within the power of the authoritative text-writers even more than of the judges; the power to seize an obscure or neglected principle, to drag it to the light, to show its important applications to the practical affairs of life, and by the mere force of convincing logic to compel its adoption by the courts."[34]

The net effect of all these writings was to increase judicial authority and prestige. Indeed everything during this period conspired to enlarge the power of the judiciary. That does not mean that this enlargement of power was without opposition. Such a view would be misleading. There was considerable opposition particularly when an opinion was rendered in the Supreme Court that affected important interest groups of one kind or another. The Income Tax case, for example, gave rise to a considerable expression of adverse opinion. Furthermore, a very active movement was at work during this period which would have increased the power of legislatures at the expense of the courts. For it is during this period that the two branches locked horns in a struggle which came to be known as the battle of the codes. Starting with a preliminary struggle in New York in 1857, the conflict raged for thirty years. In the years immediately following the Civil War the controversy between one group of jurists led by David Dudley Field (1805-1894) who favored codification of state law by the legislature, and another group led by James Coolidge Carter (1829-1905) who favored the gradual development of the law through judicial decisions was particularly bitter. Field was impatient with the over-refined technicalities, the interminable delay, and the burdensome expenses of civil justice. He was interested in establishing a method whereby simply, expeditiously, and inexpensively, litigation might perform its function of superseding private controversy.

He began his agitation for radical reform in procedure and for codification of the substantive law in 1839. His first project was the reformation and simplification of procedure and the elimination of the distinction between suits at law and equity. This project took form in the Field Code of Civil Procedure and ultimately influenced the English reforms on the same subject in the English Judicature Acts.[35] When

---

[33] "Few sentences of the book, in its interpretative parts, have failed of adoption by some courts, often by many courts. Its effect has been that of a partial codification of this most vital portion of the law, with none of the dangers, in loss of flexibility, that attend a general statutory enactment. The hope, so earnestly expressed in the author's preface, that his book might help to avert, in this country, the threatened decay and hardening of equity, appears to have been abundantly fulfilled." Lewis, *Great American Lawyers*, vol. 8, pp. 130-131.

[34] *Ibid.*, p. 131.

[35] Today this code is in one shape or another, the text, or at least the substance of legal procedure in all but a few of the states of the United States, and in most of the English-speaking commonwealths, and among some foreign nations.

he began his campaign, constitutional obstructions interfered with his plans in New York State. In 1846, a new constitution was adopted which made his project possible and established tentative machinery for the reforms he sought. After great effort, the Code of Civil Procedure was adopted in 1848.[36] He was not satisfied with this, however, since his plan involved five codes: one covering civil procedure, the second covering criminal procedure, the third a restatement of criminal substantive law, the fourth a restatement of civil or private substantive law, and the fifth a political or governmental institute.[37] It was the battle over these advanced codes that began in New York in 1857 and lasted for thirty years. Year after year, the bill came before the New York legislature and was defeated in one way or another. Field continued to fight on. Between 1878 and 1888, James Carter led a successful fight to keep the Field Code from being adopted in New York. In that year, when Field was eighty-three years old, the bill was finally defeated. The arguments used in this struggle are of interest.

Field claimed that a chaotic system resulted from piece-meal decision and emphasized the necessity for simplification in phraseology and procedure. He claimed that a crystallization of the law in statutory form would make it more systematic and intelligible.[38] Believing that our codeless myriad of precedents, our wilderness of single instances

[36] The Code of Civil Procedure went into effect on July 1, 1848. Additions and amendments were added in 1849. The foundation of this new procedure "was laid in the abolition of the separate and distinct jurisdictions of Courts of Law and Courts of Chancery and in the vesting in one tribunal, the Supreme Court of the State, jurisdiction in both Law and Equity. Previously existing forms of action likewise were abolished and in the stead of fictitious methods of pleading were to be plain, concise statements of fact. For pleadings at law, although originally oral and simple, had ultimately developed into a system of highly technical and formal rules requiring the greatest precision in their application and often by their very formality and rigidity defeating rather than aiding justice. . . . Field's Code abolished fixed forms of action and allowed facts to be pleaded without formality, the general object in this and all the changes being to make the system more simple and just in its application and to avoid the determination of rights on purely formal grounds." Lewis, *Great American Lawyers*, vol. 5, pp. 155-156.

[37] "Such a statute Field held would confer large benefits upon all men. It would settle long disputed questions, and make possible reforms which only comprehensive and simultaneous legislative acts could effect. It would render the law accessible to lawyers enabling them to dispense with the number of books which now encumber their shelves and would save an enormous amount of labor by doing away with long searches through reports, examinations of cases and deriving of inferences from decisions. Moreover it would bring justice within the reach of all, diffusing among the people in simple, untechnical language a more general and accurate knowledge of their rights and obligations than they could otherwise secure." Lewis, *Great American Lawyers*, vol. 5, pp. 155-156.

[38] He believed that "by casting aside known rules which are burdensome or unsuitable to present circumstances, avoiding repetition, rejecting anomalies, or ill-considered cases, reconciling repugnances, molding into distinct propositions and classifying according to scientific method" the different branches of the law could be brought into order and harmony, and enacted into a comprehensive code which would make known the sum of man's rights and obligations. In short, Field's conception was "all law reduced to a statute so that a man might carry in his hand all that the state ordained for the regulation of human conduct." Lewis, *Great American Lawyers*, vol. 5, p. 156.

could be reduced to form and system, he drew upon democratic America's dislike for a law which was known only by the lawyers or a class apart from the average man. He claimed that codification would remove the anachronisms of the common law, would set forth the whole body of the law in simple terminology and would eliminate the need for learned commentaries and elaborate report of cases.[39] Field's contentions received popular support from those who opposed all tendencies toward rigid precedents and who believed that the legislatures should assume new responsibilities and that judge-made law needed a readjustment to new conditions.

Opponents of codification distrusted the ability of the legislature to enact satisfactory codes, and preferred the more elastic and progressive growth from case to case in the courts. They also frowned upon the idea that each man should be his own lawyer. James C. Carter, their chief spokesman during this period, argued that in private law justice is of more importance than certainty, and that situations will arise which are unforeseeable. Consequently, he held that a system of case law, which lays down rules which are at best provisional, and which can be revised for new situations, is the only system which can properly meet our needs. The fixed rules of codification, he believed, are either guesses too wild to be risked or definitely unjust.[40] At a later date he shifted the basis of his argument from justice to inherent necessity. Private transactions, he held, are governed by certain absolute principles which cannot be made by human instinct. They are growths, he asserted, which can be discovered only by study from case to case by the judges who are the experts in discovery.[41] It was largely due to Carter's efforts[42] that the

[39] " . . . It must be remembered that the remarkable growth of our young nation early began to necessitate such immediate modifications in the common law as demanded the rapid and trenchant operation of statute rather than the slow, cumbrous methods of judicial legislation. Only through the activity of state legislatures during a long period have we thus speedily reached our present approximately stable equilibrium in which is found an almost complete adaptation of eighteenth century common law to existing social needs. Most of the sharp changes were made during the first fifty years of our national life, but even in 1850 the tendency to legislate was far from spent" and gave rise naturally to demands for codification or complete enactment, "inevitably resulting in a Field. This encroachment of legislature upon judiciary ceased, however, with the necessity for it. After the greatest positive changes had been affected, it practically confined itself to that province appropriate to statutory law—those portions of both public and private law where the general social interest demands the freest play of individual activity were left to the slow, cautious legislation of the courts." *Ibid.*, p. 167.

[40] See *The Proposed Codification of Our Common Law*, 1884.

[41] See *Provinces of the Written and Unwritten Law*, 1889.

[42] He developed his ideas still farther in *The Ideal and the Actual in Law*, 1890. His best known book, however, is *Law: Its Origin, Growth and Function*, 1907. Judges and legislators, he held, approach creative activity when they seize on tendencies and convert growing custom into positive rules. "They cannot create custom; and their attempts to declare it are experiments, futile and tyrannous" if the rule declared does not fit. Custom, he declared, is not only known, but felt. Carter's ideas approach, in many regards, those of Savigny. They received the support of most of our jurists. Indeed since

codification movement in general failed of acceptance and the courts remained as the chief interpreters of the law.

Although Field lost his fight to Carter, his civil code was adopted in California and the Dakotas and in a modified form in Georgia. His procedural (civil and criminal) codes became the model for those now in force in about two-thirds of the states while many states have also adopted penal (criminal) codes like his. In New York State, where he labored so arduously, only the procedural codes were adopted and those in somewhat modified form.[43] In England, the effect of his activities was as great, if not greater, than it was at home.[44] Toward the end of the century, a movement arose in this country, which was undoubtedly influenced in some regards by Field's codification attempts of an earlier day. This movement was concerned with a system of uniform state laws in certain, selected fields. As business tended to become even more nation-wide in its scope, and the laws of the several states were widely diversified, conferences of commissioners were held, beginning in 1890, for the purpose of framing uniform state laws.

These conferences have resulted in the preparation and adoption in many states of codified sections on important commercial branches. Uniform state laws now govern negotiable instruments everywhere except the Canal Zones and Puerto Rico; sales in thirty states and in Alaska and Hawaii; bills of lading in twenty-five states and Alaska; warehouse-receipts in forty-five states, the District of Columbia, Philippines and Puerto Rico; conditional sales in eight states and in Alaska; partnership in sixteen states and Alaska; corporations in two states; stock transfers in twenty states and Alaska; fraudulent conveyances in fifteen states; limited partnership in fourteen states and Alaska. In 1923, the American Law Institute began work on a restatement of important branches of the common law, contracts, agency, torts, and conflicts of law. These activities may prove highly important in resolving this last

Bentham's time comparatively few legalists have favored codification; although John Austin, Sir James Fitzjames Stephens, Sheldon Ames, and Sir Frederick Pollock in England and David Dudley Field in America are noteworthy exceptions.

[43] Field's proposed Code of Criminal Procedure was not adopted in New York State until 1882, while the complete Code of Civil Procedure was never enacted.

[44] Many of the leading principles of Field's reforms were adopted in England in statutes designated as "Practice Acts." In 1853, England effected a partial though slight union of law and equity. Field was called in to discuss law reform with English committees in both 1851 and 1867. Shortly after his second visit, the Judicature Acts of 1873 and 1875 were passed. They involved the adoption of a substantially statutory form of pleading and practice and abolished the Courts of Chancery, also, in conformity with Field's theory. Sixteen British colonies followed this example and enacted the Code's chief features. Field had endeavoured to provide New York State "a method whereby simply, expeditiously and inexpensively litigation might perform its function of superseding private controversy and his system was almost universally adopted by the English speaking world." Lewis, *Great American Lawyers*, vol. 5, pp. 155-156.

phase of the conflict between those who favor the common law in its
entirety and those who look with approval upon attempts at codification.

These later day movements in the direction of codification, it is
interesting to note, are largely concerned with unifying or centralizing
the law.[45] When codes were adopted in Italy, Spain, and Germany late
in the century, a number of different systems of law prevailed in these
countries, and the purpose of codification in each state was principally to
establish a system of law for the whole country. The same purpose is
at the basis of the uniform state law movement in his country. The
codification movements, which took place in the early nineteenth century, on the other hand, was largely prompted by the individualistic feeling of the times.[46] Both movements threatened the supremacy of the
common law. The early codification movement with its interest in
French legal institutions did not succeed. The attempts made in the
days of Field met with a similar result. The ultimate effect of present
tendencies in the direction of codification remains a matter of great
uncertainty. Professor Maitland was of the opinion that the possibilities
of legislation superseding the common law were great indeed.[47] Brunner
also believed that the period of the uncontested supremacy of the common law is passing away.[48] Goodhart also predicts the passing of the
common law in America, because of the tendency in this country to
depart from the doctrine of *stare decisis*.[49] Dean Pound, on the other
hand, does not believe the supremacy of the common law will be greatly
affected by codification attempts.[50] As he sees it, the real danger to the
common law comes from quite different sources.[51]

[45] Beale, "The Development of Jurisprudence During the Nineteenth Century,"
Select Essays in Anglo-American Legal History, vol. 1, p. 567.

[46] "That which we have need of (need we say it?)," says Bentham, "is a body of
law, from the respective parts of which we may each of us, by reading them or hearing
them read, learn, and on each, occasion, know, what are his rights, and what are his
duties." In his view, the code would make each man his own lawyer. The individualistic
spirit of the times was greatly pleased with a method which promised to do away with
the science of law and the need of lawyers.

[47] *English Law and Renaissance*, p. 33. With hundreds of legislatures busy at
law-making in the various common-law jurisdictions Maitland believed that the unity of
the law was threatened, and with the loss of unity, he believed the common law was
bound to be threatened.

[48] *Sources of the Law of England*, p. 176.

[49] *Essays in Jurisprudence and the Common Law*, 1931, pp. 65-74.

[50] He says: "In the first place there is little in legislation that is original. Legislatures imitate one another. . . . Secondly, everything indicates that codification as such, is
still far remote. The gradual codification now in progress is but a legislative restatement
of the common law. It promotes unity. It does not affect the system itself—its basic
dogmas and tenets—in the least. Each statute is but a fresh starting point for a new body
of case law. Moreover, general codification, when it comes, is almost certain, unless an
entire change of feeling intervenes, to be a restatement of the common law in improved
form, pruned of archaisms and antimonies, to be construed according to common law
principles, and in due time overlaid by a new body of adjudicated cases. . . . " "The
Spirit of the Common Law," *The Green Bag*, 1906, pp. 18-21.

[51] The real danger to the common law in Dean Pound's opinion, comes not from

However that may be, it is interesting to note that the Field codification movement had the effect of strengthening the development of the common law in certain regards. For one thing, it forced the courts themselves to take corrective action with regards to the common law, particularly in the field of procedure. In the very midst of Field's activities some great American jurists appeared on the scene and devoted great skill and labor to the task of improving procedural practices. Justice Charles Doe of New Hampshire, one of our greatest jurists, was particularly active in this connection.[52] Judge Doe sat on the bench almost thirty-five years. His judicial services were of longer duration than those of Marshall, Taney, or Shaw. In fact, he served on the bench for a longer time than any American judge except William Cranch of the District of Columbia Courts, Chief Justice Gibson of Pennsylvania, and Mr. Justice Field. He also served longer than Lord Mansfield, or any English judge with the exception of Judge Heath. He came upon the bench in 1859. At that time the reform movement was in progress, which was to produce various Law and Chancery Acts in England and inspire codification and practice acts in various American states. In the year before his appointment to the bench, Chief Justice Bell had drafted certain rules regulating Chancery practice in New Hampshire. They were successful and Justice Doe in his attempts to reform common law procedure was influenced by this fact. He did not attempt, however, to draft rules for adoption by the court, or for enact-

threats of codification but from the fact that the common law is for the first time not to be found on the side of the people. "When Henry II put bounds to the limitations of the church," he says, "when the barons exclaimed, '*Volumes Leges Angliae Mutare,*' when the commons petitioned against the Court of Chancery, when Coke for the judges of England told James I that he ruled *sub Deo et lege,* when the Continental Congress resolved that the several colonies were entitled to the common law of England, the common law side was the natural and popular side. But today, the popular side is not that of the individual, but that of society. Today, for the first time, the common law finds itself arrayed against the people; for the first time, instead of securing for them what they most prize, they know it chiefly as something that stands between them and what they desire." *Ibid.*, pp. 19-20.

[52] Charles Doe (1830-1897) was one of the greatest American jurists. His work was characterized by great care and precision. Sparing neither time or effort, he traced the numerous streams of law to their fountain head and then wrote elaborate and exhaustive opinions. Over a twenty year period, he delayed the publication of the official reports of New Hampshire from five to seven years. He spent this time in study and research; sometimes spending months and even years in preparation of a single case. His reforms in common law procedure were predicated on the idea that substantive common law rights exist independent of any particular unit for their enforcement and that the citizen should obtain his rights as cheaply as possible. His idea raised some fundamental questions as to the nature of the common law. They succeeded admirably in effecting their purpose in New Hampshire. "In no place on God's footstool," says his colleague Justice Carpenter, "could justice be had so cheaply as in New Hampshire through the influence of Justice Doe." Justice Carpenter believed that no judge, since Lord Mansfield had exercised "a more potent influence in the direction of judicial reform in his own jurisdiction than Justice Doe." Lewis, *Great American Lawyers,* vol. 8, pp. 243-249.

ment in the legislature. Refusing "to sit with folded hands waiting for the legislature to enact a poorly-drawn code," he proceeded to simplify procedure by court decision. His efforts were rewarded by a flexibility of procedure in New Hampshire that was unsurpassed in any of the code states.

The victory of Carter and the common law school in the struggle over codification and the increasing use of judicial review in both national and state spheres makes the period between 1865 and 1900 an outstanding one in American legal history. Toward the latter part of this period, the American judiciary becomes an important, if not a controlling factor, in the American governmental system. The decline of the importance of the legislature apparently completed "the legal structure founded by fourteenth century judges, built up laboriously by Coke, and fixed in American institutions by the Federal Constitution and the Fourteenth Amendment. We had achieved in very truth a Rechtstaat. Our government was one of laws and not of men."[53]

At the same time, as industrialism expanded during these years, the common law system, which had been received and adjusted to American conditions by the courts in the early nineteenth century, began to develop weaknesses which made its continued application to an industrialized society a matter of grave question. Thus at the very time when it was reaching the fullness of its power and strength, it became evident that a new crisis was at hand. Evidence of this state of affairs can be seen in the attacks which were made on the doctrine of supremacy of law and its accompanying judicial review of legislation.[54] These attacks were directed at the independence and authority of the courts which is a central fact in the Anglo-American legal system. The codification of the commercial law in both England and America was another threat-

---

[53] "Complete elimination of the personal factor in all matters affecting the life, liberty, property or fortune of the citizen seemed to have been attained. Nothing is so characteristic of American public law of the nineteenth century as the completeness with which executive action is tied down by legal liability and judicial review. The tendency was strong to commit matters of clearly executive character to the courts, and no small number of statutes had to be rejected for such violations of the constitutional separation of governmenal powers. (It is noteworthy that the first cases in which acts of Congress were held unconstitutional by the Supreme Court of the United States were of this character. *In re Hayburn*, 1792, 2 *Dall.* 409; U. S. Todd, (1794), 15 *Howard*, 52, note). And that reaction as the last remnants of legislative justice were disappearing, brought back the long obsolete executive justice and has been making it an ordinary feature of our government." Pound, "Justice According to Law," *Columbia Law Review*, vol. 13, 1913, p. 696.

[54] "The right of the individual and the exaggerated respect for his rights are common law doctrines. And this means that a struggle is in progress between society and the common law; for the judicial power over unconstitutional legislation is in the right line of common law ideas. It is a plain consequence of the doctrine of the supremacy of law, and has developed from a line of precedents that run back to Magna Carta." Pound, "The Spirit of the Common Law," *The Green Bag*, vol. 18, pp. 15-21, 1906.

ening influence, of greater or lesser effect. In the field of torts, various modifications took place which involved a reconsideration of principles once considered highly important to the system.

These changes reflect a movement for socialization of law that was world-wide in the latter part of the nineteenth century. Throughout the western world, at least, there was a shifting from the abstract individualist justice of the earlier part of the century to a newer ideal of justice which emphasizes the social factor.[55] In the United States the tendency was to commit everything to boards and commissions which proceeded extra-judicially. This involved the encroachment of a government of men upon our traditional government of laws; and the reshaping of our body of authoritative grounds of judicial decision and administrative action. Legal precepts and institutions which were satisfactory for our rural, pioneer society functioned badly under new conditions.

The matured common law technique "with its cautious judicial eking out of the traditional law" by interstitial law-making lost favor in "an impatient age accustomed to instant communication, super-rapid transportation and governmental activities of the first moment."[56] Legislative action, which the nineteenth century analytical school of jurisprudence put great hope in, as a means of supplementing judicial law-making, likewise ceased to command public confidence. Dissatisfaction with the legal order was based on still other important factors. The received ideals of the legal order which the courts applied pictured a society of economically self-sufficient individuals. The law they applied remained incorrigibly individualistic, despite the emergency of an economically unified world emphasizing cooperative relationships.[57] As in-

[55] "Men have changed their views as to the relative importance of the individual and society; but the common law has not changed. Indeed the common law knows individuals only. In the seventeenth and eighteenth centuries, when the theory of the state of nature was dominant, this feature of our legal system made it popular. But today the isolated individual is no longer taken for the center of the universe. We see now that he is an abstraction and has never had a concrete existence. Today we look instead for liberty through society." Pound, "The Spirit of the Common Law," *The Green Bag*, vol. 18, pp. 20, 21, 1906.
[56] Pound, "The Future of the Common Law," *American Law Review*, vol. 7, p. 36, 1933.
[57] "Hence this same obstinate individualism, which makes it fit so ill in many a modern niche, may yet prove a necessary bulwark against an exaggerated and enfeebling collectivism. When from the sixteenth to the eighteenth centuries, the whole world was turning absolutist, England alone kept alive the local, individual legal government of the Middle Ages. In consequences, the English Parliament has become the type of all the collegiate sovereignties of today. Bacon was modern and Coke was antiquated. Yet the constitutional ideas of Coke triumphed. Today the up-to-date economist and sociologist is as sure that the narrow individualism of the lawyer is a relic of the past as Bacon was that Coke's precedents from the reigns of the Plantagenets, and from the Wars of the Roses were antiquated shades by which a Stuart king could not be bound. The lawyers saved our Teutonic heritage of individual rights and individual responsibility in the

dustrialism continued to expand in the closing days of the century "new ideas of the economic order, new ideas worked out through business usages, and the product of scientific business administration" demanded recognition from the legal order. This put a tremendous strain on the courts, who continued to view the law in the light of their earlier training. In short, they continued to emphasize the goals of certainty and uniformity which were so much sought after in the early days of the century when stability was the watchword. In consequence, we find a widespread dissatisfaction with the legal order at the turn of the century for its failure to keep pace with the demands of the rapidly changing social and economic order.

---

seventeenth century, and unless our legal system is to be hopelessly decadent, they must do so once more today. Their obstinate conservatism in refusing to take the burden of upholding right from the concrete each, and put it upon the abstract all, may yet save for us a valuable—nay, an indispensable—element in our institutions." Pound, "The Spirit of the Common Law," *The Green Bag*, vol. 18, p. 24-25, 1906.

PART IV

SOME PROBLEMS OF GROWTH AND DEVELOP-
MENT IN THE PRESENT AMERICAN
LEGAL SYSTEM, 1900-1935

CHAPTER X

SOME RECENT TRENDS IN AMERICAN LAW AND LAW ADMINISTRATION

Any attempt to analyze developments in the American legal system in the first third of the twentieth century with a view to interpreting their significance for the future presents a problem of great difficulty and must remain essentially tentative and general in character. The period we are passing through is a transitional one. On every side there is a vast confusion as attempts are made to find solutions for the difficult problems forced upon us by technological change. In the political sphere, centralization of power proceeds apace, with dictatorships, one after another, superseding parliaments and checks and balances. In the legal sphere, a spirit of change raises new problems for law and law administration. Whether this movement will supplement or modify, redirect or transform, no one can say. That it is a ferment of no ordinary character few will deny. On the contrary, many competent observers believe we are in a period of major significance for the legal order.[1] Dean Pound, one of our foremost students of jurisprudence, writing in 1913, foresaw one of those great periodic swings back to justice without law, comparable to the movement which brought equity into English law, and into Roman law as well.[2] In more recent years, other writers have expressed similar views. Writing in 1934, Judge Joseph C. Hutcheson says, "We are now, in fact, in the bursting time of one of law's long, slow, but

[1] Pound, "Justice According to Law," *Columbia Law Review*, vol. 13-14, pp. 696-713.

[2] "Equity both at Rome and in England began as executive justice. . . . The executive justice of today is essentially of the same nature. It is an attempt to adjust the relations of individuals with each other and with the state summarily, largely according to the notions of an executive officers for the time being as to what the general interest and a square deal demand, unencumbered by many rules. The fact that it is largely justice without law is what commends it to a busy and strenuous age, as it was what commended it to the individualism of an England set to thinking freely and vigorously by Renaissance and Reformation. Moreover, the causes of each movement away from the common law courts and hence from the law are much the same. In each of the partial reversions to justice without law referred to, it happend that for the time being the law was not fulfilling its end. It was not adjusting the relations of individuals with each other so as to accord with the moral sense of the community. Hence praetor or emperor or king, or chancellor administered justice for a season without law till a new and more liberal system of rules developed. In part a similar situation may be remarked today. The world over a shifting of ideas as to the end of the law and the meaning of justice is putting a heavy pressure upon the administration of justice secondary to law." Pound, "Justice According to Law," *Columbia Law Review*, vol. 13-14, pp. 696-713.

greatly glorious, springs. I look for a great flowering."[3] There are several phases of this general movement to adjust our legal system to the rapidly changing conditions of twentieth century life. One recent phase, for example, involves a new approach to thought about law and its place in society. Some speak of this phase of the movement as "a scientific approach to law," others as "the skeptical movement" or the "neo-realist" movement, while still others describe it as "the functional approach" which stresses the interest in, and valuation by, effects. The "objective method" and "fact-research" are looked upon as having an important place in this movement and interest in the actuality of what happens is emphasized, and distrust of formula is expressed. Although the individuals who have taken part in this movement differ somewhat in point of view, in interest, and in emphasis, certain points of departure seem common to all.[4]

Accompanying this realistic movement in jurisprudence is a tendency to put a new emphasis on the role and importance of the judge in orienting law to life.[5] In this view, it is the duty of the judge to administer law, "not merely possessively, but dynamically and actively," adapting the law to changing social needs[6] as far as possible through the judicial process; and where the law is lacking anywhere and beyond the judicial power of repair, to cooperate with judicial councils and their agencies in getting change through other channels.[7] Emphasis on a

[3] "Judging as Administration," The American Law School Review, No. 11, April, 1934, pp. 1071.

[4] Karl Llewellyn believes any such common approach would involve: "(1) The conception of law in flux, of moving law, and of judicial creation of law; (2) the conception of law as a means to social ends and not an end in itself; so that any part needs constantly to be examined for its purpose, and for its effect and to be judged in the light of both and of their relation to each other; (3) the conception of society in flux, and a flux typically faster than the law, so that the probability is that any portion of law needs re-examination to determine how far it fits the society it purports to serve; (4) the temporary disregarding of the question of what the courts are doing; (5) distrust of traditional legal rules and concepts in so far as they purport to *describe* what courts or people are actually doing; (6) distrust of the theory that prescriptive rule-formulations are the heavily operative factors in producing court decisions. This involves the tentative adoption of the theory of rationalization for the study of opinions; (7) the belief in the worthwhileness of grouping cases and legal situations into narrower categories than has been the practice in the past; (8) an insistence on evaluation of any part of the law in terms of its effects; (9) insistence on sustained and programmatic attack on the problems of law along any of these lines." "Some Realism About Realism—Responding to Dean Pound," Harvard Law Review, vol. XLIV, No. 8, June, 1931.

[5] Judge Joseph C. Hutcheson, Jr., "The Worm Turns," Illinois Law Review, vol. 27, p. 357; Stone, "Some Aspects of the Problem of Law Simplification," Columbia Law Review, vol. 23, pp. 319-332. 5 Wigmore, Evidence (Id. Ed. 1915), Preface to Supplement Index. Judge Joseph C. Hutcheson, Jr., "Judging as Administration," The American Law School Review, vol. 7, no. 11, April, 1934, p. 1071.

[6] Judge Joseph C. Hutcheson, Jr., ibid., p. 1071.

[7] F. R. Aumann, "The Ohio Judicial Council Embarks on a Survey of Justice," American Political Science Review, vol. 24, May, 1930, pp. 416-425; F. R. Aumann, "The Judicial Council Movement and Iowa," Iowa Law Review, June, 1930, vol. XV,

conscious recognition of the factor of social control in the judging process is greatly favored by the realists.[8] It has some interesting sidelights. It is in line with the pragmatic philosophy now so widely accepted.[9] In emphasizing the factor of control, the realists do not deny that "purpose has always been an inescapable factor in determining what shall be enforced as law," but stress the point that the adaptation of means to an end ought to be self-conscious and methodical, a recognized part of the jurists' problem.[10]

Closely related to this tendency to give the judge an increased or reemphasized responsibility[11] in the sphere of conscious renovation, or judicial legislation, or judicial restatement of the law is a perceptible change of judicial attitude toward the function of precedent in our system. At the present time, there are many indications that the doctrine of *stare decisis* is undergoing a marked decline in its influence and practical application in this country.[12] This tendency[13] has been noticeable

---

pp. 425-433; F. R. Aumann, "The Ohio Judicial Council: Studies and Reports, *American Political Science Review*, vol. XXVII, December, 1933, pp. 957-964.

[8] Walter W. Cook, "Scientific Method and the Law," *American Bar Association Journal*, vol. 13, 1927, pp. 303 ff.; Herman Oliphant, "A Return to *Stare Decisis*," *American Bar Association Journal*, vol. 14, 1928, 71 ff.

[9] . . . philosophic pragmatism may be said to stand like a tripod upon the three supports of empiricism, evolution, and the instrumentalism of thought in human behavior. It accepts control as the end of knowledge and the test of its efficacy, and therefore makes purpose an ineradicable part of all thinking." Geo. H. Sabine, "The Pragmatic Approach to Politics," *American Political Science Review*, vol. 24, November, 1930, p. 866.

[10] "The object of the law is to regulate conduct for some end, and the end sought is the only criterion by which to decide what similarities are essential and what are not. The ruling consideration in making the choice ought to be the desirability of the practical results which will follow. Consequently, the jurists ought not to try to escape the consideration of ends and the means of obtaining them, but should make such matters consciously and overtly a part of his study of the law. As I understand Professors Cook and Oliphant, they mean to assert that some choice of public policy cannot practically be avoided by judges and students of the law. The objection is not that judges fail to do this, but that they do it confusedly, or ignorantly, and therefore without a full sense of responsibility for what they are doing. By setting up the fiction that cases themselves contain the principles for their own classification, they really become the victims of their own preconceptions. There is no system of formal legal logic by which cases can validly be decided, and the pretense that decisions are made in this way merely encourages clandestine ways of making them." Geo. H. Sabine, "The Pragmatic Approach to Politics," *American Political Science Review*, vol. 24, November, 1930, pp. 876-878.

[11] Judge Joseph C. Hutcheson, Jr., *op. cit.*, p. 1070.

[12] There does not seem to be such a trend in England. Justice Cardozo, in comparing the position of the doctrine in this country and England, said: "The House of Lords holds itself absolutely bound by its own prior decisions." (Gray, *supra*, Sec. 462; Salmond, *Jurisprudence*, p. 164, Sec. 64; Pound, "Juristic Science and the Law," *Harvard Law Review*, vol. 31, pp. 1053; *London St. Tramways Co.* v. *London County Council*, 1898, A. C. 375, 379.) The United States Supreme Court and the highest court of the several states overrule their own prior decisions when manifestly erroneous. (Pollock, *First Book of Jurisprudence*, pp. 319, 320; Gray, "Judicial Precedents," *Harvard Law Review*, vol. 9, pp. 27, 400.) Pollock, in a paper entitled "The Science of Case Law," written more than fifty years ago, spoke of the freedom with which this was done, as suggesting that the law was nothing more than a matter of individual opinion. (*Essays*

for some time.[14] It reflects, in some instances, a desire for a mild modification of the doctrine[15] and in others for its complete abandonment.[16] Among those interested in reappraising *stare decisis* have been members of the Supreme Courts of the United States,[17] of Kansas,[18] of Ohio,[19]

---

in Jurisprudence and Ethics, p. 245.) Since then the tendency has, if anything, increased. (Cardozo, *The Nature of the Judicial Process*, p. 158.) Arthur L. Goodhart gives a very reasonable explanation as to why the doctrine of *Stare Decisis* is losing prestige in this country and not in England. "Case Law in England and America," *Cornell Law Quarterly*, vol. 15, Feb., 1930, pp. 189 ff.

[13] "In such matters we can only speak of averages, of tendencies. And it is, I think, safe to say that in most American jurisdictions today a more rational theory as to the binding force of precedents generally obtains than that held by the British House of Lords. . . . The better class of modern lawyers and judges have in part from the very copiousness of authority come to regard precedent as their servant and not their master, as presumptive evidence of what law is rather than as absolutely conclusive evidence." Orrin McMurray, "Changing Conceptions of Law," 1915, *California Law Review*, 441, 446.

[14] In *Washington* v. *Dawson and Co.*, 264 *U. S.* 21, 238, 44 *Sup. Ct.* 304, 309 (1904). Mr. Justice Brandeis cites twelve instances in which the Supreme Court has reversed itself.

[15] Judge Cardozo says: "I think adherence to precedents should be the rule and not the exception. . . . But I am ready to concede that the rule of adherence to precedent, though it ought not to be abandoned, ought to be in some degree relaxed. . . . There should be greater readiness to abandon an untenable position when the rule to be discarded may not reasonably be supposed to have determined the conduct of the litigants and particularly when in its origin it was the product of institutions or conditions which have gained a new significance or development with the progress of the years." Benjamin Cardozo, *The Nature of the Judicial Process*, 1921, pp. 149, 150, 151.

[16] Professor Herman Oliphant takes a very advanced position in the matter. "Not the judges' opinions, but which way they decide cases will be the dominant subject-matter of any truly scientific study of law. This is the field of scholarly work worthy of the best talents, for the work to be done is not the study of vague and shifting rationalizations, but the study of such tough things as the accumulated wisdom of men taught by immediate experiences in contemporary life . . . the battered experiences of judges among brutal facts." "A Return to *Stare Decisis*," 14 *A. B. A. J.* 71, 159 (1928).

[17] "The Circuit Court of Appeals was obviously not bound to follow its prior decision. The rule of *"stare decisis,"* though one tending to consistency and uniformity of decision, is not inflexible. Whether it shall be followed or departed from is a question entirely within the discretion of the court, which is called upon to consider a question once decided. . . ." Mr. Justice Lurton in *Hertz* v. *Woodman*, 218 *U. S.* 205, 212, 30 *Sup. Ct.* 621 (1910).

"Satisfied as we are that the legislation and the very great weight of judicial authority which have been developed in support of this modern rule, especially as applied to the competency of witnesses convicted of crime, proceed upon a sound principle, we conclude that the dead hand of the common-law rule of 1789 should no longer be applied in such cases as we have here, and that the ruling of the lower courts on this first claim of error should be approved." Mr. Justice Clark in *Rosen* v. *United States*, 245 *U. S.* 465, 471, 38 *Sup. Ct.* 148, 150 (1918).

[18] "The doctrine of *"stare decisis"* does not preclude a departure from precedent established by a series of decisions clearly erroneous, unless property complications have resulted, and a reversal would work a greater injury and injustice than would ensue by following the rule." *Thurston* v. *Fritz* (91 *Kan.* 625, 194). In this case the Supreme Court of Kansas departed from the common-law rule concerning dying declarations.

[19] "A decided case is worth as much as it weighs in reason and righteousness, and no more. It is not enough to say, "thus saith the court." It must prove its right to control in any given situation by the degree in which it supports the rights of a party violated and serves the cause of justice as to all parties concerned." *Adams Express Co.* v. *Beck-*

and of New York,[20] as well as such distinguished legal scholars as Dean Roscoe Pound,[21] Dean Henry H.Wigmore,[22] Dean Leon Green,[23] Dean Orrin McMurray,[24] and Associate Justice Harlan Stone.[25] Some members of the group insist that the day will come when precedents, and especially the precedent of a single case, will no longer be considered a binding source of law which judges must accept under all circumstances.[26] Whether it goes that far or not, the tendency to relax the force of precedent is bound to give the judge a larger role in determining what the law is which shall be applied.[27] The ultimate outcome of this trend is difficult to predict. In some quarters, it is said that the final result will be a condition approximating the civil law.[28] There are several practical factors which might bring about such a result. For one thing, there is

with, 100 *Ohio St.* 348, 351, 352, 126 *N.E.* 300, 301 (1919). In this case the court overruled a doctrine which had been the law of Ohio since 1825.

[20] "In fact there has been no objection raised anywhere to the right of the wife to maintain the action for criminal conversation except the plea that the ancient law did not give it to her. Reverence for antiquity demands no such denial. Courts exist for the purpose of ameliorating the harshness of ancient laws inconsistent with modern progress when it can be done without interfering with vested rights." *Oppenheim* v. *Kridel,* 236 *N. Y.* 156, 165, 140 *N. E.* 227, 230 (1923).

[21] "Law in Books and Law in Action," 1904, *American Law Review,* vol. 44, pp. 12, 20; "Mechanical Jurisprudence," *Columbia Law Review,* vol. 8, pp. 605, 614, 1908. "The Theory of Judicial Decision," (1923) *Harvard Law Review,* vol. 36, pp. 940-943.

[22] Problems of Law, 1920, p. 79.

[23] "The Duty Problem in Negligence Cases," *Columbia Law Review,* vol. 28, 1928, pp. 1014, 1036.

[24] "Changing Conceptions of Law," 1915, *California Law Review,* pp. 441, 446.

[25] "Some Aspects of the Problem of Law Simplification," *Columbia Law Review,* vol. 23, 1923, pp. 319, 320.

[26] "Precedents, and especially the precedent of a single case, will no longer be considered a binding source of law which judges must accept under all circumstances. Only if decided cases have created a practice upon which laymen have relied will the American courts feel that they are bound to follow them. This, as I have attempted to show, is the doctrine of the civil law and directly contrary to that of the English law with its insistence upon the need for certainty. I therefore believe that, as concerns the fundamental doctrine of precedent, English and American law are at the parting of the ways." Goodhart, *Essays in Jurisprudence and the Common Law,* p. 74.

[27] Under the present system our judges have a difficult time in adjusting the law to the rapidly changing social and economic conditions of the country. "Where a rule has once been decided, even though wrongly, it is difficult or impossible to depart from it. I do not agree with those who think that *flexibility* is a characteristic of case law. The binding force of precedent is a fetter on the discretion of the judge; but for precedent he would have a much freer hand." Geldart, *Elements of English Law,* p. 28.

[28] "It is, I think, therefore safe to say that the present American doctrine is strongly away from the strict English doctrine of *"stare decisis."* But is this merely a temporary step to be followed by the reaction which so frequently succeeds legal innovations, or is it likely to be accentuated in the future? I believe that the latter is the fact, and that in no distant time the American doctrine will approximate the civil law. This will be due in large part to five reasons: (a) the uncontrollable flood of American decisions, (b) the predominant position of constitutional questions in American law, (c) the American need for flexibility in legal development, (4) the method of teaching in the American law schools, and (e) the restatement of the law by the American Law Institute." Goodhart, *Essays in Jurisprudence nad the Common Law,* p. 65.

a growing demand for speedy settlement of cases. At the same time, the volume of judicial business has continued to increase rapidly.[29] With this increase has come an expansion of case law.[30] In bulk it has now become almost unmanageable.[31] Some method of control must be devised.[32] Although there is some evidence that the courts are trying to limit their written opinions, the problem remains unsolved,[33] and some observers contend that as long as we continue to maintain what Morris Cohen calls "the phonographic theory of the judicial function," little progress can be hoped for in cutting through this wilderness. Whether the movement to modify *stare decisis* will reach the condition of the Civil Law is doubtful.[34] Such a move would involve a fundamental departure from Anglo-Saxon principles.[35] For some time, however, our

[29] "All available figures show a consistent and large growth in the amount of litigation." See *Recent Social Trends in the United States*, vol. 2, 1933, pp. 1450-1453.

[30] "Each year about 350 volumes of reports are being published, which can be compared with the five or six volumes for all of England and Wales. As far back as 1902 the President of the American Bar Association, in his annual address to the Association, (cited by Whitney, "The Doctrine of *Stare Decisis*," *Michigan Law Review*, 1904, vol. III, No. 40, p. 97) stated that the law reports of the past year contained 262,000 pages and estimated that a man by reading 100 pages a day might go through them in eighty years; by which time there would be new reports on hand sufficient to occupy him for 56 years more." Goodhart, *Essays in Jurisprudence and the Common Law*, 1931, p. 65.

[31] "As to rulings of courts, it is estimated that in America alone there are a million and a half reported decisions available as judicial precedents; and the increase each year represents 170,000 printed pages. (Elihu Root, address to American Law Institute, *Proceedings*, 1923, vol. I, p. 49; Johns Hopkins University, *The Institute for the Study of Law*, Circular, 1929, No. 7, p. 10; Y. B. Smith, *Education and Research*, New York State Bar Association Bulletin, 1930, pp. 189, 190.)

[32] *Recent Social Trends in the United States*, vol. 2, 1933, p. 1430; see also Cardozo, *The Growth of the Law*, 1924, p. 4 "Unless courts set some restraints on the length and number of published opinions, it is inevitable that our present system of making the law reports the chief repository of the unwritten law will break down of its own weight."

[33] For the percentage of cases where written opinions were reduced in U. S. Supreme Court and New York Court of Appeals see Rosbrook, "The Art of Judicial Reporting," *Cornell Law Quarterly*, vol. 10, 1925, p. 103.

[34] The European view is that the disadvantage of following an outworn precedent or one which was wrong from the first is much greater than the occasional inconvenience or injustice which may result from disregarding it. In their opinion, the development of the law should proceed along the lines of rational principles and abstract justice rather than upon the strict rule of *stare decisis*. Referring to the case system as *"la superstition du cas,"* the European turns with confidence to the methods of the Civil Law. See Kotze, *Judicial Precedent*, 1918, Law Times, 349. There will always be differences of opinion and practice in this matter, it would seem. In Dicey, *Law and Public Opinion in England*, 1905, pp. 393 ff., there is a discussion of both sides of this question. See also *Democracy in America*, vol. 2, ch. 16, in which De Toqueville criticizes American lawyers for investigating what has been done rather than what might be done; and for engaging in the pursuit of precedent rather than reason.

[35] A number of writers have asserted that the distinction between the civilian and common law systems is greater in theory than in practice. Thomas Erskine Holland is one writer who has taken this view. In his volume on *Jurisprudence* (13th ed. 1924), p. 70, he says: "There have been of late symptoms of approximation between the two theories." Dean Pound has made a similar expression. He says: "In fact, our practice and the practice of the Roman-law world are not so far apart as legal theory makes them seem." "The Theory of the Judicial System," *Harvard Law Review*, vol. 36, 1923, p. 646. Judge

judges will apparently have a much freer hand in determining the law. For not only will they be less fettered by precedents, but they will be encouraged by the power-begetting philosophy of the "functionalists" and similar groups, who are interested in the more immediate social aspects of law.

If legal history repeats itself,[36] the sphere of judicial law-making will be greatly widened by these factors. In the past, whenever it became necessary to bring the administration of justice into touch with new moral ideas, or changed social or political conditions, great emphasis has been placed on a wide judicial discretion.[37] Gradually, the ideas introduced into the law in those periods of change would result in a new body of set rules. As time passed, the methods of exercising discretion would harden, and the course of judicial action become uniform once again. Eventually, an extreme of detailed rule, rigidly applied, would replace the extreme of judicial freedom.[38] Apparently any attempt to depend exclusively upon wide judicial discretion, on the one hand, or strict confinement of the magistrate by fixed rules upon the other, is doomed to failure.[39] Despite the fact that neither method in its unlimited form can endure for long,[40] such attempts have been made repeatedly and persistently.

Robert L. Henry of the Mixed Tribunals of Egypt, who has had a wide experience with the Common Law system in the United States before taking up his duties under the Civil Law does not agree with this view, however. He says: "But from my experience in the actual application of the Civil Law, including, of course, my observation of the work of counsel before the court, I have come to the conclusion that such indices may be misleading. It is clear that the divergence in attitude as to precedents between the Civil Law and the Common Law is still great, and that there is little likelihood of its becoming substantially less for a long time to come." Henry, "Jurisprudence Constante and Stare Decisis," *American Bar Association Journal*, vol. 15, 1929, p. 11.

[36] "For the most part, the administration of justice has swung back and forth from an extreme reliance upon the one to a no less extreme reliance upon the other. In the strict law of the later Middle Ages in England, and in the maturity of American law in the last half of the nineteenth century, the stress was put upon rules. Attempt was made to exclude all individualization, and to confine the magistrate to strict observance of minute and detailed precepts, or to a mechanical process of application of law through logical deduction from fixed principles. On the other hand, in the administrative tribunals of sixteenth and seventeenth century England, in the executive and legislative justice of the American colonies, and in administrative boards and commissions which have been set up so lavishly in the present century, the stress is put upon discretion and individualization. Here, in contrast, a wide power is given to the magistrate to fit the action of the tribunal to the facts of an individual case. But already some reaction from this administrative justice is manifest. Apparently the mechanical action of legal rules may be tempered, but we may not hope to obviate it." Pound, *Criminal Justice in America*, p. 39.

[37] Pollock, *The Expansion of the Common Law*, 1904, pp. 107-138.

[38] Roscoe Pound, "The Decadence of Equity," *Col. Law Rev.*, vol. 5, p.20.

[39] ". . . the most constant and universal cause of dissatisfaction with law grows out of the mechanical operations of legal rules. A balance between rules of law and magisterial discretion, which will give effect both to the general security and the individual life, is *perhaps the most difficult problem of law.*" Roscoe Pound, *Criminal Justice in America*, p. 38.

[40] "Each has its advantages and disadvantages. The application of an unvarying

If we were to pause at this point, we would have noted in the legal field today some new approaches to the law, which place increasing emphasis upon the role which law plays in society; we would have noted also that in this period of rapid social change we are repeating ancient legal history by widening the sphere of judicial discretion to the end that law may be more easily adjusted to new social needs. If we stopped here, we would have failed to note some remarkable changes which have taken place, in the legal field particularly, from the standpoint of organization and procedure.

Of prime importance in this connection is the movement which is well under way to modify our traditional judicial method of settling controversies;[41] and establish boards and commissions[42] to handle work formerly performed exclusively by the courts.[43] During the past twenty years, this movement has made steady advances.[44] Workmen's compen-

---

rule is due to work hardship in particular cases, and the more general the rule the greater the possibility becomes. On the other hand an unvarying rule has the great merit of certainty. In discussions of the evil of the law, attention is often directed too exclusively to the problems of the just settlement of legislation, *since the great triumph of a system of law is that justice is thereby attained in the vast majority* of cases without litigation. If the rules governing rights and duties regarding persons and property are certain, there is less opportunity for dispute. It is this advantage together with the preference that men have to be subjected rather to what seems an inanimate rule than to the unbridled will of one of their fellow creatures that made it one of the great ambitions of our forefathers to create a government of laws and not of men. But those who choose this method must recognize that it will bring certain hardship with it." Samuel Williston, *Some Modern Tendencies in the Law*, 1925, pp. 1-2.

[41] Implicit in this movement is a desire to make our law and legal machinery more responsive to present social needs. Giving impetus to this movement are a number of reform groups concerned with some particular phase of the legal problem. For example, the American Judicature Society is working for unified and specialized courts and emphasizes the need for getting away from antiquated rules of procedure; the American Institute of Criminology is working for the individual treatment of criminal cases; the National Association of Legal Aid Societies is working for an adequate defense for defendants who are unable to pay the costs under the present system; the American Arbitration Society is in favor of a less formal method of settling disputes with lawyers largely displaced; and the American Law Institute is working on a restatement of the law with a view to clarifying it.

[42] W. F. Willoughby, *Principles of Judicial Administration*, 1929, ch. 3; F. R. Aumann, "The Changing Relationship of the Executive and Judicial Branches," *Kentucky Law Journal*, vol. XXII, 1934, pp. 246-260.

[43] "There is a special field of law development," says Elihu Root, "which has manifestly become inevitable. We are entering upon the creation of a body of administrative law quite different in its machinery, its remedies and its necessary safeguards from the old methods of regulation by specific statutes by the courts. As any community passes from simple to complex conditions the only way in which the government can deal with the increased burden thrown upon it is by the delegation of power to be exercised in detail by subordinate agencies, subject to the control of general directions presented by superior authority. The necessities of our situation have already led to an extensive employment of this method." *Report*, American Bar Association, 1916, pp. 368-369.

[44] Roscoe Pound, "The Growth of Administrative Justice," *Wisconsin Law Review*, vol. II, 1924, p. 321. "If one were compelled to state the most important experiment in the administration of justice made in the twentieth century; the answer would unhesitatingly be the attempt to secure justice through administrative courts. Such tribunals have

sation commissions, blue sky commissions, utility commissions, trade commissions, and zoning and building commissions are all deciding questions formerly settled by the courts. Nor is the end in sight.[45] The public sees delay, expense, and technicality in the courts of general jurisdiction[46] It is interested in speedy settlement, finality, and freedom from procedural contentions. In consequence, it experiments with new agencies and will probably continue to do so, if administrative adjudication proves satisfactory over a period of time.

The final results of this movement remains a matter of some doubt.[47] The immediate effect is to raise anew for our law, after three centuries, the problem of executive justice.[48] Despite its challenge to the

sprung up with amazing rapidity; they have taken over an enormous amount of litigation formerly handled by the courts, and the law concerning administrative justice is the most rapidly growing branch of the law in our entire jurisprudence." R. H. Smith, *Justice and the Poor*, 1919, p. 83. Frankfurter and Landis, *The Business of the Supreme Court*, 1929, pp. 184-186.

[45] Elihu Root believes that there will be no withdrawal from these experiments. "We shall expand them," he says, "whether we approve theoretically or not, because such agencies furnish protection to rights and obstacles to wrong-doing, which, under our new social and industrial conditions, cannot be practically accomplished by the old and simple procedures of legislatures, and courts as in the last generation." *Report*, American Bar Association, 1916, pp. 368-369.

[46] "A court is at the best an expensive institution. Its methods of procedure are formal and technical. It can only handle matters brought before it. It does not act upon its own initiative. In the determining of facts it has no technically trained staff of its own. The proceeding is in the nature of a duel between the parties, and almost its only method of determining facts is by the cumbersome and expensive question-and-answer device. More fundamental still the burden of inquiry is in large part thrown upon private individuals. In marked contrast with this, administrative agencies can act on their own initiative, assume responsibility for determining facts, and have expert staffs to do the work of investigating. They are not bound by formal rules of evidence and procedures as are courts, and they generally can and do act in a more direct, efficient, and economical manner, and with much greater dispatch." W. F. Willoughby, *Principles of Judicial Administration*, 1929, pp. 20-21.

[47] "The future development of this type of administrative tribunal perplexes all jurists. It is undoubtedly true that some of its present advantages are due to the fact that it occupies an extra-legal position, (Pound, "Organization of Courts," American Judicature Society, *Bulletin 6*, p. 4) and that temporarily it escapes from the limitations of justice according to law and judicial justice. It is closely analogous to the rise of equity (*ibid.*, p. 5) with the exception that instead of entrusting justice to priests in place of judges, our recourse has been to laymen. New agencies enjoy a sort of hiatus when rules and precedents are few, when the liberalizing spirit is strong, but this is transitory. (Pound, *Justice According to Law*, p 2.) It is certain that the administrative tribunals must ascertain and administer their justice according to law, and it is likely that they will ultimately become part of the regular judicial system." (*Ibid.*, p. 42; "Report of Dean Pound to the President of Harvard University for 1915-1916," p. 2). R. H. Smith, *Justice and the Poor*, p. 91.

[48] See Hon. Geo. Sutherland, "President's Address, American Bar Association," *Reports*, American Bar Association, vol. XLII, 1917, 204 ff.; Hon. Wm. D. Guthrie, "President's Address, New York State Bar Association," *Reports*, N. Y. State Bar Association, vol. XLVI, 1925, 175 ff.; John Dickinson, *Administrative Justice and the Supremacy of the Law in the United States*, 1927, p. 3.

doctrine of the "supremacy of the law,"[49] which has been so long considered as central to our legal tradition, administrative adjudication would seem to be here to stay.[50] In any event, we are not likely to return to the conditions of the nineteenth century when a growing administrative need was paralyzed by our American exaggeration of the common law doctrine of supremacy of law.[51] Some changes in form and practice may be expected as we gather more experience in this field.[52]

[49] Anglo-Saxon legal theory has placed great emphasis on the doctrine of individual rights and has assumed that such rights could only be adequately protected by the courts. It also places great emphasis on the independence of the courts. All legal controversies, according to this doctrine, should be decided by the ordinary judicial courts which should be supreme in such matters. Any notion of administrative jurisdiction such as is known and practiced on the Continent of Europe would be inconsistent with this theory. There is in Anglo-Saxon theory one law and one court for the citizen and public functionary alike. A right to sue the state is not admitted except where it is expressly conferred by statute, and when it is conferred it is usually subject to restrictions which frequently make the action difficult. (See A. V. Dicey, *Law of the Constitution*, (2nd ed.) lecture 5; and his article "The Droit Administratif in Modern French Law," *Law Quarterly Review*, vol. 17, 1901, pp. 302 ff.) The system of administrative law and jurisdiction found in European countries has been critized by commentators trained in Anglo-Saxon legal theory, as a system which is fundamentally wrong because it is based on the principle of inequality between the official class and the body of private citizens. (See A. Lawrence Lowell, *Governments and Parties in Europe*, vol. 1, p. 58; compare with later view in *Government of England*, vol. 2, p. 503.) This criticism is not convincing to some observers. (See defense of administrative law by Professor J. H. Morgan in his introduction to Robinson's Public Authorities and Legal Liability, 1925, pp. 61 ff.) Professor Morgan contends that the individual in France and Germany is better protected against arbitrary and illegal conduct of the government than he is in England. Note similar defense in Munro, *Governments of Europe*, pp. 534-47. Compare also Marriot, *The Mechanism of the Modern State*, vol. 2, 1927, pp. 273 ff.; Allen, "Bureaucracy Triumphant," *Quarterly Review*, vol. 240, 1923, p. 247; and Barker, "The Rule of Law," *Political Science Quarterly*, May, 1914, pp. 117 ff.

[50] "The development of a distinctive law is in process. Administrative law has ceased to be descriptive of the exotic." Frankfurter and Landis, *The Business of the Supreme Court*, 1929, pp. 184-186; W. F. Willoughby, *Principles of Judicial Administration*, 1929, pp. 20-21; Elihu Root, *Report*, American Bar Association, 1916, pp. 368-369.

[51] Roscoe Pound, "Justice According to Law," *Columbia Law Review*, vol. 13, 1907, p. 696: "Our government was one of laws and not of men. Administration had become 'only a very subordinate agency in the whole process of government.' Complete elimination of the personal in all matters affecting the life, liberty, property, or fortune of the citizens seemed to have been attained. What in other lands was committed to administration and inspection and executive supervision, we left to the courts. We were adverse to inspection and supervision in advance of action, preferring to show the individual his duty by a general law, to leave him free to act according to his judgment, and to prosecute him and impose the predetermined penalty in case his free action infringed the law. It was fundamental in our policy to confine administration to the inevitable minimum. In other words, where some peoples went to one extreme and were bureau-ridden, we went to the other extreme and were law-ridden. . . . Obviously it threw a great burden upon the judicial system, and despite the reaction which had taken place, will continue to put a strain upon the courts for a long time to come. . . . Nothing is so characteristic of the American public law of the last half of the nineteenth century as the completeness with which executive action is tied down by legal liability and judicial review." Roscoe Pound, "Organization of the Courts," *Jour. Amer. Jud. Soc.*, 1927, pp. 69-70.

[52] "It is important," says Walter F. Dodd, "that proper methods be established for the judicial review of decisions of such bodies. Administrative tribunals may perhaps be

Indeed, some observers are of the opinion that it will be necessary to create a system of special courts[53] similar in character to the French administrative courts,[54] whose work has been so favorably received[55] Sooner or later, it is evident, these new forms of legal control through law administering agencies will have to be adjusted, in one way or another, to our traditional system of judicial justice.[56]

---

most effectively organized as subordinate agencies in the judicial organization if the courts come to be organized in such a way to do their work effectively. In rate making today, one of the chief difficulties is that administrative bodies and courts act in substantially complete independence of each other. The utility commission investigates and fixes rates; the court, by independent methods, reaches a different conclusion and annuls the action of the commission. See *McCardle* v. *Indianapolis Water Co.*, 272 U. S. 400 (1926). For this reason efforts have been made in Virginia and Oklahoma to make the highest state court an agency in rate-making rather than a mere reversing bordy. (See pp. 68, 91). But no steps have yet been taken to work out satisfactorily arrangements between the state rate-fixing agencies and the federal courts." *State Government*, 1929, p. 341. A very interesting and instructive discussion of the problems of judicial review and administrative adjudication is found in *Recent Social Trends in the United States*, vol. 2, 1933, pp. 1467-1468.

[53] William D. Guthrie, "President's Address, New York State Bar Association," *Reports*, N. Y. State Bar Assn., vol. XLVI, 1923, 169; *League of Nation's and Miscellaneous Addresses*, 352. "The need for a coherent system of administrative law, for uniformity and dispatch in adjudication, for the subtle skill required in judges called upon to synthesize the public and private claims peculiarly involved in administrative litigation, these and kindred considerations will have to be balanced against the traditional hold of a single system of courts, giving a generalized professional aptitude to its judges and bringing to the review of administrative conduct a technique and temperament trained in litigation between private individuals." Frankfurter and Landis, *The Business of the Supreme Court*, 1927, p. 186.

[54] The principal administrative courts in France are the interdepartmental councils of the prefecture and the Council of State. There are twenty-two departmental councils of the prefecture, each serving from two to seven departments. In addition, the Department of the Seine, has a council of its own. Each interdepartmental council consists of a president and four councillors. These councils hear complaints made by individuals against the actions of subordinate officials. They deal with controversies concerning tax assessments and most of the matters which come before them are of this nature. They also have jurisdiction over questions relating to public works (especially highways) and the conduct of local elections. Procedure in these courts is simple and economical. Parallel with the interdepartmental councils of the prefecture are various special administrative courts, notably the educational councils and councils of revision. Appeals from these lower administrative courts are taken to the Council of State. This is a large body, made up of two elements, political and non-political. Questions of administrative law are heard and determined by a section of the Council which consists of thirty-five non-political members, or *conseillers en service ordinaire*, as they are called. This group includes many distinguished jurists. Every year several thousands of cases are decided by this tribunal at a minimum expenditure of time and money for the litigant. It has been successful and enjoys the respect of the French people. Munro, *Governments of Europe*, 1931, pp. 543-544.

[55] James W. Garner says: "It can now be said without possibility of contradiction that there is no country in which the rights of private individuals are so well protected against the arbitrariness, the abuses, and the illegal conduct of the administrative authorities, and where the people are so sure of receiving reparation for injuries sustained on account of such conduct." "French Administrative Law," *Yale Law Journal*, vol. 32, April, 1924, p. 599.

[56] "In any merger, and in developments in that direction, there is nothing to compel a giving up of the use by administrative tribunals of investigators, impartial physicians,

Other factors which tend to withdraw certain classes of cases from our traditional method of procedure are to be found in the movement to adopt conciliation and small claim courts and to employ arbitration for the settlement of commercial disputes. Here again the emphasis is on prompt and inexpensive findings, unhampered by technical rules of evidence. Conciliation offers a means of friendly adjustment to parties whose interests clash and places emphasis on equity rather than the strict letter of the law.[57] Indeed, the discretionary element is important in both the conciliation and small claims court. The judge is the key figure in both. The success or failure of a conciliation court depends very largely upon the man who acts as conciliator.[58] In the small claims court, the same thing is true, since the judge is in affirmative control of the whole proceedings. He is equipped not only to prevent injustice but to do justice. If he does not accomplish this purpose, the responsibility rests with him.[59]

---

simple procedures, simple forms, mail service, and the automatic settlement of claims. If they interfere with parts of the traditional machinery, such parts ought to be scrapped. Administrative tribunals have much to teach judicial tribunals about promptness, inexpensiveness, and limiting the attorney to clearly defined functions." R. H. Smith, *Justice and the Poor*, p. 91.

[57] Professor John H. Wigmore, in discussing some aspects of conciliation for the American Judicature Society, said: "The rules of technical substantive law defining in detailed logic the parties' rights and obligations, are either ignored or modified or roughly followed, as each case may seem to require, in the judge's opinion of the ethical merits of the whole case." Continuing he says: "Taking first the law of substantive rights and obligations, it signifies that there is a place, at some point, where its mass of technical details is not needed. . . . Here we face the old problem, perennially discussed by the philosophers of the distinction between law and justice. . . . Law protects us against the incompetence, whimsicality, corruption, and variability of the human judge, among thousands of whom will be few who are wise and sound enough to do justice. And justice is theoretically superior to law, in that it represents the wise and just solution which uniform rules cannot expect to attain in each individual case." *Am. Jud. Soc.*, *Bull. VIII.*

[58] Judge H. H. Sawyer, who established the Conciliation Court in Des Moines, Iowa, explains why the success of conciliation depends on the concilator in "Making Justice Less Expensive," *The American Mercury*, vol. 14, July, 1928, pp. 304-312. To be successful, he says, the concilator "must be one who believes thoroughly in conciliation, he must also have almost unlimited patience, and he must have the knack of bringing warring parties together. It is a peculiar and somewhat difficult position to fill. The success of the Cleveland Court is largely due to the clerk who started it and who acted as conciliator until his death about a year ago. Almost as much can be said of the Minneapolis Court. Many other courts have failed of complete success because they have not found the right men for conciliators." F. R. Aumann, "The Des Moines Concilation Court," *Journal of the American Judicature Society*, vol. XI, June, 1928, p. 310.

[59] "More important, in the small claim courts, the judges have won back their proper and rightful power and influence which has been so badly curtailed in our state tribunals. The small claims court judge is not an umpire, he is an impartial investigator into the truth. He is not a passive agent waiting for objections, he is in affirmative control of the whole proceedings. It has long been recognized as an anomaly that judges sitting without juries should be thrust into the straight-jacket of the rules of evidence which exist solely for the protection and guidance of lay juries. In the small claims court the judge is not shackled, he is not obliged to sit by in impatience while, as Thayer has said, 'the rules of evidence are sharply and technically used to worry an inexperienced,

In arbitration, the emphasis is also placed on the speedy, economical, and final settlement of disputes.[60] For years, England has had a system of arbitration as an integral part of its judicial system which has proved very effective.[61] In 1920, the first law to give legal force to arbitration agreements was passed by New York State.[62] This act made agreements to arbitrate irrevocable. Since then, laws of much the same character have been passed by New Jersey, Pennsylvania, Massachusetts, California, Oregon, Louisiana, Connecticut, New Hampshire, Rhode Island, and Arizona, while all the other states have passed some form of arbitration law, as has the federal government.[63] The arbitration movement was greatly stimulated by the establishment of the American Arbitration Association in 1926. Where arbitration is used, the courts

---

or ill-equipped adversary in order to support a worthless case.' He is equipped and empowered not only to prevent injustice but to do justice. The small claims courts are sound. They demonstrate what our judges can do, and will do, if they are given the needed power and responsibility." "Report of the Committee on Small Claims and Conciliation Procedure of the Conference of Bar Association Delegates, 1923," *American Bar Association Journal*, November, 1924.

[60] W. A. Sturges, *Commercial Arbitrations and Awards*, Kansas City, Missouri, 1930; W. F. Willoughby, *Principles of Judicial Administration*, 1929, pp. 53-79; F. R. Aumann, "The Lawyer and His Troubles," *North American Review*, April, 1933, pp. 310-318.

[61] "A very large proportion of all business disputes of England never come into the courts at all, but are adjusted by tribunals established within the various trade associations and exchanges. This is especially true of the vast wholesale distributing trades which are responsible for a great part of the immense volume of imports and exports constantly flowing through the ports of England and giving them the commanding position they occupy towards the sea-borne trade of the world. Disputes over the quality and condition of consignments of grain, cotton, sugar, coffee, fruit, rubber, timber, meats, hides, seeds, fibers, fats, and countless other articles of commerce, as well as every conceivable variety of dispute can arise out of contract for sale and delivery, such as questions of delays, quantities, freights, interpretation, etc.—all these are passed upon by business arbitrators selected by reasons of their familiarity with the customs of the trade and with the technical facts involved, and not submitted to juries whose ignorance would usually be equally comprehensive." Samuel Rosenbaum, "Report on Commercial Arbitration in England," *American Judicature Society, Bulletin XII*, October, 1916.

[62] "At common law, agreements for the submission of disputed matters to unofficial arbitrators for settlement were not fostered since the courts were jealous of anything tending to oust them of their jurisdiction. This hostility prevented the specific enforcement of arbitration agreements and made such agreements in effect revocable by permitting resort to the laws courts by either party. Early statutes were only of a regulatory nature but by 1920 the movement toward arbitration had gained great impetus due largely to the activities of trade associations and chambers of commerce. These organizations then began to incorporate future disputes clauses into their articles of membership and by-laws and standard contract form, a practice which had been adopted by over 150 of them by 1931." *Recent Social Trends in the United States*, vol. II, 1933, pp. 1454-1455.

[63] Statutes providing for specific enforcement of irrevocable contracts to arbitrate future as well as present statutes were in effect in eleven states, the territory of Hawaii, and in the federal jurisdiction by 1933. They have been held constitutional as against charges that they were destroying the right of trial by jury and were diminishing the jurisdiction of the courts.

are displaced; another victory is won for flexible procedure; and another defeat ensues for rules and formal procedure.[64]

Significant developments affecting our traditional forms of organization and procedure have also taken place in the developments of our juvenile and domestic relations courts. In the juvenile court, much of the evidence used is taken from outside of the court by court officials and is based in great part on the sciences of human behavior,[65] plus the observations of trained workers.[66] This is quite different from the orthodox method, where evidence is presented and arguments are made by opposing attorneys before a judge who decides each case according to established principles on the legally admissible evidence of the witnesses.[67] The tendency in the juvenile court is toward a more human emphasis, and requires a more liberal procedure in transacting the business of the courts.[68] In the course of time this procedure may affect other courts as well.[69]

The methods and organization of domestic relations courts are

[64] *American Bar Association Journal,* 1930, vol. 16, pp. 699, 805.

[65] Roscoe Pound speaking in this connection said: "The fundamental theory of our orthodox criminal law has gone down before modern psychology and psychopathology. The results are only beginning to be felt." "Criminal Justice in Cleveland," *The Cleveland Foundation,* 1922, p. 588. "Scientific diagnostic study as a regular service for delinquents and for a court began in the juvenile court in Chicago in 1909. This work which was started and continued under the name of the Juvenile Psychopathic Institute, was soon perceived to have much wider bearings and usefulness than study of merely psychopathic cases; the cases of quite normal offenders often justify as much, if not more attention given them for the sake of effective understanding." William Healey, "The Practical Value of Scientific Study of Juvenile Delinquents," *United States Children's Bureau Publication,* No. 96, 1922, p. 7. For further discussion on this subject see A. L. Jacoby, "The Psychopathic Clinic in a Criminal Court: Its Use and Possibilities," *Am. Jud. Soc. Jour.,* vol. 7, June, 1923, p. 21, 25; Harry Olson, "Crime and Heredity," *Am. Jud. Soc. Jour.,* vol. 7, August, 1923, pp. 33, 77.

[66] The probation officer assumes an important role in this process. Thomas D. Elliot, "The Juvenile Court and the Educational System," *Journal of Criminal Law and Criminology.*

[67] Generally speaking certain features are considered essential for the organization of the juvenile court. These features include (1) separate hearings for children's cases; (2) informal or chancery procedure, excluding the use of petition or summons; (3) regular probation service, both for supervisory care and investigation; (4) detention separate for adults; (5) special courts and probation records, both legal and social; (6) provisions for mental and physical examination.

[68] "When a court is acting, not as an arbiter of private strife but as the medium of the State's performance of its sovereign duties as *parens patriae* and promoter of the general welfare, it is natural that some of the safeguards of judicial contests should be laid aside." Edward F. Waite, "How Far Can Court Procedure be Socialized without Impairing Individual Rights?" p. 55, *U. S. Children's Bureau Publications,* No. 97, 1922. See further in this connection, Miriam Van Waters, "The Socialization of Juvenile Court Procedure," p. 64, *U. S. Children's Bureau Publications,* No. 97, 1922. For further comments on this subject see p. 62, *ibid.*

[69] "Today the vanguard of thought is recognizing that many of the principles of socialized treatment—such as a study of the characteristics of the individual and the environment in which he lives and constructive probation—are applicable and should be extended gradually to the whole field of criminal justice." "The Child, the Family, and the Court," *U. S. Children's Bureau Publications,* No. 193, 1929, p. 13.

of interest.[70] Viewed from some angles, they have more the character of an administrative than of a judicial agency. They differ from most other administrative agencies, however, in that they put their orders in the form of a judicial decree when necessary, with all the powers of the judicial process to enforce that decree. In performing its functions, a large discretion is vested in this type of court to fit its decree to the individual case. It is assisted in this procedure by its permanent staff of trained workers who investigated each case personally and supervise the carrying out of the decree. Formalities in bringing action, producing evidence, and conducting proceedings are not present here.[71] Indeed, some experienced observers believe the "domestic relations" court should be frankly looked upon as a social agency rather than as an agency to enforce criminal law or decide technical controversies between litigants.[72] An ideal court of this kind, they believe, would have a jurisdiction, sufficiently wide to cover all cases, civil and criminal, affecting the child and domestic relations. It would be presided over by a judge holding office permanently. He would be selected with a view to his special qualifications for the office. Hearings would be informal,[73] probation would be an important factor,[74] physical and mental examinations would be required of all children appearing before the court,[75] a close relationship with organized social agencies would be maintained, and the social data developed by the court's proceedings would be carefully recorded and preserved.[76]

In conclusion it may be said that the legal system, like the social

[70] Charles Zunser, "The Domestic Relations Court," *Annals of the Amer. Acad. of Pol. and Soc. Sci.*, vol. 124, March, 1926; Charles W. Hoffman, "Courts of Domestic Relations," *Proc. of Natl. Conf. of Soc. Work*, 1918, pp. 124-128; "Development in Family Court Work," *Proc. of Natl. Prob. Assn.*, pp. 55-58; "The Organization of Domestic Relations Court," *Proc. Natl. Prob. Assn.*, 1928, pp. 145-151.

[71] The work being done in the Domestic Relations Court of Cincinnati aptly illustrates recent developments in this field. Much of its work consists in supervising probation of children. In arriving at its decrees the court employs techniques which would seem strangely out of place in the orthodox form of court. It has drawn heavily upon the tools that modern scientific knowledge places at its disposal. In consequence social investigation and medical examination play a prominent part in its work. See Alan Johnstone, "The Domestic Relations Court of Cincinnati, Ohio," *Baltimore Criminal Justice Commission*, mimeographed manuscript, 1924.

[72] See Edward F. Waite, "Courts of Domestic Relations," *Minnesota Law Review*, vol. 5, No. 3, Feb., 1921, p. 167, quoting Judge Harry A. Fisher of the Buffalo Domestic Relations Court.

[73] All technical rules of evidence would be eliminated. Hearings would be apart from proceedings in other branches of the court and the public excluded.

[74] An adequate force of capable probation officers would be required to help the judge in cases coming before him by making personal investigations. They would also supervise those placed on probation under the controlling direction of the judge.

[75] Judge Chas. W. Hoffman, "Why the Family Court Needs a Psychopathic Laboratory," *Proceedings of the American Prison Association*, 1916, pp. 61-70.

[76] W. F. Willoughby, *Principles of Judicial Administration*, 1929, pp. 333-34; *U. S. Children's Bureau Publications*, 1929, No. 193, pp. 49-52.

system of which it is a part, is straining at its moorings. In a period of rapid social change, it repeats its history of the past and experiments with some of the devices of executive justice.[77] This trend is reflected in a critical movement in legal philosophy which challenges ancient concepts and demands that the relationship of law to modern society be reexamined with care and precision to the end that law will be more useful socially. This trend is further reflected in the movement to widen the range of judicial discretion, to the end that the law may more easily adjust itself to a changed social condition. This trend is still further reflected in the several movements which are rearranging our old forms of court organization and procedure to the end that they will be more flexible and workable in a complex modern world. The net result of this is a system which can operate quickly, economically, and free from procedural formality. The delay, expense, and technicalities of the past tend to expedite the trend to newer forms. Involved in this movement is a new attitude to the legal order and its traditional set of values, such as separation of powers in government, the supremacy of an independent judiciary, proof of every allegation according to time tried rules of evidence, testing each witness by cross-examination, deliberation, jury trial, and appeal. In times past, these rights were highly prized. In fact, the history of Anglo-Saxon political and legal institutions is replete with instances of bitter struggle for these rights. Today, however, the public has little patience with them and their delay, technicalities, and costs.[78] It is much more interested in the economy and flexibility which has always characterized executive justice.[79]

The immediate significance of these movements in the legal field is variously interpreted.[80] With far-reaching changes in social forms and controls impending, some observers are convinced that our traditional ideas and practices in the legal sphere are in for some fundamental readjustments.[81] The demands of the day in all political, social, and economic environments are for an ever-increasing centralization of power.[82] As they see it, these demands will materially affect the apparatus of law.[83] Divisions of power in government, complicated legal arrange-

[77] Roscoe Pound, *Outlines of Jurisprudence*, 1928, pp. 57-58.

[78] Robert Jackson, "An Organized American Bar," *American Bar Association Journal*, vol. 18, June, 1932, p. 384.

[79] See Roscoe Pound, *Outlines of Jurisprudence*, 1928, pp. 57-58.

[80] F. R. Aumann, "Technology, Centralization and the Law," *The South Atlantic Quarterly*, vol. 36, July, 1937, pp. 278-288.

[81] Brooks Adams, *Centralization and Law*, pp. 45-46; the *Theory of Social Revolution*, p. 34.

[82] Brooks Adams, *The Theory of Social Revolution*, pp. 19-21, 204; Lawrence Dennis, *The Coming American Fascism*, p. 117.

[83] Those who see an increasing integration of life as a major tendency of the day can point to demands for change in legal forms in the past when similar integrating tendencies were taking place. These demands sometimes demanded codification. "On the

ments, constitutionalism, and the theory of an impersonal government of human relationship—all tend to limit power and hamper the discretionary role of the governing authority; and in doing so collide violently with theories that a greater concentration of power in some central authority is a major imperative of an age of technology. This conflict of interests, it is held, threatens the future of our whole legal edifice. Others do not concur in this philosophy of pessimism.[84] In their view, the changes of today may be compared with such movements in our law as gave rise to the courts of chancery and the development of equity. These movements effected no fundamental changes in the Anglo-American legal system, whose significant and enduring characteristics have continued to be: the idea of the supremacy of the law,[85] the idea of all governmental activity as subject to requirements of reason, and the insistence upon law as reason to be developed by judicial experience in the decision of cases. These ideas not only continue to color our rules and practices but also are so interwoven into the fabric of Anglo-American thinking that much more than the recent movements in the legal and political sphere will be required to uproot them.[86]

---

breakdown of the feudal organization, the rise of commerce and the era of discovery, colonization and exploration of the natural resources of new continents, together with the rise of nations in place of loose congeries of vassal-held territories, called for a national law unified within the national domain. Starkey proposed codification to Henry VIII and Dumoulin urged harmonizing and unifying the French customary law with eventual codification." Pound, *An Introduction to the Philosophy of Law*, p. 39.

[84] *The Future of the Common Law*, Harvard Centenary Publications, 1937, pp. 3-24, 120-164.

[85] John Dickinson, *Administrative Justice and the Supremacy of the Law*, 1927, pp. 32-33.

[86] Roscoe Pound, *The Spirit of the Common Law*, pp. 215-216; see also *The Green Bag*, vol. 18, 1906, pp. 24-25; "Fifty Years of Jurisprudence," *Harvard Law Review*, vol. 51, p. 559.

BIBLIOGRAPHY

BIBLIOGRAPHY

I. COLONIAL PERIOD, 1608-1776

BOOKS

* Applegarth, A. C., *The Quakers in Pennsylvania*, Baltimore, The John Hopkins press, 182. 84 pp. (In John Hopkins University Studies in Historical and Political Science, vol. 10, 1892, pp. 381-464.)
* *Archives of the State of New Jersey*, edited by W. A. Whitehead and others. 1st series, *Documents relative to the Colonial History, 1631-1800*, 27 vols., 2nd series, *Documents relative to the Revolutionary History, 1776-1779*, Newark, 1880-1906. 3 vols.
* *Acts and Laws of the Colony of New Hampshire, 1776-1780*, Exeter, 1780.
* *Acts and Laws passed by the Great and General Court or Assembly of the Colony of the Massachusetts Bay, 1775-1780*, Boston, 1789.
* *Acts and Resolves, Public and Private, of the Province of the Massachusetts Bay*, I-XXI, Boston, 1689-1922.
* Allenson, S., Compiler, *Acts of the General Assembly of the Province of New Jersey, 1702-1776*, Burlington, N. J., 1776.
* *An Abridgment of the Laws in Force and Use in Her Majesty's Plantations*, London, 1704.
* Andrews, Charles M. "The Influence of Colonial Conditions as Illustrated in the Connecticut Intestacy Law," *Select Essays*, I, 431-366.
* Andrews, C. M., "The Royal Disallowance in Massachusetts," Amer. Antiq. Soc., *Proceedings*, N. 8. XXIV.
* "Andros Records," Amer. Antiq. Soc., *Proceedings*, XIII, 1900, 237-268, 463-499.
* Bacon, T., (ed.), *Laws of Maryland at Large, 1637-1763*. Annapolis, 1765.
* Barnes, Harry E., "A History of the Penal Reformatory and Correctional Institutions of the State of New Jersey, Analytical and Historical." In *Report of the New Jersey Prison Inquiry Commission*, vol. I, 1918, pp. 17-55.
* Barton, R. T., editor, *Virginia Colonial Decisions: the Reports by Sir John Randolph and by Edward Barradall of Decisions of the General Court of Virginia, 1728-1741*, Boston, 1909, 2 vols.
* Bates, A. C., *Connecticut Statute Laws: a Bibliographical List of Editions of Connecticut Laws from the earliest issues to 1836*. Hartford, 1900.
  Beard, Charles A., "The Justice of the Peace in England," *Columbia University Studies*, New York, 1894.
  Belknap, Jeremy, *The History of New Hampshire*, Boston, 1791-1792, 3 vols.

* References so marked have not been cited among the footnotes of this book.

Beveridge, Albert J., *The Life of John Marshall*, Boston and New York, 1916-19, 4 vols.

Beverly, Robert, *The History and Present State of Virginia*, London, Printed for R. Parker, MDCCV.

Bond, Beverly, *The Quit-Rent System of the American Colonies*, New Haven, 1919, 492 pp.

Bond, Carroll T., *The Court of Appeals of Maryland, a History*, Baltimore, 1928, 214 pp.

Brigham, W., *The Colony of New Plymouth*, Boston, 1869, 27 pp.

Brown, Alexander, *Genesis of the United States*, Boston, 1890, 2 vols.

* Browne, W. F., *Archives of Maryland*, LXLIV, Baltimore, 1883.

Bruce, Philip A., *Economic History of Virginia in the Seventeenth Century*, New York, 1895-1907, 2 vols.

Bruce, Philip A., *Institutional History of Virginia in the Seventeenth Century*, New York, 1895-1907, 2 vols.

Bruce, Philip A., *Social Life of Virginia in the Seventeenth Century*, New York, 1907, 268 pp.

Burk, John D., *History of Virginia*, Petersburg, Va., Dickson and Pescud, 1822, 3 vols.

* *Calendar of Virginia State Papers and other Manuscripts . . . Preserved . . . at Richmond, 1652-1869*, edited by W. P. Palmer and others, Richmond, 1875-1893, 11 vols.

* Candler, A. D., (ed.), *Revolutionary Records of the State of Georgia, 1769-1784*, Atlanta, 1908, 3 vols.

Candler, A. D., (ed.), *Colonial Records of the State of Georgia*, Atlanta, 1905-1916, 26 vols.

* Carey, M. and Biorer, J., *Laws of the Commonwealth of Pennsylvania, 1700-1802*, Philadelphia, 1803, 6 vols.

* Carroll, B. R., compiler, *Historical Collections of South Carolina, with many rare documents*, New York, 1836, 2 vols.

* Chalmers, George, *Opinions of Eminent Lawyers on Various Points of English Jurisdiction Chiefly Concerning the Colonies*, London, 1858.

* Chapin, H. M., *Documentary History of Rhode Island*, Providence, 1856-1865, 2 vols.

Chitwood, Oliver, *A History of Colonial America*, New York and London, 1931, 811 pp.

Chitwood, Oliver, *Justice in Colonial America*, Johns Hopkins Studies in History and Political Science, Ser. XXIII, Baltimore, 1905, 123 pp.

Colonial Laws of Massachusetts reprinted from the edition of 1660, with supplements to 1672, containing also the Body of Liberties of 1641, Boston, 1889.

Colonial Laws of New York from the Year 1664 to the Revolution, Albany, 1894-1896, 5 vols.

* *Colonial Records of North Carolina, 1662-1776*, edited by W. I. Saunders, I-X, Raleigh, 1886-1890. From 1776 to 1790 (XI-XXVI, Winston, 1895-1906), the series is called *State Records*, and is edited by W. Clark.

* References so marked have not been cited among the footnotes of this book.

* *Colonial Records of Virginia, 1619-1680*, edited by S. M. Kingbury, Washington, 1906.

* Cooper, T., editor, *Statutes at Large of South Carolina, 1682-1875*, vols. VI-X, edited by D. J. McCord. Columbia, 1836-1879, 15 vols.

Coulter, E. M., *A Short History of Georgia*, The University of North Carolina Press, 1933, 457 pp.

Court Minutes of Albany, Rensselaerwyck, and Schenectady, 1668-1680, translated and edited by A. J. F. Van Laer, Albany, 1926-1928, vols. I, II.

* Crump, Helen J., *Colonial Admiralty Foundations in the Seventeenth Century*, London, 1931, 200 pp.

* Curtis, B. R., *The Life and Writings of Benjamin R. Curtis*, Boston, 1879, 2 vols.

Dallas, A. J., compiler, *Laws of the Commonwealth of Pennsylvania, 1700-1790*, Philadelphia, 1793-1797, 2 vols.

Dallas, A. J., *Reports of Cases in the Courts of Pennsylvania . . . , 1754-1806, and in the several Courts of the United States, 1790-1800*, 4 vols. Philadelphia 1790-1807. Vol. I is entitled *Reports of Cases ruled and adjudged in the Courts of Pennsylvania before and since the Revolution.* Philadelphia, 1806, 1935, 2nd edition of vols. I, IV.

Daly, Charles P., *History of the Court of Common Pleas*, in E. D. Smith's Common Pleas Reports, I, XVII, New York, 68 pp.

Daly, Charles P., *The Nature, Extent and History of the Surrogate's Courts of the State of New York*, New York, 1863.

Davis, William Thomas, *Bench and Bar of the Commonwealth of Massachusetts*, Boston, 1896, 2 vols.

Davis, William Thomas, *History of the Judiciary of Massachusetts*, Boston, 1900, 46 pp.

* Delaware. *Laws, 1700-1805.* I-II, New Castle, 1797; III, Wilmington, 1816; *1700-1819*, New Castle, 1797-1819.

* *Delaware Archives*, Wilmington, 1911-1916, 5 vols.

Documents and Records Relating to the Province (Town and State) of New Hampshire, 1623-1800, edited by N. Bouton and others, Concord, 1867-1915, 33 vols.

* Dorsey, C. (Comp.), *General Public Statutory Law and Public Law, 1692-1839*, Baltimore, 1840, 3 vols.

* *Duke of York's Book of Laws, 1676-1682, and Charter to William Penn and Laws of the Province of Pennsylvania passed between 1682 and 1700*, Harrisburg, 1879.

* Eastman, F. M., *Courts and Lawyers of Pennsylvania, a History, 1623-1923*, New York, 1923, 3 vols.

Eggleston, Edward, *The Transit of Civilization from England to America in the Seventeenth Century, 1923*, Peter Smith, 344 pp.

* *Executive Journals of the Council of Virginia, 1680-1721*, Richmond, 1926, I-III.

* Fane, Francis, *Reports on the Laws of Connecticut*, edited by C. M. Andrews, Hartford, 1915, 200 pp.

Field, Richard S., *Provincial Courts of New Jersey*, New York, 1849, 311 pp. (Collections of the N. J. Hist. Soc., vol. III).

Fisher, E. J., *New Jersey as a Royal Province, 1738-1776,* New York, 1911, 318 pp. Published also in *Studies in History, Economics, and Public Law,* edited by the Faculty of Political Science of Columbia University, vol. XLI, No. 107.

Fisher, S. G., "The Administration of Equity through Common Laws Forms in Pennsylvania," *Select Essays,* II, pp. 810 et seq.

* Ford, W. C. and Mathews, A., *Bibliography of Massachusetts Laws, 1641-1776,* Cambridge, 1907, 186 pp.

Fowler, Robert L., *Codification in the State of New York,* New York, 1884, 69 pp.

Fowler, Robert L., *History of the Law of Real Property in New York,* New York, 1895, 229 pp.

Fowler, W. C., *Local Law in Massachusetts and Connecticut Historically Considered,* Albany, 1872, 104 pp.

* "Fundamental Constitutions of the Carolinas," John Locke's *Works,* 1823 edition, vol. X.

Gager, Edwin, "Equity," *Two Centuries Growth of American Law,* 1901, pp. 115-129-147.

Goebel, Julius, Jr., *Cases and Materials on the Development of Legal Institutions,* New York, 1932, 784 pp.

Goebel, Julius, Jr., *Some Legal and Political Aspects of the Manors in New York,* Baltimore, 1928, 22 pp.

Grimké, J. F., Compiler, *Public Laws of the State of South Carolina, 1682-1790,* Philadelphia, 1790.

Grinnell, F. W., "The Bench and Bar in Colony and Province, 1630-1776," in the *Commonwealth History of Massachusetts,* New York, 1928, II, 156-192.

* Green, E. B. and Morris, R. B., *A Guide to the Principal Sources for Early American History, 1600-1800, in the City of New York,* New York, 1929, 357 pp.

Grubb, Ignatius C., *Colonial and State Judiciary of Delaware,* Wilmington, 1897, 70 pp.

Harvard Law School Association—*The Centennial History of the Harvard Law School, 1817-1917,* privately printed, Boston, 1918, 412 pp.

Hatfield, Edwin F., *A History of Elizabeth, New Jersey,* N. Y. Carlton and Lanahan, 1868, 701 pp.

Hazard, S., *Annals of Pennsylvania, 1609-1682,* Philadelphia, 1850.

Hazard, S., editor, *Pennsylvania Register,* Philadelphia, 1825-1835, 16 vols.

Hening, W. W., *The Statutes . . . at . . . Large, being a Collection of all the Laws of Virginia, 1619-1792,* Philadelphia and New York, 1823, 13 vols.

* Hoadley, C. J. (compiler), *Records of the Colony and Plantation of New Haven, 1638-1649. Records of the Colony or Jurisdiction of New Haven, 1633-1663,* Hartford, 1858.

* Hoffman, Murray, *A Treatise Upon the Practice of the Court of Chancery,* New York, 1835, 3 vols.

* References so marked have not been cited among the footnotes of this book.

* Hood, John, *Index of Colonial and State Laws, between 1663 and 1877*, Trenton, New Jersey, 1877.
* Hough, Charles M., *Reports of Cases in Vice Admiralty of the Province of New York*, New York, 125.
* Howard, George E., *History of Matrimonial Institutions*, Chicago, 1904, 3 vols.
* Howard, J. P., *Laws of the British Colonies in the West Indies and other Parts of America, concerning Real and Personal Property, etc.* London, 1827.
* Hubbard, L. M. and Hoadley, C. J., *Report of the Secretary of State and State Librarian (of Connecticut) on Ancient Court Records*, 1889.
* Jefferson, Thomas, *Reports of Cases determined in the General Court of Virginia, 1730-1740, 1768-1772*, Charlottesville, 1829.
* Jones, C. C. (ed.), *Acts passed by the General Assembly of the Colony of Georgia, 1755-1774*, Wormsloe, 1881.
  Jones, Leonard Augustus and Reno, Conrad, *Memoirs of the Judiciary and the Bar of New England for the Nineteenth Century with a History of the Judicial System of New England*, Boston, 1900, 2 vols.
* *Journals of the House of Representatives of Massachusetts, 1715-1731*, Boston, 1919, vols. I-IX.
* *Journal of the Procedure of the Governor and Council of the Province of East Jersey from and after the first day of December, 1682-1703*, Jersey City, 1872.
  Kilty, W. (ed.), *Laws of Maryland, 1692-1799*, Annapolis, 1799-1800, 2 vols.
* *Laws of New Hampshire, including Public and Private Acts and Resolves and Royal Commissions and Instructions*, edited by A. B. Batchellor, Manchester, 1904-1922, vols. I-X, (I-VII, 1679-1801).
  Laws and Ordinances of New Netherlands, 1636-1674, compiled and translated by E. B. O'Callaghan, Albany, 1868.
  Leaming, A. and Spicer, J., *Grants, Concessions, and Original Constitutions of the Province of New Jersey, 1664-1682*, Philadelphia, 1752. Reprinted Somerville, 1881.
  Lechford, Thomas, *Plain Dealing* (London, Nathaniel Butler, 1642).
* *Legislative Journals of the Council of Colonial Virginia*, edited by H. R. McIlwaine, Richmond, 1918-19, 3 vols.
* Libby, C. T. (ed.), *Province and Court Records of Maine, I, 1636-1668*, Portland, 1928.
  Loyd, William H., *Early Courts of Pennsylvania*, Boston, 1910, 287 pp.
* Lucas, S., *Charters of Old English Colonies in America*, London, 1850, 123 pp.
* Marbury, H. and Crawford, W. M., compilers, *Digest of the Laws of the State of Georgia, from its settlement as a British Province in 1755 to the session of the General Assembly in 1800, inclusive*, Savannah, 1802.
* *Maryland Catalogue of Manuscripts and Printed Matters*, November, 1926, in the possession of the Maryland Court of Appeals at Annapolis.
* *Maryland Court of Appeals Reports, 1658-1799*, Harris and McHenry.
* *Maryland Reports, 1700-1797*, New York, 1809-1813, 3 vols.

* Mathews, A., *Notes on the 1672 Edition and 1675 Volume of the General Laws*, Cambridge, 1917.
* Maxey, V. (ed.), *Laws of Maryland, with he Charter, the Bill of Rights, etc., 1704-1809*, Baltimore, 1811, 3 vols.
* *Minutes of the Council of Delaware State from 1776 to 1792*, Dover, 1886.
* *Minutes of the Council and General Court of Colonial Virginia*, edited by H. R. McIlwaine, Richmond, 1924.
* *Minutes of the Court of Fort Orange and Beverwyck, 1652-1660*, translated and edited by A. J. F. Van Laer, Albany, 1920-1923, 2 vols.
* *Minutes of the Court of Rensselaerwyck, 1648-1652*, translated and edited by A. J. F. Van Laer, Albany, 1922.
* "Minutes of the Court of Sessions, 1657-1696, Westchester County, N. Y.," edited by D. R. Fox, Westchester County Hist. Soc., *Publications*, II, White Plains, N. Y., 1924.
* *Minutes of the Executive Council of the Province of New York (with) Collateral and Illustrative Documents*, edited by V. H. Paltsits, I-II, 1668-1673, Albany, 1910.
* *Minutes of the Orphanmasters of New Amsterdam, 1655-1663*, translated and edited by B. Fernow, New York, 1902, 2 vols.
* "Minutes of the Superior Court of Judicature, 1693-1701," N. Y. Hist. Soc., *Collections*, 1912, pp. 39-214.
  Morris, R. B., editor, *Select Cases of the Mayor's Court of New York City, 1674-1784*, The American Historical Association, 1935, VII, 777 pp.
* Morris, R. B., *Historiography of America, 1600-1800*, as represented in the publications of Columbia University press, New York, 1933, 30 pp.
  Morris, R. B., *Studies in the History of American Law*, New York, 1930, 287 pp.
* New York (state), *The Colonial Laws of New York*, Albany, 1896, 5 vols.
* Noble, John, "Notes on the Trial and Punishment of Crimes," Col. Sec. of Mass., *Publications*, III, 51-66.
* O'Callaghan, E. B., *Documentary History of the State of New York*, Albany, 1849-1851, 4 vols.
* O'Callaghan, E. B., *Documentary History of the State of New York*, Albany, 1853-87, 15 vols.
  Osgood, Herbert L., *American Colonies in the Eighteenth Century*, New York, 1924-1925, 4 vols.
  Osgood, Herbert L., *American Colonies in the Seventeenth Century*, New York, 1904-1907, 3 vols.
  Palfrey, John G., *A Compendious History of the First Century of New England*, Boston, 1872, 3 vols.
  Pennsylvania Archives, 1664-, compiled by S. Hazard and others, 91 vols. in 6 series (to 1907). Philadelphia and Harrisburg, 1852-1907.
* Pennsylvania. *Colonial Records, 1683-1790*, Philadelphia, 1852-1853. 16 vols., vols. I-X, *Minutes of the Provincial Council*; vols. XI-XVI, *Minutes of the Supreme Executive Council*, Philadelphia, 1860, General Index.
* Penn. Hist. Soc., *Charlemagne Tower Collection of American Colonial Law*, Philadelphia, 1880.

* References so marked have not been cited among the footnotes of this book.

Pennypacker, S. W., *Pennsylvania Colonial Cases, 1682-1700*, Philadelphia, 1892, 185 pp.

* Perceval, John (First Earl of Egmont), *Journal of the Transactions of the Trustees for Establishing the Colony of Georgia in America*, Wormsloe, 1866.

Plumer, William, Jr., *Life of William Plumer*, Boston, 1857, 543 pp.

Poore, B. P., compiler, *The Federal and State Constitutions, Colonial Charters and other Organic Laws of the United States*, Senate Misc. Docs., 44 Cong., 2 sess. (no number, serial numbers, 1730, 1731). Also separately, 2 parts, Washington, 1877. New Edition compiled and edited by F. N. Thorpe, House Docs., 59 Cong., 2 sess. No. 357, Washington, 1909, 7 vols.

Pownall, Thomas, *The Administration of the Colonies; Wherein their Rights and Constitutions are Discussed and Stated*, London, 1777, 2 vols.

Proceedings of the First General Assembly of "the Incorporation of Providence Plantations" and the Code of Laws Adopted by that Assembly in 1647, Providence, 1847.

Quincy, Jr., Josiah, *Reports of Cases Argued and Adjudged in the Superior Court of Judicature of the Province of Massachusetts Bay, between 1761 and 1772*, Boston, 1865.

* *Records of the Colony of Rhode Island and Providence Plantations in New England, 1636-1792*, compiled by J. R. Bartlett, Providence, 1856-1865, 10 vols.

* *Records of the Courts of Chester County, 1681-1697*, Philadelphia, 1910, 430 pp.

* *Records of the Court of Trials of the Colony of Providence Plantations, 1647-1670*, Providence, 1920-1922, 2 vols.

* *Records and Files of Quarterly Courts of Essex County, Massachusetts, 1638-1683*, Salem, 1911-1921, 8 vols.

* *Records of the Courts of Assistants*, I, 1672-1692; II, 1630-1644; III, 1642-1673. Boston, 1901-1928.

* *Records of the Governor and Company of the Massachusetts Bay in New England 1628-1686*, edited by N. B. Shurtleff, Boston, 1863, 5 vols.

* *Records of the Colony of New Plymouth in New England 1620-1692*, edited by N. B. Shurtleff and others, Boston, 1855-1861, 12 vols. IX, X, contains "Acts of the Commissioners of the United Colonies," (1643-1679); "Plymouth Colony Laws" (1623-1682) XI.

* *Records of New Amsterdam, 1653-1674*, edited by B. Fernow, New York, 1897, 7 vols.

* *Records of the Virginia Company of London; the Court Book, from Manuscripts in the Library of Congress*, edited by S. M. Kingsbury, Washington, 1906, 4 vols.

* Reinsch, Paul T., (Useful working bibliography of the secondary colonial legal material in *Select Essays*, II, 164-168.)

Reinsch, Paul S., "English Common Law in the Early American Colonies," *Select Essays in Anglo-American Legal History* (Boston, 1907), I, pp. 367-415. (Originally published as a doctoral dissertation in the *Bulletin* of the University of Wisconsin, Madison, Wisc., 1899.)

Reno, Conrad, *Memoirs of the Judiciary and the Bar of New England for the Nineteenth Century*, Boston, 1900, 3 vols.

* Richardson, Mrs. H. D., "Reports of the Public Records Commission of Maryland," *Annual Reports*, 1905, I, 367 *et seq.*

Sampson, William, *Sampson against the Philistines, or the Reformation of Lawsuits and Justice Made Cheap, Speedy and Brought to Everyman's Door; Agreeable to the Principles of the Ancient Trial by Jury, Before the Same Were Innovated by Judges and Lawyers*, Philadelphia, Printed by W. Duane, 1805. (William Duane, supposed author), 23 pp.

Sampson, William, *Sampson's Discourse, and Correspondence with Various Learned Jurists, upon the History of the Law, with the Addition of Several Essays, Tracts, and Documents, Relating to the Subject.* Compiled and published by A. Thompson. Printed by Gales and Seaton, Washington City, 1826, 202 pp.

Sedgwick, A. G., and Wait, F. S., "The History of Ejectment in England and the United States," *Select Essays*, III, 611-646.

Select Essays in Anglo-American Legal History, Boston, 1907, 3 vols.

* Scott, Henry W., *Distinguished American Lawyers*, New York, 1891, 716 pp.

Siousatt, St. George L., "The Extension of English Statutes to the Plantation," *Select Essays*, I, 416-430.

Some Records of Sussex County, Del. (Court records of Deal County, 1681-1695). Compiled by C. H. B. Turner, Philadelphia, 1909.

Statutes at Large of Pennsylvania from 1682 to 1801, compiled by J. T. Mitchell and H. Flanders, II-XIII (1700-1710), Harrisburg, 1896-1908.

* Stearns, A., *A Summary of the Law and Practice of Real Actions* (2nd ed., N. P., 1831), 495 pp.

Swift, Zephaniah, *A System of the Laws of the State of Connecticut*, Kindham, 1795, 2 vols.

Two Centuries' Growth of American Law, (Yale Univ., Bicentennial Publications), New York, 1901, 538 pp.

The Book of the General Lawes and Libertyes, Cambridge, 1648. Reprinted from the copy in the Henry E. Huntington Library, Cambridge, 1929.

* *The Laws of New Haven Colony*, edited by S. Andrews, Hartford, 1822.

Trott, N., *Laws of the British Plantations in America, Relating to the Church and the Clergy, Religion and Learning*, London, 1721, 435 pp.

Trott, N., *Laws of the Province of South Carolina before 1734*, Charleston, 1736, 2 vols. in 1.

Trumbull, J. P., and Hoadley, C. J., (compilers) *Public Records of the Colony of Connecticut, 1636-1776*, Hartford, 1850-1890. Two additional volumes of *State Records*, Hartford, 1894-1895, 15 vols.

* Updike, Wilkins, *Memoirs of the Rhode Island Bar*, Boston, 1842, 311 pp.

Vermont State Papers: being a Collection of Records and Documents, compiled by William Slade. Middlebury, 1823, 567 pp.

Warren, Charles, *History of the American Bar*, Boston, 1913, 586 pp.

Washburn, Emory, *Judicial History of Massachusetts*, Boston, 1840.

* References so marked have not been cited among the footnotes of this book.

Webb, James H., "Criminal Law and Procedure," *Two Centuries Growth of American Law, 1701-1901*, pp. 351-360.

* Weeden, W. B., *Economic and Social History of New England*, (2nd ed.), Boston, 1896, 2 vols.

Whitmore, W. H. (ed.) *Bibliographical Sketch of the Laws of the Massachusetts Colony from 1630 to 1686*, Boston, 1890, 150 pp.

Willis, William, *A History of the Law, the Courts and the Lawyers of Maine*, Portland, 1863, 712 pp.

Wilson, S. D., "Courts of Chancery in the American Colonies," *Select Essays in Anglo-American Legal History*, II, 779-809.

* Wright, Carrol D., *Report on the Custody and Condition of the Public Records*, Boston, 1889, pp. 316-332.

Wright, T. G., *Literary Culture in Early New England, 1620-1730*, New Haven, 1920, 322 pp.

MAGAZINES

Atkinson, George R., "Origin and Growth of the Jurisprudence of the Two Virginias," 2 *Va. Law Reg.* (N. S.), vol. 2, 1917, p. 722.

Bates, A. C., "Report on the Public Archives of Connecticut," Amer. Hist. Assn., *Annual Report*, 1900, II, 26-36.

Becker, A. L., "Adrian Van Der Donck, the Earliest Lawyer in New York," *Albany Law Journal*, vol. LXVI, 1904, p. 46.

Budd, Henry, "Colonial Legislation in Pennsylvania, 1700-1712," Col. Soc. of Pa., *Publications, Bulletin*, No. 1.

Chitwood, Oliver, "Justice in Colonial Virginia," *West Virginia Law Quarterly*, vol. 32, p. 204.

* Cross, Arthur Lyon, "Benefit of Clergy in the American Criminal Law," Mass. Hist. Soc., *Proceedings*, vol. LXI, 1927-28, 154-181.

Dale, R. C., "The Adoption of the Common Law by the American Colonies," *American Law Register*, 1882, N. S. XXI.

Davis, A. McF., "The Law of Adultery and Igonominious Punishments," (Worcester, Mass., 1895), with a supplement in Amer. Antiq. Soc., *Proceedings*, 1889, N. S. XIII, 67 *et seq.*

Dill, T. M., "Colonial Development of the Common Law," *Law Quarterly Review*, vol. XL, 1924, 227-244, with special references to the situation in Bermuda.

Dorland, A. G., "The Royal Disallowance in Massachusetts," Queens Univ., *Bulletin*, 1917, No. XX.

"East Hampton Book of Laws, or Duke's Laws, 1665," N. Y. Hist. Soc., *Collections*, I, 305 *et seq.*

Fisher, Sidney G., "The Administration of Equity through Common Law Forms in Pennsylvania," *Law Quarterly Review*, vol. I, 1885; p. 455, reprinted in *Angli-American Legal Essays*, 1908, p. 455.

Fowler, Robert L., "Organization of the Supreme Court of Judicature of the Province of New York." *Albany Law Journal*, vol. XIX, pp. 66, 87, 106, 149, 189, 209, 229, 309, 349, 389, 430, 489.

"Gloucester County Court Records" (1774-), Vt. Hist. Soc., *Proceedings*, 1923-1925.

Goebel, Julius, Jr., "King's Law and Local Law in Seventeenth Century New England," *Columbia Law Review*, vol. XXX, p. 474.

* Gray, Russel, "The Supreme Judicial Court of Massachusetts," *Medico-Legal Journal*, vol. XIII, 1925, pp. 225-235.

Hazeltine, H. D., "Appeals from Colonial Courts to the King in Council," Amer. Hist. Assn. *Annual Report*, 1894, pp. 299-350.

Hilkey, Charles J., *Legal Development in Colonial Massachusetts, 1630-1686*, (Columbia Univ. Studies in Hist., Econ., and Public Law, vol. XXXVII, No. 2).

* James, Eldon R., "A List of Legal Treatises Printed in the British Colonies and the American States before 1801," *Harvard Legal Essays*, 1934, pp. 159-211.

Keasbey, Edward Q., "Origin and Jurisdiction of Courts of New Jersey," *New Jersey Law Journal*, vol. 17, pp. 131, 210, 324; vol. 18, p. 69. (W. M. Clevenger, 163, 195, 228, 233, 262.)

Kellogg, L. P., "American Colonial Charter," Amer. Hist. Assn., *Annual Report*, vol. 1, 1903, pp. 175 *et seq.*

Lee, Francis B., "Early Courts of New Jersey," *New Jersey Law Journal*, vol. 14, p. 357; vol. 15, p. 4.

Lewis, Lawrence, "Courts of Pennsylvania in the Seventeenth Century," Pa. Bar Assn., *Reports*, vol. I.

Mason, Albert, "Judicial History of Massachusetts," *The New England States*, (edited by W. T. Davis), Boston, 1897, ch. CXXXIV.

Morris, R. B., "Massachusetts and the Common Law: the Declaration of 1646," *Amer. Hist. Rev.*, vol. XXXVI, 1926, 443-435.

Niles, Henry C., "Jeremiah Sullivan Black and His Influence on the Law of Pennsylvania," *9th Annual Report of the Pennsylvania Bar Association*, 1903, pp. 400-471.

Paxson, F. L., "Influence of Frontier Life on Development of American Law," State Bar Association of Wisconsin *Reports*, vol. XIII (1919-21), p. 484.

Plucknett, Theodore, Review of "Laws and Liberties of 1648," *New England Quarterly*, vol. III, 157-158.

Pope, Herbert, "English Common Law in the United States," *Harvard Law Review*, vol. XXIV, p. 6.

Prince, W. F., "The First Criminal Code of Virginia," Amer. Hist. Assn., *Annual Report*, vol. I, 1899, 399 *et seq.*

Proctor, L. B., "Origin of Chancery Courts in New York," *Albany Law Journal*, vol. 56, 1897, p. 173.

Putnam, Harrington, "The Early Administration of Equity in This Country," *Central Law Journal*, vol. 90, 1920, p. 423.

"Records of the Court of General Sessions of the Peace of Worcester County" (1731-1737), Worcester Soc. of Antiquity, *Collections*, edited by F. P. Rice. Worcester, 1882, vol. 5.

* References so marked have not been cited among the footnotes of this book.

Records of the Court of Newcastle on Delaware, 1675-1681. Lancaster, 1904., Reprinted from the Geneal. Soc. of Pa., *Collections,* LXVIII, LXIX.
"Records of the Court at Upland in Pennsylvania, 1676 to 1681," Pa. Hist. Soc., *Memoirs,* Philadelphia, vol. VII, 1860, pp. 9-203.
"Records of the Particular Court of Connecticut, 1639-1663," Conn. Hist. Soc., *Collections,* vol. XXII, 1928.
Russell, E. B., "The Review of American Colonial Legislation by the King in Council," New York, 1915. (*Columbia University Studies in Hist., Econ. and Pub. Law,* No. 155.)
Schlesinger, A. M., "Appeals to the Privy Council," *Political Science Quarterly,* vol. XVIII, pp. 440-449.
Scott, A. P., "The Criminal Law and Its Administration in Colonial Virginia," a dissertation abstracted in *Abstracts of Theses,* (Univ. of Chicago, *Humanistic Studies,* vol. 1, 1922-1923, pp. 225-229).
Siousatt, St. George L., "English Statutes in Maryland," *Johns Hopkins Studies in History and Political Science,* ser. XXI.
Stone, Harlan, "The Lawyer and His Neighbors," *Cornell Law Quarterly,* vol. 4, 1918-19, p. 175.
Tanner, E. P., "The Province of New Jersey," *Columbia Studies in History and Politics,* vol. 30, 1908, p. 460.
The North American Review, vol. 21, July, 1825, pp. 104.
The North American Review, vol. 21, July, 1825, p. 139.
Thompson, J. F., "Early Corporal Punishments," *Illinois Law Quarterly,* Dec., 1923.
"Virginia Council and General Court Records, 1640-1641," from "Robinson's Notes," in Va. Hist. Soc., *Collections, Virginia Magazine of History and Biography,* vol. II, pp. 277-284.
Washburne, George A., "Imperial Control of the Administration of Justice in the Thirteen American Colonies, 1684-1776," New York, 1923. *Columbia University Studies in Hist., Econ., and Public Law,* No. 238.)

II. The Formative Period, 1776-1865

BOOKS

Adams, Henry, *Writings of Gallatin,* Philadelphia, 1879, 3 vols.
Addresses and Orations of Rufus Choate, Boston, 1883, 529 pp.
A History of Columbia University, 1754-1904, New York, 1904, 493 pp.
A History of the Operations of a Partisan Corps, called the Queen's Rangers commanded by Lieut. Col. J. G. Simcoe during the War of the American Revolution, with a memoir of the author, etc. New York: Bartlett and Wilford, 1844.
Adams, Herbert, *Thomas Jefferson and the University of Virginia,* Washington, Govt. Printing office, 1888.
Address of Edward J. Phelps, on Chief Justice Marshall and the Constitutional Law of His Time, American Bar Association, 1879, 22 pp.
Alexander, D. S., *A Political History of the State of New York,* New York, 1906-09, 3 vols.

* Ames, James B., *The Vocation of the Law Professor*. In his *Lectures on Legal History, and Miscellaneous Legal Essays;* Cambridge, Harvard University Press, 1913, pp. 354-369.

An Address delivered at the Dedication of the Dane Law College in Harvard University, October 23, 1832, by Josiah Quincy, D.D., President of the University, Cambridge, 1832, 27 pp.

Andrews, D. J., *The Works of James Wilson*, Chicago, 1896, 2 vols.

An Inquiry into the Law Merchant of the United States; or Lex Mercatoria Americana on Several Heads of Commercial Intercourse (1802, published anonymously by George Caines, New York, 1802, 648 pp.

Austin, Benjamin, *Observations on the Pernicious Practice of the Law by Honestus (Benjamin Austin) as Published occasionally in Independent Chronicle in Boston, of April 20, 1786*, Boston, 1819, 60 pp.

Baldwin, Simeon E., *The American Judiciary*, New York, 1905, 403 pp.

Baldwin, Simeon E., "Zephaniah Swift," *Great American Lawyers*, vol. 2, 1907.

Barringer, P. B., and Garnett, J. M., (eds.), *University of Virginia*, New York, 1904, 2 vols.

Beale, Jr., Joseph H., "Lemuel Shaw," *Great American Lawyers* (edited by W. D. Lewis), vol. III, Philadelphia, 1908, pp. 455-490.

Bell, C. H., *The Bench and Bar of New Hampshire*, Boston and New York, 1894, 795 pp.

Beveridge, A. J., *The Life of John Marshall*, Boston, 1916-19, 4 vols.

* *Bibliography of Legal Education*, prepared by W. Addis. (In U. S. Commissioner of Education. Reports, 1890-91, vol. I, pp. 565-578.)

Biddle, G. W., *A Sketch of the Professional and Judicial Character of the Late George Sharswood*, printed in *Pa. State Reports*, vol. 102, 1883, pp. 601-30.

* Bishop, Joel P., *The First Book of the Law; Explaining the Nature, Sources, Books, and Practical Applications of Legal Science, and Methods of Study and Practice*. Boston, 1868, 466 pp.

* Bishop, W. G., and Attree, W. H., *Report of the Debates and Proceedings of the Convention for the Revision of the Constitution of the State of New York*, 1846.

Black, N. P., *Richard Peters: His Ancestors and Descendants, 1810-1899*, Atlanta, 1904, 145 pp.

Boardman, D. S., *Sketches of the Early Lights of the Litchfield Bar,* (1860), in Kilbourn, D. C., *The Bench and Bar of Litchfield County, Conn. 1709-1909*, Litchfield, Conn. 1909.

Bond, Carrol T., *The Court of Appeals of Maryland*, Baltimore, 1928, 214 pp.

Boutell, L. H., *The Life of Roger Sherman*, Chicago, 1896, 361 pp.

Brackenridge, H. M., *History of the Western Insurrection in Western Pennsylvania, Commonly called the Whisky Insurrection, 1794*, Pittsburgh, 1859, 336 pp.

* References so marked have not been cited among the footnotes of this book.

Breckenridge, Sophonistia, *Administration of Justice in Kentucky* (Dissertation, University of Chicago, 1897).

Brightly, F. C., *Treatise on the Equitable Jurisdiction of the Courts of Pennsylvania*, Philadelphia, 1855, 773 pp.

Brockenbrough, J. W. (editor), *Reports of Cases Decided by the Hon. John Marshall . . . in the Circuit Court of U. S. for the District of Va. and N. C., from 1802 to 1833, inclusive*, 1837, 2 vols.

Brown, S. G., *The Works of Rufus Choate*, Boston, 1862, 2 vols.

Bruce, P. A., *History of the University of Virginia, 1819-1919*, New York, 1920, 2 vols.

Bruce, W. C., *John Randolph of Roanoke*, New York and London, 1922, 2 vols.

Brunner, Heinrich, *The Sources of the Law of England. An Historical Introduction to the Study of English Law* . . . (Translated from the German with a bibliographical appendix by W. Hastre.) Edinburgh, 1888.

Bulletin of the College of William and Mary, vol. XI, 1917, No. 2.

Caines, George, *Cases Argued and Determined in the Court for the Trial of Impeachments and Correction of Errors in the State of New York*, 1805-1807, 2 vols.

Carpenter W. S., *Judicial Tenure in the United States*, New Haven, 1918, 234 pp.

Carson, H. L., "Historical Sketch of the Law Department," *Catalogue of the Alumni of the Law Department of the University of Pennsylvania . . . 1790-1882*, (1882), pp. 23-28.

* Carter, A. G. W., *The Old Court House*, Cincinnati, 1880, 466 pp.

Caldwell, Joshua, *Sketches of the Bench and Bar of Tennessee*, Knoxville, 1898, 402 pp.

Chase, Frederic H., *Lemuel Shaw*, Boston, 1918, 330 pp.

* Chester, Alden, *Courts and Lawyers of New York*, New York and Chicago, 1925, 3 vols.

Cheyney, Edward F., "The Anti-Rent Movement and the Constitution of 1846," *History of the State of New York*, (Alex. Flick, editor, 1934), vol. VI, pp. 282-321.

Chipman, Daniel, *A Memoir of Thomas Chittenden, the First Governor of Vermont, with a History of the Constitution, during His Administration*, Boston, 1846, 402 pp.

Chipman, Daniel, *An Essay on the Law of Contracts for the Payment of Specific Articles*, Middlebury, 1822, 224 pp.

Chipman, Daniel, *Reports of Cases Argued and Determined in the Supreme Court of . . . Vermont, 1789-1824*, (1824).

Chipman, Nathaniel, *Reports and Dissertations*, Rutland, 1793, 293 pp.

Chipman, Nathaniel, *Sketches of the Principles of Government*, (revised ed., 1833), Rutland, 292 pp.

Clark, Walter, "Thomas Ruffin," *Great American Lawyers*, (W. D. Lewis, editor), 1908, vol. IV.

Collins, Lewis, *Historical Sketches of Kentucky*, Covington, Ky., 1874, 2 vols.

Clevenger, W. M., and Keasbey, Edward Q., *The Courts of New Jersey: Their Origin, Composition, and Jurisdiction*, 1903, pp. 39-44, 118-126.

Cordell, E. F., *Historical Sketch of the University of Maryland*, 1891.

Cordell, E. F., *University of Maryland, 1807-1907*, New York and Chicago, 1907, 2 vols.

Cork, F. G., "Theophilus Parsons," *Great American Lawyers*, Lewis (editor), vol. II, 1907, pp. 91-92.

Cooley, T. M., *Constitutional Limitations*, Boston, 1883, 886 pp.

Corwin, Edward, *The Doctrine of Judicial Review and the Constitution*, Princeton, 1914.

Corwin, Edward S., *John Marshall and the Constitution*, New Haven, 1921, 242 pp.

Cotton, J. P. (editor), *The Constitutional Doctrines of John Marshall*, New York, 1905, 2 vol.

Curtis, William, *James Kent, the Father of American Jurisprudence*. An address delivered before the Alabama State Bar Association at Montgomery, June 15, 1900. New York Evening Post job printing house, 1900, 35 pp.

Dallas, Geo. M., *The Life and Writings of A. J. Dallas*, Philadelphia, 1871, 487 pp.

Dallas, Alexander, *Reports of Cases Ruled and Adjudged in the Several Courts of the United States and Pennsylvania, etc.* (1793-1801), 4 vols.

Davis, Andrew, *The Shays Rebellion: A Political Aftermath*, a Reprint from the Proceedings of the American Antiquarian Society for April, 1911, Worcester, Massachusetts, 1911.

Davis, William T., *Bench and Bar of the Commonwealth of Massachusetts*, Boston, 1895, 2 vols.

Davis, William T., *History of the Judiciary of Massachusetts*, Boston, 1900, 446 pp.

Day, Thomas, *Reports of Cases . . . in the Supreme Court of Errors . . . Conn.*, vol. 1, 1817, p. xxxii.

Debates and Proceedings, Massachusetts Constitutional Convention of 1853, Vol. II, pp. 706-707.

Dembitz, Lewis N., *Kentucky Jurisprudence*, Louisville, vol. 32, 1890, 714 pp.

Dickinson, John, *Administrative Justice and Supremacy of Law in the United States*, Cambridge, 1927, 403 pp.

Dickson, Samuel, "George Sharswood," *Great American Lawyers*, (Lewis, ed.), vol. VI, 1909, pp. 123-161.

Dictionary of American Biography, vol. 20, p. 293.

Dillon, J. F., "Bentham's Influence in the Reforms of the Nineteenth Century," *Select Essays in Anglo-American Legal Histoy*.

Dillon, J. F., *John Marshall, Life, Character, and Judicial Sciences*, Chicago, 1903, 3 vols.

Dillon, John F., *Laws and Jurisprudence of England and America; lectures before Yale University*. Boston, 1894, 431 pp.

* References so marked have not been cited among the footnotes of this book.

* Dodd, W. F., *Revision and Amendment of State Constitutions*, Baltimore, 1910, 350 pp.

Duer, John, *Discourse on the Life, Character, and Public Services of James Kent*, New York, 1848.

Dunaway, Wayland F., *A History of Pennsylvania*, New York, 1935, 828 pp.

Du Ponceau, Peter, *A Dissertation on the Nature and Extent of the Jurisdiction of the Courts of the United States, 1824. To which are Added a Brief Sketch of the National Judiciary Powers Exercised in the United States, Prior to the Adoption of the Present Federal Constitution*. By Thomas Sargeant, Esq., Vice-Provost, and the Author's *Discourse on Legal Education, delivered at the opening of the Law Academy, in Feb., 1821, with an appendix and notes*. Philadelphia, 1824.

Farnham, H. P. (ed.), *Ohio Jurisprudence*, vol. I, 1928, p. cvi.

Fee, Walter R., *The Transition from Aristocracy to Democracy in New Jersey, 1789-1829*, Somerville, (N.J.), 1933, 291.

* Field, H. M., *Life of David Dudley Field*, New York, 1898, 361 pp.

Findley, W. W., *History of the Insurrection, in the Far Western Country of Pennsylvania*, 1796, Philadelphia, 328 pp.

Fiske, John, *The Critical Period*, Boston and New York, 1888, 368 pp.

Foote, H. S., *The Bench and Bar of the South and Southwest*, St. Louis, 1876, 264 pp.

Foster, Robert L., *History of the Law of Real Property in New York*, New York, 1895.

Fox, Dixon R., "New York Becomes a Democracy," *History of the State of New York*, (Alexander Flick, ed.), 1934, vol. 6.

Fuess, Claude, *Rufus Choate*, New York, 1928, 278 pp.

Goodnow, Frank, *Comparative Administrative Law*, New York and London, 1902, 2 vols.

Graham, W. A., *The Papers of Thomas Ruffin*, Raleigh, 1918, 4 vols.

* Gray, John Chipman, *Restraints on the Alienation of Property*, Boston, 1895, 309 pp.

* Gray, John Chipman, *The Rule Against Perpetuities*, Boston, 1915, 714 pp.

Greenleaf, Simon, *A Collection of Cases Overruled, Doubted, or Limited in their Application. Taken from American and English Reports*, Portland, 1821, 121 pp.

Greenleaf, Simon, *A Discourse Commemorative of the Life and Character of the Honourable Prentiss Mellon, LL.D., late Chief Justice of Maine*, Maine Reports, vol. 17, p. 467.

Greenleaf, Simon, *Cruise's Digest of the Law of Real Property, Revised and Abridged for the Use of American Students*, (1849-50), 7 vols. in 5.

Greenleaf, Simon, *Reports of Cases Argued and Determined in the Supreme Judicial Court of Maine*, Hallowell, 1824. Vol. II, containing cases of the years 1822 and 1823.

Grimké, Frederick, *Consideration Upon the Nature and Tendency of Free Institutions*, Cincinnati, 1856, 670 pp.

Grimké, J. F., *The South Carolina Justice of the Peace*, Philadelphia, 1788, 510 pp.

Grinnell, F. W., "The Judicial System and the Bar, (1820-1861)," *Commonwealth History of Massachusetts*, (Hart, ed.), 1930, vol. 4.

* Hagan, H. H., *Eight Great American Lawyers*, Oklahoma City, 1923, 293 pp.

Haines, Charles G., *The American Doctrine of Judicial Supremacy*, Berkeley, Calif., 1932, XVIII, 705 pp.

Haines, Charles G., *The Conflict Over Judicial Powers in the United States to 1870*, New York, 1909, 181 pp.

Hamilton, William, *Report of the Trial and Acquittal of Edward Shippen, Jasper Yeates, and Thomas Smith . . . on an Impeachment*, 1805.

Hammond, Jabez E., *Political History of New York*, Buffalo, 1850, 2 vol.

Hart, C. H., *Memoir of George Sharswood*, 1880.

Harvard Law School Association, *The Centenniel History of the Harvard Law School, 1817-1917*, privately printed, Boston, 1918.

Hepburn, Charles M., *The Historical Development of Code Pleading*, Cincinnati, 1897, 318 pp.

Herrick, William D., *History of the Town of Gardner*, Gardner, 1878, 535 pp.

* Hicks, Frederick C., *Aids to the Study and Use of Law Books*, New York, 1913, 129 pp.

* Hicks, F. C., *Men and Books Famous in the Law*, Rochester, 1921.

Hicks, F. C., *Yale Law School: from the Founders to Dulton, 1845-1869*, New Haven, 1936, 62 pp.

Hoffman, David, *A Course of Legal Study; Respectfully Addressed to the Students of Law in the United States*, Baltimore, 1817, 383 pp.

Hoffman, David, *Legal Outlines: being the Substance of a Course of Lectures now delivering in the University of Maryland*, Baltimore, 1829, 3 vols., 626 pp.

Hoffman, David, *Syllabus of Law Lectures in the University of Maryland*, 1821, 91 pp.

Holmes, O. W., *The Common Law*, Boston, 1881, 422 pp.

Hooker, John, *29 Connecticut Reports*, 611-614.

Howe, Henry, *Historical Collections of Ohio*, 1908, I, 687.

Hume, David, *Essays, Moral and Political*, London, 1882, (new ed.), 2 vols.

Hunt, Charles H., *Life of Edward Livingston*, New York, 1864, xxiv+448 pp.

Jefferson, Thomas, *Writings*, Washington, D. C., 1903-4, 20 vols.

Jones, Leonard Augustus, and Reno, Conrad, editors, *Memoirs of the Judiciary and the Bar of New England for the Nineteenth Century: with a History of the Judicial System of New England*, Boston, 1900, 2 vols.

Kennedy, W. P. M., *The Constitution of Canada*, London and New York, 1922, 519 pp.

Kennedy, W. P. M., *Essays on Constitutional Law*, London, 1934, 183 pp.

Kent, James, *An Introductory Lecture to a Course of Law Lectures deliv-*

* References so marked have not been cited among the footnotes of this book.

ered Nov. 17, 1794. New York, Francis Childs, 1794. (Reprint by Professor William D. Guthrie, Columbia University, April 8, 1913.) First of a series of lectures delivered by Chancellor Kent while Professor of Law in Columbia College.

Kent, James, *Commentaries on American Law*, (5th ed.), New York, 1844, 3 vols.

Kent, William, *Memoirs and Letters of James Kent, LL.D.*, late chancellor of the state of New York, author of "Commentaries on American Law," etc., by his great-grandson, William Kent, of the New York bar. Boston, 1898, 341 pp.

Kilbourn, D. C., *The Bench and Bar of Litchfield, Connecticut, 1709-1909*, Litchfield,1909.

King, Rufus, *Ohio, First Fruit of the Ordinance of 1787*, Boston and New York, 1903, (new ed.), 446 pp.

Kirby, Ephraim, *Reports of Cases Adjudged in the Superior Court and Court of Errors of the State of Connecticut from the Year 1785 to May, 1788*, (1789).

Klingelsmith, Margaret, "History of the Department of Law," *University of Pennsylvania Proceedings at the Dedication of the New Building of Law, 1900*, pp. 213 ff.

Klingelsmith, Margaret, "Jeremiah S. Black," *Great American Lawyers*, ed. by Wm. Draper Lewis, Philadelphia, 1909, vol. VI.

Konkle, Burton A., *Benjamin Chew, 1722-1810*, Philadelphia, 1932, 316 pp.

Lamar, J. R., "Eugenius Aristides Nisbet, 1803-1871," *Great American Lawyers*, (W. D. Lewis, ed.), 1908, vol. IV.

* *Law Schools, a series of articles*. Articles on the following schools: Harvard, Boston University, University of Pennsylvania, Columbia, Michigan, Yale, St. Louis, Union College of Law (Chicago), University of Iowa, Buffalo, Cornell, Hastings College of Law, Cumberland University, Tulane, Albany, University of Minnesota, Law School of Osgoode Hall, Toronto, (*The Green Bag*, vol. 1-3).

Lewis, W. D. (ed.), "Ephraim Kirby," *Great American Lawyers*, vol. 2, 1907, pp. 469-471.

Lewis, William D., *Great American Lawyers*, John C. Winston and Co., Philadelphia, 1907-09, 8 vols.

Lile, William M., "The Law School of the University of Virginia," *The Centennial of the University of Virginia*, 1921.

The Litchfield School . . . Catalogue of Scholars . . . Interesting Memoranda. (In Kilbourn, Dwight C., *The Bench and Bar of Litchfield County, Conn., 1709-1909*. Litchfield, by the author, 1909, pp. 179-214.)

McAdam, D., et. el., *History of the Bench and Bar of New York*, 1897, vol. I.

McLaughlin, Andrew, *The Confederation and Constitution*, New York, 1905, 348 pp.

McMaster, John B., *A History of the People of the United States*, New York and London, 1884-1928, 8 vols.

McRee, G. J., *Life and Correspondence of James Iredell*, vol. II, 1857, p. 532.

Maitland, Frederick K., *The Materials for English Legal History*, Boston, 1908. (In *Political Science Quarterly*, vol. 4, pp. 496-518, 628-647.) Printed also in vol. 2, *Select Essays in Anglo-American Legal History*.

* Marshall, Carrington T., *A History of the Courts and Lawyers of Ohio*, New York, 1934, 4 vols.

Matlock, S. D., "John Bannister Gibson," *Great American Lawyers*, (W. D. Lewis, ed.) 8 vols., Philadelphia, 1907-1909; vol. III, p. 351-404.

Memoir and Correspondence of Jeremiah Mason, Cambridge, 1873, 467 pp.

Miller, Stephen F., *The Bench and Bar of Georgia*, Philadelphia, 1858, 2 vols.

Minor, Benjamin B. (ed.), *Decisions of Cases in Virginia by the High Court, by George Wythe, with a memoir of the author*, 1852.

Minor, John B., *Institutes of Common and Statute Law*, Richmond, Va., 1883-95, 4 vols.

Minor, J. B., *The Minor Family of Virginia*, Lynchburg, 1923, 125 pp.

Minot, George R., *The History of the Insurrection in Massachusetts*, Boston, 1810, 192 pp.

Moore, B. F., *The Supreme Court and Unconstitutional Legislation*, New York, 1913, 158 pp.

Moore, M. Herndon, "The Law Writers of the South," *The South in the Building of the Nation*, vol. 7, p. 330.

Morison, S. E., *Three Centuries of Harvard, 1636-1936*, Cambridge, 1937, 512 pp.

Morison, S. E., *The Founding of Harvard College*, Cambridge, 1935, 472 pp.

Morison, S. E., *The Life and Letters of Harrison Gray Otis, Federalist, 1765-1848*. Boston and New York, 1913, 2 vols.

Morse, S. L., *The Federalist Party in Massachusetts to the Year 1800*, (1909).

Neilson, Joseph, *Memories of Rufus Choate*, Boston and New York, 1884, 460 pp.

Niles, A. S., "William Pinkney," *Great American Lawyers*, (edited by W. D. Lewis), 1907, vol. II.

Paine, Jr., Elijah, *Reports of Cases Argued and Determined in the Circuit Court of the United States for the Second Circuit, comprising the Districts of New York, Connecticut, and Vermont*, New York, 1827, vol. 1.

Parker, Edward G., *Reminiscences of Rufus Choate*, New York, 1860, 522 pp.

Parker, Joel, *Daniel Webster As a Jurist*, Cambridge, 1852, 71 pp.

Parsons, Theophilus, *Memoir of Theophilus Parsons*, 1859. This memoir contains the obituary address of Chief Justice Isaac Parsons (also in 10 *Mass. Reports*, 521).

Pennsylvania Magazine of History and Biography, July, 1899; July, 1916; October, 1920.

* References so marked have not been cited among the footnotes of this book.

Pickering, Octavius, and Upham, C. W., *The Life of Timothy Pickering*, 1867-73, 4 vols.

Pierce, Edward L., *Memoir and Letters of Charles Sumner*, London, 1878-94, 4 vols.

* Plucknett, T. F. T., *A Concise History of the Common Law*, Rochester, 1929, 453 pp.

Pollock, Frederick, and Maitland, Frederick, *History of English Law*, Boston, 1899, 2 vol.

* Pollock, Sir Frederick, *The Expansion of the Common Law*, London, 1904, vii+164 pp.

Pomeroy, John N., *Equity Jurisprudence*, (3rd ed.), San Francisco, 1905, 6 vols.

Pomeroy, John, *Code Remedies*, (5th ed.), Boston, 1929, 1154 pp.

Porter, W. A., *An Essay on the Life, Character, and Writings of John B. Gibson*, Philadelphia, 1855, 140 pp.

Potts, S. G., *Precedents and Notes of Practice in the Court of Chancery of New Jersey*, 1841, 456 pp.

Preliminary List of Useful Articles and Chapters on Topics of Anglo-American Legal History, American Bar Assn., *Report*, vol. 30, 1906, part 2, pp. 191-203.

Purcell, R. J., *Connecticut in Transition, 1775-1918*, Washington, 1918, 471 pp.

Randall, E. O., and Ryan, D. J., *History of Ohio*, 1912, vols. IV and V.

Reed, A. Z., *Training for the Public Profession of the Law*, 1921, Bulletin No. 15, Carnegie Foundation.

Report of Joseph Story, Theron Metcalf, Simon Greenleaf, Charles Forbes, and Luther Cushing, Commissioners to Take into Consideration the Practicality and Expediency of Reducing to a Written and Systematic Code the Common Law of Massachusetts or any Part Thereof, 1836, reprinted by David Dudley Field, 1852.

Roberts, T. P., *Memoir of John Bannister Gibson*, Pittsburgh, 1890, 247 pp.

Root, Jesse, *Reports of Cases Adjudged in the Superior Court and Supreme Court of Errors . . . 1789 to . . . 1793*. 1798-99, 2 vols.

Rowland, Dunbar, *Courts, Judges, and Lawyers of Mississippi, 1783-1935*, (1935), 2 vols.

Sabine, Lorenzo, *The American Loyalists*, Boston, 1847, 733 pp.

Sanderson, John, *Biography of the Signers of the Declaration of Independence*, Philadelphia, 1822, 9 vols.

Schofield, William, "Joseph Story," *Great American Lawyers* (edited by W. D. Lewis), Philadelphia, 1907-09, 8 vols.; vol. III, pp. 123-185.

Scott, James Brown, "Henry Wheaton," *Great American Lawyers*, (edited by W. D. Lewis), 1907, vol. III.

Scott, James Brown, "James Kent, 1763-1847" in *Great American Lawyers* (ed. by W. D. Lewis), 8 vol., Philadelphia, 1907-09, vol. II, pp. 491-533.

Sedgwick, Theodore, *Memoir of the Life of William Livingston*, New York, 1833, 447 pp.

Sharswood, George, *A Compendium of Lectures on the Aims and Duties of the Profession of Law, 1854.* This work republished several times as *An Essay on Professional Ethics*, Philadelphia, 1930, 214 pp.

Sharswood, George, *An Essay on Professional Ethics* (6th ed.), Philadelphia, 1930, 214 pp.

Sharswood, George, *Lectures Introductory to the Study of Law*, Philadelphia, 1870, 262 pp.

Sharswood, George, *The Origin, History, and Objects of the Law Academy of Philadelphia*, 1883, 38 pp.

Smith, Herbert A., *Federalism in North America: A Comparative Study of Institutions in the United States and Canada*, 1923, pp. 125-126.

Smith, Jr., Jeremiah, *Decisions of the Superior and Supreme Courts of New Hampshire from 1802 to 1809 and from 1813 to 1816 . . . with Extracts from Judge Smith; Manuscript Treatise on Probate Law*, 1879.

* Stephen, J. F., *History of the Criminal Law in England*, London, 1883, 3 vols.

Stillè, Charles, *The Life and Times of John Dickinson* (1732-1808), Memoirs of the Historical Society of Pennsylvania, 1891, vol. 13.

Story, Joseph, Address delivered before the members of Suffolk Bar in 1829, *The American Jurist*, Boston, no. I, January, 1829.

Story, Joseph, *A Discourse Upon the Life, Character and Services of the Honourable John Marshall, LL.D.*, Boston, 1835, 74 pp.

Story, Joseph, *Commentaries on Equity Pleading*, Boston, 1838, xxiv+ 743 pp.

Story, Joseph, *Commentaries on the Conflicts of Laws*, Boston, 1834, xxv+ 557 pp.

Story, Joseph, *Commentaries on the Constitution*, 1833, 4th ed. with notes and additions by Thomas M. Cooley . . . Boston, 1873, 2 vols.

Story, Joseph, *Commentaries on the Law of Bills of Exchange*, Boston, 1843, xxiv+608 pp.

Story, Joseph, *Commentaries on the Law of Promissory Notes*, Boston, 1845, xxviii+675 pp.

Story, Joseph, *Commentaries on the Law of Agency*, Boston, 1839, xxiii+ 544 pp.

Story, Joseph, *Commentaries on the Law of Bailments*, Cambridge, 1832, xxxiv+411 pp.

Story, Joseph, *Commentaries on the Law of Partnership*, Boston, 1841, xxi+690 pp.

Story, W. W., *Life and Letters of Joseph Story*, Boston, 1851, 2 vol.

Sullivan, William, *Address to the Suffolk Bar*, Boston, 1825, 63 pp.

Swift, Zephaniah, *A System of the Law of the State of Connecticut*, Windham, 1795-1796, 2 vols.

Swift, Zephaniah, *Digest of the Law of Evidence, in Civil and Criminal Cases; and a Treatise on Bills of Exchange, and Promissory Notes*, Hartford, 1810, 361 pp.

Swift, Zephaniah, *Digest of the Laws of the State of Connecticut*, New Haven, 1822-23, 2 vols.

* References so marked have not been cited among the footnotes of this book.

Swisher, Carl B., *Roger B. Taney*, New York, 1936, 608 pp.

Thacher, Thomas, "Yale In Its Relations to the Law," *Yale Bicentennial Celebration, 1901* (1902), pp. 174-198.

The Centennial History of the Harvard Law School, 1817-1917, Boston, 1918, 412 pp.

Tucker, Henry St. George, *Commentaries on the Laws of Virginia*, Winchester, 1836-37, 2 vols.

Tucker, Nathaniel B., *Principles of Pleading*, Boston, 1846, 220 pp.

Twiss, Horace, *The Public and Private Life of Lord Chancellor Eldon, with Selections from his Correspondence*, London, 1846, 2 vols.

Tyler, L. G., *Early Courses and Professors at William and Mary College*, 1904, 13 pp.

Tyler, L. G., *The College of William and Mary in Virginia, Its History and Work 1693-1907*, Richmond, 1907, 96 pp.

Tyler, L. G., *The Life and Times of the Tylers*, Richmond, Va., Whittet and Shepperson; 1884-96, 3 vols.

Tyler, Samuel, *Memoir of Roger Brooke Taney*, Baltimore, 1872, 659 pp.

* Van Santvoord, *Lives of the Chief Justices of the United States*, New York, 1858, 538 pp.

Van Schaack, Henry, *The Life of Peter Van Schaack*, New York, 1842, 490 pp.

Wallace, David S., *The History of South Carolina*, New York, 1934, 4 vols.

Ward, George A., *Journal and Letters of the late Samuel Curwen, Judge of Admiralty, etc., an American Refugee in England from 1755 to 1784. Comprising Remarks on the Prominent men and measures of that Period. To which are added Biographical Notices of many American Loyalists and other eminent persons*, 1842.

Warren, Charles, *A History of the American Bar*, Boston, 1913, 586 pp.

Warren, Charles, *English Law, Law Books and Lawyers in the Seventeenth Century, . . . Early American Law Books . . . American Law Books, 1815-1910*. (In his *A History of the American Bar*, Boston, 1913.) pp. 19-38, 325-340, 540-567.

Warren, Charles, *The Supreme Court in United States History*, Boston, 1922, 3 vols.

Warren, Charles, *History of the Harvard Law School*, vol. I, 1908, pp. 299-302.

Wayland, Francis, "Law Department" in W. L. Kingsley's *Yale College: a Sketch of Its History*, 1879, pp. 90-99.

Wheaton, Henry, *Elements of International Law*, Boston, 1855, 728 pp.

Wheaton, Henry, *Some Accounts of the Life, Writing, and Speeches of William Pinkney*, 1826.

Whipple, E. P., *Some Recollections of Rufus Choate*, New York, 1879, 100 pp.

Whitehead, John, *The Judicial and Civil History of New Jersey*, Boston, 1897, 527, 611 pp.

Wilson, Woodrow, *Constitutional Governments in the United States*, New York, 1908, 236 pp.

Winters, William H., *Three Hundredth Anniversary of the Settlement on Manhattan Island, 1614-1914. A Literary and Legal Bibliography of the old Dutch Province of Nieuw Netherlandt (New Netherland) and the city of Nieuw Amsterdam (New Amsterdam)*, New York, 1914, 34 pp.

Woolsey, T. D., *Historical Discourse . . . Pronounced Before the Alumni of the Law Department of Yale College at the Fiftieth Anniversary of the Foundation of the Department*, New Haven, 1874, 47 pp.

Writings of Hugh Swinton Legare, edited with a memoir, by his sister Mary S. L. Buller, 1845-46, 2 vols.

Wigmore, John H., *A Preliminary Bibliography of Modern Criminal Law and Criminology*, Chicago, 1909, 128 pp.

MAGAZINES

Albany Law Journal, Aug. 28, 1875.

American Law Magazine, April, 1845.

American Law Review, vol. 40, 1906, p. 437.

Appel, J. W., "Gibson and Progressive Jurisprudence," Pennsylvania Bar Association, *Reports*, vol. 15, 1909, pp. 356-370.

"A System of Penal Law for the State of Louisiana," *North American Review*, vol. 43, October, 1936, pp. 297-336.

Atlee, B. C., "Jasper Yeates," *The Green Bag*, September, 1893.

Aumann, F. R., "The Course of Judicial Review in the State of Ohio," *American Political Science Review*, vol. 25, 1931, pp. 36-38.

Aumann, F. R., "The Development of the Judicial System of Ohio," *Journal of Ohio Archaeological and Historical Society*, April, 1932, p. 212.

Aumann, F. R., "The Selection and Tenure of Judges in Ohio," *Cincinnati Law Review*, vol. 5, November, 1931, pp. 408-429.

Bainard, D. D., "The Anti-Rent Movement and Outbreak in New York," *American Whig Review*, vol. 2, December, 1845, pp. 577-598.

Barton, R. T., "John Randolph Tucker," *Va. Law Register*, May, 1897.

Browne, Irving, "The New York Court of Appeals," *The Green Bag*, vol. 2, 1890, pp. 277, 278.

Columbia Law Review, vol. III, p. 330.

Corwin, Edward S., "The Establishment of Judicial Review," *Michigan Law Review*, vol. 9, 1911, 314.

Coxe, M., "Chancellor Kent at Yale," *Yale Law Journal*, vol. 17, 1907-08, pp. 311-337, 553-72.

Daggett, Leonard M., "The Yale Law School," *The Green Bag*, vol. 1, 1889, p. 239.

Davenport, F. G. (editor), "Judge Sharkey Papers," *Miss. Valley Hist. Rev.*, June, 1933.

Dilly, A. U., "The Legal Profession in America," *MacMillan's Magazine*, vol. 25, p. 209.

* Dodd, Walter F., "The Growth of Judicial Power," *Pol. Sci. Quar.*, vol. 24, p. 195.

Doolan, John C., "The Old Court-New Court Controversy," *The Green Bag*, vol. 11, 177, 1899.

* References so marked have not been cited among the footnotes of this book.

Doolan, John C., "The Court of Appeals of Kentucky," *The Green Bag*, vol. 12, 1900, pp. 342, 408, 458, 516.

Dwight, Timothy, "Columbia College Law School, New York," *The Green Bag*, vol. 1, 1889, p. 14.

Eakin, M. Q., "Hugh Henry Brackenridge, Lawyer," *Western Pennsylvania History Magazine*, July, 1927.

Eaton, Amasa M., "The Development of the Judicial System of Rhode Island," *Yale Law Journal*, vol. 14, 1905, pp. 148, 153.

Elliot, Charles B., "An American Chancellor," *American Law Review*, vol. 37, May, June, 1903, pp. 32, 347.

* Eshelman, Frank, "Struggle and Rise of Popular Power in Pennsylvania's First Two Decades, 1682-1701," *Pennsylvania Magazine of History and Biography*, vol. 34, pp. 129-161.

Everett, Edward, "Life, Services, and Works of Henry Wheaton," *North American Review*, vol. 82, January, 1856, pp. 1-32.

* Fairman, C., "Justice Samuel F. Miller: a Study of a Judicial Statesman," *Pol. Sci. Quart.*, vol. 50, March, 1935, pp. 15-44.

Farrand, Max, "The First Hayburn Case," *American Historical Review*, January, 1908.

* Franklin, M., "Concerning the Historic Importance of Edward Livingston," *Tulane Law Review*, vol. II, February, 1937, pp. 163-212.

* Gilpin, Henry D., "Biographical Notice of Edward Livingston," *American Law Magazine*, vol. 3, April, 1844, pp. 1-16.

* Grant, J. A. C., "Marbury v. Madison Today," *American Political Science Review*, vol. 23, 1929, pp. 673-691.

Gray, Russel, "The Supreme Judicial Court of Massachusetts," *Medico-Legal Journal*, vol. XIII, 1925, pp. 225-235.

Green, Frederick, "Separation of Powers," *Yale Law Journal*, vol. XIX, p. 571.

Green, Nathan, "The Law School of Cumberland University," *The Green Bag*, vol. 11, 1899, p. 63.

Hale, G. S., "Joel Parker," *Am. Law Rev.*, vol. 14, January, 1876.

Hale, J., "Edward Livingston and His Louisiana Penal Code," *Am. Bar Assn. Journ.*, vol. 22, March, 1936, pp. 191-196.

Hammond, William G., "American Law Schools, Past and Future," *Southern Law Review* (N.S.), vol. 7, 1881, pp. 400-429.

Hardy, S. E. M., "Some Virginia Lawyers," *The Green Bag*, January, 1898.

Harris, R. C., "The Edward Livingston Centennial," *Tulane Law Review*, vol. 11, December, 1936, pp. 1-3.

* Hicks, Frederick C., "Where are the Law Books?" *The Green Bag*, vol. 22, No. 9, pp. 520-522.

Hunt, Carleton, "Edward Livingston and the Law of Louisiana," *Law Notes*, vol. 7, August, 1903, pp. 88-90.

Hunt, Carleton, "Life and Services of Edward Livingston," *Proceedings*, Louisiana Bar Assn., May 9, 1903; *American Lawyer*, vol. 12, 1905, pp. 100, 154.

Jones, Francis R., "Henry Wheaton," *The Green Bag*, vol. 16, December, 1904, pp. 781-785.

Kent, James, "An American law student of a hundred years ago," (Letter from Kent to Thomas Washington, October 6, 1828.) *American Law School Review*, vol. 2, May, June, 1911, pp. 547-553.

Kent, James, "Autobiographical sketch of Chancellor Kent," *Southern Law Review*, vol. 1, July, 1872, pp. 381-391; *Virginia Law Register*, vol. 3, December, 1897, pp. 563-571.

Kerr, Charles, "If Spencer Roane Had Been Appointed Chief Justice Instead of John Marshall," *American Bar Association Journal*, vol. 20, March, 1934, No. 3, pp. 167-172.

Lamar, J. R., "History of the Establishment of the Supreme Court of Georgia," *Report of the Twenty-Fourth Annual Session of the Georgia Bar Association*, 1907.

Landes, C. I., "Jasper Yeates and His Times," *Pennsylvania Magazine of History and Biography*, July, 1922.

Law Reporter, November, 1853.

Legal Intelligencer, vol. XL, June 1, 1883, p. 220; vol. XL, June 8, 1883, pp. 230-732.

Livingston, a full bibliography in *Tulane L. Rev.*, vol. 11, p. 331.

McWilliams, Elizabeth, "Political Activities in Western Pennsylvania, 1800-1816, *Western Pennsylvania Historical Magazine*, vol. 7, pp. 225-234.

Martin, Charles S., "Chancellor James Kent," *The Green Bag*, vol. 7, April, 1895, pp. 153-165.

Maryland Historical Magazine, December, 1906, pp. 358-362.

Meader, L. H., "The Council of Censors," *Papers from the Historical Seminary of Brown University*, 1895.

Memorial of the Late James L. Pettigru, Proceedings of the Bar of Charleston, South Carolina, March, 1863 (1866).

Monson, John H., "Life of the Hon. Jeremiah Smith, etc.," *The North American Review*, vol. LXI, 1845, pp. 26-27.

Mooney, W. C., "The Genesis of a Written Constitution," *Annals of the American Academy of Political and Social Science*, April, 1871.

Moore, E. H., "The Livingston Code," *Journ. of the Amer. Instit. of Criminal Law and Criminology*, November, 1928, pp. 344-363, including a bibliography.

More, Elon H., "The Livingston Code," *Journal of Criminal Law and Criminology*, vol. 19, 1928, 344.

Morison, S. E., "The Struggle over the Adoption of the Constitution of Massachusetts, 1780," *Proc. Mass. Hist. Soc.*, vol. L, 1917.

Murray, David, "The Anti-Rent Episode in the State of New York," *American Historical Association, Report for 1896*, vol. 1, 1897, pp. 139-173.

"Nathaniel Beverly Tucker," *Richmond College Hist. Papers*, vol. 2, 1917, No. 1.

Nelles, Walter, "Commonwealth v. Hunt," *Columbia Law Review*, vol. 32, 1932, pp. 1128-69.

Patterson, S. S. P., "The Supreme Court of Appeals of Virginia," *The Green Bag*, vol. 5, 1893, pp. 310, 361, 407.

Peeling, James H., "Governor McKean and the Pennsylvania Jacobins, 1799-1808," *Pennsylvania Magazine of History and Biography*, vol. 54, pp. 320-354.

* Pound, Roscoe, "A bibliography of procedural reform including organization of courts," *Massachusetts Law Quarterly*, vol. 5, May, 1920, pp. 332-345. (Reprinted from Illinois Law Review, February, 1917, with a supplementary bibliography.)

Pound, Roscoe, "Fifty Years of Jurisprudence," *Harvard Law Review*, vol. 51, p. 557.

Pound, Roscoe, "Judge Story in the Making of American Law," *American Law Review*, vol. 48, 1914, pp. 676-97.

Pound, Roscoe, "Organization of Courts," *Philadelphia Legal Intelligencer*, vol. 70, p. 86; also in *Proc. Minn. Bar Assn.*, 1914, p. 169.

* Pound, Roscoe, "The Cause of Popular Dissatisfaction with the Administration of Justice," (American Bar Association, *Report of the Twenty-ninth Annual Meeting*, 1906, Philadelphia, Dando, 1906), pp. 395-417.

Pound, Roscoe, "The Spirit of the Common Law," *The Green Bag*, vol. 18, 1906, pp. 24-25.

Remarks on the Projected Revision of the Laws of New York, first published in *The Atlantic Monthly*, April, 1825, vol. 8, p. 19, New York.

Report of the Virginia State Bar Association, vol. IX, September, 1895.

Sharswood, George, "The Common Law of Pennsylvania," *Pa. Bar Assoc., Reports*, 1896, 135.

Shea, George, "Some Thoughts on Henry Wheaton and the Epoch to Which he Belonged," *New York State Bar Association, Reports*, vol. 2, 1879, pp. 95-103.

Smith, Eugene, "Edward Livingston and the Louisiana Codes," *Columbia Law Review*, 1902, pp. 25, 26.

Southern Law Review, (N.S.), vol. 2, 1906, p. 339.

Stinson, J. W., "Opinions of Richard Peters (1781-1817)," *Univ. of Pa. Law Review*, March, 1922.

Stockton, C. H., "Historical Sketch," 19 *Records of the Columbia Historical Society*, 1916, pp. 99, 124.

Story, Joseph, "Remarks on the Study of the Civil Law," *The American Jurist*, No. III, July, 1829.

* *The Green Bag*, vol. 1, 1889, to vol. 12, 1900.

* *The North American Review*, vol. 3, May, 1816, to vol. 65, October, 1847.

"The Supreme Court of Rhode Island," *Med. Leg. Jour.*, vol. 9, p. 86.

"The Works of Edward Livingston," *Law Magazine and Review* (N.S.), vol. 3, April, 1874, pp. 332-344.

Thompson, George J., "The Development of the Anglo-American Judicial System," *Cornell Law Quarterly*, vol. 17, December, 1931, pp. 9-42; February, 1932, pp. 203-247; April, 1932, pp. 395-458.

Trepagnier, O. B., "Bibliography on Edward S. Livingston," *Tulane Law Review*, vol. 11, February, 1937, pp. 331-343.

Tucker, H. St. George, "Patrick Henry and St. George Tucker," *Univ. of Pa. Law Review*, January, 1919.

Tucker, J. R., "The Judges Tucker of the Court of Appeals of Virginia," *Va. Law Register*, March, 1896.

"Two Letters of Chancellor Kent," *American Law Review*, April, 1878, pp. 478-490.

Utter, William, "Judicial Review in Early Ohio," *Mississippi Valley Historical Review*, vol. 14, pp. 3-26.

Utter, William, "St. Tammany in Ohio: A Study in Frontier Politics," *Mississippi Valley Historical Review*, vol. 15, pp. 321-340.

Veeder, Van Vechten, "A Century of Federal Judicature," *The Green Bag*, vol. 15, 1903, p. 24.

Washburn, Emory, "Memoir of Joel Parker," *Proceedings Mass. Hist. Soc.*, vol. 14, 1876.

Western Law Journal, May, 1844.

Whitehead, John, "The Supreme Court of New Jersey," *The Green Bag*, vol. 3, 1891, pp. 355, 401, 402.

Wilkinson, A. E., "Edward Livingston and the Penal Codes," *Texas Law Review*, vol. 1, 25, 1922.

William and Mary Quarterly, vol. 9, 1900, p. 80.

Williams, Mildred, "Hugh Henry Brackenridge as a Judge of the State Supreme Court, 1799-1816," *Western Pennsylvania History Magazine*, *1799-1816*, October, 1927.

Winslow, John, "Contest between the Judiciary and Legislature of Rhode Island," *New York State Bar Association*, 1888, p. 74.

Winslow, John, "Trial of Rhode Island Judges in 1786," *Albany Law Journal*, vol. 35, p. 338.

Wister, Owen, "The Supreme Court of Pennsylvania," *The Green Bag*, vol. 3, 1891, pp. 72-87.

Wood, George B., "History of the University of Pennsylvania from its Origin to the year 1827," *Memoirs of the Historical Society of Pennsylvania*, vol. 3, 1834, p. 109.

III. The Period of Maturity, 1865-1906, and Recent Trends, 1900-35

BOOKS

Adams, Brooks, *Centralization and the Law*, Boston, 1906, 296 pp.

Beale, Jr., Joseph C., "Jurisprudence—Its Development During the Past Century," *Congress of Arts and Sciences*, vol. III, 1906.

Boudin, Louis B., *Government by Judiciary*, New York, 1932, 2 volumes.

Bruce, Andrew A., *The American Judge*, New York, 1924, 218 pp.

* Cardozo, Benjamin N., *The Growth of the Law*, New Haven, 1924, 145 pp.

* Cardozo, B. N., *The Nature of the Judicial Process*, New Haven, 1921, 180 pp.

* Cardozo, B. N., *The Paradoxes of Legal Science*, New York, 1928, 142 pp.

* References so marked have not been cited among the footnotes of this book.

* Cardozo, B. N., *What Medicine Can Do for Law*, New York and London, 1930, 52 pp.

Carter, James, *Law: Its Origin, Growth, and Functions*, New York and London, 1907, 355 pp.

Carter, James C., *Provinces of the Written and Unwritten Law*, An address delivered at the annual meeting of the Virginia state bar association, at White Sulphur Springs, July 25, 1889. New York and Albany, Banks and brothers, 1889, 62 pp.

Carter, James C., *The Ideal and the Actual in Law*. The annual address delivered at the thirteenth annual meeting of the American Bar Association, August 21, 1890. Philadelphia, 1890, 31 pp.

Carter, James C., *The Proposed Codification of Our Common Law*. A paper prepared at the request of the committee of the Bar Association of New York, appointed to oppose the measure. New York Evening Post job printing office, 1884, 117 pp.

Dicey, A. V., *Lectures Introductory to the Study of the Law of the Constitution*, London, 1885, 407 pp.

Dicey, A. V., *Lectures on the Relation between Law and Public Opinion in England during the Nineteenth Century*, London, New York, 1905, 503 pp.

Dickinson, John, *Administrative Justice and the Supremacy of the Law*, 1927.

* Frankfurter, Felix, *Mr. Justice Holmes and the Supreme Court*, Cambridge, Mass., 1938, 139 pp.

* Frankfurter, Felix, *The Commerce Clause Under Marshall, Taney, and Waite*, Chapel Hill, 1937, 114 pp.

* Frankfurter, Felix and Greene, Nathan, *The Labor Injunction*, New York, 1930, 343 pp.

Frankfurter, Felix and Landis, James E., *The Business of the Supreme Court: a Study in the Federal Judicial System*, New York, 1928, 349 pp.

Goodhart, Arthur L., *Essays in Jurisprudence and the Common Law*, Cambridge, (Eng.), 1931, 295 pp.

* Harvard Tercentenary Publication; *Authority and the Individual*, Cambridge, 1937, 371 pp.

Harvard Tercentenary Publication; *The Future of the Common Law*, Cambridge, 1937, 247 pp.

* Hicks, Frederick C., *Men and Books Famous in the Law*, Rochester, N. Y., 1921, 259 pp.

* Maitland, F. W., *Domesday Book and Beyond, Three Essays in the Early History of England*, Cambridge, 1897, 527 pp.

* Maitland, F. W., *English Law and Renaissance*, Cambridge, 1901, 98 pp.

* Maitland, F. W., *The Collected Papers of Frederick William Maitland*, Cambridge, 1911, 3 vol.

Mariot, J. A. R., *The Mechanism of the Modern States*, Oxford, 1927, 2 volumes.

Pollock, Frederick, *The Expansion of the Common Law*, 1904, 164 pp.

* Pollock, Sir Frederick, *The Genius of the Common Law*, New York, 1912, VII, 141 pp.

* Pound, Roscoe, *An Introduction to American Law*, Cambridge, 1919, 44 pp.
* Pound, Roscoe, *An Introduction to the Philosophy of Law*, New Haven, 1925, 307 pp.
* Pound, Roscoe, *Criminal Justice in America*, New York, 1930, 226 pp.
Pound, Roscoe, *Interpretations of Legal History*, Cambridge, 1923, xx+171 pp.
* Pound, Roscoe, *The Formative Era of American Law*, Boston, 1938, 188 pp.
Pound, Roscoe, *The Spirit of the Common Law*, Boston, 1921, xv+224 pp.
Recent Social Trends in the United States, 1933, vol II.
Redlich, Josef, *The Common Law and the Case Method in American University Law Schools*, a report to the Carnegie foundation for the advancement of teaching, New York, 1914, XI, 84 pp.
Report of Dean Pound to the President of Harvard University for 1915-1916, p. 2.
Robson, William A., *Civilization and the Growth of Law*, New York, 1935, 354 pp.
Salmond, John W., *Jurisprudence*, London, 1913, 511 pp.
Smith, R. H., *Justice and the Poor*, a study of the present denial of justice to the poor and of the agencies making more equal their position before the law, with particular reference to legal aid work in the United States, New York, 1919, XIV, 271 pp. (Bul. No. 13, The Carnegie Foundation for the Advancement of Teaching).
Stone, Harlan F., *Law and Its Administration*, New York, 1915, 232 pp.
Sturges, W. A., *Commercial Arbitration and Awards*, Kansas City, 1930, 1082 pp.
* Willis, Hugh E., *Introduction to Anglo-American Law*, Bloomington, Indiana, 1926, 236 pp.
Willoughby, W. F., *Principles of Judicial Administration*, Washington, 1929, xxii+662 pp.

MAGAZINES

American Bar Association Journal, vol. 16, 1933, pp. 695, 805.
Amer. Jud. Soc. Bull. VIII.
Aumann, F. R., "The Changing Relationship of the Executive and Judicial Branches," *Kentucky Law Journal*, vol. XXII, 1934, pp. 246-260.
Aumann, F. R., "The Des Moines Conciliation Court," *Journal of the American Judicature Society*, vol. XI, June, 1928.
Aumann, F. R., "The Development of the Judicial Organization of Ohio," *Ohio Archaeological and Historical Journal*, vol. 41, April, 1932, pp. 195-236.
Aumann, F. R., "Domestic Relations Courts in Ohio," *Journal of the American Judicature Society*, vol. 15, October, 1931, pp. 89-93.
Aumann, F. R., "The Judicial Council Movement and Iowa," *Iowa Law Review*, vol. XV, June, 1930, pp. 425-433.
Aumann, F. R., "Juvenile Courts in Ohio," *Journal Criminal Law and Criminology*, vol. XII, November, 1931, pp. 556-565.

* References so marked have not been cited among the footnotes of this book.

Aumann, F. R., "The Lawyer and His Troubles," *North American Review*, April, 1933, pp. 310-318.

Aumann, F. R., "The Ohio Judicial Council Embarks on a Survey of Justice," *American Political Science Review*, vol. 24, May, 1930, pp. 416-425.

Aumann, F. R., "The Ohio Judicial Council; Studies and Reports," *American Political Science Review*, vol. 17, December, 1933, pp. 957-964.

Aumann, F. R., "Public Opinion and the Legal Technique," *U. S. Law Review*, vol. 59, February, 1935, pp. 71-90.

Aumann, F. R., "Some Changing Patterns in the Legal Order," *Kentucky Law Journal*, vol. 24, November, 1935, pp. 38-57; also published in *The Florida Bar Association Journal*, June, 1936, pp. 200-213; and in *Current Legal Thought*, November, 1935, pp. 215-218.

* Aumann, F. R., "The Supreme Court and the Advisory Opinion," *The Ohio State Law Journal*, December, 1937, pp. 21-55.

Aumann, F. R., "Technology, Centralization, and the Law," *The South Atlantic Quarterly*, vol. 36, June, 1937, pp. 277-278.

Blount, J. H., "The Three Great Codifiers," Georgia Bar Association, *Reports*, 1895, p. 190.

* Bohlen, Francis, "The Rule in Rylands v. Fletcher," *Univ. of Pa. Law Review*, vol. 59, 1911, pp. 298, 373, 423.

* Burdick, Francis M., "Half Century of Legal Education," *Cornell Law Quarterly*, vol. 4, 1919, p. 138.

* Burdick, Francis M., "The Removal of Benthamite Codification," *Columbia Law Review*, vol. 10, 1910, p. 118.

* Chase, Stuart, "The Age of Plenty; and the Imperatives Which It Involves," *Harpers Magazine*, March, 1934.

Cook, Walter W., "Scientific Method and the Law," *American Bar Association Journal*, vol. 13, 1927, p. 303 ff.

Dicey, A. V., "The Droit Administratif in Modern French Law," *Law Quarterly Review*, vol. 17, 1901, p. 302 ff.

Fiero, J. N., "David Dudley Field and His Work," *Rep. N. Y. State Bar Assn.*, vol. 18, p. 177.

Green, Leon, "The Duty Problem in Negligence Cases," *Columbia Law Review*, vol. 28, 1928, pp. 1014, 1036.

Guthrie, W. D., "President's Address," New York State Bar Association, *Reports N. Y. State Bar Assn.*, XLVI, 1923, pp. 175 ff.

Hall, A. Okey, "Reminiscences of David Dudley Field," *The Green Bag*, vol. 6, pp. 209, 244.

Healey, William, "The Practical Value of Scientific Study of Juvenile Delinquents," *United States Children's Bureau Publications*, No. 96, 1922, p. 7.

Henry, Robert L., "Jurisprudence Constante and Stare Decisis," (1929), *American Bar Association Journal*, vol. 15, p. 11.

Hoadley, George B., "Codification of the Common Law," *American Law Review*, vol. 23, 1889, p. 495.

Hoffman, Charles W., "Courts of Domestic Relations," *Proc. of Natl. Conf. of Soc. Work*, 1918, pp. 124-128.

Hutcheson, Joseph C., "Judging as Administration," *The American Law School Review*, No. 11, April, 1911, pp. 1071.

Hutcheson, Joseph C., "The Worm Turns," *Illinois Law Review*, vol. 27, p. 357.

Jacoby, A. L., "The Psychopathic Clinic in a Criminal Court: Its Use and Possibilities," *Amer. Jud. Soc. Journ.*, vol. 7, June, 1923, pp. 21, 25.

Johns Hopkins University. *The Institute for the Study of Law Circular*, 1929, No. 7, p. 10.

Judson, Frederick N., "Modern Views of the Law Reforms of Jeremy Bentham," *Columbia Law Review*, vol. 10, 1910, p. 41.

Llewellyn, Karl N., "Some Realism About Realism—responding to Dean Pound," *Harvard Law Review*, vol. XLIV, No. 8, June, 1931.

McMurray, Orrin, "Changing Conceptions of Law," *California Law Review*, 1915, pp. 441, 446.

Oliphant, Herman, "A Return to Stare Decisis," *American Bar Association Journal*, 1928, pp. 71 ff.

Olson, Harry, "Crime and Heredity," *Amer. Jud. Soc. Journal*, vol. 7, August, 1923, pp. 33, 77.

Pomeroy, John N., "The True Method of Interpreting the Civil Code," *West Coast Reporter*, vol. 3, pp. 585, 691, 717; vol. 4, pp. 1, 49, 109, 145.

Pound, Roscoe, "Justice According to Law," *Columbia Law Review*, vol. 13, 1913, p. 696.

* Pound, Roscoe, "Law in Books and Law in Action," *American Law Review*, vol. 44, 1904, p. 20.

* Pound, Roscoe, "Mechanical Jurisprudence," *Columbia Law Review*, vol. 8, 1908, pp. 605, 614.

Pound, Roscoe, "Organization of Courts," Bulletin VI, *Publication of the American Judicature Society*, pp. 11-12.

* Pound, Roscoe, "The Causes of Popular Dissatisfaction with the Administration of Justice," American Bar Association, *Report of the Twenty-Ninth Annual Meeting*, 1906, Phil., Dando, 1906, pp. 395-417.

* Pound, Roscoe, "The Decadence of Equity," *Columbia Law Review*, vol. 5, p. 20.

* Pound, Roscoe, "The End of Law as Developed in Legal Rules and Doctrines," *Harvard Law Review*, vol. 27, 1914, pp. 195-235.

Pound, Roscoe, "The Future of the Common Law," *Cincinnati Law Review*, vol. 7, 1930, p. 346.

* Pound, Roscoe, "The Theory of Judicial Decision," *Harvard Law Review*, vol. 36, 1923, pp. 340-343.

Root, Elihu, *Address to American Law Institute*, Proceedings, 1923, I, p. 49.

Rosbrook, Alden I., "The Art of Judicial Reporting," *Cornell Law Quarterly*, vol. 10, 1925, p. 103.

Rosenbaum, Samuel, "Report on Commercial Arbitration in England," *American Judicature Society, Bulletin XII*, October, 1916.

Sabine, George H., "The Pragmatic Approach to Politics," *The American Political Science Review*, vol. 24, November, 1930, p. 866.

* References so marked have not been cited among the footnotes of this book.

Smith, Eugene, "Edward Livingston and the Louisiana Codes," *Columbia Law Review*, vol. 2, 1902, p. 24.

Smith, Y. B., *Education and Research*, New York State Bar Association Bulletin, 1930, pp. 189, 190.

* Stone, Harlan F., "Some Aspects of the Problem of Law Simplification," *Columbia Law Review*, vol. 23, pp. 319-322.

Sutherland, George, "President's Address, American Bar Association, *Reports*, American Bar Association, XLII, 1917, pp. 175 ff.

"The Child, The Family and the Court," *U. S. Children's Bureau Publications*, No. 193, 1929.

Van Waters, Miriam, "The Socialization of Juvenile Court Procedure," *U. S. Children's Bureau Publications*, No. 97, 1922, p. 64.

Waite, Edward F., "Courts of Domestic Relations," *Minneapolis Law Review*, vol. 5, no. 3, February, 1921, p. 167.

Waite, Edward F., "How Far Can Court Procedure be Socialized Without Impairing Individual Rights," *U. S. Children's Bureau Publications*, No. 97, 1922, p. 55.

White, W. A., "Judicial versus Administrative Process at the Prosecution Stage," *Journal of Criminal Law and Criminology*, vol. 25, no. 6, pp. 851-858. (March-April, 1935).

Whitney, Edward B., "The Doctrine of Stare Decisis," *Michigan Law Review*, vol. 3, no. 4, 1904, p. 97.

Zunser, Charles, "The Domestic Relations Court," *Annals of the Amer. Acad. of Pol. and Soc. Sci.*, vol. 124, March, 1926.

INDEX

INDEX

Act of Settlement, 41

Adams, Brooks, 33n.

Adams Express Co. v. *Beckwith*, 222n.

Adams, John, 42, 107; on early colonial justice, 54-55; on checks and balances, 151

Adams, John Quincy, 170

Adams, Samuel, 33

Addington, Isaac, 35

Administration, and the rule of law, 194

Administrative adjudication, 227

Administrative courts, 229

Alabama, judicial tenure in, 185

American Judicature Society, 226n.

American law, nature of, in colonial period, 3-18; and the English common law, 5-18; effect of scarcity of lawyers on, 8-9; and natural justice, 9; influence of Bible on colonial, 10; books and pamphlets on, 11; colonial codification of, 12-13; effect of frontier on, 14-16, 55; and colonial law-books, 45-48; arbitration in, 48-50, 231; procedure in colonial, 50-55; and local custom, 58; influence of religion on, 58-61; the formative period of, 67-194; in the post-Revolutionary period, 67-93; early reports of, 74-77; hostility toward English decisions and precedents in, 79-86; influence of French authorities on, 86-93; codification of, in formative period, 121-129; influence of great American judges on, 127-137; influence of Story on, 128-130; influence of Kent on, 130-131; influence of Marshall on, 132-133; influence of Wheaton on, 133-136; in the years 1830-1860, 138-153; eminent state judges in formative period of, 142-149; influence of mathematics on, 149-151; and individual liberty, 151-153; the doctrine of judicial review and, 190-194; during the period of maturity, 1865-1900, 197-216; and the Civil War, 200-201; and the Reconstruction period, 201; and notable judges, during period, 1865-1900, 202-209; influence of Bradley on, 203; influence of Cooley on, 204-206; influence of Pomeroy on, 206-208; influence of David Dudley Field on, 208-210; influence of James Carter on, 209-211; codification of, in period from 1865-1900,

208-214; movement for socialization of, 215; recent trends in, 219 ff.; and *stare decisis*, 222-226; and the rise of boards and commissions, 226-229; conciliation in, 230; and judicial discretion, 234. See also Common law, Divine law, Frontier, Lawyers, etc.

American Law Institute, 211

American Legal System, colonial period of, 1608-1776, 3-63; formative period of, 1776-1860, 67-194; in the period of maturity, 1865-1900, 197-216; present period of, 1900-1935, 219-235

American public law, 132, 136

Andrews, Charles N., 15n., on colonial land tenure, 16n., 17n.

Anglo-Saxon law, 9

Anti-Federalists, hostility of, toward English institutions, 86

Anti-rent riots, 179-180

Appeals, 51-52; in Kentucky, 170

Appellate jurisdiction, 163-164

Apprenticeship, legal training through, 94-95

Arbitration, 48-50, 230-232

Arkansas, judicial tenure in, 185

Ashmun, George, 125

Austin, Benjamin, 126; attitude toward the law and lawyers, 85-86

Austin, John, 149n.

Australia, 158

Azuni, 87

Bache, Benjamin Franklin, 178

Bacon, Ezekiel, 170

Bacon, Lord, 121, 143

Baldwin, Simeon E., on the status of the colonial legal profession, 31

Bar, American, seventeenth-century, 19-26; eighteenth-century, 26-34

Barradal, Edward, 26

Barry, William T., 183

Bartlett, Josiah, 38

Bayard v. *Singleton*, 190n.

Bellomont, Lord, 24

Bentham, Jeremy, on codification, 123, 126

Berrien, John M., 156

Bibb, George M., 184

Bible, as a source of law in New England, 10; influence on American common law, 58-61